ALCOHOLISM TREATMENT

A Social Work Perspective

KATHERINE VAN WORMER
The University of Northern Iowa

Nelson-Hall Publishers
Chicago

Project Editor: Dorothy S. Anderson
Typesetter:Precision Typographers
Printer:Capital City Press
Illustrator: Corasue Nicholas, Nicholas Communications
Cover Painting: Carolyn Golden, *Coming to Life*

Library of Congress Cataloging-in-Publication Data

Van Wormer, Katherine S.
    Alcoholism treatment a social work perspective / Katherine van
Wormer.
       p.   cm.
    Includes bibliographical references and index.
    ISBN 0–8304–1387–1
    1 Social work with alcoholics. 2. Alcoholics—Rehabilitation.
    3.   Alcoholism—Treatment.   I. Title.
  HV5275.V35   1995
  362.29' 28—dc2O   94-43291
                                                         CIP

Manufactured in the United States of America

10 9 8 7 6 5 4 3 2

TM The paper used in this book meets the
minimum requirements of American
National Standard for Information
Sciences—Permanence of Paper for
Printed Library Materials, ANSI
Z39.48-1984.

To all those who have descended into the abyss of addiction and who have somehow managed to pull themselves up out of it. And to all those who have helped someone manage that difficult climb because they cared. And to my mother, Elise Talmage, who knows of these things.

CONTENTS

PART TWO

CHAPTER 9

GROUP THERAPY WITH SUBSTANCE ABUSERS   239

CHAPTER 10

ECONOMIC, SOCIOLOGICAL, AND LEGAL DYNAMICS   272

CHAPTER 11

GENERAL SOCIAL WORK WITH THE ALCOHOLIC CLIENT   305

Alcoholism Treatment

PREFACE

It is an old story and a new story. It is a story of biology, culture, and control. It is a story of despair and hope. Alcoholism and its treatment have *arrived* on the scene as a major area of legislative, public, and professional concern. Drunkenness, in general, and drunken driving, in particular, are no longer taken-for-granted as they once were. There is, in fact, an international soul-searching today about all forms of chemical abuse and dependency.

New laws are being put on the books all over the industrialized world. And where laws and enforcement of laws change, new job markets arise. And where there are new markets, persons trained in similar fields move over to meet the need. It was thus that I, as a sociologist and social worker, made the transition from Community Home Health to Community Alcohol Center. It was thus that I came to realize the lack of availability, in one source, of the information needed to practice in the field of substance abuse.

As a social worker and a person who grew up in an alcoholic home, I delved into work on family therapy with the chemically dependent family; my focus was more on relationships than on the inner psyche of the person. As an alcoholism counselor, I was interested in sobriety and the legal requirements of compliance with the deferred prosecution laws. As a sociologist, I was intrigued by causal relationships, for example, the effect of belief systems concerning control of life events on treatment outcomes. I was also drawn into close examination of roles clients played in their family, such as dependency roles and the role of scapegoat or clown. But even more intriguing, I sought a broader view of the *field* of alcoholism counseling and the varied assortment of individuals who have drifted into or chosen this line of work. What brings them here? What is their professional ideology? And what are the role demands and conflicts? Where are the rewards, and where are the challenges?

My focus has been broadened considerably by a rare opportunity I have had to work as program director at an alcoholism treatment center in Norway. Twelve-Step based alcoholism treatment is in its infancy in Norway, with programs expanding rapidly to meet the newly defined need. Denmark, Iceland, and Sweden have borrowed the Minnesota Model and adapted it to their own requirements. The need for resource material in Scandinavia on alcoholism treatment techniques is essential. This book, with its international breadth and practical, how-to-do-it focus, is designed to fill the gap in the literature of other countries as well as the United States.

The primary goal of this book is to bring together in one work the essence of alcoholism counseling treatment; the secondary goal is to provide an ecological perspective for the alcoholism/addictions field. The terms *addiction, chemical dependency,* and *alcoholism* are used as parallel and, for the most part, interchangeable terms. Addiction and chemical dependency are the broader terms, alcoholism, the narrower term. And yet, in the final analysis, addiction is addiction. There is a generalized psychology of addiction as there are generalized family patterns. Only the particulars of the substance consumed are different. Addictive people will abuse many drugs, prescription drugs and tobacco included. The loss of control, not the particular substance, is the key element. This book, therefore, is applicable to helpers in *all* fields of chemical abuse.

The terminology, ideology, and conceptual framework for this book derive from the ecological-interactionist orientation of social work. Such an orientation is offered here for two reasons. The first is to introduce to alcoholism/addictions work a *unifying* framework so vitally needed by a new and diversified field. The second reason for choosing the ecological formulation pertains to its *practical* relevance. The ecological-interactionist approach, in its person-in-the-situation conceptualization, successfully integrates the basic components of alcoholism. These components are biological, psychological, and environmental. Among the basic concepts borrowed from the science of ecology are the notions that: (1) cause and effect are intertwined and perpetually interacting and (2) the whole is greater than the sum of its parts.

Some of the smaller-range basic assumptions that underlie this presentation are as follows:

- To effect change in substance abuse work, a combination of individual/group/family treatment is needed.

- Abstinence from all mood altering drugs is conducive to effective treatment.
- According to most dictionary definitions of disease, alcoholism is a disease, as are most other addictions and ailments. My preference is the term *illness,* one that cuts across the major treatment modalities.
- There are hereditary components to addiction, making for significant individual differences.
- Much of the current criticism of the disease model is valid: most of the popular treatment models used today are not of proven effectiveness; those that are are rarely used.
- Alcoholism workers who are themselves recovering alcoholics / addicts or who have lived with an alcoholic have some advantages, especially in early-stage treatment, over other counselors. However, this kind of personal involvement is no more essential in this field than is comparable personal involvement in related fields, such as health or mental health.
- The bachelor's or master's degree in counseling, social work, or clinical psychology or the European equivalent are appropriate credentials for all kinds of therapy, including alcoholism therapy.
- Specialized training in substance abuse dynamics should be an additional requirement. This training should take place outside the treatment center and should be scientifically oriented.
- The key area for addiction therapy, consistent with the ecological framework, is in helping persons find ways of coping with stress. Treatment must be individualized to match the unique coping style of each client.

I am excited to be a specialist in addictions work. I wrote this text to share my excitement in a field that is not new, is often denigrated, is full of professional rivalries, but is stimulating and growing nevertheless. I wish to offer a concise work that summarizes both practice and theory and introduces a meaningful framework into a rapidly emerging field, alcoholism and substance abuse counseling.

Acknowledgment

Research for this book was funded, in part, by the University of Northern Iowa Summer Fellowship for research projects, sponsored by the Graduate College.

Part One

THE CONTEXT OF SOCIAL WORK PRACTICE IN ALCOHOLISM TREATMENT

Practicing social workers and clinical psychologists, not to mention addiction treatment specialists, encounter the effects of alcohol abuse and alcoholism on a daily basis. Chemical abuse often figures in domestic violence or incest situations that come to the worker's attention. The troubled, depressed young woman, who is unable to trust men and unable to like herself, may have grown up in an alcoholic home. The neglectful parent may be sipping booze all day. The bereaved father may have lost his daughter in a car crash involving a drunken driver. The veteran suffering from Vietnam stress syndrome typically has a record of extensive narcotic abuse.

There is a biology of alcoholism, a psychology of alcoholism, and a sociology of alcoholism. There is also a sociology of alcoholism treatment. This text organizes for the social worker a growing body of knowledge from multidimensional and often contradictory sources. Divided into three parts, this text addresses the context of social work practice in Part One, varied aspects of alcoholism from biology to psychology in Part Two, and the field of alcoholism treatment in Part Three. An underlying purpose of *Alcoholism Treatment: A Social Work Perspective* is to help establish the validity of alcoholism treatment as an emerging profession. A secondary purpose is to produce a text on the fundamentals of social work practice with the alcoholic client.

Part One starts with the *context* of chemical abuse. The essential definitions are here, as are the historical and temporary frameworks.

Chapter 1, "The Ecological Approach to Alcoholism Treatment," sets the stage for the more practice-oriented chapters of Parts Two and Three. Chapter 1 presents alcoholism treatment in terms of an adaptational model of stress and coping. The view of causation is interactionist—not *a* causes *b*, but *a* and *b* affect each other simultaneously.

Chapter 2 provides the history of addictions treatment. Attention is given to the cultural setting in which alcoholics were given treatment. Chapter 3 offers an overview of the contemporary context and a brief summary of the dictates of each approach along with the leading criticisms. Contributions of the religious-moral model, the psychoanalytical-psychodynamic paradigm, the Alcoholics Anonymous based Twelve Step approach, and the behavioral-cognitive framework are presented. Each framework is examined in terms of scientific findings on treatment effectiveness.

1

THE ECOLOGICAL APPROACH TO ALCOHOLISM TREATMENT

There is much joy in alcoholism treatment work and much pain and despair also. Join a gathering of relaxing alcoholism counselors and their repertoire of stories will whet your imagination. While tragedy and sorrow run through these stories, an element of amusement often characterizes the mood of these groups of workers. Each of the following vignettes captures something of the real-life challenge (and drama) facing workers in the field of alcoholism treatment.

INTERVENTION TO PREVENT BIOLOGICAL DAMAGE

Doris is an active member of the National Association of Black Social Workers in Waterloo, Iowa. A community social worker, her clients are pregnant mothers at high risk for substance abuse. Doris describes her work as follows:

> My caseload consists of twenty-five drug addicts, thirty-five who are abusing alcohol and others at risk because of an unstable life-style. The women may be referred by their doctor or an agency such as the Department of Corrections. Funding for the program is through a grant from the federal government. My working day is 8:00 A.M. to 5:30 P.M. Sometimes I go to the client's house as early as 7:00 A.M. to be sure to catch her to transport her to an appointment with the doctor or court. I work with as many as seven different

agencies which are involved with these women. The African-American out-reach program operates in the black community, providing substance abuse treatment. I work closely with this clinic. But I never tell the women I'm a social worker; when you say to them "social worker," your name is mud.

INTERVENTION AT THE PSYCHOLOGICAL LEVEL

Ron, a former director of a community alcoholism treatment center in western Washington state, experienced a serious case of professional burn-out. After some rest and travel, he decided to go into private practice. Today, from an office in his home and working mainly in evening hours, Ron conducts alcoholism assessments for court or intensive psychotherapy sessions for longterm clients. A gestalt approach with special emphasis on anger management characterizes Ron's preferred intervention style. Ron loves his work today because of the rewards of direct client/therapist contact. Many former clients of his are leading sober and productive lives.

SOCIALLY BASED INTERVENTION

"My name is Bev. I am an alcoholic." Many of the clients in Bev's treatment groups are court-referred. Because, in this state-supported treatment cen-ter, there are no medical staff, Bev does random urinalysis checks (U.A.'s) on her female outpatient clients. Bev is a senior social work major from the University of Northern Iowa. Though her field placement instructor has expressed concern over the social control nature of some of her work, Bev has managed to juggle the role demands of her position very well. As group counselor, listener, and educator, Bev is rapidly developing confidence in her ability to help alcoholics help themselves. Her active involvement in Twelve Step work is seen as a strong point in her favor. Bev has reason to anticipate a job offer by this agency upon graduation.

Inni is a social worker at a luxurious private treatment center in Norway. Having learned nothing about alcoholism or alcoholic clients at her school of social work, Inni chose to study under American profes-sionals at a new Minnesota Model based clinic. Previously married to an alcoholic, Inni is now living with a man whom she met as a client at the center. Since he was not her personal client, she perceives no irregularity in this arrangement. In her professional work as a family therapist, Inni gets to utilize the whole gamut of her professional social work skills. She does much public relations work as well, spreading information on the disease concept of alcoholism to Norway.

INTRODUCTION TO ALCOHOLISM TREATMENT

To engage the reluctant client and perhaps reluctantly sober client into a sustained treatment relationship is the primary challenge of social work

4

practice with alcoholic clients. Only when the client is engaged in treatment can the real counseling work begin. The second major challenge for the social worker is to lead the client toward healthier ways of coping with stress than through reliance on alcohol (or pills or drugs).

The multidimensional nature of alcoholism and other addictions mandates that the clinician consider the biological dynamics, as in example one (prevention of fetal alcohol syndrome); the individual's peculiar style of perception and cognitive function, as in example two (private practice); and the socially based group therapy work discussed in example three. The fourth vignette from Norway reveals the multiple variables that come into play in alcoholism treatment, whether in the United States or some other country.

Alcoholism is not merely a physical problem, it is a psychological and sociocultural problem as well. With alcoholism as with coronary artery disease (Wallace, 1989) the ingredients are all there: a genetic history, behavior that is ultimately self-destructive, and a society and culture that encourage unhealthy consumption patterns. Alcoholism, like heart disease, is a truly *biopsychosocial* phenomenon. For an understanding of the comprehensive nature of alcoholism, to provide the most effective and meaningful treatment approach for each individual, an overall biopsychosocial model is essential. The ecological framework to be described in this chapter provides a systematic foundation for integrating knowledge about human behavior into the context of the social environment.

THE ALCOHOLISM TREATMENT CENTER AS CONTEXT FOR SOCIAL WORK PRACTICE

Alcoholism treatment is a part of the health care system. The nature and form of the treatment services are shaped by the system. Both alcoholism treatment and the health care system are themselves the product of peculiar economic, social, and political arrangements in a given society.

There are today in the United States over 10,000 alcoholism and drug abuse treatment centers and programs. Over 300,000 clients are enrolled in these programs (National Institute on Drug Abuse, 1990). The alcoholism treatment center is a small but complex social structure that may operate independently as an outpatient clinic assessment agency or as a specialized detoxification wing in a major urban hospital. Recently developed structures include neighborhood clinics, health maintenance organizations (HMOs), prison alcoholism counseling services, and adolescent inpatient substance abuse treatment centers. Social workers are found practicing in most of the traditional and new structures for specialized care, but most commonly they encounter the alcoholic client in the course of some other branch of social work practice, such as family therapy or mental health.

The history of social work practice in the specialized addictions field is a history of the struggle to establish professional identity in "alien territory," to use Kurzman's memorable terminology (1983). In more traditional fields, such as child welfare, social workers have acquired a recognized degree of autonomy and influence. The chemical dependency field, on the other hand, has been defined and dominated by recovering chemical dependents, often without professional education or training (Lawson, Ellis, and Rivers, 1984). Until recent times, the chemical dependency field has shown little interest in recruiting social workers, or psychologists, for that matter, to its ranks. Nor have social workers shown much interest in specializing in addictions work.

An underlying assumption of this text is that alcoholism/addictions treatment is a major potential growth area for social work activity. The ecologically oriented social worker can utilize his or her diversified training to play an important role in helping individuals, groups, and families alter addictive patterns and life-styles. In fact, social workers are steadily building and reshaping the field of alcoholism counseling; this will be explored in chapters 3 and 8. Although only 5 percent of social workers identify substance abuse treatment as their area of specialization, the influence of social workers and social work knowledge is far out of proportion to what the percentages would indicate. The influence has come largely from writers and popularizers concerned most often with the family as a system. Hopefully, in the future, influence will be felt at the practitioner and administrative levels as well as through national social work leadership.

INTRODUCTION TO THE ECOLOGICAL PERSPECTIVE

Despite its eclecticism, the field of social work has been dominated during different periods of history by different paradigms. In the last decade, the psychosocial approach has incorporated systems theory to become the ecosystems or ecological approach. This is, in fact, the most prominent concept in social work education today (Howe, 1983; Zastrow and Kirst-Ashman, 1990).

Hartman and Laird (1983: 3) applaud the dawning of a new era in social work—the shift toward rigorous but holistic theories that broaden the parameters of social work practice:

> A revolution has been brewing for some time now, in the social sciences, in the helping professions, and in social work. Since the late 1950s and 1960s, social workers have been exploring the potential of general systems, cybernetic and ecological theories. . . . A scientific revolution has been in the making, one which in Kuhn's sense is ushering in a new paradigm.

6

FIGURE 1.1

Eco-Map

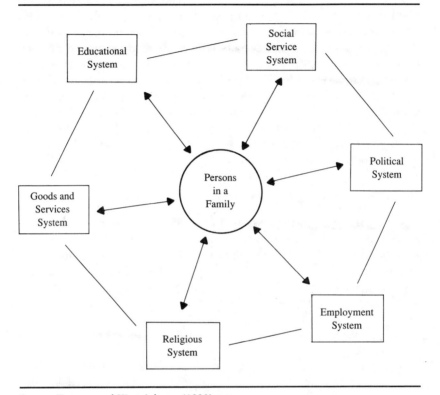

Source: Zastrow and Kirst-Ashman (1990).

An outgrowth in the biological sciences of a need to understand the interaction of the many varied components of the natural environment, the discipline of *ecology* came into being (Wessells and Hopson, 1988). The ecological framework or metaphor is interactionist; it does not view the person and the environment as separate entities but rather looks at the interaction between them (Howe, 1981). The ecological approach is holistic, biopsychosocial in its understanding of the person-in-the-environment and of the environment-in-the-person. In ecology, emphasis is on adaptation of the individual organism and of the system (such as the family system) to internal or external stress. Alcoholism in the family can be understood in terms of internal (illness within the individual) stress with a strong external-environmental component. The focal point of study would be the interaction among various parts of the alcoholic system.

The diagram in figure 1.1, from Zastrow and Kirst-Ashman (1990), illustrates the simultaneous interaction among persons and systems. The environmental factors are prominent here. The two-headed arrows represent the concept of interaction as opposed to linear causality (which would be represented by an arrow with one head). I have altered the original diagram to place the person *within* the family system instead of external to it. And I have linked the external systems with each other to indicate interconnectedness within the system. This diagram reflects a theme of contemporary social work—the complex interplay between person and environment. This is also the theme of this chapter. The presentation of the fundamentals of ecology that follows paves the way for the application of these concepts to specialized social work practice with clients who abuse, or are addicted to, alcohol.

THE ECOLOGICAL FRAMEWORK

Theories are ideas abstracted from experience and observation. Their purpose is to simplify and order the universe. Theories offer to behavioral scientists a general conceptual framework for understanding individuals in a wide range of situations. Theory from the science of ecology has been an especially promising development. Among the basic assumptions and concepts from biology are the following:

- The biological organism exists in dynamic *equilibrium* with its environment.
- Force exerted by the organism affects the environment, which in turn affects the organism. This concept is called *interactionism.*
- The organism *adapts,* partially adapts, or fails to adapt to stress induced by changes in the environment.
- Organisms work together to form a *system*: the whole is greater than the sum of the parts.

Because of its wide applicability to various aspects of the *human* condition, ecological theory provides an exceptionally good fit for conceptualizing and treating alcoholism. The key advantages of this framework are the breadth of the knowledge it encompasses, its malleability in terms of needs of various fields of study, and the environmental focus translated, in social work terms, as "the-person-in-the-situation" (see van Wormer, 1987). The emphasis on organism adaptation provides an appropriate metaphor to describe adaptation of the organism to the drug alcohol or to habituation to this drug.

Consistent with the environmental approach is the awareness that individual behavior is shaped by the biological, psychological, and social/

cultural components of human experience. Such influences have a differential impact on each individual, group, or community, depending on multidimensional experience. A change in one aspect of a person's or family's functioning has reverberating influences on other segments of reality.

Ecological theory is a framework for action, directed at the here-and-now interactions of individuals and families; work is toward altering, for enhanced functioning, the basic structure of those interactions. Unlike the *psychodynamic* approach in social work, which stresses personality or intrapsychic variables, the *ecological* approach tends to perceive personality and environmental characteristics in dynamic interaction with each other (Howe, 1981). The latter view is more complicated and psychologically demanding than the former; it goes against the natural tendency to simplify human experience. The ecological approach also goes against another tendency, which is to attribute another person's actions solely to *innate* personality characteristics rather than to a combination of factors (Bell, 1979; Howe, 1981).

SOCIAL WORK FRAMEWORK FOR ADDICTIONS WORK

As a conceptual framework for training social workers for addictions practice, the ecological perspective has the advantage of taking into account the complexities of addiction as an individual and family disturbance with strong biopsychosocial implications. Each chapter of this text is concerned with one or more dimensions of alcoholism. While the early chapters describe the environmental context and the social/historical framework for treatment activities, later chapters describe biological adaptation to alcohol abuse and the psychological and systemic components.

THE BIOLOGICAL REALM

Social workers should know that the course of addiction is chronic, progressive, and fatal in its consequences. The addiction is primary—it takes precedence over everything else. Good clinical practice is interdisciplinary. A thorough medical examination is required, to assess long-term effects of dietary and nutritional neglect. Testing for chemically induced changes may be indicated.

Use of the ecological model is invaluable for its recognition of biological components in human behavior. For successful substance abuse work, familiarity with the biochemical hereditary aspect of addiction is required as is familiarity with various techniques of relapse prevention that relate to the physical/psychological components of the disease. These issues will be dealt with in chapters 4 and 8, respectively.

THE PSYCHOLOGICAL DIMENSION

Social workers should not be doctrinaire about any one approach to the treatment of addiction for *all* clients but must recognize that what works for one individual may not work for another (Lewis, 1977). Alcohol and similar substances are powerful painkillers of both physical and psychological pain. Social workers should be aware of the self-medication function of mood-altering substances and of the need to address the psychological/emotional dimension of alcoholism/addiction.

Depression and anxiety are major factors in substance abuse. A treatment approach geared to cognitions and feelings is essential for long-term recovery. The reciprocal link between thought and affect is explored in depth in chapter 5.

Alcoholism treatment tends to be *present* oriented (van Wormer, 1987), as is contemporary ecological theory (Germain and Gitterman, 1980). Social workers, however, must never lose sight of underlying factors in the addiction process with specific individuals, such as the link between trauma in the *past* (rape, incest, war) and sedating in the *present* with alcohol and/or other numbing substances. Adequate attention to the psychological dimension includes issues of the unconscious and of the past as well as factors in the present and future.

SOCIAL DYNAMICS

Knowledge of a history of alcoholism and drug dependence in a family is essential to an informative and effective treatment intervention into the life of the alcoholic (Steinglass, 1979). The behavior of the individual alcoholic is affected by the role he or she plays in the family system and by the roles played by other family members.

The ecosystems approach (the blend common today between ecological and systems theories) is especially relevant to treatment of the alcoholic family. It is also relevant in an analysis of the client's social world, including friendship patterns and work relations. Peer group ties play a role in the development of alcoholism and in its alleviation. As the intoxication ceases, roles change, and the social system of which the client is a member can be expected to alter accordingly. Chapter 9 reviews contemporary knowledge concerning the dynamics of the alcoholic family.

THE CONCEPT OF INTERACTIONISM

"First the man takes a drink, the drink takes a drink, and the drink takes the man." Implicit in this Japanese saying is the notion of interaction or reciprocity. Interactional relationships are reciprocal exchanges between entities or between their elements in which each influences the other over time.

Both elements are changed, with consequences for both. According to linear or simple cause-and-effect thinking, however, a cause (such as mental illness) precedes an effect (abusive drinking). Where this type of causality is one-dimensional, transactional causality is circular. As Germain (1991) explains it, transactional causality occurs in a circular loop, in which an event or process may be a cause at one point and an effect at another in the ongoing flow around the loop of social, cultural, psychological, and biological process. Figure 1.2 demonstrates how the drinking/pain cycle may be conceived.

Similarly, low self-esteem may be viewed as both cause and effect of alcohol abuse. The advantage of the biopsychosocial, interactionist model over the simpler, more traditional framework is that it encourages a more complex view of the illness. As the model implies, alcoholics cannot be understood or properly treated in a social vacuum. Attention must be directed everywhere at once. The skilled social worker, like the anthropologist, seeks the pattern in the chaos, the "method in the madness." The skillful social worker is at once a theorist and a scientist.

FIGURE 1.2

Drinking/Pain Cycle

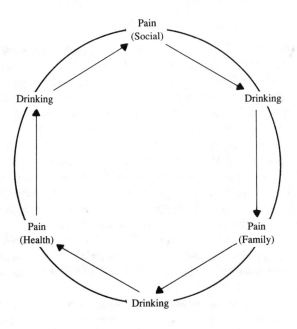

The alcoholism treatment system is under attack for its failure to deal with the multidimensional nature of alcohol addiction. Persons trained as alcoholism specialists typically are indoctrinated into a narrow disease model formulation based upon basic Alcoholics Anonymous (A.A.) principles for personal growth and recovery. Although an improvement over the psychodynamic approach to alcoholism treatment that preceded it, the traditional disease model and method are too narrow to constitute the sole treatment philosophy. Several authors have suggested that the ecological theory of human behavior holds the most promise for providing the paradigm for comprehensive appreciation of the overall context within which the alcohol-related problems are embedded (Jacobson, 1989; van Wormer, 1987; Wallace, 1989).

A central ecological concept is interactionism. Interactive or transactional in its approach, the ecological model has important implications for social work intervention into the world of the alcoholic client, a world that is both *creator of* and *created by* the alcoholic.

Another central ecological concept useful in thinking about alcoholism is *adaptation*. After a consideration of the meaning of adaptation, we will see how social work activity proceeds as theory integrated into practice.

THE ADAPTATIONAL PARADIGM
STRESS AND ADAPTATION

Adaptation is defined by Germain (1991) as an active process of self-change or environmental change or both, not a mere passive adjustment to circumstances. Adaptation comes about as human beings strive for the best person-environment "fit" possible between their needs and capacities and the requirements of the environment. Adaptation may be internal (physiological and psychological) or external (social and cultural), positive (stress conducing) or negative (stress reducing). Germain's concept of adaptation is transactional, that is, it expresses particular kinds of relationships or transactions between people and their environments. For the social worker, a dual focus on both person and environment is required.

Adaptation flows from and parallels stress, such as environmental stress. Stress may be conceived as a transactional phenomenon: the meaning of the stress itself and the experience of being stressed vary by individual. The process of behaving in conjunction with stress will modify the level of the stress and in turn produce altered behavior. Coping behavior may reduce or exacerbate the stress.

Germain's adaptational paradigm, with its interrelated concepts of adaptation, stress, and coping, provides a framework with which to view the various aspects of substance abuse—the stress (environmental), count-

12

erstress (drinking), and adaptation. Biologically, one can consider the remarkable physical adaptations by the body to enhance the ingestion and metabolism of the chemical alcohol. Both short-term and long-term adaptations may occur. Psychologically, one is impressed with the link between mental and emotional health and the drinking response. Psychological stress and alcohol abuse may be intertwined. Socially, adaptation to a pattern of drinking determines the company one keeps; likewise, the society reinforces the drinking life. In short, psychological and environmental factors have a powerful influence on the experience of stress and efforts to deal with it. It is not the magnitude of the stressor itself but the *perception* of its magnitude that is important. Germain's description of the ecology of serious illness applies to alcoholism even more than to other illnesses (1984: 64).

> Serious illness, then, represents perceived demands that other illnesses may exceed perceived resources for handling them, and so is a source of stress. The stress of illness, in turn, may lead to stress in other realms of life, especially in family, work, and community roles, thereby interfering with recovery or with management of disability.

Paralleling individual adaptation to stress by the alcoholic is the awesome set of demands imposed upon the family members. Each family will have its own peculiar style of adaptation—coping through blaming, denial, and protecting. The emotional and financial resources of the family may be almost entirely depleted by the stress of the alcoholic's illness.

In reviewing all the major scientific treatment evaluation research that has been done, Miller (1990) singles out the very few approaches of proven effectiveness. Among these are social skills training and stress management. These strategies relate to the coping dimension and to the important social work task to help clients find healthier ways of coping with pain than through self-medication.

Alcoholism, then, represents a reaction that is stressful for the individual and the family. The stress of drinking has a synergistic or multiplying effect throughout the family system and related environmental network. The family may come to serve in a mediating role between the alcoholic and other systems—work, school, larger family. But gradually, as the illness progresses, the bridges between the alcoholic and his or her social world will be broken. The family may then adapt to social isolation and continual stress of the progressing alcoholism, or members may regroup and form a reconstituted family without the alcoholic. A third alternative, of course, is treatment for the alcoholic and for the whole family. Treatment considerations would focus on healthy adaptation to the demands of familial sobriety.

The twin notions of interactionism and adaptation inform the alcoholism treatment process. Alcoholism treatment consists of three major activities—assessment/diagnosis of the illness, individual and group treatment interventions, and family systems work. At each of these levels, ecological theory, skillfully applied, will help the practitioner perceive the *total* picture of the client's situation rather than only a small part of it. Each of the major treatment areas is discussed from the ecological point of view. The brief descriptions contained in this portion of the chapter can be regarded as a preview of the chapters to come.

ASSESSMENT

The notions of causality and association are fundamental in assessment. Physiological, psychological, and sociocultural variants are all important as the clinician examines the effects of alcohol on the life of the individual. Is the individual addicted to alcohol and/or some other substance? Does the individual deny his or her condition? What are the genetic factors? What are the stresses?

Drinking and stress, stress and drinking: each is invariably cause and effect of the other. Identifying stress as the only cause of the drinking is to ignore recent research that strongly implicates a hereditary, biological factor in chemical dependency (Goodwin, 1976; Holden, 1985).

Identifying biology as the *sole* or even primary cause of the problematic drinking behavior would be a fallacy in the other direction, a failure to appreciate the situational stresses. Extreme personal loss, for example, is often seen as a factor in addiction in the aged or in parents who have lost their children. The significance of the crisis should be probed and the client encouraged to express and share feelings of loss, guilt, and fear. Assessment is of many things, including life situation, personality factors, and the meaning of drinking to the individual. The onset of the illness may be studied as the consequence of exchanges between individual characteristics and adaptation to environmental stress in the presence of a disease agent (Germain, 1984).

The assessment portion of the treatment consists of two or three initial sessions. Written tests are usually administered during the first session and diagnosis of the nature and extent of the problem given during the second session. A contract is drawn up at this time with the plan and requirements of treatment. Specifics on assessment activities are provided in chapter 11.

The ecological influence comes into play with regard to the focus of the interview and the facts solicited. Through carefully focused questions, a picture of the alcoholic's social environment and of his or her role in the environment is mapped out. Who are the other people in the picture, and how have they adapted to the client's drinking? What functions does the drinking serve for the client and the family members?

14

Some particularly useful areas for diagnostic exploration are: (1) an analysis of coping skills, including patterns that minimize and maximize stress; (2) an analysis of the subjective experiences of stress that evoke the coping response (e.g., drinking, fighting); (3) the identification of some of the specific problem solving tasks that need to be accomplished in connection with treatment; and (4) an assessment of internal and external support systems that will enhance recovery. Cultivation of hope and optimism are key ingredients in treatment from the very first professional encounter.

INDIVIDUAL TREATMENT INTERVENTIONS

Two types of bias common among practitioners as they approach social problems are the bias toward intrapersonal qualities (discussed earlier) and a bias toward extraneous or situational factors. Interventions employed reflect the bias. The former or psychodynamic orientation to alcohol abuse is considered risky so far as the client's relapse is concerned and not very conducive to recovery (Krystal, 1985). At the other extreme, the situational bias may furnish the client with just the rationale needed to drink some more. The ecological-interactionist perspective offers a framework that focuses directly and continuously upon the specific aspects of the unique social setting and the individual's dynamic role within it. The development of the "ecological therapies," as Dulfano (1982) notes, has given to alcoholism therapy tools to launch a multi-effort attack on both the intrapsychic and interpersonal components of the alcoholism syndrome.

The majority of alcoholism counselors are themselves alcoholics with many years of sobriety. Termed "recovering alcoholics" in the profession, such counselors have "learned the ropes" through their own addiction and recovery through a self-help program. There is a great deal that the professionally trained but nonalcoholic counselor can learn from the counselor "who has been there." The street-wise counselor is likely to be "an old hand" at cutting through the alcoholic's denial, rationalization, minimization, and guilt. The recovering person without professional education can learn a great deal from the professional of the ecological school. An interdisciplinary team of workers is often considered the ideal from a treatment point of view (Lawson, Ellis, and Rivers, 1984).

The ecological model provides a coherent theoretical framework based on sound empirical data and clinical experience; it is a model from which appropriate intervention techniques may be derived. Interventions are aimed directly at a client's biopsychosocial needs. The *physiological* aspects of alcoholism are integrated with psychological and social factors for a holistic and individualized approach. Major interventions to address the physiological realities are gentle confrontation and, above all else,

15

education. The therapist must educate the client in how to function in his or her social world as a person with certain physical vulnerabilities. Active involvement in a local Alcoholics Anonymous (A.A.) group may be encouraged. To help the person recover physically and mentally from years of gross physical abuse, the therapist may provide facts about general health and nutrition.

Approaching the *psychological* dimension, the practitioner will utilize all the usual techniques of social work practice—for example, intensive individual and group counseling, crisis intervention, and counseling in the areas of depression, anger management, career planning, and marital counseling. Special attention is given to clarification and identification of feelings.

Work in the *social* realm involves direct intervention in the environment to bring the newly sober person back into society.

Behind all the interventions is the therapist's awareness of the client as a person-in-situation, as a person who both shapes and is shaped by the situation he or she is in. Questions for the worker to consider are: What is the present reality (socially, culturally, economically)? What are the patterns? Questions relevant to the treatment reality are: How does the client respond to the label "alcoholic"? What are the legal constraints (driving offenses, child custody issues, parole or probation requirements) in the client's life? And to what extent is the client actively involved in maintaining some personal control over this situation? The overall treatment task is to help steer the client out of the muddy waters into clear water for smooth sailing. The worker will help the client "to make a way out of no way."

FAMILY SYSTEMS WORK

Because ecological theory is reality based, it can serve as a guide to all forms of treatment: individual, family, group, or community. Perception, goals, and patterns are the principal concerns of this approach. Attention is paid to the complex ways in which individual persons and families are reciprocally linked with each other.

The family systems concept, though sometimes presented as a separate theory, can be conceived of as one of the key components of the interactionism of ecological theory. This formulation of the family as a system, and of the individual as a subsystem in the family, is one of the most dynamic and useful developments in alcoholism counseling. Numerous recent journal articles and workshops all have pursued the theme of the importance of family systems work with the alcoholic. There are numerous journals—*Focus on Chemically Dependent Families, Focus on Educating Professionals in Family Recovery,* and *Change: For and about Adult Children*—devoted to the families of chemically addicted persons.

Unfortunately, as Dulfano (1982) observes, family treatment is given only lip service. The practice is to zero in on the individual alcoholic as we have always done. Yet for effective individual treatment, the entire family must be prepared to accept back as a member a sober and therefore changed individual.

Germain and Gitterman (1980) adapt an ecological perspective to problems in living. Their framework for examining painful life transitions is relevant to the family situation of change caused by the alcoholism treatment process itself. Life transitions, write Germain and Gitterman, hold the potential of challenge and growth for individuals and families. Life transitions may be differentiated as (1) developmental stages and tasks, (2) status changes and role demands/conflicts, and (3) the particular crises that have arisen as a result of 1 and 2.

Previously stabilized relationships and communication patterns may have deteriorated under the stress of one family member's illness. New adaptive forms have developed, and these now may be upset by the member's emerging sobriety. The therapist has a role to play in educating the family to deal with the issue of alcoholism and in preparing family members for some jolting changes. Interventions are directed toward destructive communication patterns and ruptured role relationships (Kaufman and Pattison, 1981).

The ecological approach offers to family therapy a nonlinear view of causation, a circular chain of acts and reactions. Each member in the family group may at once be victim and victimizer of the others. The alcoholism therapist may join the family unit temporarily, acting as a pseudo family member to help shape a way for healthy and adaptive family functioning.

Techniques of changing an alcoholic family nearly always involve restructuring boundaries so as to allow the alcoholic back in. While alcoholism can adversely affect family system functioning, dysfunctional family systems can promote and maintain alcoholism. Dulfano (1982) describes ways of rebuilding the spouse subsystem and the parental subsystem to provide for the necessary shifts in family equilibrium to accommodate the newly sober member.

According to the ecological view, therapists who fail to consider the entire family's structure and to intervene in this structure are unlikely to effect lasting change.

CONCLUSION

Alcoholism counseling is a field in search of a model. The model that is needed should include the physiological nature of alcoholism in addition to the personal and interpersonal dimensions. The paradigm chosen should be one that will readily provide the tools and concepts for direct practice intervention.

The ecological perspective has been proposed as a framework for improving the care provided for alcoholic persons and their families and for unifying alcoholism treatment therapy. The disease model, which is the dominant organizing framework, is actually a mere explanation and not a theory or framework at all. The A.A. Steps that focus on spiritual and psychological growth are very effective in themselves but are unrelated theoretically to the disease model with which they are associated.

The beauty of ecological theory is its sweep; it can subsume within its framework other theoretical models and treatment orientations. There is no "either-or" with this formulation—viewing the person-in-the-situation includes the total biopsychosocial reality. The concepts of ecology—adaptation, equilibrium, systems, interaction—are not unique. What the ecological perspective can bring to counseling alcoholics is an increased capacity to conceptualize the environmental components in interaction and an awareness of the ways in which the social environment shapes and is shaped by the individual alcoholic. Further research is needed to elaborate on adapting ecological principles to each of the specific areas of diagnosis, individual and group therapy, and family counseling.

SUMMARY

This chapter presented an overview of pertinent theoretical concepts and how they organize the social work task of reshaping the person-environment configuration for healthy, nonaddictive living. The ecological framework, with its biopsychosocial conceptualization of alcoholism, is offered as a truly comprehensive framework appropriate for treating an illness of complexity.

The multidisciplinary and interdisciplinary nature of the alcoholism treatment field was explored. The medical component is of most obvious significance during the early period of sobriety; the cognitive/emotional components are more easily addressed during the middle and later stages of treatment; and the social aspects of addiction are apparent at every level.

Because the leading paradigm of social work today is the ecological or ecosystems framework, social work practitioners should be ideal candidates for direct practice with clients who have alcohol problems.

Working with clients troubled by compulsive and addictive behavior requires extensive knowledge of the health, social, and psychological complexities. Specific training is also required in the fundamentals of alcoholism treatment work. Familiarity with the ecological concepts of interactionism and adaptation help the worker overcome narrow professional biases so as to intervene in a holistic fashion.

This chapter has provided a brief description of some of the roles and functions required of the social worker in this field. Assessment of alcoholism, individual and group intervention, and family systems therapy are the three activities described. Parts Two and Three will draw on the ecological concepts introduced in this chapter to examine the specific skills required for professional practice with alcoholic clients. The remaining chapters of this section will provide an overview of the alcoholism treatment apparatus: the historical context is covered in chapter 2 and the dynamic, contemporary context in chapter 3.

REVIEW QUESTIONS

1. What are some of the basic assumptions of the ecological school of social work?

2. How do social work's psychodynamic approach and the ecological approach differ?

3. How would the traditional psychodynamic approach view alcoholism?

4. How does the ecological approach view alcoholism? Discuss each of the three dimensions of human behavior: biological, psychological, and social.

5. Define the ecological concepts of interactionism and adaptation. What is the connection between drinking and stress, stress and drinking?

6. How can assessment be multidimensional? What are the major fallacies made by social workers with regard to causation?

7. What are the types of interventions that can be used to address alcoholism as a physical disease? How about the *psychological* realities?

8. How can the ecological framework account for the perpetuation of alcoholism within the dysfunctional family system?

2

HISTORICAL CONTEXT

Drink is in itself a good creature of God, and to be received with
thankfulness, but the abuse of drink is from Satan.
　—Increase Mather, 1673

America's Puritan tradition could never be reconciled with the
American's thirst.
　—D. W. Goodwin, *Alcohol and the Writer*, p. 203

　　Cultural and historical forces have shaped the understanding and
treatment of alcoholism. But before alcoholism came, there was alcohol.
Alternatively worshipped, tolerated, and reviled, alcohol has played a
vibrant role in the history of humankind. While alcohol has influenced
the social, political, and economic life of societies, the social, political,
and economic aspects of life have influenced the partaking of alcohol.
This chapter offers a brief overview of the historical uses and abuses of
this powerful substance. We will look at the earliest civilizations through
the Middle Ages to the modern world as represented by the United States
with respect to the nature and impact of alcoholic beverages. At times,
the technological advances have exceeded the human capacity to absorb
them—the introduction of wine was one thing, the discovery of distilled
spirits quite another. To control liquor consumption, stringent social sanctions were sometimes applied.
　　We will trace the course of how *alcoholism* became defined and,
over time, redefined. From evangelism to criminalization to medicalization, the course has been paved with many ill-fated attempts at social

control. Finally, we examine the treatment responses in historical context. Treatment will be viewed as offering a clever compromise between the forces that say "no one should drink" and those that say "live and let live." The compromise promotes abstinence for the few (alcoholics) who cannot drink and unmitigated enjoyment for the large numbers who can.

EARLY CIVILIZATIONS

No one knows what kind of intoxicant came first—wine, beer, or mead. Fermentation, a combustive action of yeasts that occur naturally on plants in which the sugar is converted to alcohol, can occur any time grapes, berries, or honey are left exposed long enough to the warm air. So it is no wonder that the making of wines and beers developed in ancient societies. A plethora of customs and regulations accompanied their use. Drinking was central to customs and rites of passage such as births, marriage, feasts, magic, and hospitality. As an aid to a society's simple expression of communal values, alcohol was looked upon as a beneficent beverage. The level of tolerance for women's drinking—as well as for men's—reflected cultural attitudes toward alcohol itself.

While most of the pre-Columbian Native American peoples lacked knowledge of alcohol, several of the cultures of northern Mexico and the southwestern United States consumed wine and beer. Columbus found the Caribbean Indians drinking beer from fermented maize. Limited to communal fiestas, drunkenness was socially sanctioned and therefore not disruptive.

The Egyptians goddess, Isis, was promoting beer in 3,000 B.C. (Royce, 1989). As we know from papyri, Egyptian doctors included beer or wine in their prescriptions, as did the Sumerians. Ancient Romans had their god of drink, Bacchus, and the Greeks their Dionysus. The Graeco-Roman classics abound with descriptions of festive drinking and often drunkenness. While the men of classical Greece enjoyed their revelry and *symposia* ("drinking together"), women's abuse of alcohol was linked to its harmful effects on unborn children (Sandmaier, 1992).

From the Old Testament of the Bible, we learn of drinking practices of the Hebrews. Abundant wine made from grapes was regarded as a blessing that could "gladden the heart of man" (Psalms 105:15, King James version). That it also had the property to wreak some havoc is revealed in Genesis 9:20:

> And Noah began to be an husbandman, and he planted a vineyard: And he drank of the wine and was drunken; and he was uncovered within his tent.

Similarly, Proverbs 33: 29–30 provides a strong cautionary note:

> Who hath woe? Who hath sorrow? Who hath contentions? Who hath babbling? Who hath wounds without cause? Who hath redness of eyes? They that tarry long at the wine; they that go to seek mixed wine.

Whereas the large majority of the Hebrews rejoiced in wine and used it for medicinal and nutritional purposes, there were only occasional lapses into excess. In religious practices, wine was relegated to a sacred and symbolic role. The New Testament depicts this common association.

While the Hebrews condoned drinking but not drunkenness, a different kind of religious control was adopted later in the seventh century by Islam. The Koran simply condemned wine altogether, and an effective prohibition against all alcoholic beverages prevailed. In the Far East, India and China, alcohol consumption was secularized and widespread (Levin, 1990).

The long road from the sacred to the profane was shortened by a tenth century discovery of an Arabian physician (Kinney and Leaton, 1991). The word *alcohol* itself is derived from the Arabic *al-kuhul* (Ayto, 1990). The discovery of distilled spirits, which made possible the manufacture of much stronger alcoholic concoctions, is an instance of the reach of technology exceeding its grasp. The devastation unleashed with this new development, however, did not occur suddenly but took place over centuries of use (Orford, 1985).

Originally, this distilled alcohol was a powder, not a liquid. It was used as a cosmetic for darkening the eyelids and as a medicine. Use of distilled liquors gradually became common in Europe.

MODERN EUROPEAN HISTORY

Before liquor reached Norway in earnest in the seventeenth century, beer brewed from oats and barley was the predominant alcoholic beverage. Peasants were required to brew this substance for harvest festivals. With grains somewhat scarce at these northern latitudes, beer must have been in short supply (Brun-Gulbrandsen, 1988). As time went by, distilling to make stronger alcoholic beverages was done on most of the farms.

The early to mid-eighteenth century in England offers a prime example of the impact of technology on society. Founded in 1575, the oldest distillery in the world still in operation is in Amsterdam. From a concoction of grains, herbs, and juniper berries, *jenever* or gin was produced. (The word *booze* is thought to be a corruption of the middle Dutch *busen*—"drink much alcohol.") The availability of cheap gin, combined with the population displacement caused by industrialization and associated with the growth of an urban proletariat, contributed to an epidemic of drunkenness (Levin, 1990). The devastation was so great, in fact, that a staggering infant mortality rate and child starvation rate combined to prevent a growth in population from 1700 to 1750. Crimes of violence and immorality among all social classes, but most evident among the poor, gave the age a debaucherous character, preserved in political commentary and the early novel.

ON NORTH AMERICAN SHORES

Drinking had been a part of the European cultural scene. Transplanted to what used to be considered the "new world," the drinking culture took on some peculiarities of the new land. The pilgrims chose to land at Plymouth, in fact, in order to dispense the dwindling supplies of beer with all due speed. A fight between the settlers who faced a long cold winter and the sailors who faced a long dry return home was averted when supplies were divided up. In these early days, beer was considered indispensable to health and life. The early settlers did not plan to rely on water for subsistence. It is not surprising, therefore, that more beer than water was carried on the *Mayflower* (Lender and Martin, 1982). The colonists did learn to drink water, but they also learned to make a brew from Indian corn which satisfied their needs for a time. Improvements in the technology of the manufacture of distilled beverages, however, was to change all this.

With the passage of time, liquor came to be valued for both its high alcohol content and its shipping advantages. The Puritans regarded rum as "God's good creature." Although an occasional drunk was placed in the stocks, the tavern was the center of social, economic, and political activity (Levin, 1990). As time passed, Jamaican rum seemed to have become the solution to the new nation's thirst. For rum's sake, New Englanders became the bankers of the slave trade that supplied the sugar cane and molasses needed to produce rum (Kinney and Leaton, 1991).

As the colonists turned to distilling hard liquor, they proved as adaptable as they had earlier in producing passable beer. Honey, corn, rye, berries, and apples were used in domestic production. A general lack of concern about alcoholism and its problems was one of the most significant features of the colonial era (Lender and Martin, 1982). Strong drink was thought to protect against disease and to be conducive to good health. Since good drinking water was not always available, there was some substance to this argument. And as long as the social norms were followed, drinking excesses could be tolerated. Unlike beer, however, the stronger stuff soon acquired a dubious reputation.

The relationship of alcohol abuse, the availability of cheap spirits, and the weakening of social controls in a given society or culture can be easily documented (Levin, 1990). In both England and her colonies, moral depravity, especially among the poor, was seen to be both the cause and effect of habitual intoxication. Distilled spirits in early America appeared side-by-side with easy money, the image of manliness, and all-round good cheer (Moynihan, 1993). Drinking whiskey at breakfast became routine; laborers digging the Erie Canal were allotted a quart of whiskey a day.

Severe restrictions, on the other hand, were placed on drinking by slaves. Although masters might reward slaves with alcoholic beverages, especially at holiday times, drinking was seen as a hindrance to work. Besides, there was a deep-seated fear among whites that blacks, like Indians, were especially prone to violence when intoxicated (Lender and Martin, 1982). Slave codes mandated harsh measures against slaves who drank without permission. The typical drinking pattern taught to the slaves by their masters was a long period of abstinence punctuated by a binge. Abolitionist Frederick Douglass declared that one might just as well be a slave to man as to rum.

EARLY ATTEMPTS TO REGULATE ALCOHOL IN THE UNITED STATES

Of religious groups during the eighteenth century, only the Quakers, who were persuaded for rational reasons, and the Methodists, who were moved more by faith and morals, opposed the drinking of distilled spirits. Yet the period 1725 to 1825 was notorious for the extent of the hard drinking that took place (nearly a half pint of hard liquor per man each day) and for the kind of ribald and bellicose behavior often associated with this practice. When the government attempted to impose an excise tax upon whiskey (seen as the poor man's drink), mass discontent broke out, culminating in the Whiskey Rebellion of 1794. The measure was rescinded.

After 1800, drinking in groups to the point of total inebriation had ideological overtones. Such drinking was a symbol of egalitarianism. The guest at an evening party who refused to drink, reports historian Rorabaugh (1979), might be physically forced to do so. Refusal could be downright dangerous. Some drinking party guests were even killed because of such stubborn abstinence. The wildest celebration of the year came with Independence Day—the Fourth of July—which evoked a national intoxication, according to Rorabaugh. To be drunk was to be free.

The male drinking cult was pervasive. Adolescents perceived drinking brandy in a tavern as an initiation rite of manhood. Early exposure of white male children to alcohol was encouraged as an educational experience. Parents intended to help their infants and small children get used to the taste of strong alcohol as soon as possible.

THE TEMPERANCE MOVEMENT

Social commentators decried the ruination of the young nation, the death of family life. The seeds for a counterrevolution were sown. Royce (1989),

24

tracing "the temperance to abstinence movements" during the years 1825–1919, describes how, out of a general concern for community life and for disciplined work, the temperance movement was born. The word *temperance* means "moderation." The temperance movement opposed only spirits, not wine and beer, which were considered harmless. A Calvinist clergyman spearheaded the movement. The ministers of the day, especially the descendants of Puritans, aligned with concerned citizens to condemn the wasteful and debaucherous behavior that was characteristic of the day. The new focus was on saving the family (Metzger, 1988).

Two currents of thought, the temperance and medical approaches, were inextricably interwoven in the nineteenth century as in recent times. At the time, these views—the one stressing evil and the other illness—appeared in opposition. While one stressed the supply side of the drug alcohol, the other focused on reducing the need for the drug. Unity came because of awareness of a major social problem and the urgent need to address it.

The temperance proponents, in order to reduce habitual drunkenness, promoted taking an abstinence pledge. Public confession figured in the decision to take this pledge. In Britain, the temperance movement acquired following under the leadership of a charismatic priest, Father Matthew. Ireland was practically transformed into a nation of teetotalers during this period. (The word *teetotaler* came from "T = total abstinence," which was put next to a person's name on the society's rolls.) In Scotland, the Presbyterian ministry led the way toward total abstinence, which became common among the middle classes in the early 1900s (Plant, et al., 1992). Father Matthew's well-publicized work had a large following in North America, especially among the Irish. In Norway, strong anti-alcoholic measures were put into effect; distilling at home was outlawed.

The temperance woman represented the Victorian ideal of purity; she fought alcohol as a rude intrusion upon the family, a threat to the family's very survival. As Sandmaier (1992) indicates, the temperance woman was in fact more radical than her image suggests. She fought against men's drunkenness and for the liberation of women from the tyranny of this drunkenness. Eventually, the volunteer army of church women led into another movement of renown, the women's suffrage movement.

The way a society views alcoholism is culturally constructed and culturally bounded. Different historical periods promote distinctive dominant models of treatment, and different cultural groups within one historical period favor one or another social construction, in terms of which excessive drinking is dealt with. Alasuutari (1992) draws on Levin's (1990) concept of the temperance cultures. Such cultures, characteristic of North America, Britain, Australia, New Zealand, and all of Scandinavia, developed ongoing temperance movements in the nineteenth and early twentieth centuries. These temperance cultures have been shaped by the cultures of Protestantism and have been or still are places where people drink a considerable portion of their alcohol as liquor. According to Levin, in the "neotemperance" era of today, the original temperance cultures retain a distinctive and strong cultural focus on the problematic consequences of alcoholic drink.

THE MEDICAL VIEW

The medical approach was the forerunner of a social movement that was to revolutionize thinking on a serious concern of the day. Doctors Thomas Trotter in Britain and Benjamin Rush in the United States took widely reported scientific positions on the subject of "inebriety." Dr. Rush received his medical education at the University of Edinburgh, where he came to realize that the healthful qualities of rum and other hard liquors were overrated. His role as surgeon general in the Revolutionary War strengthened his convictions. The army's traditional rum ration, Rush asserted, caused diseases and a lack of vigor (Rorabaugh, 1979). With the publication of several influential pamphlets, Rush became the first in modern times (the Roman, Seneca, had equated uncontrolled drinking with insanity) to treat alcohol abuse as a medical problem and as a disease (Levin, 1990). Congruent with the teachings of the temperance movement, Rush blamed the use of *hard* liquor for socially disruptive drinking. For a cure, he prescribed psychotherapy and even flogging. His scientific treatises on the nature of the compulsive loss of control over drinking and on the addictive qualities of distilled beverages provided a rational foundation for the philosophy of abstinence that was to be the solution of the future.

THE PROHIBITION MOVEMENT, 1825–1920

During the nineteenth century, the drinking preferences of Americans were altered by the thousands of immigrants to the United States (Helzer and Canino, 1992). A tremendous amount of beer was consumed by the large numbers of German immigrants. The Irish immigrants also carried their drinking habits with them. Unlike the Germans, the Irish tolerated a pattern of regular intoxication. The anti-immigrant and anti-Catholic xenophobia combined to give the temperance movement a new and fierce momentum. Saloons, which were frequented by working classes and immigrants, were feared as threats to the middle-class home and as forums for labor union organizers (Helzer and Canino, 1992). The Anti-Saloon League grew out of these sentiments and became a strong lobbying group.

Next to the movement to abolish slavery, the most popular and influential social movement of nineteenth century America concerned the effort to limit and prohibit the use of alcohol (Moynihan, 1993). The struggle between the "wets" and the "drys" was the main focus of American politics and religion in the late nineteenth and early twentieth centuries. Emotionally heated debates pervaded American life, drinking in moderation being condemned as strongly as alcohol abuse. From congregations to the ballot box, a fervor to eliminate all access to alcohol got underway. Ever-increasing numbers of abstainers began to bombard state legislatures with demands for the abolition of demon rum. As early as 1846, temperance forces in Maine persuaded the legislature to outlaw the manufacture and sale of distilled liquors (Lender and Martin, 1982).

Following the Civil War and the dramatic social changes inherent in industrialization and urbanization, skid rows began to appear in the poorest sections of towns. The term derived from Seattle's Skid Road, which lumbermen had built to "skid" timber downhill (Lender and Martin, 1982). The urban saloon derived its name from the French word *salon*, meaning "room."

Whether or not to employ legal remedies for social ills was the burning question as the century drew to a close. The greatest popular orator of the pulpit of his day, the Reverend T. Dewitt Talmage, addressed the "liquor question" in these words:

> I believe we must bring into greater prominence moral suasion in overcoming this evil and expect less of legal enactment. People have made the question for temperance too much a legal question and have neglected moral suasion, without which all laws of creation would amount to nothing. (Rush, 1902: 184)

However, legal forces ultimately prevailed. By the time World War I broke out, anti-German sentiment was overwhelming. Since many of the brewers had German names, the antiliquor forces were able to capitalize on this connection to link prohibition with patriotism. The support of the corporate world, which had an interest in promoting sober worker habits and reducing spending on alcohol, was instrumental in the passage of the Eighteenth Amendment to the Constitution establishing national prohibition in 1919 (to begin in 1920).

RESTRICTIVE MEASURES IN VARIOUS OTHER COUNTRIES

Outside North America, the blame was put on the alcohol rather than the consumer. Efforts, therefore, were geared toward restrictions of access. Orford (1985), in a review of policies in Europe and elsewhere, relates how the British government became involved in alcohol control through taxation in the eighteenth century, and governments around the world involved themselves in establishing controls two centuries later. Belgium, Denmark, and Sweden all introduced—and Britain reintroduced—regulations during or just after the First World War. Unusually comprehensive, they included a ration book system, taxation controls, licensing restrictions, and temperance boards to forbid alcohol sales or driver's licenses to problem drinkers. Denmark's taxation was drastic: the tax on spirits was increased thirty-four-fold, and the consumption decreased markedly. In varying degrees, as Smart and Mora (1986) note, the sale of alcoholic beverages has been prohibited in the United States, in all but one province in Canada, and in all Scandinavian countries. Temperance sentiment, in contrast, seems never to have existed in Latin American countries, religious festivals being times of great drinking and inordinate drunkenness.

In Ireland, in the North as well as the South, there are strong social pressures for an individual to take a teetotal pledge. Particularly strong normative prohibitions discourage adolescent drinking in Ireland (Christiansen and Teahan, 1987). Northern Ireland, in fact, has the highest level of total abstinence in Europe. Yet alcoholism is a persistent problem. Consistent with Irish cultural norms, total abstinence is regarded as a realistic and necessary goal for alcoholics (Davidson, 1991). In both parts of Ireland, the rate of abstinence is higher than in England, yet drinking, when it does occur, is problematic and associated with aggression. In short, drinking is an issue generating much emotion and significant social but not legal sanctioning in Ireland.

Totalitarian methods in the Arab countries include a range of severe punishments, often physical. In parts of the world dominated by Islam, prohibition efforts have been strictly yet successfully applied. These efforts have had the sanction of religion and culture. They are effective to the present day.

THE PROHIBITION EXPERIENCE IN THE UNITED STATES

Of attempts throughout history to control the use of alcohol, the most resounding failure was that of the United States from 1920 to 1933 (*Encyclopaedia Britannica*, 1993). The American experiment with prohibition—the "noble experiment"—gave drinking the allure of the forbidden and led to the burgeoning and glamorizing of crime, the growth of organized crime, the corruption of the police and politicians, and the criminalizing of ordinary citizens.

The brother of Mafia godfather Sam Giancana gives, in *Double Cross* (1992), a graphic account of what began in Chicago during the years of Prohibition—the Mafia/Hollywood/Las Vegas/Washington, D.C., connection that continues to the present day:

> [Joseph] Kennedy's ties to the underworld intersected a hundred points. Besides making a fortune in bootlegging, Kennedy had made a financial killing in Hollywood in the twenties—with the help of persuasive behind-the-scenes with New York and Chicago muscle. When Prohibition came to a close, as part of a national agreement between the various bootleggers, Kennedy held on to three of the most lucrative booze distributorships in the country—Gordon's gin, Dewar's, and Haig & Haig—through his company, Somerset Imports. (Giancana and Giancana, 1992: 227)

If the attempt was noble, the end result was sad. Although the quantity of alcohol consumed did go down and the cirrhosis of the liver rate with it, the overall social consequences were devastating. As Thornton (1992) argues, the potency of the alcohol that was manufactured increased about 150 percent or higher compared to what was produced before or after Prohibition. Those products also were likely to contain dangerous adulterants. The death rate from poisoned liquor was appallingly high at this time. Homicide rates in large cities increased by 78 percent over the pre-Prohibition figures. As Thornton notes, the lessons of Prohibition remain important today. They apply not only to the debate over the war on drugs but also to such issues as censorship and bans on insider trading, abortion, and gambling.

Economic interests played a role in the impetus to repeal, as they had in the impetus to criminalize. Corporate moguls such as John D. Rockefeller believed that Repeal would lower income taxes by substituting taxes on alcohol (Helzer and Canino, 1992). The widespread disrespect for the law that had developed made people realize that the cure had become worse then the original problem. Moreover, the Depression created a desperate demand for more jobs and government revenue, and a hope that perhaps the reestablishment of the liquor industry could help in this regard. Besides, the new immigration quotas stemmed the tide of immigration. In 1933, the Eighteenth Amendment was repealed.

Today, the legacy of Prohibition prevails. Age-restrictive laws have been instituted. In the South, dry counties and townships still outlaw the sale of alcohol, while Sunday sales of alcohol are illegal in many places. The war against other drugs is still waged on legal fronts, sometimes by means of well publicized semi-military style operations.

THE SCIENTIFIC APPROACH

Along with the changes in sanctions and social control, there is a corresponding change in definition of the deviant act. As alcohol became freely available, the punishment impulse diminished. Also, the fault could not be located in the alcohol itself. A new model was needed.

The American disease model served as a useful transition from the period of prohibition to the period of legalization (Miller and Hester, 1989). Models do not so much arise suddenly to fill the gap as they are rediscovered and reinvented. The medical thinking had not changed substantially since the writings of Dr. Rush. Recently, the *Journal of the American Medical Association* reprinted an essay, "Inebriety among Women in this Country," written in 1892. The editorial, in concurrence with its British counterpart, states:

> As a periodical drinker, profound neuroses come on and the drink craze changes. The *British Medical Journal* urges, very wisely, that this "National folly" of arresting and sending to jail these victims, should cease. A new departure is demanded, and they should be recognized as diseased and sent to hospitals, under the care of physicians. (*JAMA,* 1892: 530–31)

And well before this, in 1849 in Sweden, the physician Magnus Huss introduced the term *alcoholism* in his classical essay, "Alcoholismus chronicus." And it was in 1790 that the influential pamphlet, *An Inquiry into the Effects of Spirituous Liquors on the Human Body,* by Benjamin Rush, was published. So the philosophy was hardly new when Alcoholics Anonymous espoused it or when Jellinek gave it form and substance. What was significant was the dominance that the medical view was to assume.

THE IMPACT OF ALCOHOLICS ANONYMOUS

Nan Robertson (1988), in her affectionate and humorous portrait of the founding of Alcoholics Anonymous, records a momentous event. Bill W., a stockbroker from New York, was transplanted in 1935 in Akron, Ohio, and in his loneliness he had a desperate desire to drink. Seeking the help of an Oxford Group member (a religious sobriety group) he was referred to Dr. Bob, not because Dr. Bob was sober but because Dr. Bob could not stop drinking. The Oxford Group member, Henrietta Seiberling, brought these two together in her home. Dr. Bob arrived reluctantly in the company of his wife. From his wife he extracted a promise, "We will not stay over fifteen minutes."

Bill W., sixteen years younger than Dr. Bob, was dramatically different in temperament. A flamboyant person, he indulged in overstatement and fantasy. Later his compulsive womanizing would be a constant source of despair to fellow A.A. members. Dr. Bob, on the other hand, was scholarly, formidable, and somewhat cold. Somehow the chemistry worked. In the end, this unlikely pair talked together until almost midnight; they talked together in order to stay sober. On that historic night in 1935, the two men who became the founders of Alcoholics Anonymous set a pattern that has been followed by millions of alcoholics all over the world.

Bill W., as a stockbroker, had the personality to spread the word of the miracle of A.A. His four books, beginning in 1939 with *Alcoholics Anonymous* (known as the Big Book), gave the movement its name. (For more of the early days of the A.A. legacy, see *Getting Better: Inside Alcoholics Anonymous* by Robertson, 1988.)

With the founding and spread of Alcoholics Anonymous was born the American disease model of alcoholism (Miller and Hester, 1989). Unlike the temperance approach to drinking, this model assumes that there are some people who are more susceptible to alcohol than others and that these individuals cannot drink, in contrast to other individuals who can always drink in moderation. The alcoholic suffers from loss of control over alcohol.

Although no one knows how many alcoholics have failed to recover through Alcoholics Anonymous, there are over a million recovering alcoholics who are members of A.A. throughout the world to attest to its success. Lender and Martin (1982) explain the success in terms of structure and sense of community given to A.A. members. Members help each other stay sober and in so doing reinforce their own sobriety. The basic precepts of A.A. are spelled out in the next chapter.

The phenomenon of Alcoholics Anonymous had a rebound effect on scientific research into alcoholism, which, in turn, provided acceptance for the treatment of alcoholism as a disease. The caliber of research grew more rigorous over time. The Yale University Center of Alcohol Studies was founded in the late 1930s and included an experimental, treatment counterpart. The establishment of this august body of research stimulated exciting scientific exploration into the new field. In 1940, the *Quarterly Journal of Studies on Alcohol* (now the *Journal of Studies on Alcohol*) became the first specialized journal of this nature. Today, it remains the most empirically based and prestigious of the American alcoholism journals. In Britain this distinction would go to the *British Journal of Addiction,* which had its inception in 1884 as the *British Journal of Inebriety.* The Scandinavian countries were among the first to conduct scientific research into alcoholism. The Yale Center has moved to Rutgers, the State University of New Jersey, and has become the Rutgers Center for Alcohol Studies.

THE PIONEERING WORK OF JELLINEK

The popularization of the disease concept is attributed to the work of E.M. Jellinek, whose affiliation with the Yale Center spanned the 1950s and early 1960s (Lender and Martin, 1982). Jellinek conducted research

31

on A.A. members. His worldwide travels for the World Health Organization helped provide him with an international perspective for research, a perspective that provided the basis for his typology of alcoholics.

Jellinek's sociocultural analysis of alcoholism was the theoretical basis for his book, *The Disease Concept of Alcoholism*, published in 1960. The cultural patterns that differentiate one country from another, according to Jellinek, help account for the drinking patterns. Thus, the Italian contempt for alcohol intoxication is in contrast to the French tolerance for intoxication, accompanied by an insistence that everyone drink. Furthermore, as Jellinek observed, the drinking patterns are to a large extent ascribable to the beverages that contain the alcohol—that is, wine or beer are associated with continual use and distilled spirits with "concentrated" consumption over short periods.

Using letters of the Greek alphabet, Jellinek singled out five "species of alcoholism" that he considered to be disease-related:

- *Alpha alcoholism* represents an undisciplined use of alcoholic beverages. Drinking may relieve emotional disturbance, but relationship problems are caused thereby. There is no progression.
- *Beta alcoholism* involves heavy drinking, causing physical complications such as gastritis or cirrhosis of the liver, yet without physical or psychological dependence on alcohol.
- *Gamma alcoholism* is characterized by increased tissue tolerance, withdrawal symptoms when drinking is discontinued, and loss of control. A marked progression occurs, with interpersonal relations impaired to the highest degree. This variety predominates in Great Britain and northern Europe. Most A.A. members have experienced this kind of alcoholism.
- *Delta alcoholism* is similar to gamma alcoholism but without the loss of control over the amount consumed, only an inability to abstain for even one day. There are no distressing social problems over the quantity consumed, though health problems may result. This is the predominant pattern in France.
- *Epsilon alcoholism* is periodic alcoholism. In their periodic bouts, binge drinkers suffer a great deal of physical and emotional damage.

Of all the types of alcoholism, according to Jellinek, only the gamma and delta varieties can be considered to be addictions and/or diseases. Miller (1986) applauds the Jellinek formulation for its versatility, while deploring the trend in the U.S. to single out the gamma type as *the* definitive description of alcoholism to the exclusion of all other variations. Jellinek (1960) himself warned against the exclusiveness in the definition of alcoholism propounded by members of Alcoholics Anonymous.

The profound impact of Jellinek's formulation was in getting the public and professionals alike to accept that alcoholism was a diseaselike entity. Offering the most articulate and scholarly statement of alcoholism to date, *The Disease Concept* had a profound impact on the conceptualization of alcoholism. That alcoholics are not immoral but persons with a disease (or diseaselike condition) and that once addicted, the problem drinker is no longer able to control his or her drinking—these were the basic conclusions of Jellinek's work. These conclusions jelled nicely with the basic premises of A.A. and gave the rapidly growing organization a considerable boost.

The political implications of the disease concept should not be underestimated. The assumptions that alcoholism is a pathology that lies within the individual and that the pathology can be measured and treated are basic to the medical or disease model. When the World Health Organization acknowledged alcoholism as a medical problem in 1951 and the American Medical Association declared alcoholism an illness in 1956 and a disease in 1966, the transformation to the medicalization of alcoholism was complete. The hospital now had replaced the church and legislators as the center of social control of a newly designated disease. Rather than punitive, the social response to alcoholism had become therapeutic. The new ideology provided a rationale for costly complex medical approaches and for an extensive treatment apparatus. It absolved alcoholics of responsibility for the etiology of the disease but gave them the responsibility to seek treatment. Moreover, the disease model appealed to moderate drinkers in its implication that only alcoholics are at risk. Finally, the American disease model was promoted by the alcohol beverage industry because it removed the blame from the alcohol and its sale and distribution (Miller and Hester, 1989).

The disease concept has spread throughout the world, especially Western Europe. In 1968, the German Supreme Court recognized alcoholism as a disease; statutory health insurance schemes pay for all treatment. Based on the principles of Alcoholics Anonymous, the Twelve Step programs of treatment have become predominant in Sweden and Iceland. In Canada, the illness concept has received a favorable reception, and A.A. there has grown to have one of the largest memberships in the world. The Canadian health system has instituted generous treatment reimbursement policies.

The International Council on Alcohol and Addictions holds a congress each year for the discussion of academic scholarship and dispersion of research findings. The Canadian Addiction Research Foundation in Toronto and the Finnish Foundation for Alcohol Research represent noteworthy regional efforts to bring a scientific bearing to alcohol problems and alcoholism. Some of the top scientific research in the world has come from Sweden and Denmark.

33

THE HUGHES ACT AND NIAAA

The founding of Alcoholics Anonymous in 1935, the dissemination of their teachings through the publication of the "Big Book," the establishment of the Yale Center to conduct research, and the key role of Jellinek and the medical community all contributed to the eventual enactment of the Hughes Act in 1970. This Act allowed for major research funding by the federal government and for the founding of the National Institute on Alcohol Abuse and Alcoholism (NIAAA). The role of Harold Hughes is an interesting story in itself. As related in his autobiography (1979), Hughes was a popular reformist governor of Iowa; he was also a recovering alcoholic who made no secret of his early battle with alcoholism. As a U.S. senator, Hughes was able to follow through on his personal mission, which was to mobilize public and political support for legislation to fund extensive treatment programs, state level information offices, and scientific research. Later, the federal government, under a conservative administration, shifted the treatment responsibility to the states. However, NIAAA continues to finance extensive research activity and to distribute the results, often free of charge, to interested persons. Figure 2.1

FIGURE 2.1

U.S. per Capita Consumption of Beer, Wine, and Spirits, 1977–1987

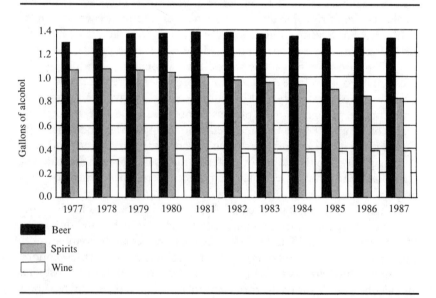

Source: NIAAA (1989).

distributed by NIAAA, shows the U.S. per capita consumption of alcohol trends from 1977 to 1987.

SUMMARY

American drinking patterns reflect a conglomeration of attitudes and customs brought to the continent from other lands. The first settlers, the English, drank more beer than water. The later arrival of German beer drinkers, Irish drinkers of distilled spirits, and French and Italian drinkers of wine all helped shape the alcohol response, a response that varied with the age. Race added another dimension to drinking in America. Most Native Americans, who had little or no experience with alcohol, were encouraged to trade furs and land for "firewater." Slaves, on the other hand, were alternately denied alcohol or supplied with too much of it all at once. The American drinking experience, in short, can be characterized in terms of ambivalence and confusion.

Other countries have had similar responses to alcohol, yet their homogeneous character makes these responses easy to identify. The type of prohibition hysteria that emerged in the United States did not take place elsewhere. All countries discussed in this chapter, however, have used various means of regulating alcohol, usually in the form of taxation.

Because of the mass availability of distilled spirits in the eighteenth century, drinking got out of control in many countries. While gin addiction in England affected poor families, and infants and small children through neglect, the American colonies were experiencing a breakdown in stability and values. A systematic sociological study of Oslo, Norway, housing conditions revealed widespread drunkenness at all class levels (Kerry, 1973).

A moralistic outcry ensued. While most governments sought regulation through taxation, the United States made total elimination the aim. This development took time. The temperance movement at first advocated moderation, then total abstinence for all by the latter part of the 1800s. Finally, in the mood of anti-immigrant fervor, a constitutional amendment was passed making the manufacture or sale of alcoholic beverages illegal. Although liquor consumption went down during Prohibition, the widespread corruption of some of the major institutions of society, coupled with the desperate need of a depressed economy to open up new industry, sowed the seeds of Prohibition's demise. The government was missing out on a source of revenue from an operation that was making a fortune for participants in organized crime (a development echoed today in the growth of drug syndicates). Vaillant (1986: 142) surveys the course of Western history and alcohol and reaches the following conclusion:

In Western societies one of the most obvious but least useful means of combating alcoholism has been to forbid drinking. Stated differently, *proscriptions* against alcohol use have rarely been as effective as social *prescriptions* for alcohol use. First, cultures that teach children to drink responsibly, cultures that have ritualized when and where to drink, tend to have lower rates of alcohol abuse than do cultures that forbid children to drink.

A new model, which was a reworking of scientific understandings that had been present for some time, offered an alternate approach to alcohol. The focus shifted from alcohol to the *individual* who had a problem with alcohol. This conceptualization was to render alcoholism a respectable subject of scientific investigation and professional attention. Whereas the concern of the nineteenth century was the control of *alcohol*, the concern of the twentieth century has been the control of *alcoholism*. Ameliorative treatment was found in Twelve Step self-help groups and A.A.-inspired medical treatment programs. Treatment for alcoholism today is dominated by A.A.'s ideology and comradery. Indeed, A.A. has become the focal point in the institutionalization of treatment relationships among medicine, the courts, and the work place.

With the legalization of alcohol use, bureaucratic control has shaped the sales, distribution, and consumption of alcohol in the United States. Strict control over advertising was enacted. The Hughes Act of 1970 defined a role for the federal government in treatment and research.

This brief survey of the history of alcohol reveals the extraordinary role one potent beverage has played among peoples everywhere. The study of alcohol is a study of social values, personal choices, and business enterprises, both legal and illegal. It is a study of successful and unsuccessful attempts at social control. These attempts are by no means over, nor is American society's continuing ambivalence over alcohol.

REVIEW QUESTIONS

1. Surveying this chapter as a whole, describe the historical cycle of punishment of the abuser, restriction of the source, and treatment of the ill.

2. What was the role of alcohol in preliterate times?

3. What role did wine play in the lives of ancient Greeks, Romans, and Hebrews?

4. How can the invention of distilled spirits be considered an example of technology exceeding its grasp?

5. Describe the epidemic that plagued Britain in the eighteenth century. How was the population affected?

6. How do the pilgrims and the *Mayflower* relate to the history of drinking? What was the European tradition?

7. What were the advantages of distilled liquor over beer and wine? What were the disadvantages? Describe life in eighteenth century England.

8. Describe the period 1725 to 1825 in terms of drinking in America. What was the cause of the Whiskey Rebellion?

9. How were slaves introduced to alcohol?

10. Discuss the "temperance to abstinence movements," 1825–1919. What were the two seemingly opposing currents of thought?

11. What was the role of the temperance woman?

12. What was the contribution of Dr. Benjamin Rush?

13. How did xenophobia figure in Prohibition?

14. How can Prohibition be considered a failure? What is its legacy today?

15. How did economic interests figure in the repeal of Prohibition?

16. How did the disease concept of alcoholism fill the void? What was the role of Alcoholics Anonymous? Describe the inside story of Dr. Bob and Bill W.

17. How are the *delta* and *gamma* varieties of alcoholism different from the others? What was Jellinek's contribution?

18. How did the disease concept of alcoholism influence countries other than the United States?

19. What was Harold Hughes's contribution? What is the task of the NIAAA today?

20. Trace the origins of the words *alcohol, booze,* and *gin.*

3

THE CONTEMPORARY CONTEXT
IN TREATMENT OF ALCOHOLISM

Within the field of social work, the psychoanalytical paradigm and the individual treatment modality were dominant from the 1920s until the early 1970s. And the gap between professional treatment and the local Alcoholics Anonymous meetings was wide indeed. While A.A. chalked up notable success stories, the low status accorded treatment of alcoholics by the helping professions ensured social work's continuing lack of interest in alcoholism treatment.

The legacy of this earlier lack of interest is still reflected in the numbers of social workers employed in the addictions field today. The most recent survey of primary practice areas reveals that only 5.4 percent of social workers identified substance treatment including occupational counseling as their specialty (Gibelman and Schervish, 1993). Social workers who are not NASW members are not included in this survey. Although this figure represents a small increase over the past decade, addictions is still not regarded as a major social work specialty.

A scientific study by Peyton, Chaddick, and Gorsvek (1980) indicates that graduate social workers in the study tended to ignore indicators of alcoholism in simulated situations while focusing on other kinds of information. Second-year students did no better on measures of perception of alcoholism than did first year students. According to Plaut (1977), alcoholism remained the most neglected major social medical problem in the United States.

The way a discipline perceives a disorder and the paradigm used to understand the disorder profoundly influences the practice of that discipline. External forces, too, define the professional enterprise. The economic policies of the day, political/military trends within the society, the amount of information available, and funding all shape the nature of work that is done as well as the nature of the problems addressed.

This chapter surveys the contemporary context of social work addictions practice. First, the current paradigm of social work is defined, and how addictions practice fits into this model is demonstrated. Alcoholism is defined within the context of current social work ideology. To further place the model in a contemporary context, social and economic aspects of alcoholism treatment are pinpointed.

A discussion of current treatment modalities includes a description of the moralistic/religious approach, the psychoanalytical/psychodynamic orientation, A.A.'s disease-model conceptualization, and finally, modalities for the behavioral/cognitive school. Each approach is analyzed in terms of treatment implications and empirical findings concerning effectiveness. The conclusion proposes a reorganization of available knowledge under the *ecological* framework.

THE CURRENT PARADIGM OF SOCIAL WORK PRACTICE

In the "house" of social work, there are "many mansions." Specialization may be by size of population—group work, family therapy, or individual counseling. Or specialization may be according to substantive area of expertise—geriatrics, health, or mental health. Third, social problems—drug addiction, alcoholism, crime, or poverty—may define the parameters. Social work, unlike related fields such as psychology or sociology, is known for its eclecticism. Borrowed from psychology is the behaviorist/cognitive approach; from sociology, the systems framework; and from law, advocacy on behalf of the client.

TERMINOLOGY FOR ALCOHOLISM TREATMENT

Terminology in the field of alcoholism treatment is imprecise and inconsistent. Sometimes several terms are used to convey identical meanings; conversely, at times the same term carries alternate meanings. In fact, much of the controversy in the field—such as whether or not alcoholism is a disease—centers on the various definitions utilized.

The American Psychiatric Association *Diagnostic and Statistical Manual of Mental Disorders*, 4th edition (*DSM-IV*), has set out to codify knowledge in the mental health field for practical and universal usage. The term *substance dependence* is used in place of addiction. The symptoms of dependence are clearly summarized in figure 3.1.

To specify the extent of recovery, the *DSM-IV* uses the categories "early full remission" to indicate abstinence outside of a controlled environment and "partial remission" to indicate a significant reduction for over twelve-months duration in substance use. The categories of "sustained full remission" and "sustained partial remission" refer to longer periods of time.

Social workers often utilize the *DSM-IV* criteria as a means of justifying insurance reimbursement for their clients. The physical, psychological, and social aspects of dependence are spelled out succinctly in this formulation. The scheme clearly demonstrates the importance of continuity of diagnostic criteria over time.

FIGURE 3.1

Criteria for Substance Dependence

A maladaptive pattern of substance use, leading to clinically significant impairment or distress, as manifested by three (or more) of the following, occurring at any time in the same 12-month period:

(1) tolerance, as defined by either of the following:
   (a) a need for markedly increased amounts of the substance to achieve intoxication or desired effect
   (b) markedly diminished effect with continued use of the same amount of the substance
(2) withdrawal, as manifested by either of the following:
   (a) the characteristic withdrawal syndrome for the substance (refer to Criteria A and B of the criteria sets for withdrawal from the specific substances)
   (b) the same (or a closely related) substance is taken to relieve or avoid withdrawal symptoms
(3) the substance is often taken in larger amounts or over a longer period than was intended
(4) there is a persistent desire or unsuccessful efforts to cut down or control substance use
(5) a great deal of time is spent in activities necessary to obtain the substance (e.g., visiting multiple doctors or driving long distances), use the substance (e.g., chain-smoking), or recover from its effects
(6) important social, occupational, or recreational activities are given up or reduced because of substance use
(7) the substance use is continued despite knowledge of having a persistent or recurrent physical or psychological problem that is likely to have been caused or exacerbated by the substance (e.g., current cocaine use despite recognition of cocaine-induced depression, or continued drinking despite recognition that an ulcer was made worse by alcohol consumption)

Source: American Psychiatric Association, *Diagnostic and Statistical Manual of Mental Disorders,* 4th ed. (Washington, DC: APA, 1994), p. 181. Reprinted with permission.

FIGURE 3.2

Criteria for Substance Abuse

A. A maladaptive pattern of substance use leading to clinically significant impairment or distress, as manifested by one (or more) of the following, occurring within a 12-month period:
   (1) recurrent substance use resulting in a failure to fulfill major role obligations at work, school, or home (e.g., repeated absences or poor work performance related to substance use; substance-related absences, suspensions, or expulsions from school; neglect of children or household)
   (2) recurrent substance use in situations in which it is physically hazardous (e.g., driving an automobile or operating a machine when impaired by substance use)
   (3) recurrent substance-related legal problems (e.g., arrests for substance-related disorderly conduct)
   (4) continued substance use despite having persistent or recurrent social or interpersonal problems caused or exacerbated by the effects of the substance (e.g., arguments with spouse about consequences of intoxication, physical fights)
B. The symptoms have never met the criteria for Substance Dependence for this class of substance.

Source: American Psychiatric Association, *Diagnostic and Statistical Manual of Mental Disorders,* 4th ed. (Washington, DC: APA, 1994), pp. 182–83. Reprinted with permission.

Unlike the criteria for substance dependence, the criteria for substance abuse do not include tolerance, withdrawal, or a pattern of compulsive use. Substance *abuse*, therefore, is defined in the absence of physical and psychological adaptation: the contrast between dependence and abuse is clarified in the criteria presented for substance abuse (see figure 3.2).

For everyday social work usage, Moncher, Schinke, and Holden (1992) prefer the flexibility of the word *addiction* in place of *DSM*'s substance dependence. The term addiction, they believe, is more amenable to the biopsychosocial model, which attends to the subjective compulsion to continue the behavior pattern. Freeman's (1992:252) definition of addiction is the one that will apply in this book:

> *Addiction:* A behavior pattern of compulsive substance abuse, relationships, or other nonconsummatory and consummatory behaviors characterized by overinvolvement with the relationship or abuse as well as a tendency to relapse after completion of withdrawal.

The concept of addiction is useful because of its emphasis on the *process* rather than on the substance itself. The word *pattern* utilized in this definition refers to symptomology as well as the fact that the addiction may be to a behavior (such as sex, work, exercise) as well as to a substance (alcohol, food, tobacco).

The term alcoholism is used in this book to signify a loss of control over the substance alcohol. Loss of consistent control is sufficient for diagnosis (Royce, 1989). The American Medical Association in 1967 offered the following definition, which is still widely used:

> Alcoholism is an illness characterized by preoccupation with alcohol and loss of control over its consumption such as to lead usually to intoxication if drinking is toward relapse. It is typically associated with physical disability and impaired emotional, occupational, and/or social adjustments as a direct consequence of persistent and excessive use. (American Medical Association, 1967, p. 6)

The AMA definition identifies the three basic areas of ecological concern— the physical, the psychological, and the social. Thus it is the definition chosen for this text. The selection of the word *illness* to describe alcoholism provides a clear acknowledgment of alcoholism as a medical problem with widespread ramifications (social and moral). Illness is a nonjudgmental, non–victim-blaming term.

The word *disease,* originally used by Jellinek (1960) as a metaphor, unfortunately has taken on a meaning far beyond the historical formulation. The short road from "like a disease" to "a disease" is paved with politics favoring the medicalization of disorders. Today, this trend has gone further as a host of complaints have become medicalized (e.g., codependency). Simultaneously, a countertrend toward stress on individual responsibility carries some risk of "throwing the baby out with the bathwater." Criticism of the disease concept may be utilized by political and legal forces to restrict treatment access. (Chapter 11 looks at future trends in some depth.) According to most dictionary definitions, alcoholism certainly qualifies along with diabetes and various heart conditions as a disease:

> *Disease:* 1. A condition of the body in which there is incorrect function. 2. deranged condition, as of the mind, society, etc. (*Random House,* 1980: 251)
>
> *Disease:* (Old French) Absence of ease, uneasiness. (*Oxford Universal Dictionary,* 1955: 524)

To denote the extensive pain and suffering wrought by the condition of alcoholism, I favor the word *illness* over *disease,* however. Illness, to Conrad and Kern (1981), is the experience of being sick or diseased; it is a social psychological state caused by the disease. Thus, pathologists treat *disease,* whereas patients experience *illness.* The subjective level of illness makes this the term with more relevance to the social work focus on the person-in-the-environment and the interactional nature of the internal world of the human body and the world outside.

THE NATURE OF ADDICTIONS SOCIAL WORK

The pain and suffering—the biopsychosocial reality—of alcoholism and other addictions are the concerns of the following chapters. First is the *biology* of chemical dependency—the formidable hereditary components in the etiology of the illness and the physical consequences of substance abuse. Chapter 4 reviews and explores recent scientific research, which is compelling in its implications. The *psychological* component in chemical dependency, the thinking that leads to the drinking, is the aspect of the disease with important treatment implications; this is the subject of chapter 5.

The *social* component in alcoholism is the third critical dimension. If the biological dimension is the *why* and the psychological dimension is the *what,* the social dimension is the *where.* Where is the impact of this illness manifested? The family comes to mind as the key arena of social strain. The dynamics of the family system is explored in depth in chapter 9. Peer group ties and the work setting also come to mind as part of the social aspect of alcoholism.

Roles for the addictions worker that directly correspond to the biopsychosocial framework are (1) the *educator* in the facts of the biology and chemistry of addiction, (2) the educator or *coach* in healthy thinking and control of irrational, obsessive thought patterns, and (3) the *family therapist* in alcoholism prevention, treatment, and preparation of the whole family for the recovery of the individual member.

Social work practice with alcoholics takes place in a wide range of social work settings. Hospital social workers, for instance, encounter both the early and late stage effects of heavy drinking in patients. The estimate is that one hospital bed in four is occupied by a patient whose ailment is alcohol related. Alcohol abuse is the third leading cause of death after heart disease and cancer.

Social workers at mental health settings can expect that 20 to 40 percent of their clients will have problems stemming from their own or a family member's alcoholism (Googins, 1984: 161). From my own experience, I would raise the estimate to around 50 percent. Crowley, Chesluk, Dilts, and Hart (1974) found that over one-third of adults in a psychiatric hospital had alcohol and/or other drug problems. In a more recent study, Holloway (1991) reports a correlation between substance abuse and mental disorders at over 50 percent.

Alcohol abuse figures widely also in marital counseling. Workers in child welfare observe firsthand the toll on the victims of neglect and abuse due to parental alcohol abuse. Forensic social workers encounter the effects of alcoholism in the course of their treatment of offenders. A survey of state prisoners found that 34 to 45 percent of offenders convicted of a violent crime described themselves as very heavy drinkers (Kalish, 1983). Social work, in short, can neglect alcoholism in the *abstract* but cannot avoid the victims of alcoholism.

Just as social workers in a variety of specializations encounter much substance abuse, those who specialize in direct work with the chemically

---

FIGURE 3.3

Alcohol's Toll

- An estimated million U.S. adults exhibit some symptoms of alcoholism or alcohol dependence and an additional 7.2 million abuse alcohol, but do not yet show symptoms of dependence.
- Alcohol use is associated with a wide variety of diseases and disorders, including liver disease, cancer, and cardiovascular problems.
- Cirrhosis of the liver caused almost 27,000 deaths and was the ninth leading cause of death in the United States in 1984.
- Fetal exposure to alcohol is one of the leading known causes of mental retardation in the Western world and can be totally prevented.
- Accidental death, suicide, and homicide are significant causes of death, particularly for young men under age thirty-four; nearly half of these violent deaths are alcohol-related.
- More than 20,000 alcohol-related motor vehicle fatalities annually are attributed to alcohol abuse and these deaths are relatively more frequent among younger Americans.
- In 1986, alcohol abuse in the U.S. was estimated to cost $128.3 billion, including alcoholism, liver cirrhosis, cancer, and diseases of the pancreas.
- It is estimated that 20 to 40 percent of all U.S. hospital beds are occupied by persons whose health conditions are complications of alcohol abuse and alcoholism.
- Blacks, especially males, are at extremely high risk for acute and chronic alcohol-related diseases such as cirrhosis, alcoholic fatty liver, hepatitis, heart disease, and cancers of mouth, larynx, tongue, esophagus, and lung.
- Chronic alcohol abusers can develop clinical signs of cardiac dysfunction, and up to 50 percent of excess mortality in alcoholics and heavy drinkers can be attributed to cardiovascular disorders.
- Chronic alcohol consumption is associated with a significant increase in hypertension.
- Heavy alcohol consumption is a well-documented cause of neurological problems, including dementia, blackouts, seizures, hallucinations, and peripheral neuropathy.

Source: U.S. Dept. of Health and Human Services, *Seventh Special Report to the U.S. Congress on Alcohol and Health* (Washington, DC: U.S. Government Printing Office, 1990).

dependent encounter a variety of problems related to the dependency. Addictions work, therefore, includes much of the social work mentioned above—for example, working with families in trouble or working with offenders for whom drug involvement has had legal ramifications. Addictions work is multifaceted in its focus (domestic violence, child-rearing, employment) and in its population size (individual, family, group).

Under the auspices of a chemical dependency treatment agency, the worker might find him- or herself directing a family intervention to bring an identified alcoholic into treatment. The worker might work with battering men to teach them anger management skills. The worker might conduct a group for alcoholic women who have histories of sexual abuse. Practitioners might be called on to testify in court either as expert witnesses or on behalf of clients. They might engage in public speaking programs to enlighten the public on chemical dependency issues.

Thus, addictions work is infinitely broad and requires all the general skills of social work counseling plus the acquisition of a special expertise in detecting and preventing substance abuse. A characteristic of addictions work that sets it apart from other aspects of social work, however, can be encompassed in one word—*denial.*

Unlike the ill or mentally ill or retarded or depressed client, the chemically dependent person is apt to be slow to acknowledge the source of the problem(s). A great deal of early treatment time, accordingly, is spent in overcoming psychosocial barriers to treatment. Only when, in the words of A.A.'s First Step, the client has recognized his or her "powerlessness over alcohol" is the treatment process ready to begin. And then social workers must be ready to draw upon their wide array of practitioner skills and diversified roles to prepare the alcoholic for life as a nonintoxicated, nonsedated person.

Hence, this text is not just about treating alcoholism but also is about treating the person or family suffering from alcoholism or other addictions—addictions-centered social work practice in a variety of treatment settings.

A NEW AWARENESS OF AN OLD PROBLEM

Help Wanted. Chemical dependency counselor. Certification (C.A.C.) required. Bachelor's degree in social work or related field required, master's degree preferred.

This type of ad is commonly found in the Help Wanted column of the Sunday classified section. Today, unparalleled opportunities exist for social workers in the administration and provision of alcoholism counseling services. A glance through the classified section of the telephone book reveals an extensive activity in this direction. Inpatient, outpatient, long-term, short-term—competing facilities offer a wide variety of treatment modalities for the *insured* alcoholic consumer. This is the big business aspect of what has become a billion-dollar-a-year industry (Fingarette, 1988).

ECONOMICS

The economic aspect of chemical dependency counseling should not be overlooked. Alcoholism treatment is big business. Few fields in health care, in fact, have grown as rapidly as has addictions treatment. Throughout the 1980s, third-party payers, state welfare systems, and employers recognized the value of rehabilitating chemically dependent persons (Siddons, 1985). Capitalizing on the new legal requirements and social atmosphere, alcoholism treatment centers have sprung up throughout the country. Articles in *U.S. News and World Report* (Lord, 1987), *Forbes,* (Sherrid, 1982), and *Time* (Lee, 1985) chronicled the boom. Treating alcoholism for profit has been one of the fastest growing markets in health care (Sherrid, 1982). Treatment for adolescent drug abusers, the family members of the chemically dependent, and those suffering from eating disorders (Peele, 1989) are recent areas of high profit. Scherman (1990) makes fun of this phenomenon in his Minneapolis newspaper column: "Within 30 days of arrival in Minnesota you must enroll in some twelve-step program."

Yet today, the hard-pressed insurance companies are balking. In the interests of saving money, reimbursement policies provide coverage for the least restrictive and least expensive of programs: Inpatient is out and outpatient is in. The dollar, rather than patient need, may determine the treatment protocol. "Managed care" is the latest buzzword in health care. Decisions for the future, which will influence the shape of the alcoholism treatment enterprise, have to do with the willingness of federal and state funding sources to set up and finance treatment efforts. Changes in the emerging health care system will also have definite impact. The best prediction that can be made at the present time is that before a corporation or legislative body will invest in treatment, some stringent measure of success outcome will be required. The days of massive spending without accountability are over.

The American mass media both reflect and reinforce a keen interest in substance abuse issues by the general public. In Norway, by contrast, there is relatively little interest in such concerns, although interest is growing. Russia under capitalism is rediscovering the intransigence of alcoholism in its population. In North America, the attention given in the press and on television to various aspects of addictions—the alcoholic family, children of alcoholics, driving under the influence (DWI, DUI, OWI) legislation—is considerable. Today, as formerly, self-help groups are mushrooming to meet the public demand.

PROFESSIONAL CONCERNS

For a variety of reasons—lack of training, prejudice, competing interests—social work ceded the turf in alcoholism treatment to others. And once a paraprofessional network of A.A. enthusiasts came to dominate the treatment industry, entry into the profession was controlled while, internally, dissent was stifled. The role of social workers was effectively limited to referral of alcoholic clients to the specialized, socially inbred agencies that resulted (Googins, 1984).

Today, however, as alcoholism counseling becomes more professional, there is a strong impetus to hire Bachelor of Social Work (B.S.W.) and master's level (M.S.W.) counselors. Third-party payers create strong economic incentives for agencies to hire workers with degrees over recovering alcoholic workers without degrees. A widening interest in recruiting social workers for alcoholism treatment is paralleled by a widening interest by the social work profession in employment opportunities for B.S.W. graduates within the addictions field. Near major university centers, a surplus of social work graduates has encouraged Social Work Departments to explore options for field placement and subsequent employment for their majors. Staff members from the agencies, in turn, often take courses or attend workshops at the university. A mutual interest in personal growth and recovery and family systems theories unites the two fields.

Two rapidly expanding areas of alcoholism treatment are pregnant drug-abusing women and work with the dually diagnosed (alcoholism plus mental illness). Experienced social workers often have expertise in meeting the specialized needs of these populations.

The strength of social work has been its ability to grow and change with the times. Social work is a field broad in its vision and amorphous in its framework. Social work is both of the world and in the world; representatives are very politically involved. Like doctors, lawyers, and teachers, social workers lobby for congressional recognition of their profession's and their clients' interests. Because of this active community involvement, social work in all probability will begin to move beyond what Googins has accurately termed "the avoidance of the alcoholic client" and look in new directions. *Economically,* in the form of new job opportunities, *politically,* in the form of relevant legislation, and *socially,* in the form of heightened public consciousness, the social work profession may be expected to move into the addictions area.

Social workers at mental health centers and at family treatment agencies are attending workshops to sharpen appropriate assessment and treatment skills in alcoholism. In-service programs are now common. While many social workers are gaining certification as alcoholism counselors, many alcoholism counselors are professionalizing through social work education. Expansion by schools of social work in alcoholism/ addictions treatment course offerings are underway; the range is from isolated course offerings to full concentrations in alcoholism/addictions treatment (still uncommon at the undergraduate level, however).

The National Association of Social Workers (NASW) in 1988 adopted a new substance abuse policy outlining treatment for alcoholism and drug addiction as a primary rather than a secondary disease (*NASW News,* Jan. 1987). The significance of this is in the rejection of the traditional social work belief that alcoholism is a symptom of some underlying disturbance such as stress or depression (Brown, 1985:5). Finally, alcoholism is recognized as a disease in its own right.

Major changes in the alcohol treatment field and in social work involvement in these changes are underway. As social work alters its conceptualization of alcoholism as a treatable disease, and as the treatment industry continues to grow and develop, social workers can begin to reexamine their earlier biases concerning addiction and addictions work. In the next section, we look at some treatment modalities (major and minor) utilized in addictions work today.

CURRENT TREATMENT MODALITIES

Many forms of alcoholism treatment exist. For instance, transactional analysis, reality therapy, and gestalt methods have all been modified for chemical dependency work. For the sake of simplicity I have singled out four major forms of treatment that have special relevance for the alcoholic. Since these are *ideal-types* of treatment modalities, oversimplified for the purpose of contrast, they do not correspond exactly to reality. In actual practice, one finds a remarkable overlap and flexibility in modalities used even at a single agency.

The four most significant past and present treatment modalities are: the moralistic/religion approach, psychodynamic orientation, the A.A.-based Twelve Step approach, and the behavioral/cognitive framework. Each will be described with attention to theoretical framework and empirical evaluation studies.

RELIGIOUS/MORAL MODEL—TWO EUROPEAN EXAMPLES

In the United States there are religiously oriented shelters and halfway houses (missions) for recovering alcoholics or "reformed drunks." Funded by private donations, churches, and community resources, treatment is in the form of preaching, praying, and "work therapy." Drunkenness has long been viewed by major North American religions as sinful behavior. The criminal justice system takes a punitive stance toward those who commit offenses while intoxicated.

Despite the official disease-model rhetoric, there is in the United States an undercurrent of moralism that coexists with the belief that the alcoholic is suffering from a disease. This issue of personal responsibility for alcohol problems is currently unresolved (Royce, 1989).

According to the moralistic view, alcohol abuse is "willful misconduct" deriving from weakness in moral character. The position is vehemently enunciated today in the prolific writings of Stanton Peele. In this essay, Peele (1988:202) expresses the view that:

> Appetitive behavior of all types is crucially influenced by people's preexisting values and that the best way to combat addiction both for the individual and the society is to inculcate values that are incompatible with addiction and with drug- and alcohol-induced misbehavior.

The proof for Peele's moralistic position is given in scientific research showing: (1) ethnic and social class differences in the successful socialization of moderate consumption of every kind of substance; (2) the tendency for abusers to display other antisocial and self-destructive behaviors; (3) developmental studies that repeatedly discover value orientations to play a large role in styles of drug use in adolescence and beyond; and (4) the relationship between personal sobriety and changes in life-style and belief system. Example after example is provided to illustrate that those individuals and cultures that achieve moderation are those that regard the state of intoxication as an intolerable absence of control.

Addiction, according to this argument, is part of a panoply of self-destructive behaviors that fit larger patterns in people's lives. Significantly, Peele uses the word *reformed* in place of recovering, as in "reformed addicts" and "reformed overeaters." In creating and preventing addiction, the role of morals and values should never be discounted, declares Peele (1988).

Two modern manifestations of treatment modalities derived from the moralistic framework are found in Norway and Russia. While Norway's approach relies on religion, the former Soviet republic relies on punishment.

NORWAY

One of the prime examples of the state-sanctioned use of the religious/moral model of addiction occurs in Norway, an otherwise extremely secular state (Selbyg, 1987). This position is not so much articulated as it is implied in the harsh mandatory sentences for driving under intoxication and in the high degree of shame expressed toward alcoholism.

A well-known Norwegian psychologist of the "controlled drinking" school, Fanny Duckert, pursues the Norwegian moralistic perspective in combination with behavioral techniques. In Norway, writes Duckert (1985), the moralistic model is the oldest model, the most unique, and the one with great appeal. In the final analysis, according to this theory, it is the individual will that is in control of the alcohol. Substance abuse indicates a weak moral character. According to the model, this weakness is inherited. However, the tenets of this model are lacking in scientific support, and some professionals object to the heavy moralism.

Duckert blasts the disease model as amoral. In placing the individual problem ahead of the community, the disease model (*sykdomsmodellen*), according to Duckert, frees the individual from responsibility for good behavior. The disease model can, by implication, lower the moral standards of the community.

In sharp contrast to trends in the United States and other Western countries, Norway has not "demoralized" addiction. Today, a few private, for-profit (but not profitable) treatment centers struggle to popularize the Minnesota Model (now standard in Sweden) in Norway. I was one of a handful of experienced alcoholism counselors recruited from the United States to bring the principles of the Minnesota Model to clients, staff, and the community.

Stenius (1991), a Finnish sociologist and editor of *Alkoholpolitik*, has conducted extensive research on the introduction of the Minnesota Model into the Nordic Countries. She describes Norwegian treatment as divided among conflicting approaches. These include the commercialized Minnesota-style clinics; professionally run clinics based largely on the psychological approach; and/or clinics utilizing the moral or "moralistic layman approach."

A highly reputable, religious-based organization, Norway's Blue Cross is responsible for most of the treatment provided in Norway. Blue Cross operates long-term residential programs throughout the country. Due to extensive state funding, administered through each local Social Office, there is no cost to the client. The majority of the clients suffer from severe alcoholism; many are derelicts who have lost everything in the course of their addiction.

Although the psychiatrists and psychologists are employed by Blue Cross, the emphasis is on moral values and self-control. Alcoholism is not seen as a disease or even sickness, which is the Norwegian translation for disease (*sykdom*). This emphasis is consistent with the Norwegian repugnance toward problem drinking, the legacy, perhaps, of an earlier religious moralism, incongruous with the secularism and sophistication of today. Brun-Gulbrandesen (1990: 25) ponders the cultural climate mandating social control for every occasion except for the rare festive event:

> Is it the harsh living conditions of former times that have burned deep into the "soul" of the Norwegian people, making such qualities as industriousness, frugality, and self-control such central values and ideals that they have, to a certain extent, survived in the modern, affluent society? Is it reminiscences of "the Protestant ethic" that can explain why Norwegians in the secularized society of the 1980s only drink half as much alcohol as is common in the rest of Europe?

In short, in Norway, alcoholism is widely viewed as a moral weakness. Treatment methods tend to be individualistic and authoritarian, even when the modality used is group therapy. Strong guilt feelings may be aroused in the course of the treatment. Future change can be anticipated, however, as the Norwegian Social Department strives to offer alcoholics a choice of treatment modalities. Norwegian social work journals have recently begun to highlight work with alcoholics as an area requiring much professional help and training.

RUSSIA

The country that absolutely epitomizes the moral, primitive approach to alcohol abuse is the former Soviet State of Russia. This part of the world has moved from complete denial of a problem to harsh, publicized punishment. According to the earlier Marxist formulation, alcohol abuse was a remnant of capitalism; once capitalism disappeared, so would these kinds of social problems.

Like Norway, the authorities in Russia (and the Commonwealth States) do not so much articulate their moralistic position as live it. While the Russians officially recognize alcoholism as a disease, their basic definition of alcoholism differs significantly from that of U.S. authorities. As Powell and Fuller (1991) report, Russian factories regularly post photographs of the plant's "resident alcoholics," persons whose work was terminated because of drinking on the job. Russian society finds principles of confidentiality and self-referral as culturally alien. A.A. meetings, recently introduced from America, are regarded with suspicion. According to a graphic photograph essay in *Mother Jones* (1991: 52)

> Instead of a twelve step program, the Soviet government forms three steps: incarceration, involuntary aversion therapy, and forced labor.

Already, however, as Russian society faces massive social change, the reaction to the problem of alcohol abuse is beginning to change also. In short, the Norwegian system is characterized by moralism mixed with kindness, the Russian system by harshness and stigmatization. Both countries register alcoholics in an official capacity.

STRENGTHS OF THE MORALISTIC APPROACH

Personal values and personality traits clearly play a role in one's relationship with alcohol. Alcohol abuse is associated with the psychological traits of impulsiveness and risk-taking, and these with psychopathic or antisocial behavior (Peele and Brodsky, 1991). Sobriety and discipline and acceptance of responsibility are obvious correlates of one another (Jellinek, 1960).

In placing emphasis on individual responsibility and religion as a source of strength higher than the self, the moralistic program may work wonders with clients of strong religious faith.

I remember one seemingly "hopeless" case in Washington state, a former alcoholism counselor who had spent several years of his life as a client in alcoholism treatment. At a tearful commitment proceeding, the man's lawyer and I decided, out of desperation, to commit this person to a religious shelterlike facility operated by a religious group. The client not only recovered but later took a job at the facility. For me, the lesson in the experience was that clients are individuals who must be carefully matched to programs that can meet their needs at that particular time.

A final strength of the religious-based clinic program is in its ability to draw on the resources of a church, including the resources of men and women engaging in "service to God."

CRITICISMS OF THE MORALISTIC APPROACH

Detractors of this approach point to the lack of proven effectiveness; the risks of "teaching" people to drink as is done in Norway with alcoholics who perhaps would have an easier time giving up the addictive substance altogether; the stress on sin and moralism that can exacerbate feelings of depression and guilt; and finally, the lack of a unitary, integrated model offering consistency from one treatment center to the next. The punitiveness and blaming, in short, may impede healing rather than promote it.

A WORD ABOUT EFFECTIVENESS STUDIES

The most appropriate way to evaluate treatment efficacy is, according to the principles of the scientific method, to assign subjects randomly to treated and control groups. The overwhelming majority of alcoholism treatment outcome evaluations fail to do this. The effect of pretreatment demographic characteristics, therefore, often confounds the research findings. According to Vaillant (1983), author of the landmark follow-up study of alcoholics' progression over time, the single, most important variable associated with remission among treated alcoholics is *stability of life-style*. For this reason, upper income, paying clients treated at Center A cannot be compared on outcome results with unemployed, nonpaying clients at Center B.

Miller (1990), in scholarly pursuit of the truth about treatment effectiveness claims, has organized and analyzed over six hundred of the most rigorous studies of treatment outcome results. What Miller and his colleague, Reid Hester, were seeking was the well-designed experiment, one that utilized random assignment of clients to alternative treatment conditions. In the end, approximately two hundred carefully controlled studies were found to yield fairly consistent results. These research findings are utilized throughout the remainder of this chapter to validate treatment effectiveness claims.

TREATMENT EFFECTIVENESS AND THE MORAL/RELIGIOUS MODEL

Harsh penalties applied universally and immediately can deter social deviance such as crime. Thus, in countries with instant penalties for driving "under the influence" there is a reduced rate of driving-while-drinking offenses. This is not necessarily a deterrent, however, to drinking itself.

In Norway, rigorously controlled treatment effectiveness studies have not been done. Internal measures (by the treatment centers themselves) of treatment effectiveness indicate an extremely low recovery rate of alcoholics in conventional moralistically based treatment. The rate of 15 percent is the highest rate cited (Stenius, 1991). Since treatment is free and available for all, the most severe cases of alcoholism are represented in these results.

One aspect of the Norwegian traditional approach that *has* been rigorously tested is the controlled drinking learning model. This modality is utilized under both the behavioral and moralistic schools. When the conceptualization is moralistic, the element of control over weakness is emphasized.

Moderation-oriented treatment, which is highly controversial in the United States, is an accepted treatment option in European countries. The offering of such an option flies in the face of the disease model and its dictates: once an alcoholic, always an alcoholic; the alcoholic is powerless over the substance alcohol; and abstinence is essential. Scandinavian researchers Nordstrom and Berglund (1987) conducted a systematic research follow-up study on sixty male alcoholics twenty years after treatment. Of the 50 percent who recovered, most participated in moderate drinking. Hester and Miller (1989), in their extensive review on moderation studies, reach the following conclusion: Current data suggest that moderation is most likely to be achieved by clients who, at the beginning of treatment, were experiencing less severe alcohol problems and dependence, whereas abstinence is a more stable outcome among more severe alcohol abusers.

THE PSYCHODYNAMIC ORIENTATION

Personality theorists stress personality variables conducive to the development of addiction. Terms like *alcoholic personality* or *addictive personality* are often used to describe the phenomenon. Although researchers generally agree there is no single alcoholic personality, systematic studies do indicate high instances of depression, sociopathy, and hyperactivity as forerunners of alcoholism (Gorenstein, 1987: 310).

Recent biochemical research reveals that a highly serious form of alcoholism, the Type 2 or male-limited variety, is associated with impulsiveness, excitability, and heightened sensitivity to pain. Stimuli are perceived more strongly by Type 2 alcoholics; drinking is one way to adapt to this sensitivity (NIAAA report, 1988). Peele and Brodsky (1991: 65), in their critical analysis of the Cloninger et al. (1987) genetically oriented study, are impressed by the significance shown by the *personality* dimension in the development of alcoholism: children most likely to become alcohol abusers were relatively fearless, novelty-seeking, and indifferent to others' opinions of them. At the other end of the scale, boys who were very "harm avoidant" or very sensitive to others' opinions of them also had a fairly high risk of alcohol abuse.

Cunynghame (1983) reviews the literature on alcoholic personality traits and draws from her own observations to conclude that a high percentage of alcoholics in these studies were diagnosed as having character disorders. Character disorders include the passive-aggressive personality, the paranoid personality, and the explosive personality. A drawback to these kinds of observations, however, is the failure to distinguish between cause and effect in alcohol abuse.

The determination of the role depression plays in the onset of alcoholism is another area of confusion of cause and effect. Since alcohol acts as a depressant on the nervous system, depression is a correlate of alcohol consumption. Scientific research consistently shows a high relationship between drinking and depression. The basic psychodynamic position is that depression is the underlying cause for drinking, alcohol being used for self-medication (Forrest, 1985) and cocaine and other "uppers" to lift the spirits.

In Norway, treatment for alcoholism is primarily in terms of the psychological dynamics of substance abuse (Duckert and Aastand, 1988).

Accordingly, psychologists are the counselors of choice at most treatment centers. Treatment consists of confrontation on various items in the "self-biography" that is presented in the group. Emphasis is on individual responsibility in restoring control over one's life. Recently, however, the disease model has made some inroads in shaking the dogma of the pure psychiatric position (Laberg, 1988).

Basic assumptions of the psychodynamic approach are:

- Alcoholism/addiction is not a disease but a symptom of an underlying psychological condition.
- Alcoholics have less self-control and less emotional stability than do nonalcoholics.
- Drinking problems may be alleviated through abstinence or learning techniques of controlled drinking.
- Treatment is through helping the client achieve self-understanding; this may be done in group or individual therapy.
- Treatment focus is on early childhood trauma as well as on psychological coping mechanisms that were learned during childhood.
- Treatment providers are professional psychologists, usually not recovering alcoholics themselves.

STRENGTHS OF THE PSYCHODYNAMIC APPROACH

Psychological components play an important role in the etiology and continuation of alcoholism. Identical-twin studies reveal that the identical twin of an alcoholic has a 60 percent probability of also being alcoholic (Gordis, 1988). Presumably the other 40 percent had a psychological resistance to development of the disease, which hindered its occurrence.

Research into personality traits commonly associated with alcoholism has run into difficulty in separating cause and effect. Nevertheless, there is some indication that obsessive-compulsive traits, rigidity of thinking, low frustration tolerance, perfectionism, and impulsiveness may precede development of alcoholism (Royce, 1989). In terms of treatment implications these studies are promising.

Whether the various psychological symptoms are perceived as the creator or the result of the alcoholism, virtually all the literature in the field mentions the psychological symptoms associated with the disease. The characteristic defense mechanisms, including denial, projection, and externalization, are a significant part of the treatment process. Much attention in the literature is devoted to new techniques specifically designed to be effective against the rigid defense mechanisms that counselors commonly encounter (Chernus, 1985).

Psychological dependence on alcohol, as Royce (1989) correctly notes, is probably more devastating than physiological dependence. Compulsive cigarette smoking and coffee drinking, and susceptibility to a wide range of other addictions may be indicative of an underlying psychological predisposition to behavior in the extremes.

Components of psychological theory have successfully been incorporated into treatment programs at most treatment agencies. At its core, the A.A. program is ingeniously cognitive (Brown, 1985) with a strong thrust toward the eradication of "stinking thinking." Attention to the psychological component in addictive behavior is an essential aspect of successful treatment. Emphasis on the thinking and feeling dimensions of the destructive emotional state of depression is incorporated into relapse prevention efforts.

CRITICISMS OF THE PSYCHODYNAMIC APPROACH

Detractors of the psychodynamic approach point to the narrowness and rigidity of focus and lack of a central philosophical theme for self-improvement such as the Twelve Steps; history of failure in the early days in utilizing a psychological approach; guilt-producing belief system that stresses self-control and, by implication, moral shortcomings as causing alcoholism; the lack of a clear link with the A.A. program of recovery; the lack of attention to family and systems dynamics. Finally, reliance on treatment staff trained in psychology and social work without any addictions training are cited as deficiencies. Such staff are said to feel educationally and theoretically superior to staff of the A.A. school.

TREATMENT EFFECTIVENESS

Treatment effectiveness studies utilizing psychodynamic psychotherapy are rare. In fact, according to Forrest (1985), because most psychotherapists fail to maintain a constant addictive focus throughout the course of their treatment relationships, they fail in their efforts with addicts and abusers. Forrest claims an approximate 50 percent success rate with chronic alcoholic patients where long-term psychotherapy is combined with adjunctive self-help modalities.

Psychodynamic approaches that are infused with A.A. teachings clearly contaminate the treatment effectiveness research design. Most psychotherapists with a psychoanalytic insight orientation, however, do not utilize other resources because of a deliberate inattention to the drinking. This orientation, claims Pattison (1985), often leads to failure. In any case, the long-term intervention within the psychodynamic framework is psychotherapy to resolve basic underlying conflicts and to alleviaite low self-esteem. The length of time required precludes comparative research evaluations including this approach.

Insight-oriented psychotherapy, according to Miller (1990) in his extensive review of the research literature, has failed to demonstrate any therapeutic value. There is some indication, however, that psychodynamic treatments are helpful during the post-treatment, relapse prevention phase (Shaffer and Gambino, 1990). The influence of unconscious processes cannot be disregarded entirely.

THE A.A. TWELVE STEP APPROACH

The path to sobriety, according to the A.A. model, is a journey of many small steps. It is a journey not of one individual in isolation but of an alcoholic in the fellowship of recovering alcoholics. To keep the transition from being overwhelming, the journey is conceptualized as "one day at a time." The itinerary for the undertaking is outlined in A.A.'s twelve basic steps to recovery.

This journey to sobriety parallels an earlier descent into the despair of addiction. Most practitioners in the field perceive this progression in the terms first delineated by Jellinek (1952, 1960). Basing his description on a survey of over two thousand members of A.A., Jellinek drew up a series of ever-worsening characteristics in the direction of absolute and total ruin. This down- and up-hill progression is commonly known as the Jellinek curve (see figure 3.4). Four sequential phases of alcohol addiction constitute the Jellinek curve: the pre-alcoholic, prodomal, crucial, and chronic phases.

The *Pre-alcoholic* phase is a period characterized by social drinking. The individual actively seeks out occasions where drinking occurs. Blackouts or prolonged lapses in memory accompanied by bouts of severe guilt signal the start of the *prodomal* phase. The *crucial phase* is characterized by increasing loss of control. In the final *chronic phase,* the drinker's physical impairment is evident. Tremors, reversal of the tolerance for alcohol acquired earlier, and major alcohol-related illness may all be present at this stage.

The disease model of alcoholism, which chronicles such a progression symptomology, is widely accepted in alcoholism treatment circles. The disease model has helped remove the stigma associated with alcoholism and placed emphasis away from the vulnerable self and onto a highly structured program.

Persons engaged in a Twelve-Step program hold meetings on a regular, even daily basis ("Ninety meetings in ninety days" for beginners). The only requirement for membership is the willingness to stop drinking. A tremendous bonding takes place in a fellowship where all are united in their battle against the enemy that is their disease.

More people are recovering from their alcoholism through Alcoholics Anonymous than through any other treatment program. Founded in 1935

FIGURE 3.4

Alcohol Addiction and Recovery: The "Jellinek Curve"

To be read from left to right

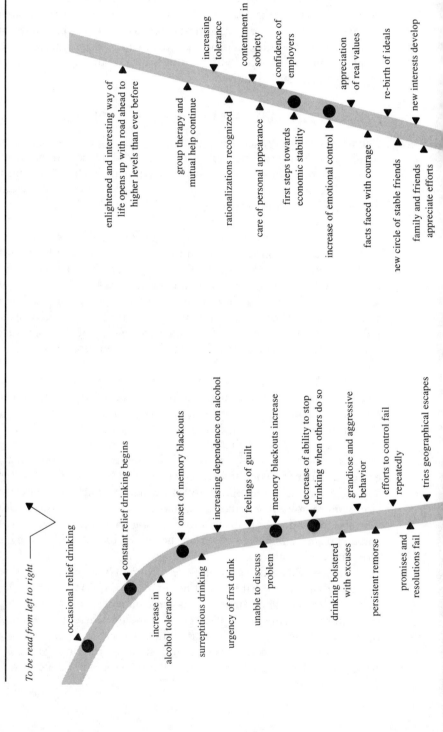

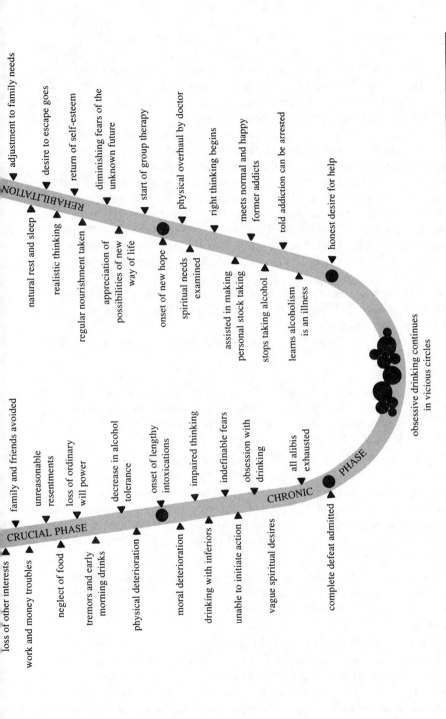

The chart shows the progression and recovery stages of alcoholism along a U-shaped curve.

CRUCIAL PHASE (descending, left side):
- loss of other interests
- work and money troubles
- family and friends avoided
- unreasonable resentments
- neglect of food
- loss of ordinary will power
- tremors and early morning drinks
- decrease in alcohol tolerance
- physical deterioration
- onset of lengthy intoxications
- moral deterioration
- impaired thinking
- drinking with inferiors
- indefinable fears
- unable to initiate action
- obsession with drinking
- vague spiritual desires

CHRONIC PHASE (bottom):
- all alibis exhausted
- complete defeat admitted
- obsessive drinking continues in vicious circles

Recovery / REHABILITATION (ascending, right side):
- honest desire for help
- learns alcoholism is an illness
- told addiction can be arrested
- stops taking alcohol
- meets normal and happy former addicts
- assisted in making personal stock taking
- right thinking begins
- spiritual needs examined
- physical overhaul by doctor
- onset of new hope
- appreciation of possibilities of new way of life
- start of group therapy
- regular nourishment taken
- diminishing fears of the unknown future
- realistic thinking
- return of self-esteem
- natural rest and sleep
- desire to escape goes
- adjustment to family needs

Source: M. M. Glatt, "Group Therapy in Alcoholism," *British Journal of Addiction 54*(2). Used by permission of the Society for the Study of Addiction, Edinburgh, Scotland.

by an Ohio physician and a New York stockbroker, A.A. now has more than 73,000 chapters in 115 countries. In the United States, membership is an estimated 750,000. In Norway, however, where the disease model is less widely accepted, A.A. membership is a mere 1,000 (Krogh, 1988). According to data from an international collaborative study, 53.8 percent of all A.A. members are from the United States and Canada, 34.5 percent are from Latin America, 1.3 percent are from Scandinavia, and 5.2 percent are from other English-speaking countries (Makela, 1993).

The A.A. formulation is antitherapy and antiprofessional. Yet, paradoxically, A.A. teachings have worked their way into the core of the predominant treatment modality. The grandfather of alcoholism inpatient treatment (not the first but the best known), the Hazelden Treatment Center of Minnesota, introduced in the late 1940s the Twelve Step "Minnesota Model" to the United States and the world. This model promotes the philosophy of the alcoholic helping alcoholic in extensive group therapy work. Today, through the international publishing unit headquartered at Hazelden, a massive amount of educational material ("inspiration and information in the Twelve-Step tradition") keeps the message of purposeful recovery alive.

The Minnesota Model is described in detail by Anderson (1981: 29) as follows:

> What we have done is successfully integrate the spiritual philosophy of Alcoholics Anonymous into the professional treatment program. And in doing this, something profound has happened. It seems that all we have done is to humanize our programs with the interpersonal mutuality found in most Alcoholics Anonymous relationships.

Prior to the 1970s, chemical dependency treatment was based on a "tear 'em down, build 'em up" philosophy. Aggressive, confrontational counseling was regarded as the only way to break the denial system of the alcoholic/addict. Today, Hazelden favors a program emphasizing individualized respectful care. "Patients need to be nurtured to have their health built up," according to an editorial in the *Hazelden Professional Update* (1985: 2).

> We're concerned because many treatment programs still use these confrontational techniques. Some even call themselves Hazelden or Minnesota models. It's true that we once used confrontation. But we found a better way and we went with it.

Social work students doing field placement at treatment centers in Iowa report the use of various "humiliation" rituals, among them: new clients are forced to wear pajamas to group therapy sessions; clients "in denial" are forced to wear pajamas; a childish client is told to wear a pacifier around his or her neck. On the southern coast of Norway is a

"Minnesota Model" treatment center that utilizes shouting and badgering of clients as a regular part of the group process. These rituals of social control can be viewed as sad anachronisms.

Treatment groups in the A.A. tradition are task-oriented groups; members help each other move toward a sober and fulfilling life. The knowledge and philosophy are borrowed from Alcoholics Anonymous ; the format is not. Therapy groups are smaller than most A.A.meetings; there is a designated leader or counselor, and everyone actively participates. In the task-oriented treatment groups the first three or four of A.A.'s Twelve Steps are explored in depth during the intensive period of professional treatment; the remaining steps are followed in the months and years ahead under the guidance of the local A.A. chapter.

Written by the founders and early members from their actual experiences, the classic Twelve Steps to Recovery are as follows:

1. We admitted we were powerless over alcohol—that our lives had become unmanageable.
2. Came to believe that a Power greater than ourselves could restore us to sanity.
3. Made a decision to turn our will and our lives over to the care of God *as we understood Him.*
4. Made a searching and fearless moral inventory of ourselves.
5. Admitted to God, to ourselves, and to another human being the exact nature of our wrongs.
6. Were entirely ready to have God remove all these defects of character.
7. Humbly asked Him to remove our shortcomings.
8. Made a list of all persons we had harmed, and became willing to make amends to them all.
9. Made direct amends to such people wherever possible, except when to do so would injure them or others.
10. Continued to take personal inventory and when we were wrong promptly admitted it.
11. Sought through prayer and meditation to improve our conscious contact with God *as we understood Him,* praying only for knowledge of His will for us and the power to carry that out.
12. Having had a spiritual awakening as the result of these steps, we tried to carry this message to alcoholics and to practice these principles in all our affairs.

The Twelve Steps are reprinted and adapted with permission of Alcoholics Anonymous World Services, Inc. Permission to reprint and adapt this material does not mean that A.A. has reviewed or approved the contents of this publication. A.A. is a program of recovery from alcoholism. Use of the Twelve Steps in connection with programs and activities which are patterned after A.A., but which address other problems, does not imply otherwise.

There is a gold mine of knowledge in this laconic program for recovery. There are whole books, in fact, written on each one of the steps (see the recent Hazelden educational materials catalogue). But not until the 1970s did most alcoholism treatment centers, staffed with recovering alcoholics, incorporate the principles of the A.A. Twelve Step plan in their treatment. Counselors who work at these centers generally are expected to be able to recite the Twelve Steps verbatim.

Makela (1993) draws on the literature for estimates of the number of alcoholism treatment counselors who are also members of Alcoholics Anonymous. Estimates are between 60 and 72 percent. Few treatment professionals with advanced degrees, however, according to Makela, are recovering alcoholics, and the A.A. Twelve Step program is not an integral part of American professional treatment regimens. Only 25 percent of alcoholism treatment centers in England base their work on a disease model of alcoholism (Klingemann, et al., 1993).

BASIC ASSUMPTIONS OF THE A.A. APPROACH TO TREATMENT

Alcoholism is a disease. This is the most basic assumption of the A.A. school. Alcoholism is regarded as a progressive, incurable disease that will only get worse if untreated. Step 1—We admitted we were powerless over alcohol—is the step of surrender to the disease alcoholism. *Surrender* is the positive admission that one's life has become unmanageable as a result of one's preoccupation with alcohol. With the surrender comes a full acceptance of the label *alcoholic* or *addict*. Alcoholics Anonymous proper does not debate causation. The treatment counterpart, however, offers information on the biochemistry of alcoholism: the latest scientific research is introduced to bolster the disease concept of alcoholism. Alcoholism counselors, moreover, receive intensive training in the physiology of chemical dependency.

Total abstinence from all mood-altering substances is required. Abstinence alone, however, is not sufficient for recovery. *Sobriety* is regarded as the desirable state of psychological acceptance of the reality of the disease and of a full recovery program.

Group confrontation and support of individual members are considered vital for recovery. The group process dominates treatment to the exclusion of much individual therapy. Group work follows the logical sequence of the early steps. Unconditional nurturance is provided to the newly sober client in the early stage of adjustment to the disease. As time passes, however, increasing demands are made for the development of self-awareness and the rejection of self-defeating behavior and attitudes.

62

The comprehensiveness of A.A.'s goals encourages personal growth in emotional, behavioral, and spiritual spheres.

"The Program" for one addiction is "The Program" for all addictions; the principles of Alcoholics Anonymous serve as the cornerstone for Narcotics, Overeaters, Emotions, and Gamblers Anonymous and their auxiliary family groups. The provision for easy and inexpensive training of counselors is inherent in the simplicity of the A.A. program. The tradition of on-the-job training supplies a ready source of cheap yet enthusiastic labor.

Detractors of the A.A.-based treatment point first and foremost to the heavy religious flavor of the A.A. message—the use of the word *God*, saying of prayers, and so on—as unappealing to many individuals. Feminist critics are especially put off by the reference to a male God and to notions of powerlessness, surrender, and humility. The concept of people as victims (of genes and family history) who must be regulated by punitive, external forces has been singled out as counterproductive by those of the individual-responsibility school. Others resent the rigidity and intolerance of the A.A. creed, which offers a uniform view of alcoholism and of recovery. Heavy reliance on dogma in treatment obviates use of current scientific findings concerning effective treatment modalities.

Lack of an individualized approach to meet each client's idiosyncratic needs is seen as an additional shortcoming. Nonalcoholics are annoyed by the perceived sense of superiority by recovering alcoholic staff to nonalcoholic staff who, it is said, "don't know what they're talking about." Counselors as models of recovery often suffer from other addictions such as smoking, food, and relationship addictions. The sense is that when the director is a recovering person without professional education, often the door is closed to job entry by "nonrecovering" professionally trained staff.

Finally, stigmatization of young problem drinkers may be harmful; the too-early diagnosis of alcoholism may be incorrect. Confrontation of persons who may be of an introverted nature and not comfortable in an almost exclusively group-oriented program may cause a setback for those who could benefit by an alternative approach.

From the late 1980s until today, the criticism of the disease model of alcoholism as advocated by most alcoholism treatment centers has become more emotional and vitriolic (see Fingarette, 1988; Peele, 1989; Peele and Brodsky, 1991; Kasl, 1990). The days when scientists, humanists, and social workers blindly accepted the platitudes espoused by hardliners "of the old school" are over. The Twelve Steps are no longer considered sacrosanct. Chapter 7 includes the feminist response to a program designed by males for males. The rift between the A.A. school and the professionally trained nonalcoholic personnel is explored further in chapter 11. Here we will look at the scientific criticism. What is the *scientific evidence* for the efficacy of this model?

TREATMENT EFFECTIVENESS

The tenets of the disease-model treatment school are grounded in tradition, not in empirical research. As Peele and Brodsky (1991) in their extensive review of the treatment literature make clear, the forms of treatment that are most effective are not the ones that have become popular in the United States. Treatment, according to the Twelve Step model that predominates, has received less in the way of scientific support for effectiveness than comparable treatment modalities.

Peele and Brodsky, for the most part, draw upon the comprehensive research of Hester and Miller (1989) described previously. Of two hundred controlled studies analyzed, only four involved controlled trials of A.A. strategies. Strikingly, none of these demonstrated a beneficial treatment effect (Miller, 1990).

Miller's explanation for poor results concerns the confrontational style typical of traditional alcoholism counseling. This style of therapy is associated with poorer outcomes than the empathic style such as that described by Carl Rogers or by most social work practice textbooks. Another traditional treatment component—prescription of the drug Antabuse (disulfiram), which renders drinking virtually impossible—has not been correlated with high recovery rates. Use of educational films and lectures has no demonstrated treatment validity. In short, concludes Miller, the uncontrolled evaluation studies done by individual Twelve Step treatment programs based on follow-up telephone calls cannot be regarded as creditable reports of treatment effectiveness.

Vaillant's (1983) extensive longitudinal study, covering a low SES (socioeconomic status) population of males for over a forty-year period, is widely cited by supporters and detractors alike of the traditional Twelve Step approach as the study *par excellence* in the literature. Tracking a large contingent of adult alcoholics identified from a community sample, Vaillant (1983) concluded that factors associated with recovery in middle age were attribution of recovery to willpower, active church membership or other group membership such as A.A., stable marital relationships, and hobbies. Over half of the subjects in Vaillant's inner city sample had recovered; most became sober outside of treatment in Alcoholics Anonymous.

The best evidence in support of the Twelve Step program is provided by the independent evaluation service for the chemical dependency field, CATOR (Comprehensive Assessment and Treatment Outcome Research) (Hoffman and Harrison, 1987). Approximately 53 percent of 1,975 adult patients (male and female) were followed for two years after discharge. Of those interviewed, only 28 percent relapsed significantly. Statistically correcting for the patients who could not be contacted, the study concluded that at least half of the men and women treated at the inpatient treatment centers maintained sobriety for two years (study summarized by Blume, 1990).

What we do not know is how many of these individuals (or individuals of the same high socioeconomic class) would have recovered on their own. And the results, presumably, would not have been as good if the clients could not have returned to the stability of the middle-class environment. The need is for rigorously controlled treatment evaluation designs studying a variety of treatment modalities and population characteristics.

THE BEHAVIORAL/COGNITIVE APPROACH

Whether or not alcoholism is a disease or is of biological origin is irrelevant to this approach of the here-and-now school. Nor are the bouts of intoxication dealt with as symptoms of some other illness. Instead, the focus is on the problematic behavior (Akers, 1992) and on the thinking that underlies this behavior. The focus is on changing behavior. Treatment may be direct conditioning of the stimulus/response variety or it may center on analysis of cognitions.

The behavioral school is much more grounded in empirical research than is any other school. The model is a conglomerate of approaches, all united by the concept of drinking as learned, problematic behavior. Treatment consists of learning new techniques of management, reversing the dysfunctional drinking process, and/or changing the conditioning factors. This approach is at once simple and highly intellectual.

AVERSION THERAPY

The oldest behavioral conditioning approach to alcoholism is aversion therapy. This type of therapy is based on Skinner's operant conditioning principles: if drinking alcohol leads to rewarding consequences it is likely to continue; if it leads to punishment it is likely to be discontinued. For effective results, the punishment must be closely connected to the act. The hangover the day after or bankruptcy a year later is too far removed from the stimulus to yield to aversion therapy.

Treatment relies on nausea-inducing drugs (apomorphine, or Emetine) given in conjunction with alcohol. When this is repeated over time, ideally, the alcohol itself will elicit nausea. The Shadel Hospital in Seattle utilizes this approach, purportedly with high success rates. For clients with heart conditions or who are in poor health, shock treatments are

BOX 3.1: An A.A. Meeting

Alcoholics Anonymous is a remarkable human organization. Its chapters now cover every part of the United States and most of the world. There is more caring and concern among the members for one another than in most other organizations. Group members work together to save the lives of each other and to restore self-respect and sense of worth. A.A. has helped more people overcome their drinking problems than all other therapies and methods combined.

Alcoholics Anonymous is supported entirely by voluntary donations from the members at meetings. There are no dues or fees. Each chapter is autonomous, free of any outside control by the A.A. headquarters in New York City or by any other body. There is no hierarchy in the chapters. The only office is that of group secretary. This person chooses a chairperson for each meeting, makes the arrangements for meetings, and sees that the building is opened, the chairs set up, and the tea and coffee put on. The group secretary holds office for only a limited time period; after a month or two the secretary's responsibilities are transferred to another member.

The only requirement for membership in Alcoholics Anonymous is a desire to stop drinking. All other variables (such as economic status, social status, race, religion) do not count. Members can even attend meetings while drunk, as long as they do not disturb the meeting.

A.A. meetings are held in a variety of physical locations—churches, temples, private homes, business offices, schools, libraries, or banquet rooms of restaurants. The physical location is unimportant.

When a newcomer first arrives, he or she will usually find people setting up chairs, placing ashtrays, putting free literature on a table, and making coffee. Other members will be socializing in small groups. Someone is apt to introduce himself or herself and other members to the newcomer. If someone is shy about attending the first meeting alone, he or she can call Alcoholics Anonymous and someone will take the person to the meeting, and introduce him or her to the other members.

When the meeting starts, everyone sits down around tables or in rows of chairs. The secretary and/or chairperson and one or more speakers sit at the head of a table or on a platform if the meeting is in a hall.

The chairperson opens with a moment of silence, which is followed by a group recitation of a prayer that is nondenominational. The chairperson then reads or gives a brief description of Alcoholics Anonymous and may read or refer to a section of the book *Alcoholics Anonymous* (a book that describes the principles of A.A. and also gives a number of case examples).

Then, the chairperson usually asks if anyone is attending for the first, second, or third time. The new people are asked to introduce themselves according to the following: "Hello, my name is (first name), and this is my first (second, third) meeting." Those who do not want to introduce themselves are not pressured to do so. New members are the lifeblood of A.A., and the most important people at the meeting in the members' eyes. (All the longer term members remember their first meeting and how frightened and inhibited they felt.)

If the group is small, the chairperson usually then asks the longer term members to introduce themselves and say a few words. If the group is large, the chairperson asks volunteers among the longer term members to introduce themselves by saying a few words. Each member usually begins by saying, "My name is (first name); I am an alcoholic" and then discloses a few thoughts or feelings. (The members do not have to say they are alcoholic, unless they choose to do so. Each member sooner or later generally chooses to say this, to remind him- or herself that he or she is an addictive drinker who is recovering and that alcoholism is a lifelong disease, which must be battled daily.) Those who introduce themselves usually say whatever they feel will be most helpful to the newcomers. They may talk about their first meeting, or their first week without drinking, or something designed to make the newcomers more comfortable. Common advice for the newcomers is to get the phone numbers of other members after the meeting so that they can call them when they feel a strong urge to drink. Alcoholics Anonymous considers such help as vital in recovering. The organization believes members can only remain sober through receiving the help of people who care about them and who understand what they are struggling with.

A.A. members want newcomers to call when they have the urge to drink, at any time day or night. The members sincerely believe that by helping others they are helping themselves to stay sober and grow. Members indicate that such calling is the newcomer's ace in the hole against the first drink, if everything else fails. They also inform newcomers that it is good to call others when lonely, just to chat.

In his own words, a newcomer explains how Alcoholics Anonymous began to help him:

> Here's what happened to me. When I finally hit bottom and called AA for help, a U.S. Air Force officer came to tell me about AA. For the first time in my life, I was talking to someone who obviously really understood my problem, as four psychiatrists had not, and he took me to my first meeting, sober but none too steady. It was amazing. I went home afterward and didn't have a drink. I went again the next night, still dry, and the miracle happened a second time. The third morning my

(continued on next page)

BOX 3.1 (continued)

wife went off to work, my boys to school, and I was alone. Suddenly I wanted a drink more than I had ever wanted one in my life. I tried walking for a while. No good. The feeling was getting worse. I tried reading. Couldn't concentrate. Then I became really desperate, and although I wasn't used to calling strangers for help, I called Fred, an AAer who had said that he was retired and would welcome a call at any time. We talked a bit, he could see that talking on the phone wasn't going to be enough. He said, "Look, I've got an idea. Let me make a phone call, and I'll call you back in ten minutes. Can you hold on that long?" I said I could. He called back in eight, asking me to come over to his house. We talked endlessly, went out for a sandwich together, and finally my craving for a drink went away. We went to a meeting. Next morning I was fine again, and now I had gone four days without a drink.[1]

After such discussion speakers may describe their life of drinking, how drinking almost destroyed their life, how they were introduced to Alcoholics Anonymous, their struggles to remain sober one day at a time, how Alcoholics Anonymous has helped them, and what their life is now like.

At the end of a meeting the chairperson may ask the newcomers if they wish to say anything. If they do not wish to say much, that is okay. No one is pressured to self-disclose what they do not want to reveal.   Meetings usually end after the chairperson makes announcements. (The collection basket for donations is also passed around. New members are not expected, and frequently not allowed, to donate any money until after the third meeting. If someone cannot afford to make a donation, none is expected.) The group then stands, usually holding hands, and repeats in unison the Lord's Prayer. Those who do not want to join in this prayer are not pressured to do so. After a meeting the members socialize. This is a time for newcomers to meet new friends and to get phone numbers.

A.A. is a cross-section of people from all walks of life. Anonymity is emphasized. It is the duty of every member to respect the anonymity of every person who attends. Concern for anonymity is a major reason for two kinds of meetings in A.A., open and closed. Anyone is welcome at open meetings. Only people with drinking problems are allowed at closed meetings. Therefore, if a person feels uncomfortable going to an open meeting and has a drinking problem, then closed meetings are an alternative.

1. Clark Vaughan, *Addictive Drinking* (New York: Penguin, 1984), pp. 75–76.

Members do not have to believe in God to get help from A.A. Many members have lost, or never had, a faith in God. A.A. does, however, assert that faith in some Higher Power is a tremendous help in recovery because such a belief offers a source of limitless power, hope, and support whenever one feels one has come to the end of one's resources.

How does A.A. help? New members, after years of feelings of rejection, loneliness, misunderstanding, guilt, and embarrassment, find they are not alone. They feel understood by others who are in similar predicaments. Instead of being rejected, they are welcomed. They see that others who had serious drinking problems are now sober, apparently happy that way, and are in the process of recovering. It gives them hope that they do not need alcohol to get through the day and that they can learn to enjoy life without alcohol. They find that others sincerely care about them, want to help them, and have the knowledge to do so.

At meetings they see every sort of personal problem brought up and discussed openly, with suggestions for solutions being offered from others who have encountered similar problems. They can observe that group members bring up "unspeakable" problems without apparent embarrassment, and that others listen and treat them with respect and consideration. Such acceptance gradually leads newcomers to share their personal problems and to receive constructive suggestions for solutions. Such disclosure leads individuals to look more deeply into themselves and to ventilate deep personal feelings. With the support of other members, newcomers gradually learn how to counter strong desires to drink, through such processes as calling other members.

Newcomers learn that A.A. is the means of staying away from that first drink. A.A. also serves to reduce the stress that compels people to drink by: (a) providing a comfortable and relaxed environment and (b) having members helping each other to find ways to reduce the stresses encountered in daily living. A.A. meetings and members become a safe port that is always there when storms start raging. A.A. helps members to be programmed from negative thinking to positive thinking. The more positive a member's thinking becomes, the more stress is relieved, the better he or she begins to feel about him- or herself, the more the compulsion to drink decreases, and the more often and more effectively the person begins to take positive actions to solve his or her problems.

Source: Zastrow, C., and K. Kirst-Ashman, *Understanding Human Behavior and the Social Environment* (Chicago: Nelson-Hall, 1993). Reprinted with permission of Nelson-Hall, Inc.

substituted for the vomiting inducing drug. Treatment at this center is solely in the hands of medical personnel.

Infliction of pain, nausea, sickness, and electric shock in order to condition aversion to alcohol in the patient raises serious ethical concerns (Akers, 1992). Reports in the late seventies of high deaths among elderly clients caused several of these types of treatment centers to close their doors.

COGNITIVE MODELS

Also based on learning theory, the cognitive approaches treat abusive drinking as a learned habit that must be changed. These models focus on interactions between the individual and the environment in shaping patterns of alcohol use. Social learning perspectives emphasize cognitive processes, such as the thinking that leads to the drinking.

Various kinds of anxiety-management techniques have been attempted. Clients suffering from anxiety have been trained to relax through biofeedback and systematic desensitization. Problem drinkers have been taught social skills for coping with threatening situations without resorting to use of chemicals. Cognitive restructuring is used to teach clients to replace unhealthy thoughts with healthier ones; this technique is widely used in all relapse prevention programs.

Each of the models utilized is slightly different in focus. The Rational Emotive Therapy (RET) model by Ellis provides an illustration of how cognitive principles are applied to alcoholism treatment. Further examples will be provided in chapter 5, "Alcoholism as a Way of Thinking."

Rational emotive therapy is based on the following premises as enunciated by Ellis, McInerney, DiGiueseppe, and Yeager (1988). Irrational beliefs associated with low frustration tolerance are present in addictions. In order to remove the emotional pain accruing from thinking that is often hysterical or depressed, persons with drinking problems will drink. Upsetting situations for such persons often lead to intoxication. Such intoxication is but one symptom of an underlying antisocial personality for a minority of people, while for others, the substance abuse itself leads to antisocial behavior.

Ellis et al. (1988) conceptualize addictive thinking, like other forms of irrational thinking, as often automatic, not conscious, overlearned, and continually practiced. To aid clients in reshaping their thinking distortions, the therapist takes the role of teacher, actively labeling and challenging irrational self-statements. Special attention is paid to high-risk situations and to the feelings aroused. Always, the cognitive focus is on the here-and-now of *present* thinking.

There is very little of a critical nature that can be said about this form of treatment. Believers in the disease model disagree with a treatment strategy that does not make use of the label "alcoholic" or even the concept of illness. Some say that this treatment modality is "all head and no heart." Despite the mild criticism, virtually every alcoholism treatment center provides coping techniques and relapse prevention training derived directly from this framework.

TREATMENT EFFECTIVENESS

Well-designed treatment studies attest to the effectiveness of various cognitive-behavioral modalities. Aversion therapy consistently produces favorable results, even when researchers control for the effect of SES. At the six-month follow-up assessment, Bromet, Moos, Wuthmann, and Bliss (1977) determined that patients functioned well on drinking variables although their social and psychological functioning were below that of most graduates from therapy programs. Miller (1990) confirms the effectiveness of this controversial form of therapy.

Oei, Lim, and Young (1991) studied treatment effectiveness studies utilizing a cognitive-behavior therapy. Empirical studies utilizing a cognitive restructuring approach to acquire a more positive outlook, a stress management approach to teach coping techniques, and social skills training to teach alcoholics to handle difficult social situations all provided evidence of effective treatment of problem drinking. Similarly, Miller (1990) singles out stress management approaches and social skills training as of high efficacy in maintaining treatment benefits. The majority of relapse prevention programs today incorporate various cognitive exercises in their treatment (Marlatt and Gordon, 1985).

CHALLENGE TO THE SOCIAL WORK PROFESSION

The current paradigm in vogue in social work is the ecosystems or ecological approach. Unlike the four modalities described in this chapter, this is not a treatment modality. Instead, this is a framework for viewing human phenomena. Thus, the ecological framework may incorporate aspects of the disease model for the biological side of addiction, while the social aspect may be addressed through stress on self-help groups. The cognitive modalities relate well to the psychological factors in addiction. This biopsychosocial paradigm, in short, has unique capabilities of addressing alcoholism in terms of both conceptualization and treatment (van Wormer, 1987).

The social work profession should be at the forefront of the emerging addictions field because of the relevance of its multidimensional approach to human behavior. Alcoholism, which may well be the one condition above all others that requires an approach that attends to the physiological, psychological, and social realm, has been shrouded in controversy and what Parihar (1982) terms "cultural ambivalence." Social workers and other professionals have ceded the territory to those whose major qualification has been "first hand experience" with alcoholism and recovery. Often former clients were recruited to conduct group therapy (this is still true in Norway, at the private treatment centers where the use of the Minnesota Model is in its infancy).

Alcoholism counseling and treatment for drug abuse and eating disorders are steadily gaining in respectability and credibility. And there is the need for multidisciplinary trained professionals sensitive to the complexities of this diversified field. Social work, newly equipped with a multifaceted theoretical focus and ever interested in challenging career opportunities, is in an ideal position to meet this need. The task for the following chapters is to adapt the contemporary theoretical model of social work to the treatment demands of the alcoholic/addict as client.

CONCLUSION AND SUMMARY

Unfortunately, the U.S. alcoholism treatment field remains largely mired in competition, with each program or approach asserting its superiority (Miller and Hester, 1989). Internationally, there is vast disagreement over the causes of alcoholism and over the manner of treatment (if any) to be provided.

Treatment that may be effective for one individual or social or ethnic group may not be effective for another. Yet factors of limited resources, professional loyalties, and third-party reimbursement serve to limit the program options available.

This chapter has provided a survey of the field of alcoholism treatment, a field recently opened up to social worker involvement and leadership. Four approaches to the disorder of alcoholism were described in terms of underlying assumptions, treatment modalities, and scientific backing for the treatment and assumptions.

The moralistic/religious approach is largely out of fashion now in North America (but is being revived under a scientific umbrella). This approach still survives in Norway where policies are of a caring nature, and in Russia, where a punitive philosophy still prevails. The recovery rate is reportedly quite low under both systems. The psychoanalytical or psychodynamic approach is also largely defunct today as a popular model of treatment for alcoholism. Delving into the past carries risks for the unrecovered drinker. Intoxication and psychotherapy are rarely compatible, in any case.

The A.A.-based Twelve Step approach has dominated the field to the neglect of any other possibilities. The dominance has been shown to be based on a fluke of history and professional neglect rather than on scientific support. Nevertheless, the intense group work and recent family communication programs have brought personal growth and sobriety to many. Finally, the behavior/cognitive scheme is responsible for the introduction of two modalities—stress management and social skills training—the effectiveness of which is scientifically verified by an increasing array of controlled follow-up research studies.

In practice, of course, each of these strategies is not entirely separate. Thus, the behaviorist will enroll his or her client in an active Twelve Step group. The A.A.-based approach provides training in how to deal with stress. Moral concerns are not overlooked by any orientation, and even the psychological dimension is beginning to be reidentified in light of the recognition of childhood trauma as a common correlate of later addiction.

The challenge for future research is to determine which treatment strategies relate best to which categories of people (Hester and Miller, 1989). The matching of client to treatment mode should be scientifically perfected for optimum results. Effective treatment is individualized treatment; alternative treatment offerings are therefore essential. The overall ecological or holistic framework of social work lends itself well to understanding the complexities of alcoholism in a multidimensional light.

REVIEW QUESTIONS

1. What, according to Hartman and Laird (1983), is the revolution brewing in the social sciences?
2. Define the following terms: *addictions worker, addiction, alcoholism,* and the *psychological component* in alcoholism.
3. Discuss the idea that in the "house of social work" there are "many mansions."
4. List the three criteria of *DSM-IV*'s diagnosis of substance dependence that distinguish this disorder from substance abuse.
5. Define *addiction, disease,* and *alcoholism.*
6. Explain how the biological component is the *why,* the psychological component is the *what,* and the social part is the *where* of alcoholism.
7. Which of the social worker specialties will most likely encounter clients with chemical dependency problems?
8. How is specialized addictions work not really so specialized after all?
9. What are some indications that social workers are beginning to get interested in the addictions field?

10. Name some economic, political, and social factors impinging upon substance abuse treatment.

11. What is the policy of NASW, adopted in 1988, regarding the nature of alcoholism?

12. Discuss the moral/religious approach in its American and European counterparts.

13. Who founded Alcoholics Anonymous and how did its philosophy shape alcoholism treatment programming?

14. Discuss the basic assumptions of the Twelve Step approach. What is *surrender*? How is sobriety a higher level of recovery than mere abstinence?

15. Argue the pros and cons of Twelve Step treatment.

16. What is the psychodynamic orientation? How does it differ from the A.A. approach? Name several basic assumptions of this model.

17. What do identical-twin studies show about the development of alcoholism?

18. Name various personality traits that may be forerunners of alcoholism.

19. Discuss advantages and disadvantages of the psychodynamic approach.

20. What is aversion treatment? What is the link between this approach and the cognitive framework?

21. Which two cognitive modalities emerge with the best empirically based evidence for treatment effectiveness? Why do you think these strategies are so effective? What is the challenge to the social work profession regarding the emerging addictions field?

Part Two

ASPECTS OF ADDICTION

Whereas the chapters of Part One presented the social and historical context for alcohol abuse, the task for Part Two is more varied. The three chapters of this section consider the *biology* of alcohol consumption and alcohol abuse, the *thinking* that may figure in its correction, and finally, the *grieving* factor—the loss and grief associated in the development of alcoholism and in letting go of this chemical dependence. Another way of summing up the content of the following chapters is to say the concern is with the *micro* realm of drinking, with the chemical properties of alcohol, its effects on the body—the physiology of addiction, and the psychology of chemical abuse. While Part One is largely theoretical and Part Three focuses on professional issues, the subject matter of this middle section is more practical.

4

THE BIOLOGY OF ALCOHOLISM
AND ALCOHOL ABUSE

They that tarry long at the wine. . . .
—*Proverbs*, 23

INTRODUCTION

Before pursuing the physiology of addiction, we will look at the biochemical aspects of alcohol consumption. We will first consider the normal process of drinking; later, we will examine the abnormal processes.

What is alcohol and how does it work on the body? Alcohol is a chemical and a drug; the kind that people drink is ethyl alcohol, or ethanol (C_2H_5OH), popularly abbreviated as ETOH. Ethyl alcohol is a colorless, flammable, volatile liquid with a burning taste (Royce, 1989). The same alcohol is found in beer, wine, and spirits distilled from wines and beer. Most U.S. beer contains between 4 and 5 percent alcohol; European beer is stronger. Natural wines contain between 8 and 12 percent alcohol. Fortified wines have had alcohol or brandy added for a higher alcohol content. Spirits such as vodka, gin, whiskeys, and rum usually contain between 40 and 50 percent alcohol. The word *proof* in the United States refers to twice the percent of alcohol: 100 proof liquor is 50 percent ethanol. In Canada and Britain, 100 proof liquor is 57 percent ethanol. Beverage alcohol consists of ethanol, various byproducts of fermentation known as congeners, flavorings, colorings, and water.

METABOLISM

When swallowed, alcohol's beverages are diluted by stomach juices. No digestion is required; alcohol is simply absorbed into the body. Approximately 20 percent of alcohol is absorbed by the stomach and 80 percent by the small intestine. Alcohol, unlike other nutrients, rapidly enters the bloodstream from the stomach and small intestine (Levin, 1990). The amount of food in the stomach affects the rate of absorption; food dilutes the alcohol and reduces the level of irritation. The higher the concentration of alcohol in a beverage, the more quickly it is absorbed (Kinney and Leaton, 1991). Consumed with carbonated beverages, alcohol will have an increased intoxicating effect.

Once alcohol enters the bloodstream, it is transported to every cell in the body. Alcohol is diffused in the body in proportion to the water content of the various tissues and organs (*Encyclopaedia Britannica,* 1993). Alcohol's small molecule and its solubility in water make it readily transportable across cell membranes with the effect of harm to many different organs (Levin, 1990).

The breakdown or metabolism of alcohol mostly takes place in the liver. Since this metabolic activity takes place at a fixed rate, only part of the alcohol being pumped through the liver is metabolized at a time, while the rest continues to circulate (Royce, 1989). The first step in the process is formation of a poison called *acetaldehyde.* The chain of events is as follows:

Alcohol → Acetaldehyde → acetic acid → carbon dioxide and water

This metabolism is controlled by enzymes or proteins that can cause chemical changes in other substances. The breakdown of alcohol that occurs in the stomach differs significantly in men and women. Schlaadt (1992) summarizes recently published findings that point to the important role of the enzyme *alcohol dehydrogenase* (ADH) in metabolizing alcohol. In male chronic alcoholics and in all women the amount of alcohol metabolized by ADH is lower than in nonalcoholic men. This action takes place in the stomach; more pure alcohol is delivered, therefore, into the blood streams of women and of chronic alcoholics than of nonalcoholic men. Women will have higher blood alcohol levels than men given equal consumption of alcohol.

The toxicity of acetaldehyde is not usually a problem. There is a drug, however, prescribed by doctors which stops the breakdown of acetaldehyde by blocking ADH. This drug is Antabuse (disulfiram). The usefulness of this medication is in preventing drinking. Once Antabuse is ingested, if a person drinks, a severe physical reaction of nausea, flushing, and shortness of breath occurs. Even if alcohol is placed on the skin, such as that contained in perfume, a strong reaction will occur. Although consumption of alcohol is dangerous to most alcoholics who have ingested Antabuse, some chronic alcoholics will "brag" that they can drink freely, with no negative consequences. There is as yet no substantiation of these claims, however, in the literature.

The flushing response of some Orientals and a minority of Caucasians to drinking is thought to derive from a low ADH level. This may prevent these people from imbibing too much alcohol.

BLOOD ALCOHOL LEVEL

To determine the concentration of alcohol in the body at any given time, it is necessary to assess the alcohol concentration (BAC), the amount of alcohol in the blood. The continued accumulation of alcohol faster than it can be metabolized leads to increasing degrees of intoxication. A healthy person, according to Schlaadt (1992), can break down or oxidize approximately one drink per hour. However, as Royce (1989) indicates, the "one drink an hour" rule can be very misleading. The average man's liver can metabolize only .33 ounce of alcohol per hour. According to Royce, this one drink can include only one 8-ounce can of beer, 2.6 ounces of dry wine, or .67 ounce of 100 proof liquor.

A BAC of .10 percent is a ratio of 1 part alcohol to 1,000 parts blood. As of 1993, thirty-seven states and the District of Columbia use this level to indicate intoxication; nine states use a .08 blood alcohol concentration, while four states and the Commonwealth of Puerto Rico have no illegal limit. In Scandinavia, if there is any evidence of alcohol in the blood of a driver, he or she may be dealt with harshly. This is in recognition of the fact that inefficiency in performing some tasks may begin at a low concentration, such as .03 percent (*Encyclopaedia Britannica*, 1993). Most people are quite intoxicated at .15 percent and comatose at .4 percent. Individual differences, however, are striking, with high-tolerance alcoholics functioning well up to levels of .3 percent when others would appear visibly drunk. When alcohol levels are between .5 and 1 percent, the breathing center in the brain or the action of the heart may be anesthetized. If vomiting does not prevent intoxication at this level, death will swiftly follow.

EXCRETION

Approximately 95 percent of the alcohol ingested is absorbed and metabolized, according to Levin (1990). Carbon dioxide and water are eliminated as end products of the metabolic process. An insignificantly small proportion of alcohol is exhaled through the lungs, and a tiny amount is excreted in sweat. About 5 percent of the alcohol is eliminated unmetabolized in the urine. The increased urinary frequency that accompanies drinking is related to fluid intake. Father Martin's story as recounted in the film *Chalk Talk* (1972) comes to mind:

BOX 4.1: One Drink Can Be Too Many

It's Not a New Problem

The year was 1904. The horseless carriage had only been around just a few years.

Alcohol had been around for centuries. When the two got together there was trouble.

An editorial in the *Quarterly Journal of Inebriety,* dated 1904, stated:

"We have received a communication containing a history of 25 fatal accidents occurring to automobile wagons. Fifteen persons occupying these wagons were killed outright, five more died two days later. . . . A careful inquiry showed that in 19 of these accidents the drivers had used spirits within an hour or more of the disaster. The other six drivers were all moderate drinkers, but it was not ascertained whether they had used spirits preceding the accidents."

That year 375 more persons died in auto crashes, but it's unknown how many had been using "spirits."

Today there are more than 193 million vehicles on the nation's roads. Approximately 40,000 persons will die in auto crashes this year. Alcohol will be a major factor in almost half of these deaths.

Types of Drinkers

It's estimated that two-thirds of the more than 172 million American drivers drink alcoholic beverages at one time or another before driving.

Social drinkers and alcoholics can be "problem" drinkers on the highway. Even one drink can be too many—a "social" drinker can be a menace on the highway.

Extensive evidence indicates people who drink often and heavily are predominantly responsible for alcohol-related collisions. It's believed there are approximately 41 million drivers in this category of high-volume heavy "escape" drinkers and alcoholics.

Generalities Are Misleading

The blood alcohol level will not give a true indication of the drinker's ability to drive. In fact, the driver may be much further down the road to intoxication and impairment than even a breathalyzer, blood or urine test may indicate.

Today's safety specialists make a concerted effort to explain the relationship between blood alcohol level and the probability of a fatal crash. Research data shows drivers under the influence of alcohol are at greater risk of a fatal crash than a personal injury crash. Several factors such as time of day, day of the week, type of crash, miles driven, drinking frequency, marital status, sex and age account for different levels of risks.

Of course, the *major factor* in determining driver capability is *the amount of alcohol consumed.* The greater the blood alcohol concentration, the greater the risk of being involved in a fatal crash. For instance, young drivers ages 16 to 19 with a BAC of .02 percent to .05 percent—one to two drinks—are at least seven times more likely to be killed in a crash than a sober driver of any age. At .085 percent BAC—three to four drinks—young drivers are 40 times more likely to be killed than a sober driver and 20 times more likely to be killed than a 55-year-old driver with the same BAC level. By .12 percent BAC—four to six drinks—a 16- to 19-year old is 90 times as likely to die in a traffic crash as a sober driver. The risk of a crash increases even before drivers are considered legally impaired or intoxicated.

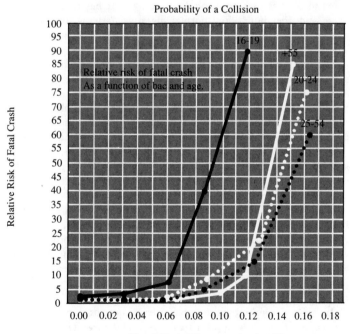

Probability of a Collision

Available research indicates that the level and duration of alcohol's effects on females is greater than on males. Women have smaller quantities of the enzyme *alcohol dehydrogenase* that breaks down

(continued on next page)

BOX 4.1 *(continued)*

alcohol in the stomach. As a result, women absorb about 30 percent more alcohol into their system. Adjusting for weight, a woman who consumes two ounces of liquor will experience about the same effect as a man who consumes four ounces.

But there are many other variables that enter into the picture, including how tired the driver is, food that was consumed, medication of any kind, and the driver's emotional state. These and other factors help determine how any amount of alcohol affects the driver's ability. Even under similar conditions, alcohol may have completely different effects each time the driver drinks. There is only one thing a driver can be certain of: The effect of alcohol on his or her ability to operate a motor vehicle is detrimental.

Alcohol Takes Effect Quickly and Wears Off Slowly

Ethyl alcohol is used in alcoholic beverages. It has no nutritional value and does not follow normal digestive patterns. Instead, it's immediately absorbed into the bloodstream through the walls of the stomach and small intestine.

Alcohol is retained in organs in proportion to the amount of water each organ contains. Because the brain has a high concentration of blood—which is 90 percent water—the effects of alcohol on the central nervous system are soon apparent, usually within minutes.

Alcohol reduces control, judgment and coordination, in addition, perceptual abilities, speech and speed of reflexes can be impaired.

Although alcohol is rapidly absorbed into the system, it takes a long time for the body and brain to return to normal. All the age-old remedies—black coffee, cold showers, fresh air and exercise—are useless and only result in a more wide-awake drunk.

Once in the bloodstream, alcohol must be broken down by the liver and oxidized—turned into water and carbon dioxide. The liver converts less than one-half ounce of alcohol per hour. For example, a 160-pound man having one $1^{1}/_{2}$-ounce drink per hour during a six-hour period would have blood-alcohol levels of .05 percent—still legally sober in some states. Taking other factors into consideration, the man may already be greatly impaired.

Increase alcohol intake to two bottles of beer or two $1^{1}/_{2}$-ounce shots of bourbon each hour for six hours, and the blood alcohol level would be .191—definitely an impaired level.

At two drinks per hour, the drinker's blood alcohol level would be .047 percent at the end of the first hour. But because the rate the body absorbs alcohol is higher than the rate the body oxidizes it, the cumulative effect causes a person to be intoxicated in a short time. With all other variables eliminated—the man has taken no medication, had plenty of rest the night before, got along well with his boss and his family, ate a full meal and was in perfect physical and mental condition—he could still become impaired after consuming one or two drinks in a short period of time.

The Effects of "Spirits"

It's a scientific fact that alcohol has a definite effect on a person's motor abilities. Medically classified as a depressant drug, alcohol acts like an anesthetic on the central nervous system, slowing the activities of the brain and spinal cord. The drug causes a person to relax and produces a feeling of euphoria—that "everything-is-pleasant-and-the-world-is-good" feeling.

This may not be bad in itself, but it can make dangerous situations seem less dangerous and make a driver feel more capable than he or she really is.

Reactions are slower after several drinks. The time required to move one's foot from the accelerator to the brake pedal increases by a fraction of a second. With more alcohol, a driver may miss the brake pedal completely—a sometimes fatal mistake.

One of the most dangerous effects of alcohol is impaired vision. Human vision is controlled by a delicate system of muscles that move and focus the eyes. Slowing these responses sends a fuzzy picture from the eyes to the brain.

Alcohol also reduces the muscles' ability to control the amount of light entering the eye. And like camera film, too much or too little light spoils the picture. These factors can cause such impairments as faulty depth perception, poor peripheral vision, distorted color vision and reduced night vision.

None for the Road Is Best

A clear mind, excellent reflexes and good vision are essential to being an alert, safe driver. Under the best circumstances—excellent physical, mental and emotional conditions—alcohol clouds the mind, delays reactions and blurs vision. Any of these can result in a crash with grave consequences.

The best advice is don't drink and drive. But even in the face of tragic statistics, there are those who still drive after drinking.

Despite how well they control their drinking, it is important for those people to realize they are likely to have had one drink too many—even after just one drink.

Reprinted by permission of the American Automobile Association.

"Have you heard the one about the man pouring beer in the toilet?"
"Why are you pouring beer in the toilet?" someone asked.
"I'm tired of being the middleman."

ALCOHOL-RELATED PHENOMENA

BLACKOUTS

Blackout is a term used by both alcoholics and health researchers to describe the total inability to recall events that occurred when the person was drunk, even though the person appeared normal at the time. There is no lapse of consciousness with a blackout. The inability to store knowledge in long-term memory (Sweeney, 1990) is attributed to a high blood alcohol level, usually over .30 BAC. When blackouts are studied experimentally, they are found to be neither selective nor predictable; nor can they be anticipated by observed behavior. To have a blackout, the person must have considerable tolerance; hence, having blackouts is probably a good indicator of alcoholism. The exact neurological process of this loss of memory is not fully understood.

Get a group of recovering alcoholics together, and the casualness with which they discuss blackout episodes can be daunting. Often, the blackout is a source of amusement if not amazement. Women talk of waking up in a bed in a strange place with a strange man; men talk of having to search endlessly for a "lost" car. One man proposed marriage; this led to an altercation later. Friends later said these people seemed to be acting normally. A typical difficulty encountered by the alcoholic is hiding liquor, then searching high and low for it later, to no avail. A memorable scene in the classic film *The Lost Weekend* graphically depicts the alcoholic hero's utter joy on leaning far back in the chair and spotting the coveted bottle directly overhead in the ceiling lampshade.

When experiencing a blackout, it is said, one can remember something for perhaps fifteen minutes, long enough to drive a car to a destination. One can think and plan. But nothing is stored in the memory; there is no way to retrieve the memory once lost. This is in contradistinction to repression, wherein the memory is buried in the unconscious. The legal implications of this are discussed in chapter 10. A fictional crime case is presented here. Mark Twain, not an alcoholic himself but familiar with the ways of drunks, lays out in the *Adventures of Tom Sawyer* (1876) an invitation to tragedy.

Potter trembled and grew white.
"I thought I'd got sober. I'd no business to drink tonight. But it's in my head yet—worse'n when we started here. I'm all in a muddle; can't recollect anything of it hardly. Tell me, Joe—honest now, old feller—did I do it?

Joe, I never meant to, 'pon my soul and honor, I never meant to, Joe. Tell me how it was, Joe. Oh, it's awful—and him so young and promising."

Fortunately, there were witnesses to the scene with proof that not Potter but Joe had committed the murder.

TOLERANCE

High tolerance for alcohol may show up immediately in the alcoholic or it may build up over time. Part of the "macho culture" says that a man who can hold his liquor is a *real* man. Such a man may be an alcoholic. His nervous system has been accommodated to, or become less sensitive to, the effects of alcohol. His liver is so efficient at metabolizing the alcohol that he has to drink excessively to get a "high."

Low sensitivity to modest amounts of alcohol—as indicated by good performance on a test of coordination and balance—shows a strong link to future alcoholism among the sons of both alcoholic and nonalcoholic fathers, according to a longitudinal study by Schuckit, reported in *Science News* (Bower, 1994). At age thirty, ten years after the tolerance measures were taken, alcoholism afflicted 43 percent of those who showed the least response to alcohol compared to only 11 percent of those deemed most sensitive to alcohol.

Tolerance, according to Royce (1989), means the ability of brain cells to function in the presence of alcohol. The individual admitted to the hospital or arrested for driving while intoxicated may have a high blood-alcohol level and yet still function normally. He or she is *behaviorally* tolerant. Behaviorally tolerant individuals, if experienced drivers, can perform remarkably when legally drunk. Others who are not legally drunk may be unable to walk a straight line. Some people may still be living and breathing at a blood alcohol level (BAL) of .7 or .8, but if the alcohol happens to be mixed with other drugs, especially sedative drugs, a dangerous multiplying effect is produced. Seixas (1975) states that one-fifth of a lethal dose of alcohol combined with one-twentieth of a lethal dose of a barbiturate can be fatal.

Alcoholics who once had high tolerance for the drug may experience a jolting intolerance as they age. This odd reversal in tolerance takes place in older, chronic alcoholics. The liver is no longer efficient, and the experienced alcoholic now gets drunk on the first drink. The integrity of the nervous system is compromised. As one of my elderly former clients moaned, "I might as well stop drinking. It doesn't do anything for me anymore." And another said, "What do I need treatment for? My drinking days are over."

CROSS-TOLERANCE

Levin (1990) describes how, with prolonged heavy drinking, a different process from the usual one comes into play, an alternate pathway for metabolizing alcohol. In this situation, the microsomal ethanol oxidizing system, or MEOS, changes alcohol to acetaldehyde. Since the MEOS also metabolizes other drugs, *cross-tolerance* is built up. Cross-tolerance means that the tolerance developed for one drug generalizes to another drug in the same pharmacological class. Barbituates, general anesthetics, and alcohol are all sedative-hypnotic drugs, so tolerance for one is tolerance for all.

Pathological intoxication, or alcohol idiosyncratic intoxication, is the occurrence of a marked personality change, as when the ordinarily mild-mannered person becoming aggressive and assaultive after one drink. Predisposing factors are brain injuries as from trauma and encephalitis. Although *DSM-IV* has now dropped use of this categorization and incorporated it under the broad term "alcohol intoxication," practitioners and clients commonly report the phenomenon of extreme individual reactions to alcohol consumption.

DEPENDENCY AND WITHDRAWAL

In the *DSM-IV* (American Psychiatric Association, 1994), substance dependence is defined to include withdrawal symptoms that may accompany the cessation of drinking. When the depressant effects of a sedative drug such as alcohol are removed, there is a rebound effect, and the central nervous system becomes hyperactive.

Black coffee and other favorite remedies do nothing to speed up the brain's recovery from a night or weekend of indulgence. Caffeine plus alcohol creates a wide-awake drunk; reaction time is still impaired. Even the next day after a binge, functions involving coordination and concentration are seriously altered. The most common or least debilitating of the postintoxication withdrawal syndromes is the *hangover* (*Encyclopaedia Britannica*, 1993). The hangover simply has to be lived through; the condition is unpleasant but not dangerous.

Withdrawal from alcohol is characterized in *DSM-IV* by the development of withdrawal symptoms twelve hours or so after the reduction of intake following prolonged use. Withdrawal consists of such symptoms as tremor of the hands, tongue, or eyelids, nausea or vomiting, anxiety, depressed mood or irritability, illusions, headache, or insomnia. Seizures may occur. The patients who have gotten into serious trouble with alcohol may be found in the detoxification wards of most local hospitals. Several complications of withdrawal are experienced only by about 5 percent of individuals with alcohol dependence, according to the *DSM-IV*.

Donald Gallant (1987) emphasizes the importance of teaching treatment and hospital personnel to recognize the potential dangers of delayed treatment for alcohol withdrawal. Although it is usually not necessary to admit a conscious, intoxicated patient to a hospital, when the patient is semicomatose or comatose, hospitalization is required. Immediate steps may be necessary to sustain the airway, assure a regular respiratory rate, and maintain the circulatory system. The blood alcohol concentration is useful as a diagnostic guide.

The more serious kind of withdrawal, often known as the "DTs" (*delirium tremens*) develops after drinking stops, usually after several days. Only a tiny fraction of even heavy drinkers enter this stage of withdrawal. Those most susceptible are people who are still alert and who have a high BAC level. Marked hyperactivity, often accompanied by hallucinations and sweating, is common. If seizures appear, they usually precede the delirium. This disorder usually occurs after five to ten years of heavy drinking. If untreated, the DTs would result in a mortality rate of 15 to 20 percent. Today, if this advanced stage of withdrawal is reached, the mortality rate is 1 to 2 percent. Medication is essential at an early stage to prevent the patient from having withdrawal difficulties. Gallant recommends placing vulnerable patients on one of the benzodiazepines, since they have anticonvulsive as well as sedative properties.

FACTORS IN THE ETIOLOGY OF ALCOHOLISM

Why does alcoholism seem to run in families? Is alcoholic behavior learned or inherited? The search for genetic links began in earnest in the early 1970s with adoption studies in Scandinavia. The aim of these studies was to separate out environmental from hereditary determinants. Goodwin (1976) sought an answer by interviewing 133 Danish men who were adopted as small children and raised by nonalcoholics. Health records were used to substantiate the interviews. The findings are striking: the biological sons of alcoholics were shown to be four times as likely to have alcohol problems as were the children of nonalcoholics. That result, according to an article in *Time* magazine (Desmond, 1987), helped put to rest the popular assumption that alcoholics took up drinking simply because they learned it at home or turned to it because of abuse suffered at the hands of an alcoholic parent.

Cloninger's research in Sweden (1989) helped clarify the role of environment as well as heredity in the development of alcoholism. In the early 1980s, Cloninger joined a team of Swedish researchers and began gathering extensive data on a large group of adopted-away sons of alcoholics. Sweden was chosen, as Denmark before, because of the availability of thorough records on each citizen kept by the government.

In Cloninger et al.'s study of 259 male adoptees with alcoholic biological fathers (out of a total of 862 male adoptees), it was found that a somewhat larger proportion of the adoptees with alcoholic fathers were

BOX 4.2: Diary of a Drunk

What is it like to suffer from alcoholism? The writer of the following article, who spent twenty-eight days in a treatment center in northeastern United States, offers his reflections:

Dying of alcoholism normally takes years. But before a final, prolonged bout of uncontrolled drinking caused my physical collapse and led to treatment, there was no doubt I was well on my way. My appearance was shocking. I was about 20 lbs. underweight and malnourished, the result of giving up almost all forms of food except coffee, sugar and, of course, alcohol. I was in the early stages of delirium tremens, the DTs. I sometimes heard faint ringing noises in my ears and suffered unexpected waves of vertigo. I felt near constant pressure in my lower back and sides from the punishment my liver and kidneys were taking. My personality was also seriously diseased. I was nervous, reclusive, by turns extravagantly arrogant and cringingly apologetic. I tried to cover my extremes of mood with brittle cheerfulness, even though I was desperately afraid. If you asked me how I was feeling, I usually lied, "Just fine."

I now see "just fine" as a key phrase that encompassed my diseased physical and mental condition. At the nadir, my addiction to a chemical that was killing me was nearly complete. I knew that something was very wrong with me. I even knew I was an alcoholic, but I had long since come to believe there was nothing I could do about it. I had decided that it was perfectly appropriate—just fine—that I should die. In fact, I honestly hoped that I would, sparing further grief for many people I loved. Dying, I thought, was the best thing I could ever do for them. The idea of living without alcohol could not occur to me. I preferred the idea that I was a hopeless case.

No one finds alcoholism more mysterious than the suffering alcoholic, and I was no exception. I had no idea why I was an alcoholic at all, though I should have: my father was one. But from his illness I had gained only a morbid fear of the substance, which lasted until I reached college. I would never touch the stuff. That prolonged abstinence while my adolescent peers experimented with liquor only made what happened to me more mystifying. I thought I could take alcohol or leave it.

Why did I ever start to drink at all? The short answer is that initially it made me feel better. Alcohol numbed my self-awareness, the same trick that it performs for nonalcoholic drinkers at cocktail parties. The difference is that normal drinkers dull their self-consciousness only slightly, the better to socialize. I very quickly tried to send all my thoughts and feelings about myself to oblivion. Psychologically, I was undoubtedly depressed when I began to overcome my well-founded but ill-understood fears about alcohol: my father died when I was a sophomore. For whatever reason, I spent the better part of two decades trying to stay emotionally and physically numb.

Even in those early days, signs might have pointed an expert on alcoholism toward my growing problem. One hint was my immediate tendency to drink to unconsciousness. At parties, I would often fall asleep in mid-hullabaloo on the couch. That drew plenty of jokes at the time. Only much later did I recognize that I had been passing out. Another signal was an initial, abnormally high tolerance for alcohol, at least until the passing-out stage. I thought I could hold my liquor pretty well. Now I think it means that my body was being less dutiful than most in handling overdoses of a hazardous chemical. (Years later, when only a couple of drinks would overload my toxified liver, causing slurring of words and other drunken symptoms, I finally joined the company of those who "can't hold a drink.")

Exactly when did I become addicted to alcohol? I don't know that either. The addiction was preceded by a delusion: I thought I drank to socialize. Maybe I did. My alcoholism took years to develop into a chronic affliction, and during much of that time I went to bars after work, one of the guys. The delusion was gradually reinforced by gravitation. I mingled more and more with other persistent drinkers who took longer and longer to call for their bar tabs. Most of us were actually alcoholics in varying stages of development. The nonalcoholics had long ago selected themselves out. Those of us who remained agreed that we were "normal." Unhappy, but normal.

Alcohol perception is like that, in a hundred insidious and distorting ways. All of them are aimed at protecting a drunkard's notion that he is possessed of free will. My drinking buddies and I agreed that we did not have a drinking problem. Everything in our increasingly narrow world, though, was a problem that required drinking: the wife, the kids, the boss, the government. In dingy watering holes from which everyone with a healthy life to lead had gone home, we conspired to overlook the obvious, that our bodily cells were addicted, and our minds were along for the ride.

Inexorably, the need for alcohol grew, while the lies wore thin. As my alcoholism accelerated, I abandoned most drinking partners and joined the ranks of solitary topers bellied up to countless bars. I lost any sense at all of what would happen after I started drinking; I became completely unpredictable. Sometimes I would go home after a couple of drinks (there was usually more booze there). More often, I would join the lineup of other alcoholics at the bar telephone stalls, fumbling with worn-out excuses about unexpected visitors and urgent business meetings. Sometimes I would simply hole up in my office

(continued on next page)

BOX 4.2 *(continued)*

with a bottle after everyone else had gone home. There simply wasn't anything else in my life. Most frightening of all, I began to suffer alcoholic blackouts during drinking episodes. I would swim back into consciousness with no recollection of where I had been or what I had done. Once, I came to late at night on a downtown city street with my suit trousers slashed down one side by a razor.

Bizarre incidents like that left me petrified but unable to stop drinking. None of the growing physical pangs of alcoholism—the retching, nervous spasms, sweaty and sleepless nights, dehydration—matched the moments of hammering panic I felt every morning for months on end, as I tried to remember exactly what I had done the night before. At one point, terrified that I might kill someone with my car, I gave up driving, but never alcohol. Along with the fear came sudden rages—at my wife, at my friends, at anyone who tried to stop me from drinking. My homelife became a nightmare. Creeping paranoia set in.

No one wanted me to stop drinking more than I did. What I could not say was that I did not know how to do it. Every day, the inability inspired waves of remorse and self-loathing. But in my fearfulness, I stayed willfully ignorant of alcoholism. I would walk out of the room if a television commercial mentioned the subject. I was convinced that getting sober was merely a matter of personal willpower—and that, through some unfixable flaws of character, I lacked the power. I never wanted to be reminded of what was, to my mind, a moral affliction. Who would?

I still consider the fact that I did not die to be a miracle, meaning that some kind of providence intervened. For me, it took the form of a friendly superior at work who confronted me. I finally broke down and admitted that I needed help. That simple admission, so long in coming, brought an enormous release. Suddenly, alcoholism was no longer something I had to endure in private. Somehow, in that encounter, a powerful psychosis dissolved.

Years later, after hundreds of Alcoholics Anonymous meetings and many hours of intensive counseling, I am happy to acknowledge that I have a serious, progressive ailment, with no cure. Alcohol is no longer a terrifying, destructive force in my life. It is just another chemical, fine for you, perhaps, but deadly for me. I avoid it, but without a sense of panic or fear. Friends say I am a completely different person now. Only, sometimes, I remember the feelings of hopelessness and shame from those terrible years, and I still have to struggle to hold back the tears.

registered with Swedish authorities for alcohol abuse than of those adopt-ees with nonalcoholic fathers. Alcohol abuse in the adoptive parents, however, was not a determinant of alcohol abuse. The adopted men were subdivided according to the frequency and severity of their registered abuse. Herein lies the major significance of the study—it demonstrated that there is more than one kind of alcoholism.

Cloninger's first group of alcoholics, the Type 1 alcoholics, about 75 percent of the total, developed the illness gradually over time. In this type of alcoholism, also known as milieu-limited alcoholism because of the environmental influence, low socioeconomic status of the adoptive father seemed to be the key influence. Type 1 alcoholics have personality traits that make them susceptible to anxiety. In response to the anti-anxiety effects of alcohol, they rapidly become drug-tolerant and dependent and have difficulty terminating drinking binges once they have started. The individual prone to this type of alcoholism avoids situations involving harm or risk and seeks approval from others. Guilt feelings are associated with the drinking and with its consequences.

The Type 2 alcoholic, on the other hand, is a risk-taker. Type 2 alcoholism is also called male-limited alcoholism because of the male dominance in this category. Traits that distinguish this type of drinker are: early and sudden development of alcoholism, hyperactivity, antisocial personality, and a history of fights while drinking. Type 2 alcoholism is highly hereditary, passing from father to son, and is associated with low levels of serotonin and dopamine in the brain. Cloninger recognizes that the Types 1 and 2 are not completely discrete categories and that there is much overlap between categories.

Elsewhere (reported in *Substance Abuse Report,* 1987) a correlation is drawn between pain sensitivity and Type 2 alcoholism. According to this study, researchers have shown that all alcoholics perceive stimuli strongly as do children of alcoholics. Drinking may be one way to adapt to the sensitivity.

Twin studies, brain wave studies, and animal studies are other areas of research linking genetics and alcoholism. Studies of identical twins indicate a likelihood that if one of a set of identical twins is alcoholic, the other is likely to be alcoholic also (Begleiter and Porjesj, 1988).

Electroencephalographic (EEG) tests of sober alcoholics reveal ex-cessive high-frequency brain waves. Researchers have found that male children of alcoholics also have fast EEG activity, indicating a possible susceptibility to alcoholism (reported in *Substance Abuse Report,* 1988).

Rat studies supply widely reported evidence for genetic factors in alcoholism. As described in the *Eighth Special Report to the U.S. Congress on Alcohol and Health* (1993), scientists have bred strains of rats with different levels of susceptibility to alcohol effects. Through selective breeding, one strain voluntarily works to acquire large amounts of alcohol. Alcoholic rats get excited when mildly intoxicated; the nonalcoholic strains of rats do not. EEG patterns may vary also. When the drug fluoxetine (Prozac), which raises serotonin levels, is administered to alcoholic rats, alcohol consumption is reduced accordingly.

MEDICAL EFFECTS

Ethanol has a harmful effect on nearly every organ in the body. The development of adverse medical consequences from alcohol consumption is related to the duration of the drinking, the amount consumed, and the pattern of consumption. There are vast individual differences in the ability to withstand harmful consequences.

Whereas moderate drinking may be associated with pleasure and even some health benefits, occasional excessive drinking produces a variety of temporary biochemical disturbances in the body—the stomach may be upset, the head may ache, and the metabolism and equilibrium of the liver may be disturbed. These effects pass, however. Severe and regular intoxication, on the other hand, may produce more serious changes in body chemistry and be associated with acute hepatitis and damage to the tissues of the mouth, esophagus, and stomach. Of the organs, the liver, the site of most metabolizing activity of alcohol, is the most vulnerable to serious damage.

Because the alcohol molecule is so small, it easily penetrates most body tissues. Within minutes of entering the bloodstream, alcohol finds its way into every organ of the body, including the brain.

THE BRAIN

The brain and the spinal cord together make up the central nervous system. The brain and spinal cord are hollow structures filled with cerebral-spinal fluid (Levin, 1990). Alcohol, as a drug affecting the central nervous system, belongs in a class with the barbiturates, minor tranquilizers, and general anesthetics—all depressants. At low levels of alcohol ingestion, an excitement phase may set in, with emotional expression uninhibited and erratic. A gradual dullness and stupor may occur. The effect of the alcohol on motor activity is seen in slurred speech, unsteady gait, and clumsiness. Effects on functioning at the higher level—thinking and remembering and making judgments—are tangibly impaired by alcohol. Before considering some of the grave neurological consequences of long-term alcohol abuse, we will consider how alcohol affects the brain at the cellular and biochemical levels; these levels directly affect one's emotions.

92

Each nerve cell of the brain is separated from its neighbor by a narrow gap called a *synapse*. Nerve cells communicate with one another via chemical messengers called *neurotransmitters*. Some drugs prevent the formation of neurotransmitters; most commonly, however, drugs disrupt neurotransmitter functions by mimicking the neurotransmitter itself (Schlaadt, 1992). Alcohol decreases the level of the inhibitory transmitter *GABA*; GABA normally regulates anxiety in the brain.

Cocaine, like alcohol, brings about marked changes in brain chemistry. According to the *Harvard Mental Health Letter* (1993), accumulated

FIGURE 4.1

The Digestive Tract

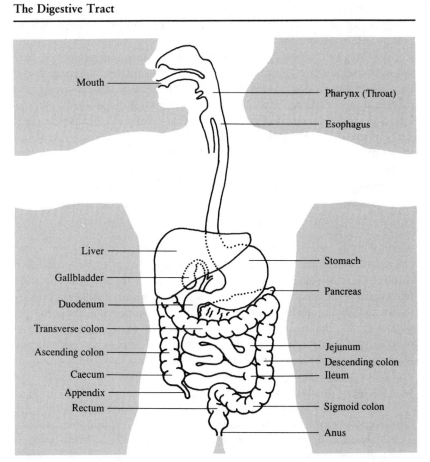

Source: *Alcohol, Health and Research World,* 10(2) (1985/86): 8.

evidence indicates that cocaine's chief biological activity is preventing the reuptake (reabsorption) of the neurochemical transmitter dopamine. Laboratory rats will ignore food and sex and tolerate electric shocks for the opportunity to ingest cocaine. A depletion of dopamine following cocaine use probably accounts for cocaine binges, tolerance, craving, and the obsessional behavior of cocaine users.

Serotonin is another neurotransmitter highly influenced by alcohol; it is involved in sleep and sensory experiences. Serotonin has received a great deal of attention by researchers and the popular press. Decreased levels of this neurotransmitter have been linked to behaviors associated with intoxicated states, depression, anxiety, poor impulse control, and aggressiveness, and with suicidal behavior (Kotulak, 1993).

Monkey research shows that there are specific biochemical anomalies in the brains of violent monkeys, that the more aggressive monkeys have low levels of serotonin and the least aggressive have high levels. As Rensberger (1992) in his review of current research indicates, men convicted of premeditated murder have normal serotonin levels; repeat arsonists do not. Drugs that reduce re-uptake of the serotonin by neurons, and thereby increase the activity of this neurotransmitter, have shown promising results in influencing behavior in primates and people. Fluoxetine (Prozac) reportedly has been used with favorable results for depression, obsessive compulsive disorders, and eating disorders (Kramer, 1993). One major drawback is that once the drug is in the body, its effects remain for a long time—two weeks is required to eliminate this drug from the body.

BRAIN IMPAIRMENT

Alcohol contributes to brain damage both directly and indirectly. Levin (1990) provides a threefold classification of damage to the nervous system through alcohol abuse: (1) damage in the form of a shrinking of the brain from the toxic effects of the alcohol itself; (2) poisoning of brain cells by toxins circulating in the blood as a result of the failure of a diseased liver to metabolize them; and (3) damage to the nervous system because of nutritional deficits associated with alcoholism. Wernicke's syndrome and Korsakoff's psychosis are thought to derive from a lack of thiamine, or vitamin B_1. Some researchers, however, believe the effect of alcohol per se is partially involved (Levin, 1990).

Wernicke's syndrome is characterized by paralysis of normal eye movements, mental confusion, and problems with walking and balance. This syndrome, according to Kinney and Leaton (1991), affects one part of the brain—the midbrain and third and fourth ventricles. Korsakoff's psychosis results from damage to areas of the brain important to memory function. Wernicke's syndrome is often associated with *peripheral neurop-*

athy, or damage to the peripheral nerves. Numbness in one's lower legs is the consequence. If the numbness does not disappear with vitamin therapy, this is an indication that the damage to the nervous system is permanent and irreversible.

Korsakoff's psychosis, sometimes called Wernicke-Korsakoff's syndrome and popularly known as "wet brain," is the long-term result of brain damage over time. Patients with this disease experience much confusion and severe short-term memory deficits. They may not retain information. *Confabulation* is a unique characteristic that involves fantasizing to fill in the gaps of memory. Although the "tall tales" seem to be ridiculous fabrications or downright lies, there appears to be no "method in this madness" other than an inability to distinquish fact from fiction. Although individuals with this affliction can become paranoid on occasion, generally they have a carefree unconcern about the present or future.

Oliver Sachs, neurologist and author of *Awakenings* and *The Man Who Mistook His Wife for a Hat,* provides rich case histories of persons with neurological disorders. In the second of these books, portraits of

FIGURE 4.2

The Brain

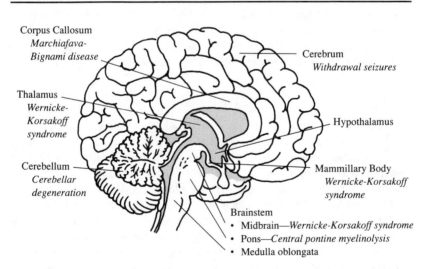

Areas of the brain that are particularly vulnerable to alcohol and the associated alcohol-related disorders.

Source: *Alcohol, Health and Research World,* 17(4) (1993): 306.

two individuals with Korsakoff's psychosis are given. Mr. Thompson, an ex-grocer with severe Korsakoff's, was institutionalized for his memory problems. Sachs (1985: 111) describes the workings of Mr. Thompson's mind: "Deprived of continuity, of a quiet, continuous, inner narrative, he is driven to a sort of irrational frenzy—hence his ceaseless tales, his confabulations, his mythomania." Lack of feeling is one characteristic that stood out. To Sachs, this man had become de-souled. Such patients fail to realize that anything has befallen them.

Jimmy G., a Korsakoff's patient, lived in the past. To him, Truman was president; no one had landed on the moon. When his brother came to visit, Jimmy G. could not believe how "old" he looked. Meeting his brother was always a truly emotional experience and the only connection between the past and the present. Sachs followed Jimmy G.'s case for years; neurologically, he never changed. Jimmy both was and was not aware of the deep, tragic loss *in* himself and *of* himself.

My father has the same rare and bewildering condition of Korsakoff's psychosis. Confined to a bustling and surprisingly cheerful nursing home, he has the "run of the place" and is the manager of the television electronic control device. Although his legs are numb from peripheral neuropathy, in his mind he is the outstanding tennis player of his middle years and youth. Moreover, he has recently signed a contract with Hollywood to film a movie at his house. Believing he has been only temporarily confined for a mysterious leg problem, he has no awareness of the recent past or of the future. Every detail, however, is recorded from the long ago, so that visitors can share in reminiscing about what to others would be ancient history. For my father, there is no sense of time or of loss.

THE LIVER

Because the liver metabolizes alcohol ahead of anything else, the toll to the body through alcohol abuse is enormous. Fatty liver, the first stage of liver disease, results from an increase in the production of fatty acids and a decrease in their elimination from the liver (Schlaadt, 1992). About one in three heavy drinkers eventually develops scars in the liver associated with cirrhosis—a disease in which liver cells are destroyed and the organ no longer is able to process nutrients in food. Scarring of the liver tissue also interferes with the task of filtering toxins from the blood.

Alcoholic hepatitis (not the same as general hepatitis, which has a different etiology) can be considered the second stage of alcoholic liver disease. This highly dangerous condition is characterized by liver swelling, jaundice, and fever. With abstinence, this condition can be reversed. If the condition is not reversed, Laennec's cirrhosis or cirrhosis of the liver can occur. With the progression of this disease, all of the liver's functions are compromised. The devastation caused to the bodily functions by cirrhosis is an indication of the important role of the liver. Royce (1989: 63) summarizes the functions as follows:

> It [the liver] *manufactures* bile, glycogen, albumin, globulin, prothrombin, and other substances for fighting infection, blood clotting (hence alcoholics show more bruises and bleeding), and general health. In vulnerable persons, drinking can trigger a painful gouty arthritis due to excessive uric acid. The liver controls the levels of cholesterol, fatty acids, and triglycerides, which harm both liver and cardiovascular systems.

The liver detoxifies many substances in the blood and thus is an important part of the immune system. The scarred liver, unable to handle the usual blood flow, causes the body to seek alternate routes to the heart. A tremendous pressure builds up in alternative vessels. When bulging veins emerge on the surface of the esophagus, the potentially fatal condition called *esophageal varices* occurs. Spidery veins may appear on the face and chest; hemorrhoids may develop. The patient may die from hemorrhaging. Edema, which is fluid accumulation in other parts of the body, is another serious consequence of cirrhosis. Large amounts of fluid can collect until the abdomen is shockingly distended.

Treatment of alcoholic cirrhosis consists of total abstinence from alcohol and careful attention to diet. For terminally ill patients, a liver transplant provides the only possibility of survival. A summary of empirical research results on liver transplantation for alcoholics reveals a survival rate equal to that of nonalcoholics who get liver transplants (National Institute on Alcohol Abuse and Alcoholism, 1993). Scientific policy evaluation, in this case, went against popular opposition to providing replacement for alcoholics who had destroyed their livers through drinking.

It is well known that some persons with liver disease take on a yellow color; the yellow comes from excessive amounts of bile that circulate in the bloodstream. I well remember, at the Norwegian treatment center, the day a new client, Terje, arrived; he was completely yellow. Even with sobriety and a long follow-up period in the halfway house, the yellow cast remained. A much-liked client, he was affectionately known as Yellow Terje or "The Yellow Submarine." One year later, healthy and rosy complexioned, he became a trainee ("therapist"). However, the name stuck, and he is called Yellow Terje to this day.

Another client at the treatment center was reminded by a confrontive counselor that because of his liver disease, his days were numbered if he drank again. "That doesn't worry me," he said, "I'll have to just rely on the *other* liver." This led to a beefed-up lecture on the medical consequences of alcoholism using a chart of the body and its organs. This client was facetiously referred to as "the man with two livers."

Writing in *That Place in Minnesota,* an autobiographical account of alcoholism treatment at St. Mary's, journalist Ed Fitzgerald (1990: 65–66) provides the following description of an after-dinner educational program:

> The seven o'clock lecture was scary enough to make Ernest Hemingway never want to take another drink. It was on the physical consequences of alcoholism and the doctor who gave it used slides to illustrate his stories of what the bogeyman would do to you if you didn't watch out. He talked mostly about the liver and how dangerous it was to think complacently that it would always regenerate itself if you just stopped drinking for a while. "There comes a time," he says, "where you've used up all of its regenerative powers, and when that happens, you've had it. There is no treatment, no medicine, for a rotted liver. When it's gone, it's gone." He showed us slides of livers partly destroyed, almost completely destroyed, and just plain destroyed. They were frightening. What made it worse for us was that Cal Scheidegger's group had a man who was suffering from cirrhosis and whose skin actually glowed with a bright yellow color. I tried not to look at him as we walked out of the hall. According to the lecture, he was a dead man.

The pancreas is another trouble spot for abusers of alcohol. A major organ of the body, the pancreas secretes digestive enzymes and insulin, which converts blood sugar. Diabetes may result from the cell damage. *Acute pancreatitis,* often caused by alcohol-induced inflammation, is an extremely painful and dangerous condition.

THE GENITOURINARY TRACT

In both sexes, problems with urination may result from excessive alcohol use. Indirect interference in the filtration process and in the elimination of the wastes produced by the kidney seems to be the problem. When *kidney failure* follows, according to Kinney and Leaton (1991), the trouble is not in the kidneys themselves, but in a circulating toxic factor resulting from the associated liver disease.

Effects on the *reproductive system* are widely known to accompany alcohol abuse. *The Eighth Special Report to the U.S. Congress on Alcohol and Health* (1993) reviews the most up-to-date clinical and endocrine studies in the literature. The few clinical studies of alcoholic women suggest ovulation and menstrual difficulties are caused by alcohol-induced hormonal imbalance. In men, impotence, low testosterone levels, low sperm count, and testicular atrophy are widely reported. Breast enlargement has been observed in alcoholic men, as has an absence of body hair accompanied by a lower rate of baldness.

Inasmuch as intoxication lowers inhibitions and caution may be "thrown to the wind," the risks of both AIDS contraction and unwanted pregnancy multiply. Perhaps the most tragic consequences of substance abuse in one generation are seen in birth defects of the next generation. The effects of intoxication on male sperm has only recently been studied. Sperm susceptibility to environmental hazards, such as pesticides, has been known for years; recent studies link male smoking to the birth of underweight infants. Mice experiments reveal learning difficulties in offspring of morphine-exposed fathers (*Economist,* 1991). Data on cocaine's ability to bind to sperm (*Science News,* 1991) indicate the need for further studies on the long-unrecognized impact of male intoxication on development of the fetus.

First officially identified in 1970, *Fetal alcohol syndrome* (FAS) is now recognized as a leading cause of mental retardation. Medical reports confirm that the fetus takes in alcohol from the mother's blood. Whereas classified fetal alcohol syndrome may be readily identified by physical characteristics in the child—small upper lip, flat nose, and small head—milder defects, classified as *fetal alcohol effects* (FAE) are properly diagnosed only rarely.

Although the percentage of hard-drinking mothers who have spontaneous abortions or babies with FAS is not known, it *is* known that habitual or even occasional drinking by an expectant mother can endanger the health of her fetus. The effect on neurological development is the greatest in the first three months of pregnancy. By the time a fertile woman confirms her pregnancy, the damage may already have been done.

A large dose of alcohol given to a pregnant mouse experimentally produces severe abnormalities in the developing fetus. The eye damage, stunted brain, and facial deformities that result are reminiscent of human babies with FAS (Steinmetz, 1992).

Longitudinal studies indicate that FAS and FAE exist on a continuum of cognitive-behavioral defects. Children of school age years born of heavily drinking mothers are found to be highly distractible in their learning operations. Hyperactivity, subnormal intelligence, and mood problems are found to persist over time (*Eighth Special Report to the U.S. Congress,* 1993). Long-term treatment for high-risk pregnant women is one of the greatest unmet needs of alcoholism prevention efforts today. Help for adults who suffer the effects of FAS is hard to come by also.

THE IMMUNE SYSTEM

The body is protected from infectious disease and cancer by an extraordinarily complex, intricately regulated, and highly efficient network of cellular and biochemical activities (Grossman and Wilson, 1992). The body's *immune system* consists primarily of white blood cells that fight bacterial

FIGURE 4.3

Fetal Alcohol Syndrome

A

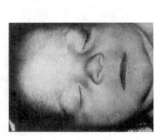

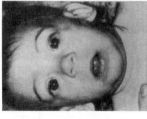
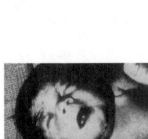

The first patient to be given the diagnosis of FAS at birth as a newborn and at ages five, ten, and fourteen years. He has been growth deficient and microcephalic throughout his life. As he has aged, his nose has shown considerable relative growth, resulting in a high, wide nasal bridge. His philtrum has remained smooth.

B

Adolescent girl whose condition was diagnosed as FAS at birth, with later intellectual functioning in the borderline range, as a newborn, at nine months, and at five and fourteen years of age. Although her facial features are gradually maturing, she still has small palpebral fissures; a relatively long, smooth philtrum; and a narrow upper lip.

C

Woman whose condition was diagnosed as FAS at four years of age; she now has an IQ level of 85 to 90. Photographs show her at nine, thirteen, and nineteen years. Her early FAS facial manifestations have evolved into a fairly normal phenotype by adult life. At nineteen, her head circumference was below the 1st percentile, her height was below the 5th percentile, and her weight was around the 10th percentile.

Source: Streissguth et al., "Fetal Alcohol Syndrome," *Journal of the American Medical Association, 265*(15): 1963. Reprinted with permission of AMA. Copyright 1991 by Streissguth et al.

FIGURE 4.4

Facial Features Characteristic of Fetal Alcohol Syndrome (FAS)

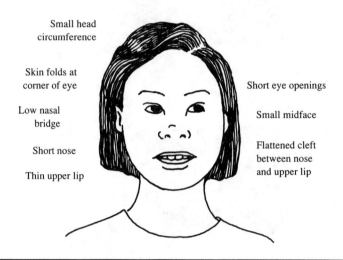

Small head
circumference

Skin folds at
corner of eye

Low nasal
bridge

Short nose

Thin upper lip

Short eye openings

Small midface

Flattened cleft
between nose
and upper lip

Source: *Alcohol, Health and Research World, 15*(3) (1991): 245.

infection and antibodies that defend against viral infection. Alterations in one or both of these protective mechanisms such as through alcoholic degeneration, however, can cause rapid deterioration in the body's immune defenses. The cause of any mysterious infection, such as mysterious skin eruptions, is often revealed through sobriety, when almost overnight, the "incurable" condition simply goes away.

Alcoholics, especially those with liver disease, suffer a host of infections. Since alcohol interferes with the function of white blood cells, heavy drinkers are highly susceptible to colds and pneumonia. Skin diseases such as psoriasis may cover the entire body. Alcoholics also are inclined toward malnutrition, itself related to liver dysfunction. Malnutrition in alcoholics is related to poor food intake and poor metabolism of the food taken in. Additionally, digestive abnormalities and chronic diarrhea contribute to the overall susceptibility to disease. Poor nutrition, in itself, influences all aspects of immunity (Mendenhall, 1992).

Although the incidence of tuberculosis has declined dramatically in the United States and has been eradicated in many European countries, pockets of disease among the indigent, alcoholic population have been a major factor in its perpetuation (Jacobson, 1992). Treatment noncompliance among the afflicted population presents a major challenge to treatment providers.

AIDS

Biglan et al. (1990) explored the relationships between drinking and practicing high-risk sexual behaviors. Such activity brings a person in contact with semen, blood, or vaginal secretions of a person already infected with the human immunodeficiency virus (HIV). Specific risk behaviors listed are failure to use a condom, having multiple partners, and engaging in receptive anal intercourse.

Not only high-risk behavior but the added strain to the immune system caused by prolonged alcohol abuse makes for an increased risk of initial infection for people exposed to HIV (Kruger and Jerrells, 1992). And once infected, there is an increased risk of AIDS development. Finally, HIV-infected persons who drink heavily are at heightened risk for developing further medical complications such as pneumonia or cancer.

THE HEART

The heart pumps blood throughout the body. Alcohol in large quantities asserts a toxic effect on the heart. Heart muscle may come to be replaced in time with fat and fiber. Hypertension or high blood pressure is a common component of chronic abuse of alcohol; this increases the risk of strokes and heart attacks. Alcohol's inhibition of the manufacture of red blood cells may result in anemia.

The heavy smoking associated with heavy drinking in 80 to 90 percent of cases—some alcoholics smoke as many as three packs a day—puts a tremendous strain on heart function and blood pressure. Because of the propensity to continue to smoke in recovery from alcoholism, the leading cause of death for recovering alcoholics is tobacco-related illness (Varner, 1992).

CONCLUSION

This chapter has shown some of the ways in which excessive alcohol consumption shortens the lives of alcoholics, by ten to twelve years on average. Our concern has been with the impact of toxic substances on the body. Lives are further needlessly shortened, however, through the high-risk behavior accompanying alcoholism. Thus, premature death may result through car crashes, overdoses, homicide, suicide, falls, polydrug abuse, and drowning.

William Faulkner once said, "There's a lot of nutrition in an acre of corn." One could paraphrase that and say, by the same token, there is a lot of malnutrition and despair in that same acre.

103

BOX 4.3: Mental Health's Special Cases Get Lost in Funding Shuffle

ERIC WOOLSON
Courier Staff Writer

WAVERLY—Michael sat behind the screen in the Bremer County Jail visitors' room and rocked back and forth, recalling what happened when he was taken from a Waterloo group home after shoving a counselor.

"They tried to get me in (the Mental Health Institute in Independence), but the door was slammed on my face. It makes me feel bad.

"I just felt an emptiness inside me, like I wasn't worth nothing," said Michael, who needs intensive supervision because of the learning and behavioral disorders caused by his mother's heavy drinking during pregnancy.

Michael, not his real name, suffers from fetal alcohol syndrome. Mary Nicholas has been one of his supervisors during his two years with Exceptional Persons Inc., which provides a range of services for people with mental retardation, developmental disabilities or brain injuries.

Michael, who is in his 20s, was placed under EPI's supervision for five years after he was convicted of burglary, and court officials determined he is mentally unable to be on self-probation or to fit into the prison population.

He was jailed for about a week and a half before being allowed back in the group home on a judge's "tight restriction" that he not violate any more group home rules or he would be back in jail, said Gary Mattson, executive director of EPI.

He has made progress in the group home for people with mental retardation and developmental disabilities, but he still has occasional angry outbursts. It was during the most recent episode, the shoving of his counselor, that group home leaders made a professional judgment call to temporarily remove Michael.

Nicholas says the Mental Health Institute has been there in the past when Michael became abusive. He could receive proper care and medication, and then return to the group home.

"We'd have every right to terminate (his placement at the group home), but his behavior is uncontrolled. It's a physiological thing, so the bottom line is: He's welcome," she explained.

That option disappeared when patients at the Mental Health Institute in Mount Pleasant were transferred to Independence. There's no longer room for Michael at Independence now, Nicholas said.

On top of that, Harold Templeman, deputy administrator of the Department of Human Services Mental Health, Mental Retardation and Developmental Disabilities Division, questions whether the Independence psychiatry facility is appropriate for someone with mental retardation.

But the State Hospital-Schools at Woodward and Glenwood aren't an option, either.

The facilities have been discharging residents, not admitting new ones, for some time. The trend has been accelerated by a 3.25 percent budget cut last July.

"We've had to reduce staff at both hospital-schools. To maintain staffing ratios that we must have to meet . . . certification standards, we have to very severely limit the populations of the two places.

"At this point in time, I don't know there's any viable, easy solution. Obviously, this places more responsibility back on communities to look at solutions," Templeman said.

Unfortunately, according to Nicholas, there aren't any alternatives in the metro area because group homes for people with mental illness aren't equipped to handle Michael.

"Doors went slam, slam, slam, slam," she said.

Mattson says Michael's case illustrates the failure of the system to adequately provide for people like Michael who have a combination of mental and emotional disabilities.

And, Mattson believes Michael may be a messenger of things to come as Gov. Terry Branstad and the General Assembly try to attack their deficit by shuffling mental health services.

Black Hawk County alone has several other people who could end up in the same situation as Michael.

"Then there's the problem of the state not providing funding for programs that are suited for these situations, so it really leaves a person like him in limbo.

"Someplace, they've got to develop a special unit to deal with these special, in-between cases," Mattson said.

There will be more of those special cases as the wave of crack babies and children with fetal alcohol syndrome swells and reaches school age, he said.

"(State and federal officials) are not looking . . . at how to prevent these situations. If we do that, we'll have fewer of these problems to deal with in live-long situations," Mattson said.

Asked to describe the incident that led to his jailing, Michael replied, "I don't know. One minute I was happy and cheerful and then bang! It's like I couldn't focus on anything.

"All I wanted to do was get out."

He pushed the counselor, and she called the police. "It was sad," Michael said.

(continued on next page)

BOX 4.3 (continued)

He was taken to the Black Hawk County Jail and transferred to Bremer County.

"I miss the group home. I miss everybody in it," Michael said while jailed. "I don't want to be snappy at people, and I don't want to go to prison because prison is mean."

Michael fully understands the reason for his behavioral disorder, which only adds to his frustration.

"I can't focus real good. . . . I have a hard time staying in control.

"If somebody says something to me and I'm not in a good mood, I bite their head off. I don't mean it," he said. "It's the alcohol (from his mother). It's the confusion in my mind."

The disability also has taken a heavy toll on Michael's self-esteem. "I'm not nothing," he said at one point.

Later, he added, "I don't know why I always think negative."

But he keeps trying to improve his outlook and his abilities.

"I don't want to go to prison. I want to learn.

"I know deep down inside, everybody knows I can do it," he said. "I just have to get that confidence back."

Mattson emphasizes Michael's outbursts are caused partly by physiological factors and partly by frustration.

"It's like saying to paranoid people, 'trust me.' They can't because they're incapable.

"If we can have (Michael) in an appropriate program we can help get some of those behaviors under control where he will not be harmful to other people and property," Mattson said.

That's one reason young men and women like Michael are in group homes. But there are others.

"Even in good families, there reaches a time when they need to leave home. Whoever it is, when you're 20 or 25 years old, it's time to start to establish some independence.

"Our residential facilities assist them with living in the community in a less restrictive environment, with the ultimate goal of getting out into the community on their own," Mattson said.

Jail life would only make Michael's negative behavior worse, Mattson said.

"He's going to have outbursts and (other prisoners) are going to react. He's going to come out a loser by far either with serious injuries or perhaps by getting killed in prison," Mattson said.

FAS leading mental retardation cause

Fetal alcohol syndrome is now recognized as the leading known cause of mental retardation in the U.S., according to a report in the Journal of the American Medical Association.

The journal said a study of 61 adolescents and adults with FAS showed IQ scores varied widely but averaged 68, which is just into the mentally retarded range.

Most functioned at the second- to fourth-grade levels.

As many as one of 50 live newborns in some areas are affected by FAS. The national average is one of 500 newborns or more than 7,500 a year.

"Maladaptive behaviors such as poor judgment, distractibility and difficulty perceiving social cues were common," the report concluded. "Fetal alcohol syndrome is not just a childhood disorder; there is a predictable long-term progression of the disorder into adulthood, in which maladaptive behaviors present the greatest challenge to management."

The report also recommended future studies evaluate FAS adults' trouble with the law and substance abuse.

Tom O'Rourke, director of the Black Hawk County Public Health Department, said he does not have hard numbers on FAS children and adults in the metro area. But he said the numbers are on the rise across the nation.

"Those kids are hitting the school system, and the millions of dollars we're going to have to spend on special education is still uncalculated," O'Rourke said.

He noted there is a growing understanding about the effects of alcohol on newborns.

"The standards have changed to the point we're starting to recognize mama can't get drunk without doing some lifelong damage to the baby," O'Rourke said.

Source: *Waterloo Courier* (Iowa), Jan. 27, 1992, A7. Reprinted with permission of the Waterloo Courier.

REVIEW QUESTIONS

1. Explain the metabolism process and the role of acetaldehyde.

2. Account for the male/female differences in metabolizing alcohol.

3. What are some typical examples of behavior at certain levels of BAC?

4. Explain the flushing response to drinking.

5. "I'm tired of being the middleman." Identify this quote.

6. Explain the phenomenon of "blackout." Relate your explanation to the excerpt from *The Adventures of Tom Sawyer*.

7. Define *tolerance, tolerance reversal,* and *cross tolerance.*

8. What brings about the DTs? What preventive measures can be taken?

9. What is the significance of the adoption studies in regard to the etiology of alcoholism?

10. Describe the characteristics of Type 1 and Type 2 alcoholics.

11. Discuss some of the experimental studies indicating hereditary aspects of alcoholism.

12. What are the effects of alcohol on the brain?

13. What is the role of serotonin in human behavior?

14. Differentiate Wernicke's syndrome from Korsakoff's psychosis. What were Dr. Sachs' findings?

15. Describe the role of the liver in metabolizing alcohol and some of the problems that occur with liver damage.

16. What is the impact of abusive drinking on the male and female reproductive systems? Discuss the signs and symptoms of FAS.

17. How does heavy drinking break down the immune system? What are some of the consequences?

18. How can the heart be damaged by alcohol abuse? What is the role of smoking in this process?

5

ALCOHOLISM AS A WAY OF THINKING

> If men define situations as real, they are real in their consequences.
> —W. I. Thomas, 1928

Social work's ecological approach is concerned with the three aspects of a disorder—biological, psychological, and social. This chapter looks at the *psychological* side of alcoholism—alcoholism as a way of thinking.

INTRODUCTION

The social worker who works with alcoholics will come, at some point, to a recognition that there is something strange and distinctive about the way that most alcoholics think about things. The *intensity* of feeling behind the thinking is not always as evident; sometimes it emerges in the form of extreme withdrawal or anger. In either case, communication difficulties hinder the best of therapeutic efforts. Sometimes the feelings have to be deduced from behaviors, behaviors that stand out as bizarre overreaction to rather ordinary circumstances. How can the worker separate the feelings from the actions and untangle this knot of pain and self-destruction and more pain? The place to start, according to Beck et al. (1979), is with the *thinking*. Fortunately, the thinking level, for work

---

Many of the ideas expressed in this chapter appeared in K. van Wormer, "All-or-Nothing Thinking and Alcoholism: A Cognitive Approach," *Federal Probation* (June 1988): 28–33.

with persons with drinking problems, is a relatively easy and concrete place to start. Alcoholics Anonymous (A.A.) does it all the time (Brown, 1985).

Stinking thinking is the term used by A.A. members to characterize the type of irrational mind-set with which they are so familiar. *Cognitive distortion* is the term used by social workers and psychologists for this phenomenon. With regard to the syndrome of alcoholism, cognitive distortions prevail at every phase of the drinking history. At the outset of the drinking episode is the intense reaction to some event coupled with the rationale to drink. Later come the justifications—the denial and minimization of the consequences. The tendency to excess is pronounced at every step along the way.

This chapter begins with a review of research findings on personality characteristics of alcoholics. Then the role of cognitive distortion in alcoholism is examined. Special attention is paid to the client's distortions in terms of all-or-nothing thinking, negativism and depression, and denial of the presenting problem of alcoholism. The section on cognitive treatment (various modalities combined as one) looks at the therapist's role in identifying and breaking unhealthy patterns of coping with reality. The use of cognitive restructuring, self-talk, love and addiction, and humor in addictions work are described. The final portion of the chapter discusses prevention implications of the cognitive approach. Key emphasis is placed on relapse prevention through the learning of stress management techniques and social skills for life satisfaction.

RECENT RESEARCH STUDIES ON PERSONALITY CHARACTERISTICS

Writers in the field of alcoholism generally agree that there is no unitary phenomenon known as "the alcoholic personality" (Metzger, 1988). Thousands of alcoholics have been interviewed and tested with such instruments as the Minnesota Multiphasic Personality Inventory (MMPI) and the Rorschach inkblot test. Evidence of one personality type that can be called the alcoholic personality has not been forthcoming. Nor can alcoholics be distinguished from nonalcoholics on the basis of scores on personality tests.

This is not to say, however, that certain aspects of personality are not relevant in the development of addictions problems. Recent research points in the direction of some sort of cognitive-perceptual deficit that manifests itself in early childhood long before the onset of problem drinking. Hyperactivity, poor impulse control, and antisocial conduct are cited as precursors of alcoholism in several neurologically based studies (Goodwin, 1976; Gorenstein, 1987; Mannuzza et al., 1993; Kinney and Leaton,

1991; von Knorring et al., 1987). Gorenstein (1987) speculates that alcoholism, hyperactivity, and antisocial behavior somehow may be derived from the same predisposing factor. Depression, similarly, has been widely cited as antecedent to drug abuse, a finding consistent with the "self-medication" explanation of alcohol use (Deykin, Levy, and Wells, 1987; Royce, 1989).

Scientists are not able to determine how much of the cognitive pattern in a person is the result of learned behavior and how much the result of neurological predisposition. To what extent the substance alcohol is itself related to cognitive distortions is not known.

THE BIOLOGICAL COMPONENT

Studies reviewed in chapter 4—twin studies, adoption studies, brain chemistry studies—all suggest a strong biochemical/heredity component in alcoholism. Twin studies indicate a likelihood that if one of a set of identical twins is alcoholic, the other is likely to be alcoholic also; the congruence in fraternal twins is consistently less (Begleiter et al., 1984).

That a biological component figures in the development of obsessive-compulsive personality disorder is evidenced in the at least partial success of medication to remedy the worst of the symptoms occurring with this disorder (Kramer, 1993). The antidepressant Prozac (fluoxetine) is prescribed for individuals thought to suffer from serotonin imbalance. Drugs such as Prozac work by slowing the re-uptake of serotonin, thus enhancing its effect. Prozac therapy reportedly has had good results with patients suffering from depression, obsessive-compulsive behavior, and eating disorders, according to Kramer. Serotonin may be a common thread linking disorders as seemingly diverse as depression, substance abuse, and chronic pain (*Psychology Today*, 1992).

The *DSM IV's* diagnostic criteria of the obsessive-compulsive disorder are listed in Box 5.1. The pattern of perfectionism and inflexibility manifest with the obsessive-compulsive personality disorder is often seen in alcoholism treatment. Perhaps this composite of symptoms and the tendency for impaired control over addictive substances are linked neurologically in some way.

If one of a pair of identical twins is alcoholic, the chances are approximately 60 percent that the other twin is alcoholic (Gordis, 1988). Numerous twin studies all point to the same thing—an addiction found in one twin is often found in the other twin. This fact is often cited to show the strength of the biological aspect in addiction. A more interesting interpretation of these findings is the fact that the genetic component is clearly *far less than* 100 percent. Even when identical twins share the same environment and general life experiences as well as genes, there must still be

BOX 5.1: Diagnostic Criteria for 300.3 Obsessive-Compulsive Disorder

A. Either obsessions or compulsions:

Obsessions as defined by (1), (2), (3), and (4):

(1) recurrent and persistent thoughts, impulses, or images that are experienced, at some time during the disturbance, as intrusive and inappropriate and that cause marked anxiety or distress

(2) the thoughts, impulses, or images are not simply excessive worries about real-life problems

(3) the person attempts to ignore or suppress such thoughts, impulses, or images, or to neutralize them with some other thought or action

(4) the person recognizes that the obsessional thoughts, impulses, or images are a product of his or her own mind (not imposed from without as in thought insertion)

Compulsions as defined by (1) and (2):

(1) repetitive behaviors (e.g., hand washing, ordering, checking) or mental acts (e.g., praying, counting, repeating words silently) that the person feels driven to perform in response to an obsession, or according to rules that must be applied rigidly

(2) the behaviors or mental acts are aimed at preventing or reducing distress or preventing some dreaded event or situation; however, these behaviors or mental acts either are not connected in a realistic way with what they are designed to neutralize or prevent or are clearly excessive

some other factor at work. It is controversial to talk of *will,* but undeniably there is some inner force at work that may defy biology and somehow resist the pathway of addiction.

My favorite example is the case of the original Siamese twins, Chang and Eng (Drimmer, 1973). Discovered in the early 1800s swimming in the waters of Siam, these boys were bought by Barnum and Bailey Circus to be displayed in America as freaks. Years passed, and the conjoined twins moved to a farm in North Carolina, marrying Quaker sisters. One (Chang) drank alcohol; the other did not drink at all. Each man had a house where his wife stayed. Chang and Eng moved from one house to the other every three days. Chang was drunk during the days at his house and got scarcely a drop to drink at his brother's house. The more irritable of the two, Chang, when under the influence of alcohol, experienced

B. At some point during the course of the disorder, the person has recognized that the obsessions or compulsions are excessive or unreasonable. Note: This does not apply to children.
C. The obsessions or compulsions cause marked distress, are time consuming (take more than 1 hour a day), or significantly interfere with the person's normal routine, occupational (or academic) functioning, or usual social activities or relationships.
D. If another Axis I disorder is present, the content of the obsessions or compulsions is not restricted to it (e.g., preoccupation with food in the presence of an Eating Disorder; hair pulling in the presence of Trichotillomania; concern with appearance in the presence of Body Dysmorphic Disorder; preoccupation with drugs in the presence of a Substance Use Disorder; preoccupation with having a serious illness in the presence of Hypochondriasis; preoccupation with sexual urges or fantasies in the presence of a Paraphilia; or guilty ruminations in the presence of Major Depressive Disorder).
E. The disturbance is not due to the direct physiological effects of a substance (e.g., a drug of abuse, a medication) or a general medical condition.

Specify if:
With Poor Insight: if, for most of the time during the current episode, the person does not recognize that the obsessions and compulsions are excessive or unreasonable

Source: American Psychiatric Association, *Diagnostic and Statistical Manual of Mental Disorders,* 4th ed. (Washington, DC: APA, 1994), pp. 422–23. Reprinted with permission.

moodiness and general deterioration. Once the inseparable pair got into a terrible altercation, and the police were summoned. With the victim and the offender joined together, no effective sanction could be applied. Finally, Chang died, and being attached to same body, Eng died also. They left twenty-two children behind, and today are survived by over one thousand descendants in rural North Carolina.

The bizarre tale of Chang and Eng shows that even when genes and environment are seemingly identical, there can still be considerable individual differences in the development of alcoholism. Though one may be biologically susceptible to alcoholism, one does not have to drink.

A probable biological link between alcoholism and a plethora of other ailments—chronic pain, obsessive-compulsive disorder, depression, and eating disorders—should be underscored. The favored contemporary explanation is that these interrelated tendencies all stem from an imbalance of serotonin in the brain.

THE COGNITIVE COMPONENT

The individual can do nothing to change his or her brain chemistry. "Pick your ancestors carefully," the cynic would say. There is much one can do, however, to shape situations one can control and to emotionally handle those situations over which one has no control. The A.A.'s Serenity Prayer says this beautifully: "Help us to change the things we can." In Norway, the word for serenity is *sinnsro*, "mind's peace." Peace of mind is what effective treatment must teach; for this reason an entire chapter is devoted to cognitive interventions. More significant than the biological disposition to addiction is the consistent finding that not all persons biologically inclined to alcoholism have addiction problems. Where one identical twin is alcoholic, for instance, why is the other one *not also alcoholic?* Why do some in a family drink addictively while others abstain entirely and still others drink moderately? What is the key to the insulating factor in prevention of alcoholism? Researchers might look to the cognitive realm for answers.

The cognitive or thinking component in alcoholism is an integral part of the dependency. At the heart of the problem of alcoholism (and of drug abuse and bulimia) are underlying thinking and belief disturbances conducive to self-defeating behavior. Self-defeating thinking, in short, leads to self-defeating behavior. Thinking shapes the course of the drinking: thinking determines the when, where, why, and how much.

SENSITIVITY AND THOUGHT PATTERNS

Alcohol, chemically a liquid form of ether, has been known as a painkiller for thousands of years. Alcohol dulls the senses and numbs the mind. Worries are literally washed away. A recent report from the National Institute on Alcohol Abuse and Alcoholism (NIAAA) highlights the relevance of sensitivity to physical and psychological pain in alcoholics. Both sons and daughters of Type 2 alcoholics (the highly hereditary and most severe form of alcoholism) tend to be unusually sensitive to pain, and this may be why they drink—to deaden the pain. Researchers have reported that all alcoholics are "stimulus augmenters," that is, they tend to perceive stimuli more strongly than others. As the NIAAA report states, alcoholics seem to be prone to suffering, and drinking is one way to adapt to this sensitivity (*Substance Abuse Report*, 1987). The link between serotonin imbalances in the brain and alcohol abuse is an intriguing avenue for research (*Psychology Today*, 1992).

O'Connor, Hesselbrock, and Bauer (1990) summarize recent findings comparing groups at high and low risk for alcoholism in terms of their response to a stressor. A greater heart-rate response to unavoidable electrical shocks has been found in men at higher versus lower risk for alcoholism. Family-history-positive men also have been shown to exhibit greater changes in perspiration level in response to a sudden auditory stimulus at a slower rate than age-matched controls.

The trait of sensitivity among alcoholics is a possible explanation for the high rate of alcoholism among artists, including poets and novelists. Ernest Hemingway, William Faulkner, Jack London, F. Scott Fitzgerald, and James Agee are a few examples of writers whose alcoholism was well known. Robert Burns, James Joyce, Henrik Ibsen, and Oscar Wilde are others. Dostoyevsky was intoxicated with the risks of gambling (Leonard, 1990). Five out of seven Nobel Prize-winning American writers became alcoholics. Goodwin (1988: 195) accounts for the phenomenon as follows:

> Their storytelling gifts as children, their tortured sensitivity, their inability to mature completely, the incongruities in their personalities—all may reflect an inability to feel at home with people. . . . All had insomnia. . . . All were hypochondriacs. . . . Were any of the alcoholic writers nonsmokers? Yes, Hemingway.

Sensitivity to psychological pain leads to overreaction to pain. An example from the life of James Agee, a famous American writer who died prematurely of alcoholism-related heart failure, spells out personality characteristics that were unique to him and reminiscent of others whose lives became consumed by alcohol. "The slightest insult, real or imagined, sent him into paroxysms of rage" (Bergreen, 1984: 63). Here is a classic description of hypersensitivity in combination with overreaction to pain. The author of Agee's biography describes his early character accordingly:

> By now some of the young man's principal characteristics were evident: his fascination with death, an oppressive and unfathomable sense of guilt, a tendency toward extreme behavior, an alternation of cruelty with compassion, acute intelligence, and a hopelessly frustrated longing for his mother. (Bergreen, 1984: 30)

The *tendency toward extreme behavior* can be seen as an almost universal characteristic of persons who are addicted to alcohol consumption. In fact, according to Peele (1989), substance abuse may be but one form of compulsive and excessive behavior, the exact type being determined by socialization and environmental opportunity. Moreover, it seems plausible to Peele that life forces differentially impact on the person, depending on his or her constitutional characteristics.

Granted, individual differences are strong and highly relevant to one's relationship with alcohol, but cultural forces are equally compelling. Sociologists have long observed cultural differences in drinking rates and styles.

THE CULTURAL CONTEXT

Why do some countries or cultural groups with very high alcohol consumption rates have relatively low alcoholism rates, while groups with the low consumption rates often have high alcoholism among those who drink? Why do some groups that perceive any kind of drinking as a sin have high alcoholism rates for those who do decide to drink? Why are there likely to be teetotalers and alcoholics in the same family?

For the answers, cross-cultural data on alcoholism are informative, if of questionable reliability. Because of differences in international measurements, cross-cultural comparisons of alcoholism rates are difficult to make. Such comparisons are confused by possible biological differences in susceptibilities to alcoholism. Orientals, for instance, who are physiologically very sensitive to alcohol ingestion and who tend to show a flushing response, have relatively low alcoholism rates. The Chinese, who reportedly exhibit a "fast-flushing" response to alcohol (Park et al., 1984), are at the low end of the spectrum for drinking problems. In some Asian countries, such as Japan and Korea, however, new drinking customs are taking shape. Afterwork drinking, often to the point of intoxication, has become almost mandatory among Japanese and Korean business executives (Helzer and Canino, 1992). Arguing against biological resistance to alcoholism, Peele (1989) points out that while Native Americans tend to flush "under the influence," they are apparently not prevented from drinking by this innate response.

Milam's hypothesis (1974) offers a biologically based explanation of differential alcoholism rates among cultural groups. The longer the period of time a people has been exposed to alcohol, according to this formulation, the lower the vulnerability to alcoholism. Hence the low rates of alcoholism among the Mediterranean peoples—Jews, Greeks, Southern Italians—in contrast to high rates among Native Americans, Irish, Russians, Poles, and North Americans in general. Over many centuries of exposure to wine, according to this theory, the fit have survived; the unfit have died before they could pass on their genes.

If one theory stands out as the most plausible explanation of alcohol susceptibility, it is Jellinek's pioneering explanation (1960). Where others pinpoint biology, Jellinek demonstrates a grasp of the interaction between sociocultural and biological forces in forging an understanding of the alcoholism process. In Jellinek's conceptualization, culture influences the manifestation of alcohol problems by creating a milieu for those with predisposing personality traits.

116

An alternative rationale for the striking intercultural differences that Milam identified is the more holistic argument that tribes and nations of people exposed to alcohol over thousands of years have developed a cultural (and possibly biological) resistance to its damaging effects. In the temperate society the use of alcohol will be nurtured and ritualized, not feared and forbidden.

Attitudes toward alcohol help shape the course of conformity to drinking norms and the course of deviance as well. Jewish traditions and Greek and Southern Italian cultures evoke an appreciation for the use of wine as an integral part of mealtime and religious rituals. Liquor is viewed as an ordinary thing; no moral importance is attached to drinking or to not drinking (Kinney and Leaton, 1991). Drunkenness is neither condoned nor expected. Inhabitants of the northern latitudes (far away from grape growing regions), on the other hand, experience strong ambivalence toward drinking, and the tendency to go to extremes is ingrained. The use of distilled spirits tends to be concentrated in Northern Europe. What distinguishes the drinking patterns of countries such as Sweden and Poland is the separation of drinking from dietary functions, the deliberate use of alcohol to produce intoxication, and the concentration of heavy drinking in a relatively small portion of the male population (Babor, 1992). Specific attitudes toward drinking in the northern climes tend to be of the all-or-nothing, drink nothing or drink-to-get-drunk variety.

The Irish, when they left their homeland, developed an alcoholism rate that is legendary. The clash of cultures combined with the traditional Irish ambivalence toward alcohol and drunkenness are cited by Kinney and Leaton (1991) as factors in their susceptibility. Orford (1985) notes the strong pull of the Pioneer Total Abstinence Association, founded in Ireland in the 1800s and a significant influence to the present day.

With one of the highest alcohol consumption rates in the world, the French have an extremely high rate of cirrhosis of the liver. Continual indulgence and drinking outside of mealtime are tolerated. In Mexico, on the other hand, per capita consumption of alcohol is low. As in Ireland, a high proportion of the population do not drink. Yet "alcohol-related problems are numerous because of the way alcohol is consumed" (Institute of Medicine, 1990: 553). Similarly, alcohol consumption rates are low in Norway. Extremely high taxes on alcoholic beverages help keep drinking levels low. Attitudes toward drinking are marked by ambivalence and a tendency to excess. When people do drink, the drinking is inclined to be problematic.

The Mormon religion forbids the consumption of substances with mood-altering properties. Mormons, accordingly, have a very low consumption rate and a low cirrhosis of the liver rate (Lyon, 1992). When a lapsed Mormon ("a jack Mormon") does drink, however, he or she drinks with a vengeance. An earlier study of drinking patterns among Christians, Jews, and Mormons indicated an extremely high incidence of social complications among those few Mormons who were users. Jews have had an extremely low rate of such complications (Straus and Bacon, 1962).

When drinking is labeled as bad and ruinous, a self-fulfilling prophecy apparently operates to make it so. Another way to view the situation is to consider total abstinence and periodic drunkenness as opposite sides of the same coin. Both responses actually have more in common with each other than with moderate drinking. They may both derive from the same source—polarized thinking—and the same obsessive concern about the beverage alcohol. As a young female alcoholic told me:

> My father always said to me, don't ever take that first drink. Once you take that first drink you will not be able to stop. And it will wreck your life. . . . And it almost has.

THE ROLE OF ABSTINENCE

A logical question that could be asked is, Inasmuch as moderate drinking is associated with healthy attitudes and life-styles, why don't treatment programs teach controlled drinking instead of abstinence? The answer is that many of them do (outside of the United States), but reported effectiveness does not appear to be high for the habitual alcoholic. The same statement may be made for alcoholism as for chain smoking: beyond a certain point of addiction, it would seem to be simpler to give up the substance altogether than to cut down. Abstinence has the advantage of getting the intoxicant out of one's system. Otherwise, the obsessiveness associated with craving remains. Learning to drink moderately may be effective early in one's drinking history, however, and may offer an attractive option for the young.

An interesting innovation in the United Kingdom is the development of Drinkwatchers groups. These groups are intended for people who want to do something about their pattern of drinking before it gets out of hand. Through the group meetings and reading the Drinkwatcher manual, attenders learn ways of cutting down (Sparks et al., 1990). Research is needed to determine the results of such an approach. More research is needed also into individual variation in the characteristic of obsessiveness. With such knowledge of individual differences, the matching of treatments to individual requirements could be scientifically directed.

FORMS OF COGNITIVE DISTORTION

Three forms of cognitive distortion or ways of thinking are commonly associated with alcoholism. These are: polarized or all-or-nothing thinking, negativism, and denial of the drinking and its consequences.

ALL-OR-NOTHING THINKING

The all-or-nothing thrust ("Give me liberty or give me death") involves an extremeness in word and deed. It is a caricature of the American obsession with being number one. "Whatever you do, be the best at it," the saying goes. Related to perfectionism, the all-or-nothing (black or white, or dichotomous) syndrome is broader than perfectionism because it tells what you will have if you are less than perfect—*nothing*. The all-or-nothing perspective is a split into either/or as opposed to both/and: *either* I am the greatest *or* I might as well quit; you are *either* my best friend *or* my worst enemy. Note the extreme elements in the following former alcoholic clients' statements:

> I'll stay in jail until my time is served. No probation for me. When I get out, I want to be completely free. Otherwise, forget it!

> I expect to get an A in any course I take. Otherwise I'll drop it. Or just plain fail.

> I never tolerate any dirt in the kitchen. I say if you're going to clean it up, make it spotless.

> When I drink it's not to get high. It's to get rolling-on-the-floor drunk. Or else why drink at all?

> What do you mean I haven't completed my hours of court mandated therapy? Just send me to jail then!

> I said to my daughter, "Either you mind me or get out of this house."

Because of the lack of compromise generated, such pronouncements are a prescription for failure. It is easy to understand the degree of problematic behavior that would accompany such an outlook. Rigid, uncompromising, the all-or-nothing person sets a trap for him- or herself before a particular task is even under way. Burns' (1980: 34) study of "the perfectionist's script of self-defeat" is relevant here:

> Reaching for the stars, perfectionists may end up clutching at air. Studies show that these compulsives are especially given to troubled relationships and mood disorders. They may even achieve less than others.

Ingrained in the near-hysteria of the all-or-nothing framework is a mandate to "end it all" or escape. The destructiveness that ensues is immortalized in ancient and modern drama and recorded in the daily obituary column. Depending on an individual's tendency to internalize or externalize pain, the means to end it all may range from merely quitting a job or running away to the ugly extremes of suicide or murder. A pattern of escape from difficult situations is an early clue of possible untimely death. The seeming desire to bury oneself in substance abuse can be conceived of as merely another avenue of escape into nothingness. Whatever the form the escape mode takes, the danger to the self and others is incalculable.

POLARIZED THINKING

Research on the thought processes of substance abusers indicates that such individuals are plagued with dysfunctional thinking patterns and that these dysfunctions precede the use of mood-altering substances (see Begleiter, Porjesj, and Kissin, 1984; Deykin, Levy, and Wells, 1987; Gorenstein, 1987). Alcoholism, as conceptualized by Brown (1985), is "primarily a behavioral and cognitive disorder maintained by a faulty core belief." Alcoholic thinking, for Brown, makes the drinking reasonable and secondary to cognitive considerations. Numerous other studies describe the peculiar kind of logic that precipitates alcoholic behavior (Ellis, McInerney, DiGiuseppe, and Yeager, 1989; McCourt and Glantz, 1980; Snyder, 1975). None of these, however, elaborates on the role of the all-or-nothing, or dichotomous, thinking framework in drinking. Several writers, however, have observed its occurrence among alcoholics in treatment (Glantz, 1987; McCourt and Glantz, 1980). Significantly, writers on depression—a strong component in substance abuse—define the all-or-nothing framework in detail (Beck, Rush, Shaw, and Emery, 1979; McCourt and Glantz, 1980). In common with other addictions, alcoholism may be a normal escape response to an abnormal way of framing reality (van Wormer, 1988). Absolutist patterns of thinking can lead to drinking in two fundamental ways: (1) the all-or-nothing attitude in itself mandates excess, and this can lead to addiction, and (2) the overreaction to life's cruelties can encourage drinking. (And the drinking doesn't do much for the thinking either, but this is another story.)

NEGATIVISM AND DEPRESSION

A poetic description of what depression feels like is contained in the writings of James Agee:

> I'm sometimes really forced to believe I have a dirty and unconquerable vein of melancholia in me. . . . I know the most important faculty to develop is one for hard, continuous and varied work and living; but the difference between knowing this and doing anything consistent about it is often abysmal. Along with the melancholia, or a part of it, is rotten inertia and apathy and disgust with myself. (Bergreen, 1984: 63)

The *DSM-IV* (1994) characterizes a chronically depressed mood in terms of poor appetite or overeating, insomnia, low energy or fatigue, low self-esteem, poor concentration or difficulty making decisions, and feelings of hopelessness. Cognitive therapy is based on the theory that the way a person thinks determines how he or she feels and behaves. For instance, a person's depressed state of mind may be tied in with harboring recurring negative thoughts about him- or herself. Self-defeating self-talk ("I will never be able to do it," "I am a born loser") inclines the individual toward depression characterized by a general flatness of affect. The utter pessimism and, in some cases, the hopelessness that are common symptoms of depression stand in the way of a strong commitment to sobriety (Murphy, 1992).

Frequently associated with chemical abuse, depression may be both cause and effect of chemical use. Stimulants such as cocaine and depressants like alcohol and heroin deplete the system of natural chemicals and exacerbate the depression the drugs were used to combat. Depression has been isolated in empirically controlled studies as a major variable of relapse (Hatsukami and Pickens, 1980). Whether depression is the cause of alcohol abuse or the alcohol abuse is the cause of depression is a debate that has been waged by researchers for decades. Whereas psychiatrists and social workers have been inclined to look for depression as the underlying cause of alcoholism, specialists in alcoholism research have perceived that recovery from alcoholism results in disappearance or marked diminution of psychiatric symptoms (Royce, 1989). Large numbers of alcoholics who have been prescribed antidepressants may be able to function quite well without these medications once the residual toxic effects of the alcohol have disappeared.

Severe organic depression may be effectively treated with antidepressants such as tricyclics for unipolar depression and lithium for bipolar personality syndrome. In the large majority of cases, however, the mode of despondency can be overcome through a systematic program of controlled thinking and believing (Beck et al., 1979).

Depressed alcoholics and abusers of other substances are at high risk for suicide (Chabon and Robins, 1986; Murphy, 1992). Severe depression, in fact, often brings the alcoholic into treatment. In a systematically conducted study of suicide and alcoholism, Murphy (1992) identified the following attributes of clients that may be regarded as a red flag: feeling depressed, having a lack of social support, having a history of suicide attempts, experiencing loss, living alone, and being unemployed. Suicidal ideation has in common with heavy drinking the sense of hopelessness leading into a destructive means of escape. In its life-threatening qualities, heavy drinking is sometimes regarded as a slow form of suicide. In four-and-a-half years of alcoholism counseling, I lost four clients or ex-clients to suicide and numerous former clients to alcohol-related health problems (far more ex-clients, however, died in sobriety from tobacco-related illness than from alcohol-related illness).

Since depression is a serious problem in a significant number of alcoholics, appropriate intervention should help alcoholics to maintain sobriety as well as improve their quality of living. Determination of whether the depression preceded or followed the alcoholism, however, is difficult and even pointless in light of the confounding factors due to the effects of alcohol (Hatsukami and Pickens, 1980). In all likelihood, the proclivity to drink and the depression stem from a common organic source. Ecological theory, which stresses the interactive effects of variables, offers a helpful framework for viewing the depressive role in alcoholism (or the alcoholic role in depression). Consistent with ecological theory, one can view the negativism in thinking, the depression, and the drinking as mutually dependent and expect that work in one area will help alleviate problems in another area. Changes in the way a depressed person views the self, the world, and the future should go far in preventing future episodes of depression. And the elimination of the what-difference-does-it-make mentality should go far toward stemming bouts of intoxication.

DENIAL

Denial of the problem and alcoholism go hand-in-hand. One of the basic human defense mechanisms, denial helps a person function in the face of a truth too big for the mind to handle. The first of Kübler-Ross's stages of reaction to news of terminal illness, denial may be a temporary and healthy coping mechanism. With addictive problems, however, the denial may continue indefinitely. Even in the face of mounting evidence, the alcoholic may insist, "I can quit anytime I want. There is no problem." My clinical observation is that denial persists in proportion to the degree of desire for the substance and the extent of guilt over its consumption.

In contrast to other cognitive distortions, such as polarized thinking and negativism, denial can be considered to be an outgrowth of the addictive behavior itself. Shielding the mind from recognition of reality, denial eases the passageway from past overindulgence to future overindulgence. It is the intransigent defense of denial that alcoholism treatment centers must go to such lengths to quash.

Sometimes the alcoholic's defense system borders on the pathological. *Minimization, rationalization,* and *projection* are the three basic components of denial. As toxicity takes over, the extent of the drinking is minimized. The rationalization is the use of logic to convince the self and others of the need for just one more drink. Any sense that there is a problem may be projected onto another person or source as the real problem.

"I only drink six pints of beer a day" is an example of minimization. "My family has nothing to complain about" is another. Minimizing the severity of the drinking problem becomes an essential part of the alcohol-

122

ic's life-style. The rule of thumb, in alcoholism treatment circles, is to multiply the amount of alcohol claimed to be consumed by three (or four or five). Many alcoholics, even in advanced treatment, continue to deny the extent of the problem. As one Norwegian woman, for instance, told the family treatment group, "Of course I wasn't drunk. It wouldn't be proper for a woman to get drunk, would it?"

When it comes to minimization, family members are among the worst offenders. In the classic study on the family progression into the alcoholic's illness, Jackson (1954: 562) describes the following situation:

> The husband, in evaluating the incident [of drunkenness], feels shame also and vows such episodes will not recur. As a result, both husband and wife attempt to make it up to the other and, for a time, try to play their conceptions of the ideal husband and wife roles, minimizing or avoiding other difficulties which arise in the marriage.

The ability to *rationalize* the drinking is a major stumbling block in treatment. No rehabilitation effort will have lasting success if recovering alcoholics are not prepared in a realistic and practical way to go back and live in their own environment with its specific drinking practices and values (Royce, 1989).

Rationalizing often begins with such words as, "I drink because of my miserable childhood," or, "You have to be drunk to live with a drunk." There is generally an element of truth in the rationalization, a fact which makes the alibi more convincing than it would have been otherwise. Rationalization and self-pity, induced through a certain line of thinking, constitute the perfect alibi to allow the drinking to dominate one's life.

Projection is the defense mechanism of placing the blame for the substance abuse anywhere other than where it belongs—with the individual. With teenage substance abusers, projection is very common. "My father makes me feel so low with his criticism that I go out and get drunk" is a typical example. Or, "After I heard those drunkalogs at the A.A. meeting, I got so obsessed with alcohol that I wound up at the bar after the meeting." Projection is widely used among the aggressive and antisocial type of alcoholic, less so among those with strong feelings of guilt and remorse. Projection is the defense *par excellence* of the externalizer—one who tends to look to external sources for the cause of his or her problems.

RELEVANT PRINCIPLES OF ALCOHOLICS ANONYMOUS

Alcoholics may cease to drink (often because of life-threatening health problems or under court order) and still think alcoholically. This is known in A.A. parlance as "the dry drunk." Membership in A.A. does a great deal to quell the "stinking thinking" of addiction. A study of the principles widely used by all self-help groups may provide a clue to their success.

The tendency to excess in the alcoholic is well recognized in the simplicity and practicality of A.A.'s oft-repeated themes:

> Easy does it.
> One day at a time.
> Make things simple.

Each meeting begins with the aptly named Serenity Prayer: "God grant me the serenity to accept the things I cannot change, courage to change the things I can, and wisdom to know the difference." Many A.A. members and others carry copies of the prayer with them and refer to it often.

The success of Alcoholics Anonymous can be attributed to its simple, universally appealing rhetoric that focuses on replacing unhealthy thoughts with healthy ones. When one member's thinking begins to sound irrational, there is always an experienced member who will offer a slogan such as "Easy does it." Such slogans, however simplistic they may sound, are an attempt to replace harmful thoughts with helpful ones. They are an attack on destructive all-or-nothing thinking. In short, as Brown (1985) correctly notes, the new language of A.A. begins to provide its own form of cognitive control.

PITFALLS

A.A. members are apt to be authoritarian (Peele and Brodsky, 1991). Three related tenets of the A.A. belief system, whether they are true or false, are all absolutist in nature: (1) the only way to recovery is through total abstinence; (2) only through active and continual A.A. involvement can recovery occur; and (3) effective counselors must themselves be recovering alcoholics of the A.A. school.

One of Brown's clients, Sally, sums up the popular thinking: "A.A. is all or nothing. You're either sober or you might as well drink" (1985: 144). The dichotomous thinking reflected in these words is striking. Such thinking, which undoubtedly has its functional side in maintaining sobriety, is often reinforced by the professional alcoholism counselors who tend to be of the A.A. school. A co-therapist once berated a resistant group of clients with the following words: "Either you're an alcoholic or not. Tell me, can you be a little bit pregnant?" Alcoholism counselors are a singularly dedicated lot. When they err, however, they err in the direction of rigidity.

The inclination to excess clearly does not depart with the cessation of the drinking: One alcoholism counselor, for instance, displayed his motto with *four* "Easy Does It" stickers on his car. Many A.A. members, nevertheless, successfully utilize humor as an antidote to the tendency to overdo, to overreact. Fortunately, the rapid professionalization of the field is under way, and a revolutionary examination of the occupation's traditional premises is evident.

COGNITIVE TREATMENT

The cognitive-behavioral approach is founded on the principle that a person's emotional and behavioral reactions are determined by his or her conceptualizing of reality. Alcohol abuse, according to this model, is associated with a multidimensional defect in thinking that constricts reality in a rigid, polarized fashion. Whether or not these distortions of reality originate in some underlying organic disorder, they may lead to a "what the heck," self-defeating drinking pattern. The heavy drinking, in turn, further distorts thinking. An intensive treatment program utilizing cognitive theory and techniques can offer a powerful mechanism for change. Intervention in the cognitive realm is relatively easy to do, non-threatening, and conducive to short-term, demonstrable results.

Dysfunctional beliefs, cognitive distortions, and maladaptive behavior patterns receive the emphasis in cognitive therapy with alcoholics. Designated roles for the cognitive therapist are teacher, clarifier, and coach. Didactic instead of dogmatic, the mode of cognitive-behavioral therapy is both egalitarian and empirical in nature. The client is taught the skills of testing and examining underlying assumptions and beliefs so that he or she can take responsibility for his or her own behavior and thoughts. A thorough grounding in maladaptive thinking processes including all-or-nothing characterizations is provided. Glantz succinctly states the challenge facing the alcoholism worker:

> The maladaptive conceptualizations of the alcoholic have a crucial role, not only in the etiology of alcohol abuse, but also in its maintenance and exacerbation; most relevant here, the maladaptive conceptualizations of the alcoholic are the primary target of the cognitive-behavioral psychotherapy. (1987: 55)

From the earliest stages of treatment, absolute sobriety is a must; if one is to work with the mind and clarify thinking, the thinking must not be muddied with intoxicants. Diagnosis of the alcoholic client's particular psychopathology is, as Glantz indicates, the logical starting point in applying cognitive theory to practice. Specific attitudes and conceptualizations arise naturally through early therapy discussions of the client's interpersonal and personal problems. That it is within the power of each client to control thinking processes so as to shape feelings and behaviors is a basic theme of instruction.

125

To help the individual combat extreme elements in thought and to enjoy a more flexible and tolerant outlook, both individual and group therapy are recommended. Specific cognitive techniques are available from Beck et al. (1979) and Glantz (1987) to this end. Techniques of relapse prevention are described later in this chapter.

Consistent with the therapist's teaching role, homework assignments are given to enable the client to monitor his or her own behavior beyond the formal therapy hours. The keeping of a daily log of events and the thoughts they engendered and emotional reactions to the thoughts is a useful exercise. The counselor may review the journal as a means of helping the client see if and when the absolutist thinking occurs and ways in which his or her thinking may or may not be unhealthy.

SELF-TALK AND POSITIVE RESTRUCTURING

Through the learning of positive self-talk and cognitive restructuring, clients can be actively helped to replace unhealthy thought processes with healthy and productive ones. Positive self-talk is taught by the counselor's juxtaposition of the client's defeatist cognition—"I might as well quit"— with more encouraging pronouncements—"I can do it; I've done it before!" The client is trained to use the word "*Stop*" when the old words appear, then to very deliberately substitute new formulations for them. Often the client may have been previously unaware of the destructive nature of the thoughts that were going through his or her head as well as of their emotionally draining powers.

Cognitive restructuring is a related strategy for inculcating in the client cognitive techniques for coping with difficult situations in the future. By means of cognitive restructuring, the counselor reframes life events in a more positive and realistic light. Thus, a setback will be redefined in terms of a challenge rather than as "the beginning of the end" or an "evil omen." And the fact that a client does not achieve the "all" in the all-or-nothing framework will be reinterpreted in light of what has been achieved rather than in terms of what has been lost. The occasion of a relapse provides a typical illustration. Through cognitive reframing, the recovering alcoholic will be encouraged to view the relapse not as failure but as a normal process in recovery. A review of the client's progress will be undertaken.

RATIONAL EMOTIVE THERAPY WITH SUBSTANCE ABUSERS

Trained as a psychoanalyst, Albert Ellis discovered that his clients' disturbed feelings and behaviors largely changed in conjunction with their newly acquired thinking. Ellis's Rational-Emotive Therapy (RET) (Ellis et al., 1989) is systematically applied to substance abuse problems in a practitioners' guidebook. RET with alcoholics and other addicts assumes that it is largely clients' self-defeating thoughts and resulting feelings and actions that sabotage their lives. RET is a flexible and persistent approach to disputing the irrational beliefs that are concomitant with addictive thinking. Addictive thinking tends to be automatic, nonconscious, over-learned, and continual.

Low frustration tolerance stems from and coincides with the irrational beliefs. According to writers of the RET school, the irrational belief that pain, discomfort, or unpleasantness is unbearable is almost ubiquitous with people who have addiction problems. Examples of typical irrational beliefs may be conceptualized addictive terms such as:

- I cannot function without a drink.
- I am not strong enough to resist alcohol.
- Life is so hard I deserve a drink.
- I must have a drink or I can't go on.
- I must end this pain—I can't stand it.

This panicky attempt to escape an emotionally disturbing situation is termed by Ellis *discomfort anxiety*. Clients in treatment need to be taught to label the feelings that occurred just *before* the last drinking episode. Ellis et al. (1989: 28) instruct the therapist to ask the client to put in words exactly what he or she was thinking when he or she "drank, snorted, popped . . . or smoked." The RET mode of treatment as detailed in the Ellis et al. text, *Rational-Emotive Therapy with Alcoholics and Substance Abusers* (1989) is highly applicable to everyday addictions therapy. Useful exercises can be found here; for example, relapse prevention and shame attacking exercises are provided for direct counselor use.

Because of the power of collective feedback, the group setting is ideal for cognitive work. Clients can so easily see the fallacies in another's thinking and behavior patterns. As clients contrast one another's frameworks and defenses, they learn about their own frameworks and defenses. Once, in my treatment group, a member was going on and on about his myriad revenge plots. There seemed to be no way to get this overwrought man to see reason. Then a fellow alcoholic ex-logger confronted him: "I think you're a great guy. But sometimes you don't have too much up here" (knocking audibly on his own head). The group laughed in spontaneous recognition, and the speaker laughed too and acknowledged at once his bullheadedness.

For "getting the ball rolling" in a group there are list-making exercises: "Count all your friends younger than yourself who are making more money" and "Think of all the hurtful things your spouse has said to you." These exercises reveal the pain that can be aroused by certain deliberate lines of thought. Group members are generally willing to offer their own favorites.

Results of cognitive therapy for depression disorders have been empirically substantiated (Beck et al., 1979). Used by itself or in conjunction with psychotropic medications, cognitive therapy has been shown to effectively alleviate depression. Controlled thinking is therefore a reality—the mind can take conscious control over the body; the intellect can quash the emotions. The success of A.A.'s simple (though not simplistic) sloganizing gives credence to the efficacy of the power of reason.

Recovering alcoholics periodically must wrestle with urges and cravings to drink. Recurrent intoxication dreams are common. The survivors, according to Ludwig (1988), tend to be those who, through either trial-and-error learning on their own or instruction from others, have discovered a variety of mental techniques for effectively coping with temptation.

IRRATIONAL THINKING IN THE SPHERE OF LOVE

Through art, music, and literature, Western culture encourages the notion of all-consuming love between two people who are joined together as one. We all know of couples who speak with one voice. And we all know of widows and widowers whose own life ends with the death of the spouse, sometimes literally. "Their two hearts beat as one," it is said.

The mature person can enjoy the romanticism in our culture, cry at the opera, and disregard the implications of the message at the same time. Thus, romantic fantasy can be an exciting and healthy escape from the drudgery and monotony of everyday life.

The immature, compulsive life of love is described by Leonard (1990) in her portrait of Dostoyevsky, who in his writings depicts his own private hell. In *The Gambler,* the leading character, Alexei, goes beyond all limits. An addict in love as in gambling, he pledges he will risk his life for his love—he will dive head first from a cliff if she gives the word. According to Leonard, "Alexei is an extremist; he plays the game of all or nothing" (p. 39).

Hartman and Laird (1983: 78), contrast the differentiated (independent) person from the one who is fused in a relationship that knows no boundaries:

> The well-differentiated person is provident, flexible, thoughtful, and autonomous in the face of considerable stress, while the less differentiated, more fused person is often trapped in a world of feeling, buffeted about by emotionality, disinclined to providence, inclined to rigidity, and suscepti-

128

ble to dysfunction when confronted with stress. . . . The differentiated person, interestingly, is the one who can risk genuine emotional closeness without undue anxiety.

In my work with alcoholic families (Family Week in an inpatient setting), I found it helpful to include a session on love relationships. I found that as clients and their family members prepared to resume their relationships with their loved ones, they were often on a disaster course. Expectations of the relationship were too high. The level of interdependency was also too high. In my mind's eye is a picture of two cartoon characters—lovers in a boat—about to enter the Tunnel of Love. Ahead, out of the lovers' view, is a steep waterfall. This is my image of the post-treatment alcoholic couple blindly heading down life's course. Whether addicted to alcohol or to a newfound relationship, the potential for destructiveness is the same. Many a recovering client has returned abruptly to the treatment center after a "slip" or relapse precipitated by a disastrous, all-consuming love affair, often with a fellow recovering alcoholic client. The "abstinence romance" or a romance between two newly sober people makes for some odd coupling indeed.

To avoid such problematic alliances, some treatment centers (such as Hazelden) totally segregate men and women in treatment. Others make up rules about "fraternization," which are invariably difficult to enforce. There is much wisdom in the unwritten A.A. rule—no new involvements during the first year of sobriety. Newly recovering clients in treatment would do well to be helped to get some perspective on the nature of relationships.

Leonard (1990) likens romanticism and alcoholism; both are attempts at escape and a longing to forget. While the alcoholic is hooked on a chemical, according to Leonard, the romantic is hooked on a fantasy of love that is projected on some person (1990: 67).

> The archetypal figure of the Romantic, the one who wants absolute merger with the loved one, is present when the addict seeks to escape the stresses of the everyday practical world through a drink, a love fantasy, or whatever helps to give the absolute feeling of being at one with the universe.

The all-or-nothing component is prominent in romantic love notions. Zastrow and Kirst-Ashman (1993) contrast idealized love, which is built on pretenses, and rational love, which is not. Irrational thought patterns that are culturally ingrained but that most mature people would not take literally are as follows:

- I cannot live without you.
- You are the only person for me.

- I'm never going to get involved with anyone else again.
- We must agree on everything.
- We should be happy in each other's exclusive company.
- Everything that is yours is mine and everything that is mine is yours.
- (And among alcoholics) You keep me sober.

The extreme element inherent in this kind of logic corresponds to a certain frantic quality underlying any addiction. The love partner, like the source of any addiction, will be used to satisfy a deep, aching need for some sort of escape. And although the initial euphoria may be long departed, the dependency prevails. According to Peele (1975: 88) in his analysis of love and addiction, the addictive foundations of a dependency relationship are revealed when it ends in an abrupt, total, and vindictive breakup. "Because the involvement has been so total," declares Peele, "its ending must be violent." Out of love so powerful grows a hatred most vile.

A positive concept of love is offered in Erich Fromm's classic *The Art of Loving* (1956). True love is realized only when a man or woman has realized himself or herself to the point of being a whole and secure person. Mature love welcomes growth in the partner.

To say "I cannot live without you" may sound romantic on a moonlit night, but this reflection veils a threat, possibly even of suicide. To the alcoholic this kind of attitude signifies a loss of control, a lack of inner stability. The person who loves the least in this relationship has all the power. And when the well-meaning alcoholic says to his or her partner, "You keep me sober," this places a tremendous burden on the partner. The other is now responsible for the alcoholic's sobriety. A healthier mode of thinking promoted in self-help circles is to say, "My sobriety comes first." Only through sobriety is true love possible.

THE USE OF HUMOR

To break depression, denial, all or nothing, the social worker who is able to utilize humor has a rare and invaluable gift. Humor is as basic to group work with alcoholics as is insight. In fact, through humor comes insight and vice versa. Shared laughter is a natural and constructive part of a group's life, instrumental in establishing initial trust, reducing individual tension, and enhancing group solidarity (Napier and Gershenfield, 1981).

At the Community Alcohol Center in Longview, Washington, the majority of my clients were court mandated. They were sentenced by the court to 104 hours of professional treatment! Both in individual sessions and groups, these captive, but not always captivating, clients were angry— angry at the system, at the alcoholism center, at themselves. Under such circumstances, I found that defusing the anger through humor was the most effective way of dealing with it.

In chemical dependency treatment, a major goal is the development in individual clients of social awareness and self-awareness as well as self-esteem. A secondary goal is to impart, as a coping mechanism, the ability to perceive some light in the darkness. Humor has a major contribution to make in both of these regards. And fortunately, a sense of humor is a *learned* as opposed to an inborn trait. The actively working and laughing therapy group, like the more serious therapy group, can be a potent force in effecting individual change and growth. A counselor who is too serious, on the other hand, is neglecting a vital modeling role in showing *how* and *when* to laugh.

Important goals for addictions workers are to topple barriers to spontaneous, emotional expression in clients and to offer new and sober means for coping with the everyday cruelties of life. Humor can be introduced as an easily accessible and harmless equivalent of alcohol. And what does humor do for the welfare of the addictions worker? Keep in mind that the burnout rate and return to drinking rate among alcoholism counselors is high (Kinney, 1983; Valle, 1979). Burnout, in general, is associated with a working structure unrelieved by fun. A humor-oriented approach, therefore, can benefit both alcoholic clients and treatment personnel alike.

PREVENTION IMPLICATIONS

The power of controlled thinking is in directing life toward moderation and away from the counterproductive extremes. The application of these techniques goes beyond mere alcoholism, because alcoholism is but one manifestation of the sensitivity that disguises itself in thought disorders. By identifying and reformulating the entrenched pattern, the counselor is able to offset many of the violent and harmful consequences of a certain line of reasoning. Additionally, work in this area is far less threatening to the average involuntary client than is work in the area of feelings, morals, or prejudices. I have found it to be especially effective in working with the resistant alcoholic male client once some kind of rapport has been achieved.

Cognitive treatment of cognitive distortions is relevant to a wide range of populations, among which are: (1) adult children of alcoholics who have been shown to have tendencies of perfectionism and addictions problems; (2) families with alcoholic members who ask, "How can we prevent our children from growing into alcoholics?" and who can benefit from clear guidelines on empowering children to control the course of their thoughts; (3) persons addicted to sex, love, gambling, and so on, because they have as their starting point some kind of irrational notion about self-worth in an absolutist framework; (4) those who have attempted suicide, probably out of the belief that complete escape was the only recourse; (5) criminals and ex-cons whose "crimes of passion" were their way of closing the door on a failed relationship and criminals who committed extreme acts to "get rich quick"; and finally (6) persons suffering from anorexia and/or bulimia as different but related eating anomalies. What all these diverse situations have in common is a compulsion that seems to take over and obscure all sense of proportion.

By helping victims of these disorders to think more clearly and find some balance, their many strange compulsions and behaviors can be offset. To treat the immediate symptoms of any one disorder is not enough: new symptoms will simply spring up somewhere else. The primary focus is on thought processes, their patterns and content. There is perhaps more wisdom in the alcoholic client's simply thumping his head than in much of the lengthy erudition on alcoholism.

RELAPSE PREVENTION

The Dr. Jekyll and Mr. Hyde phenomenon is a well-known aspect of chemically induced transformation of the personality. Robert Louis Stevenson (1886/1964: 114) grasps the full horror of the loss of control in the words of Dr. Jekyll:

> But I had voluntarily stripped myself of all those balancing instincts, by which even the worst of us continues to walk with some degree of steadiness among temptations; and in any case, to be tempted, however slightly, was to fall.

Preventing such a fall, the prevention of relapse, is perhaps the primary issue in alcoholism treatment today (Gordis, 1989). Sometimes, as in medicine, the word *remission* is used to describe the absence of the symptoms of a disease. Obtaining remission or a continuous state of sobriety is the primary goal of alcoholism treatment. One might argue, in fact, that treatment *is* relapse prevention, that every goal and concern of treatment is designed for the primary purpose of equipping clients to wrestle with the daily assaults without turning to chemical relief. Virtually every alcoholic who comes into treatment has a history of drinking and stopping, drinking and stopping. This is the game that alcoholics are programmed to play. The road to recovery is paved with relapses.

The kind of relapse with which we are concerned is not a mere drinking episode but rather the loss of control after the first drink is consumed: the first leads to a second and a third and a fourth. If the alcoholic has already been through treatment, further treatment may be required. The course that this additional treatment takes is determined by the theoretical orientation of the practitioner and treatment center.

"You failed to work Step One" is the typical response of the Twelve Step–oriented counselor in the places where I have worked. "You failed to acknowledge your powerlessness over alcohol, that your life had become unmanageable." My personal observation is that all those still toxic and forlorn former clients were well aware of their loss of control over alcohol. What they could not manage was the overwhelming and irresistible urge to escape. The answer seemed to lie not in Step One but in the clients themselves.

Relapse prevention specialist Emil Chiauzzi (1989: 17) (see Box 5.2) looks to a "combination of biological, psychological, and social weak spots that lead to distinct and destructive patterns of thought and behavior." An individualized treatment approach would seek to locate the weak spot and the kind of thinking pattern that immediately preceded the drinking episode. Typical examples of thoughts that precipitate drinking in former clients are:

- Life is not worth living. Who cares anyway?
- What is the point of going on?
- I cannot stand this nervous strain.
- My life is just one big mess.
- I will never get through this ordeal without a drink.
- I cannot go on without (Kari, Joe, etc.).
- If I take one drink, I have failed totally.

Ludwig (1988) depicts the kind of disturbed reasoning that is associated with the buildup to a drinking spree. Typical of the thought processes during the buildup or "dry drunk phase" are tendencies toward self-pity and blaming others for whatever goes wrong, nursing grievances, becoming preoccupied with petty concerns, brooding, catastrophizing, and obsessing about things.

Several relapse prevention models emphasize coping strategies that are directly aimed at the cognition or thought dimension. The point of curbing the thought is to curb the feeling, and thereby curb the drinking response. The two prevention models presented here are chosen in light of Miller's (1990) exhaustive treatment effectiveness evaluation findings. Of all the modalities examined in this systematic survey of the literature, *stress management* techniques and *social skills* training were the most consistently validated forms of relapse prevention. What these techniques have in common is that interventions are aimed at teaching alcoholics to cope with common everyday occurrences. The enemy is not the bottle, asserts Ludwig (1988), but the "slippery thinking" that is responsible for a "slip."

STRESS MANAGEMENT

The level of stress is determined by an individual's *perception* of the situation. Anxiety, fear, anger, and depression are all examples of responses to stress. (A thorough discussion of the nature of feeling work is contained in chapter 6.) To quell anxiety and to dull the senses are the most common

---

BOX 5.2: Breaking the Patterns That Lead to Relapse

Our age of addictions boasts countless treatment programs and glowing testimonials from recovering alcoholics and addicts. Some programs report that as many as 90 percent of their "graduates" give up completely the substances that once governed their lives.

But research disagrees. Roughly 60 percent of alcoholics relapse within three months of their treatment, and the outcome for cocaine abusers is even more disillusioning: A recent study by Barbara Wallace, assistant professor at John Jay College of Criminal Justice, found that 78 percent return to the highly addictive drug in about that same time.

Why do so many people struggle to quit using alcohol or drugs— and then go back to their initial substance or one just as harmful? Some who treat them feel that many of their patients lack the powerful motivation needed. Others hold that addicts are so physically vulnerable to withdrawal symptoms and cravings that they can't hold out. Another popular explanation for relapse is peer pressure.

My research suggests that most people relapse because of a combination of biological, psychological and social weak spots that lead to distinct and destructive patterns of thought and behavior. Heading off a relapse means evaluating and targeting these various patterns that can make addiction so difficult to overcome.

Over the past three years I have intensively interviewed ninety relapsed alcoholics and addicts who were originally dependent on a variety of drugs, particularly alcohol, cocaine and marijuana. Their periods of abstinence ranged between three months and seven years, with an average of about a year and a half. All of them had received professional help for their addictions, with averages of two courses of treatment—as inpatients, outpatients or at halfway houses. They had also attended, again on average, 586 Alcoholics Anonymous (A.A.) or Narcotics Anonymous (N.A.) meetings.

Despite all this help, I found, these people harbored misconceptions, misunderstandings and just plain wrong information about themselves and what causes people to resume their addictions—errors that put them at greater risk of doing just that.

---

reasons given by problem drinkers for their behavior (Stockwell and Town, 1989).

Stress management techniques are geared to preventing the cycle of interpersonal stress leading into negative emotions, which lead to relapse into heavy drinking, which leads back to more stress. Relaxation exercises,

---

Four Ways Back to Addiction

Four major trouble spots seem to set up a relapse: troublesome personality traits, substitute addictions, a narrow view of recovery and a failure to see danger signs.

Many of my patients were not aware of detrimental personality traits that frequently interfered with their recovery. Compulsiveness, for example, often causes people to be perfectionistic, orderly and inexpressive. This makes it difficult for patients to organize their feelings and admit the powerful role addiction plays in their lives. A minor slip while they recuperated could, and did, send those who expected a smooth recovery back to their original addiction.

Dependency also hampered recovery. This trait makes it hard for people to reach decisions, assert themselves and take responsibility for their actions. Since recovery involves self-growth and emotional risk-taking, the dependent people I studied often felt ill-equipped to manage themselves outside of their closest relationships. When they found they could lean only so much on others, they sought comfort in alcohol or drugs.

Passive-aggressive tendencies led people to express anger indirectly by complaining, shifting blame, making excuses and procrastinating. When faced with the openness and directness recovery requires, those who are passive-aggressive tend to feel threatened. They start to avoid treatment sessions or people who are trying to help them. Then, alone with feelings of frustration, they often retreat into their addiction.

Narcissism took a toll on recovery as well. Such people view themselves as desirable and talented. They find it hard to accept constructive feedback or go beyond superficial relationships; they feel entitled to special recognition and unconditional acceptance. Narcissistic people I studied usually relapsed because they overestimated their progress and underestimated the severity of their addictions.

Others who relapsed were antisocial. They resisted societal norms, rules and obligations, and they attempted to control others by using manipulation or aggression. Generally, these people are impulsive or thrill-seeking. On the road to relapse, they reject help from others

(continued on next page)

BOX 5.2 (continued)

and try unsuccessfully to control substance use on their own. I often heard them say, "I wanted to do things my way."

Sometimes, these personality traits are reflected in a second trouble spot—a substitute addiction (either a substance or a behavior) different from a person's original addiction that signals a step back toward it.

Compulsive patients, for instance, who generally prefer concrete tasks such as work to abstract concepts such as recovery, tend to drift into "workaholism." When they become fatigued, many return to their initial addiction for relief. One recovering alcoholic I treated put in one-hundred-hour work weeks before relapsing. He said he didn't need the money but simply enjoyed the "high" of work.

Those who were unusually dependent found the solo effort needed in recovery daunting. When they felt unable to go it alone in their program, they formed "addictive" connections to others—expecting their partner to solve their problems for them—in place of substance use.

Workaholism and addictive relationships, along with spending and eating disorders and caffeine abuse, were the most common replacement addictions. I found that 19 percent of my patients turned to one new addiction before a full-blown relapse, while 43 percent developed two or more.

Unfortunately, a substitute addiction only leads to a false, temporary sense of security. When that wears off, the momentum toward relapse may build until it becomes inevitable, as all-or-nothing thinking leads patients to reason, "I might as well go all the way."

One recovering alcoholic I saw successfully avoided drinking for a year. But in the meantime, he ran up $16,000 in credit-card charges. Understandably, he got depressed. Then he turned to heroin because he felt guilty about drinking again.

Early in recovery, several female addicts began gorging and purging junk food or using laxatives to avoid weight gain. Some became "exercise addicts," working out for hours each day to burn excess calories. As their guilt and preoccupation about weight loss intensified, many of them sought relief in alcohol or drugs.

A third weak spot for many relapsers was a limited view of recovery. They equated it most commonly with abstinence (34%) or A.A. attendance (29%). While preventing relapse clearly means avoiding alcohol or drugs, those who have the most successful recoveries also learn the importance of understanding themselves. Relatively few relapsers I interviewed referred to self-awareness—or other necessary components of healing, such as positive feelings, coping skills and personal growth.

Even when a relapse was imminent, many fell into the fourth trouble spot: missing the warning signals. Negative thoughts, for instance, such as craving or a desire to spend time with drug-using friends, were unnoticed or played down by 87 percent of my patients. They also overlooked negative emotions, such as irritability, depression and uncertainty (79%); poor physical functioning, such as headaches, fatigue and insomnia (51%); and a loss of structure in their daily routines (62%). Unable to deal with such negative reactions, they turned to the problem-solving methods they knew best—alcohol or drugs.

Heading Off Relapse Step-by-Step

Preventing relapse means treating the four components that help initiate it. For example, recovering alcoholics and addicts can learn to recognize harmful personality traits. One way is to go through the "fearless and searching moral inventory" suggested by A.A.—a process of self-exploration and learning from others who are also recovering from an addiction. Psychotherapy also can help people identify behavior patterns that might contribute to a relapse.

In early recovery, it's also important to look for signs of substitute addictions, such as compulsive eating and gambling. Such behavior is cause for concern only if it's excessive; some replacements, such as moderate eating and work, are important parts of healthy living.

As alcoholics and addicts recuperate, they need to focus on the meaning of recovery—working on personal growth, intimacy in relationships, coping skills and a sense of purpose in life, as well as overcoming the addiction.

I've found that it helps patients to view a relapse as a process rather than an event, something that begins well before they return to alcohol or drugs. By monitoring the changes (often subtle) in behavior, thoughts and emotions that precede a relapse, they have a better chance of stopping themselves before they resort again to alcohol or drugs.

It's also important to realize that a relapse is neither a mark of defeat nor evidence of moral weakness. It doesn't erase the growth that was achieved before it happens; it's often just a mistake anyone could make without sufficient understanding of themselves. A relapser simply needs to bolster his or her particular weak spots by learning the language of relapse.

Many of those who've achieved true sobriety seem to avoid these pitfalls spontaneously. But what they realize early on in recovery can be taught to alcoholics and addicts who find it more difficult to deal with the issues that make the healing process so complex. Understanding how personality, thoughts, feelings and actions may lead people back to an addiction can save them from going through that traumatic experience time after time.

Source: Emil Chiauzzi, "Breaking the Patterns That Lead to Relapse," *Psychology Today,* Dec. 1989. Reprinted with permission from *Psychology Today* Magazine. Copyright (c)1989 (Sussex Publishers, Inc.)

behavioral strategies, cognitive strategies, and life-style management are all approaches that enable individuals to gain control of their reactions to stress. Stockwell and Town (1989) describe each of these approaches in considerable depth.

During the first days and weeks of emergence from an intoxicated state, a cardinal rule in treatment is to "keep it simple." Avoidance of any and all situations involving alcohol, such as parties, is essential during the first six weeks to four months of sobriety. Then, later in recovery, as Stockwell and Town recommend, active coping strategies for refusing drinks and drugs can be taught. Such a didactic approach originated from the behavioral-cognitive school but is commonly incorporated into many treatment programs.

Mastery of relaxation techniques can serve to aid the recovering alcoholic in handling real-life anxiety-provoking situations. Use of these techniques provides a sense of control and reduces the tendency to panic. Learning to recognize incorrect breathing patterns and to take a series of controlled, deep breaths is conducive of a calming effect. A classic exercise taught at treatment centers is the alternate tensing and relaxing of various muscles (one at a time). Instruction usually begins with the counselor saying in a low, calm voice, "Place both feet on the floor, arms at your side, close your eyes and take a deep breath. As I count to ten, gradually tense the following muscles." Sensations of warmth and heaviness are induced.

Again, to teach control, active behavioral strategies are helpful. Directed toward specific fear-arousing situations, these techniques are highly practical for alcoholic clients who often suffer from a variety of phobias and related anxiety disorders. Because of the strong emotions that are aroused, however, these strategies should be taught only after the client has had a steady period of sobriety. The theme of this treatment of irrational fears is to expose the client to the fear-arousing situation long enough for the fearfulness to subside. Thus a client afraid of snakes could go with the counselor to a zoo to watch snakes. Longer periods of exposure are more effective than shorter periods.

As discussed earlier in this chapter, cognitive strategies are geared toward identifying distorted patterns of thinking that are apt to trigger negative mood states, and then teaching methods of replacing those negative thoughts. Through the use of diaries, role playing, and contrived exercises, the therapist can study the client's thought process. Clients can be conditioned to catch their lapses into the negative thinking and to challenge these constructions through use of an inner voice. Such reframings as "I've lived through this before; I can live through it again" are helpful.

The final area for intervention described by Stockwell and Town is life-style management. This entails careful planning of one's life so as to reduce avoidable experiences of stress. Pressure to take on unrealistic workloads and leisure-time responsibilities, for instance, must be resisted. I have found it helpful to teach clients the well-known acronym from A.A.—HALT! Don't ever let yourself get too *Hungry*, too *Angry*, too *Lonely*, or too *Tired*.

SOCIAL SKILLS TRAINING

Teaching particular coping skills for life functioning is closely related to teaching stress management techniques. Chaney (1989) describes the kind of practice in coping skills that should be provided. In group therapy, rehearsal of upcoming real-life situations motivates clients to practice their interpersonal skills in a supportive and safe setting. In this way, clients are prepared to communicate their needs. Utilizing a series of hypothetical situations, Chaney (1989: 210) has group members enact what they would do. For example:

> It is Monday morning and you are out of work. You are sitting around thinking about getting out and looking for a job. You know you are running out of money, but the idea of looking for work turns you off. What do you do?

Practicing such practical stress management and social skills techniques can be likened to the situation of the foreign traveler rehearsing the words and phrases for typical situations: "Where is my luggage?" "I want a taxi, please." Through practice in contrived situations, the student acquires mastery and control. For the alcoholic, the practice is for control over his or her life. Many alcoholism treatment providers offer this kind of instruction in their relapse prevention and after-care programs.

CONCLUSION

Although personality characteristics of alcoholics are known to vary enormously, a certain similarity in thought mechanisms leads the way to excess. Alcoholic thinking and alcoholic drinking are in constant and dynamic interaction with each other. Although the hereditary predisposition to addiction may be strong, there is no way to alter heredity. But the thinking component in drinking can be studied and changed.

A focus on prevention is more productive and less expensive than a focus on treatment after the fact. Prevention efforts, ideally, would begin during the school years. Instead of films showing the horror of drug abuse and the tragedy of suicide, the focus would be on how a person can organize his or her thoughts for greater coping power against the cruelties of life. In literature and health classes, a cognitive exploration of a play such as *Romeo and Juliet* could get the necessary points across in a way that is dynamic and nonthreatening. A deemphasis on educational competition, in general, and on the perfectionism sometimes associated with sports and schoolwork would also be in order. Support and cooperation should be actively fostered.

The cognitive approach to alcoholic treatment has the advantage of offering a solution as well as an explanation. The more we learn of the applicability of the cognitive mode, the more we will be prepared with specific interventions.

To the extent that the cognitive approach to alcoholism is currently utilized, it is utilized sporadically and often inadvertently (as in the A.A. tradition). In alcoholism treatment circles, the disease model of alcoholism receives the overriding emphasis, sometimes to the neglect of direct treatment approaches. Conversely, social workers and others who emphasize self-control and willpower often overlook the important physiological/biological components. That there is no contradiction in these basic truths of causation, that alcoholism is at once an illness with a biological base and a cognitive disorder, is one of the basic contentions of this text.

The need for further research to demonstrate the efficacy of directing interventions along cognitive lines is not only indicated but urgent. Addiction problems take their toll every day, even while the treatment industry flourishes. There is a need for carefully controlled studies of cognitive work in prevention and treatment, of cognitive work with people of different ages and educational levels, and for short-term and longitudinal studies alike. Refinement of certain conceptual modes such as the all-or-nothing dichotomy would be both exciting and conducive to improved alcohol education and treatment programming.

REVIEW QUESTIONS

1. What is "stinking thinking"?
2. What is the evidence concerning the existence of the "alcoholic personality"?
3. What do twin studies and adoption studies reveal about alcoholism? How do they show that biology is not the only determinant of alcoholic drinking?
4. What are the characteristics of the obsessive-compulsive personality disorder? What is this disorder's link with alcoholism?

5. Disproportionately high numbers of novelists and poets are known to have been alcoholics. Discuss this phenomenon in terms of sensitivity to pain.

6. What is the cultural component in drinking? What is Milam's hypothesis? What is an alternative cultural explanation?

7. Show variation in drinking practices in Ireland, France, Mexico, and southern Italy. What can we learn from the Mormon pattern of total abstinence?

8. Give some examples of all-or-nothing thinking. What are the psychological functions of this type of thinking?

9. What is the "perfectionist's script for self-defeat"?

10. How can absolutist patterns of thinking lead to drinking?

11. Relate cognitive distortion to depression.

12. Discuss some of the guiding principles of Alcoholics Anonymous. How do these principles relate to "stinking thinking"?

13. What are some of the pitfalls of the A.A. belief system?

14. Illustrate minimization by alcoholics and their families. How does this differ from rationalization? What is projection and how is it a defense?

15. How does the cognitive approach theoretically view addiction?

16. How can romantic love notions be risky for recovering alcoholics?

17. Define self-talk and cognitive restructuring. How is the group process ideal for cognitive restructuring?

18. Discuss the use of humor in breaking down unhealthy defenses. What does it provide for the addictions worker?

19. Describe the basic techniques of stress management. How do they relate to relapse prevention? What does HALT stand for?

20. What does social skills training offer alcoholism treatment?

6

LOSS, GRIEF, AND SPIRITUAL HEALING

I once was lost, but now am found
  Was blind, but now I see.
  —"Amazing Grace," John Newton, 1725–1807

The organization of this chapter is based on a lecture I gave each month at the Norwegian treatment center for alcoholic clients and their family members. The lecture concerned loss—early and recent—and grief over the loss. The idea for the lecture grew out of my work with male alcoholics. Much of the therapy work revolved around unrecognized grief over severe losses of early childhood. The idea also came out of my therapy with female alcoholics whose early losses had to do with loss of trust, often through sexual violation. My earlier work with American alcoholics involved a theme of loss—of a child, of a parent, of friends and siblings. A common theme that transcended the cultural milieu was the denial of feelings and of grief. Self-blame, associated with internalized guilt, was also common.

Loss is a universal human phenomenon, experienced by everyone older than twelve years and by many who are far younger. There are even sad tales of animals who suffered greatly because of loss. There are many kinds of losses—loss of a spouse through divorce, the loss of one's job, the loss of health, the loss of one's innocence as a result of crime, the loss of trust, and the loss of sobriety. For family members, there is the loss of a loved one to the pain and obsession of alcoholism.

This chapter utilizes a phase approach to analyze the dynamics of loss. The major concerns at each stage of treatment are presented. Thus, for early recovery the loss of alcohol is the chief, overriding concern. Next comes awareness, in the harsh morning hours of sobriety, of the losses incurred because of the alcohol. Grief work and feeling work are tasks to be accomplished at this stage.

The focus then shifts to the challenges of middle and later stages of treatment, when the early losses may come to the forefront. The realization of the need to say good-bye to a life-style and to old friends may appear overwhelming. The task to be considered for this period is additional feeling work on the deeper emotions. In addition to intensive work on the appropriate expression of anger and anxiety, attention is paid to the dynamics of guilt, depression, and jealousy. The chapter concludes with a discussion of the spiritual dimension of recovery.

ISSUES OF EARLY STAGES OF RECOVERY

The loss of alcohol, to the alcoholic, is the loss of the ultimate pacifier, the source of solace when there is trouble, a "best friend." Who does the alcoholic go to in times of worry and sorrow? The bottle. Who is the alcoholic married to? Booze.

Clients enter alcoholism treatment when the pain of drinking outweighs the pleasure, when friends, relatives, and colleagues have had all they can endure. To the client newly arrived in treatment, the pain of not drinking seems to outweigh the pain of drinking. Initially experienced as a physical loss, a disorienting disruption in routine and habit, the break with alcohol leaves the alcoholic in a state of fumbling helplessness. This period, before grief has set in, is a time of confusion and cruel preoccupation. If feelings are verbalized, they come out in the form of denial.

As physical discomfort lessens, mental anguish may set in. Emerging from the toxic stupor of those first days of almost physical pain, the novice client begins to see before him or her a cavalcade of losses. These are losses caused directly or indirectly by alcohol: loss of health, loss of money, loss of friends. A favorite group exercise for early treatment is to write out the cost of addiction. How much money did it cost? How much lost time? How many broken relationships?

The client may retreat into denial of the consequences. Although other clients will see through the ruse, this client will hang on to the futile defense mechanism until he or she is psychologically (and physically) ready to "see." One loss that can be acknowledged at this time is the loss of freedom by virtue of coercion into treatment. Within the treatment process there is the loss of freedom of privacy; addictions treatment can be regarded as a particularly invasive sort of therapy. For alcoholics who usually have problems in expressing feelings, sitting in a circle of intimate strangers is a major jolt in itself.

TASKS OF EARLY STAGES OF RECOVERY

Paralleling the stages of addiction that involve a progressive loss of control (Jellinek, 1960) are the stages of the recovery process, which involve a progressive regaining of control. Treatment interventions ideally are time-oriented to reflect the physical stages of recovery. Neurological and nutritional recovery from extensive alcohol abuse requires a period of six to twenty-four months, according to estimates (Gorski and Miller, 1983). The physical symptoms have an emotional/cognitive component that mandates sensitive and specialized treatment at each step of the growth-recovery process.

The first task of the abstinence stage is to help clients come to grips with their need to face life without the crutch of alcohol. Following involvement in various therapeutic exercises addressing the personal consequences of alcohol abuse, clients are ready to begin the process of saying good-bye to the source of the chemical addiction.

Goldberg (1985) wisely recommends that grief work focused on the loss of alcohol be a priority in therapy in order for the alcoholic to have a better chance to sustain sobriety. Without proper expression of grief, the client may decide that he or she cannot live without the lost object. Goldberg describes the breakup of the strong love relationship between the alcoholic and the alcohol in this manner:

> Pathological grief reactions occur most frequently when the relationship with the lost object is not anticipated, where the relationships had been highly ambivalent and stormy, where the loss was caused by self-destruction, where the lost object evokes oppressive feelings of guilt and where the real world left behind changes without the lost object. (1985: 41)

The gravity of the loss of the object of one's addiction is well expressed in these words. Some treatment centers in North America conduct a full burial ceremony. In such a ceremony a hole is dug on the grounds of the treatment center, prayers are said, and each patient buries an object that has held great meaning to him or her. Drug paraphernalia, empty tranquilizer bottles, and empty whiskey bottles are among the typical items parted with in this good-bye ceremony. The ritual becomes a symbolic recognition of the grief in letting go and of the tremendous courage required to face life without the chemical relief. In providing a funeral-type service for grieving the loss of alcohol, the therapist is teaching the use of a ritual to express deep feelings; the therapist is helping prepare clients to face the future losses in the world beyond treatment.

In the days or weeks following the burial ritual, the grieving work can begin in earnest. This time the grieving may go beyond the loss of alcohol. Emotions that the client may not have experienced in years may surface. The indifference of the initial denial may give way to a wealth of anger. (The dynamics of anger, including a look at what the anger represents and how it may be expressed, are discussed later.) Group bonding helps offset feelings of loneliness. Clients come to understand that through self-help groups or other sober groups such as religious gatherings, new friendships will emerge.

PROBLEMS AND TASKS IN THE MIDDLE AND LATER STAGES

Deeper feelings come to a head during the middle and later stages of treatment. The client starts looking back—on a lost youth or on losses early in life. Feelings of guilt may arise coupled with feelings of anguish over the loss of drinking friends and the loss of social habits associated with drinking.

A grueling requirement at some treatment centers (this is practically a mandate in Norway) is to produce a life story, or autobiography. Such a story may be reconstructed in consecutive homework assignments. A sample outline may provide space to fill in details on early childhood joys and losses, spiritual beliefs and growth, and later events such as losses and close relationships. Questions can be asked concerning feelings related to the joy or the loss, and how the feelings were coped with and/or shared. Many clients find the production of such an effort excruciating; many seem unable to find or to verbalize the appropriate feeling. The sharing of life traumas can evoke a pain that is almost intolerable.

Tasks for the last half of treatment are self-awareness and understanding of the reasons for pain and overwhelming feelings such as anger and guilt. The positive side of a whole new identity—"I am a recovering alcoholic"—is emphasized. The client who is willing to listen and grow gradually comes to realize that through treatment there are many losses and gains, but mostly there are gains.

There are several purposes in the assignment to construct an autobiography. Clients can learn that it is possible to look back at and learn to live with the horrors and shames of the past. Clients learn that they can experience emotional pain in the absence of alcohol and that pain and shame can be verbalized and shared. The relationship between loss and drinking and further loss may become apparent. In looking at themes in their lives with the help of an insightful and creative social worker, clients come to realize their own potential to redirect their lives. Storytellers can emerge with a new awareness of themselves as survivors rather than as passive victims of life's woes and despair. Workers can help clients perceive strengths where they once saw only weaknesses.

FEELING WORK

At the heart of treatment is labeling feelings, understanding loss and emotions generated by loss, and understanding that successful coping with one loss can help pave the way for successful coping later on. To know one's feelings is to know oneself.

In clients seeking treatment (perhaps forced into treatment) for substance abuse, there is usually a major issue centering around a feeling that requires work. Thus, one person may drink to curb feelings of anxiety, another to dull the agony of depression, and another out of loneliness and boredom. Many don't have a clue to what triggers their drinking. All clients can benefit from education about their feelings.

The most basic task for the social worker or counselor at a treatment center is to help the client set goals for treatment; such goals are later evaluated to determine treatment progress. Goals can derive directly from the feelings that seem to be problematic. For instance:

> CLIENT: I'm so nervous. I can't eat or sleep. I need alcohol or a sedative or something.
> WORKER: I wonder, if you could learn to get these feelings of anxiety under control, would that help your urge to drink go away?
> CLIENT: Yes, but it doesn't seem very likely that I could ever calm down.
> WORKER: Well, let's see if we can set a goal for you. How about setting the goal "to reduce feelings of anxiety"?

In much the same way, the goal of anger management can be set, or, for depression, the goal may be to reduce feelings of depression. The worker can explain to clients, in Ellis' terminology, that it is not the event but *one's view of the event* that is important. Thus, even in the same family, where members are experiencing the same events, one child may grow up with a healthy view of his or her childhood and focus on the positive, one may deny the pain through repression, while still another may brood and obsess continually about the same phenomena.

Knowledge of feelings and the thought processes connected with these feelings (My mother never loved me as much as Cindy; I have always gotten a bum deal) will help clients work toward change. Sheafor, Horejsi, and Horejsi (1991: 334) describe four guidelines for helping clients think in a healthy fashion. These can be summarized as:

1. Identify what you are feeling and thinking right now.
2. Listen to your self-talk. Look for extremes in thinking—avoid use of words such as *never, can't, always,* and *everybody.*
3. Examine objective reality. Once the facts are identified, relax, take a deep breath, and repeat them *out loud* three times. (For example, "I failed one math test. I have a B average in college. My parents will get over this. My life is not ruined.")
4. Note when your feelings change.

There is no *one* feeling that characterizes or produces alcoholism. Thus, one person may drink in hopes of cheering up, another drinks in order to express his or her anger, another seeks courage in the bottle. Once drunk, individuals vary in their behavior. Father Martin's formulation in the lecture-film *Chalk Talk* offers a colorful classification schema and one much enjoyed by alcoholics. According to Father Martin there are four types of drunks:

- the *jocose* drunk, who is a barrel of laughs
- the *amorose* drunk, who can't keep his hands to him- or herself
- the *bellicose* drunk, "the new man with the new teeth"
- the *lachrymose* or crying drunk, who is full of self-pity

When I have asked clients to pick one of these labels to describe themselves most have chosen "the jocose drunk." Family members, however, almost never choose this category to describe what they have seen. Sometimes in the course of an evening, an alcoholic will move through all these stages, the good feelings coming in early intoxication, and inappropriate behavior and a flood of tears finishing the evening off. Drug induced, such outbursts of passion may or may not be significant as a gauge of an individual's innermost feelings. Revelation of how feelings display themselves under conditions of intoxication can serve as a starting point, however, to an awareness of feelings and how they are expressed or suppressed.

The first step in feeling work is to learn to identify and label the ordinary, everyday emotions that people experience. Clients can be encouraged, often in groups, to name a feeling, then describe it in physical terms, providing a gut-level, *visceral* description. Rudimentary feelings of special relevance to alcoholics are: anger, guilt, depression, fear and anxiety, and jealousy.

ANGER

There are so many myths about anger in alcoholism treatment that it is hard to discover the facts. Two facts on which most members of Western societies agree is what anger looks like from the outside and what it feels like from the inside. When asked, children can draw an angry face or imitate an angry parent's expression quite readily. Children also can usually describe how they feel and act when they are angry. Clients (and students) typically describe the following physical responses to anger:

I can feel myself turn red all over.

I'm told I go completely white. (Indicates readiness to fight.)

I feel hot, I'm boiling over, and can hardly breathe.

My body tightens up.

I don't know what anger feels like. (Female response.)

I cry. (Female response.)

Some people take out the anger on themselves or feel themselves seething inwardly. Others report that they externalize their anger; they are ready to attack. In answer to a question on what evokes the feeling of anger, responses range from being stuck in slow traffic to witnessing an injustice against someone undeserving. Some let go of the anger rapidly; others stay angry and let it build.

Writing in *Psychology Today,* Tavris (1982) examines the scientific evidence or lack of evidence concerning anger, the misunderstood emotion. Myths pertaining to anger that are demolished in this article are: suppressing anger is dangerous to health; anger "can be uprooted as if it were a turnip"; and anger invariably is the *key* factor in depression, hysteria, bad dreams, and so on. In fact, anger often builds on itself; ventilating anger is cathartic only if it restores your sense of control, argues Tavris.

Some typical goals and means of achievement related to control of anger are shown in table 6.1. Establishing empathy with the individual who is angry often has the effect of reducing anger. Thus, the parent can come to understand the adolescent rebellion phase, which he or she undoubtedly also passed through. If the client can understand the motivation for other's actions and learn not to take them personally, the irrational wave of anger should diminish.

Often the anger that surfaces is a cover for another, deeper emotion, such as a feeling of betrayal or even insecurity. An intriguing question to ask the perpetually angry client is, "If you weren't feeling anger, what would you be feeling?" The answer may be a revelation to the client as well as to the therapist.

148

TABLE 6.1

Dealing with Anger

Goals	Means of Achievement
Learn to control angry outbursts	Use "time out"
Reduce feelings of anger	Find healthy outlets for feelings of anger
Lessen periods of angry thoughts	Use healthy self-talk to replace angry thoughts
End violent angry outbursts	Learn to verbalize reasons for anger; join anger management groups
When appropriate, feel the anger	Explore socialization history of suppressing anger; assertiveness training

Many clients, especially females, have difficulty labeling or expressing anger. Some become compulsive house cleaners, energizing themselves in the endless war on dust and dirt. Such individuals need coaching to help them learn to absorb the angry feeling without fear and to mobilize that energy in pursuit of assertive, corrective action. Generally speaking, anger-avoiding individuals should work on expressing anger, while those who have difficulty containing their anger should work on the de-escalating techniques of anger management.

Addictions workers themselves are sometimes given to angry responses. When the worker feels him- or herself reacting to an individual client with an inappropriately strong sense of anger or rage, it is helpful to explore the possibility of countertransference. The worker can ask, Who does this client remind me of? What does the situation represent to me? Putting him- or herself in the client's place is also helpful in dispelling destructive reactions and overreactions.

GUILT

Healthy in small doses, guilt feelings when too strong can be extremely damaging to an individual and to interpersonal relationships. In his classic study on prejudice, Gordon Allport (1954) defines the sense of guilt as, "I blame myself for some misdeed." However, since blaming oneself can be unacceptable to the individual, guilt may be manifested as anger or depression. As a feeling, guilt is hard to describe viscerally. When asked the question, "How does your body tell you you're feeling guilty?" perceptive clients may describe a sense of pain in the stomach or head, a feeling of being down yet nervous at the same time. The body may be described as feeling sort of slumped over. One thinks of the look of guilt in the child who in found taking a cookie from the forbidden cookie jar or even of the body language of a dog that is being scolded.

People may feel guilty because they *are* guilty—because they have acted badly, deceived someone, or hurt others. This is the guilt of culpability. Most people recognize the feeling if they stop to analyze it. But in many people, the guilt-generating situation produces anger, grief, and denial. In such cases, the guilt may come out as displaced anger or pathological grief or compulsive denial of wrongdoing.

The prime example of underlying guilt occurs with loss and grief. In the grieving process, such as in the loss of a loved one, the family members and friends must often deal with feelings that are disturbing and unfamiliar. In the bereavement literature, guilt is commonly mentioned as an underlying source of disturbance to families. Writing in the journal of death and dying, *Omega,* Miles and Demi (1984) studied parents coping with grief. The parents all identified guilt as the single most distressing feeling they had experienced since the death of their child. Similarly, Kübler-Ross (1969) discusses guilt as "the most painful companion of death." And Lindemann's classic bereavement study (1944) describes the surviving relatives' intense reaction to sudden death of their loved one. Lifton (1967) wrote movingly of the survivors of Hiroshima and of their guilt about the fact that they had lived while others died.

Abnormal grief is associated with alcoholism. As alcoholics share their life histories in treatment, the link between grief and loss and guilt feelings becomes apparent. Typically, an early loss was associated with a later pattern of seeking relief through some form of substance abuse. Then the original guilt feelings were compounded with guilt about the drinking.

Three types of guilt are experienced in the families of those who are dead or dying (van Wormer, 1985). These aspects of guilt are also found in the families of alcoholics, who are faced with the loss of a formerly sober and healthy member.

Survivor guilt occurs when one person is spared death or a calamity and another or others are not. The one who is spared may go into a depression marked by obsessive thoughts. The "Why me?" syndrome of the victim has its counterpart in the "Why not me?" reaction of the survivor. The survivor, such as the person who lived through Hiroshima or a plane crash, may feel a need to justify his or her own survival. Underneath, there may be a feeling of unworthiness.

Parents who have lost children, children who have lost parents, and surviving siblings all experience their own version of survivor guilt. For parents who survive their children, their failure to carry out the most fundamental task of protection arouses a special, overwhelming sense of despair. Children who lose their parents invariably interpret the parents' death as a form of punishment for their own misbehavior. Siblings, often ignored in the grieving process, likewise suffer their own special torment. Acknowledgment of these feelings and professional intervention are needed to help the survivor resolve the guilt he or she feels. Without intervention the guilt may be displaced as anger or self-destructiveness. Poignant literary portrayals illustrate the impact of sibling guilt. Holden Caulfield, in *Catcher in the Rye,* smashes his hand through a pane of glass upon hearing of his brother's death. Growing progressively more self-destructive, he finally enters into therapy to resolve the debilitating guilt. *Ordinary People,* a popular novel and film, describes a family's turmoil when the eldest son accidentally drowns. The manner in which the surviving son deals with the death is, however, paramount to the story. "Why was I the one to live?" he asks. Until he gets the professional and emotional help he needs, the boy is bent on a suicidal course. Parents who have survived small children sometimes take to drinking out of grief. The drunken actor played so unforgettably by Bing Crosby in the film *The Country Girl* (1954) illustrates the phenomenon of a man who lost his son in an accident.

Parents of alcoholics who seem bent on self-destruction or who do kill themselves experience the guilt of all parents who survive their children. Such parents, moreover, will reproach themselves for their inability to stop the drinking. The most typical kind of survivor guilt seen in alcoholism treatment circles is that of alcoholics (especially males) who have suffered a major childhood loss, especially of a sibling. Often, their families concealed their grief; occasionally the name of the child was never mentioned again. The survivor child, usually a boy, grew up with a sense of guilt and unworthiness.

Ambivalence guilt describes the feelings of those family members who love the alcoholic dearly on the one hand, but who deeply resent all the suffering, impoverishment, and helplessness he or she causes on the other hand. As the alcoholic sinks into the ravages of the illness, the family is pulled down as well. The conflict that results—sometimes called approach/avoidance conflict—becomes lodged in the spouse's or relative's unconscious as guilt. One regrets the source of love that brings such pain, then regrets the regretting. Hearing that the alcoholic has a *disease* and should not be blamed may only exacerbate the guilt feelings. The alcoholic, in turn, resents all those stressed-out people who make him or her feel guilty about drinking. The guilt most likely will be expressed as anger. This is the anger that treatment personnel will see in early encounters.

Guilt due to helplessness and failure is the counterpart of a person's desire to feel needed and helpful. Family members generally feel responsible for helping each other in times of trouble. When a family member is stricken with an illness and nothing can be done to alleviate it, a sense of helplessness may prevail. All activities geared toward helping the alcoholic stop drinking only seem to make the problem worse.

The feeling of *shame,* which is the public aspect of guilt, compounds the feeling of self-blame. Shame is placed on the whole family. The antisocial type of alcoholic, needless to say, does not suffer from inner turmoil at causing others grief or public humiliation. Interventions aimed at the guilt-ridden and grief-stricken will be singularly ineffective in dealing with the con artist who is incapable of empathy and devoid of conscience.

The vast majority of alcoholics, however, are plagued by guilt feelings and concomitant feelings of self-blame, sometimes stemming from early life experiences. Extensive therapy work is required to alter the deep-seated feelings about the self. Feelings of guilt associated with early childhood sexual victimization and physical abuse also need to be addressed. *The Courage to Heal Workbook* (Davis, 1990), is an excellent resource to help both men and women reframe their early life experiences. Clergy can play an invaluable role in helping alcoholics come to terms with themselves and their drug-induced acts of omission and commission. Some clients derive a sense of self-forgiveness through prayer and through working the Twelve Steps. The eighth and ninth steps cover listing all persons harmed and making amends where feasible.

Many of the self-esteem boosting exercises described in chapter 10 are directed toward reducing feelings of guilt and achieving a more positive perspective on a person's life and experiences. Group support is found to be tremendously helpful in boosting a person's sense of self.

DEPRESSION

A leading cause of drinking and relapse are feelings of hopelessness, fatalism, and loneliness. Verbalized as "I'll never be able to stop drinking," "I guess I was just born to be drunk," and "Who cares if I live or die?" these thoughts clearly run contrary to recovery.

Depression is experienced physically as a sensation of heaviness, an utter inertia and sluggishness. Victims describe a feeling of being "down." The dynamics of depression, often an organic condition, are explored in depth in chapter 5. This chapter establishes the link between thinking— one's self-talk—and the depression caused in part by the drinking used to alleviate it.

The sense of feeling good can be enhanced by the natural highs that come with exercise, by being in exciting company, and by engaging in hobbies that are fun. With guidance, clients can learn ways to avoid setting themselves up for disaster. Realistic and fulfilling goals can be set to replace grandiose or self-defeating ones. Energy-producing activities, such as taking a brisk walk or going swimming or even altering breathing patterns (to breathe high in the chest), can pick up one's spirits considerably. Self-destructive relationships and high-risk business investments can be avoided. The goal—to reduce feelings of depression—is a standard goal for clients whose bodies are recovering from chemical abuse and malnutrition. Similarly, those who have grown accustomed to the artificial high of a stimulant such as cocaine can expect to experience considerable depression at the outset of recovery. Above all, learning what to expect from group members and counselors who have had experiences in "getting clean" can be reassuring during those rough early weeks and months.

FEAR AND ANXIETY

The compliant but *fearful* child of today might be at risk for alcoholism tomorrow. Conversely, the *fearless* child of today might be predisposed to drug and alcohol abuse. Cloninger, Sigvardsson, and Bohman (1988) discovered that at each extreme—the timid boy and the high risk taker—children show traits of the Type 1 and Type 2 alcoholics. Whereas the ability to feel some degree of fear is healthy, obsessional fear can be problematic. The misery caused by chronic fearfulness is unhealthy and destructive to the body organs ("Cowards die many times before their deaths," *Julius Caesar*, II, ii). The loss of life through daredevil exploits is a commonly reported event.

Physically, fear is experienced as a rush of energy as the body prepares itself for "fight or flight." Physical strength and attentiveness are intensified. Some who have experienced fear can remember hearing and/ or feeling a loud heartbeat and/or a stabbing sensation in the stomach. Outpouring of sweat, tightening of the throat, and irregular breathing are also reported.

There is a difference between fear and anxiety. With fear, the source of the feeling is clearly identified: the growling dog, the deep water, the crashing car. With anxiety, the source of the distress is often not clearly known or defined. The stress is less severe, perhaps, but more enduring. Anxiety is often chronic. Responses to anxiety are subject to much individual variation. There may be an inability to swallow and digest food (perhaps associated with dehydration). Binge eating also may be anxiety related. Physiologically, anxiety may be experienced in the stomach, throat, sweat glands, and breathing. In most people an alcoholic beverage or tranquilizer "kills the worry," and the anxiety temporarily goes away. As Father Martin puts it in *Chalk Talk*, "The rent is still due, but you don't care." Eventually, the solution to the problem—use of chemicals—becomes the problem itself.

The perpetual nervousness that plagues some individuals can be readily reduced through cognitive therapy techniques. Worrying, anxiety-provoking self-talk ("I'm going to fail the test; my parents will kill me") can be replaced with new ways of thinking ("I'll do my best; I can always repeat the course; my parents weren't the greatest students in their day").

Some commonly set goals in therapy pertaining to fear and anxiety are learning to handle fears, managing to face fears calmly, identifying what one is truly afraid of, and being emotionally prepared for likely outcomes. Imagining the worst possible thing that can happen is often helpful. For clients who have *phobias,* or irrational fears, the origins of the phobias should be traced. Behavioral treatment provides for exposure to the feared source (e.g., a snake) in slow steps until the panic-response is extinguished.

Through cutting down in the use of stimulants, such as coffee and tea, physical anxiety can be reduced greatly. A drink of warm milk at any time can produce a quieting effect. When adrenaline is high, brisk exercise can aid in using up the excess energy and enhancing relaxation. The usefulness of physical exercise as a treatment intervention was verified in an empirically conducted study utilizing a control group (Palmer, Vacc, and Epstein, 1988). Results indicated a significant difference in post-test scores on reduced levels of both anxiety and depression by virtue of the physical training provided.

JEALOUSY

An emotion obvious in small children and covered up by a wide variety of subterfuges in adults, jealousy involves certain physical symptoms that seem to be related to tension and anger. The existence of jealousy is often inferred through its expression in some form of behavior. Freud believed that jealousy was universal and was a continuation of painful childhood experience stored in the unconscious (Freud, 1922).

The relevance of jealousy to alcoholism treatment is in the heightened sensitivity and relationship insecurity of many alcoholic clients. Years of "drinking their troubles away" rather than facing problems head on has reduced clients' levels of maturity accordingly. Perhaps for this reason, clients may experience jealousy of their partners' or spouses' friends, and this reaction may be expressed in selfish possessiveness. Moreover, clients may behave toward their own children with jealousy over attention paid them by the other parent.

In cases of domestic violence, common under conditions of alcohol abuse, jealousy is a key emotion to consider. Marano (1993) summarizes recent research linking wife abuse with difficulty handling jealousy reactions. Violent men were found in hypothetical jealousy-provoking situations to consistently misinterpret their wives' motives as intentionally hostile. Nonviolent men in a comparison group did not feel personally threatened by the scenarios presented. Abusive men, according to Marano, may go into a rage when their wives go out with friends. Treatment consists of getting abusers to see that as long as they give their spouses undue power over their emotions and behavior, they will continue to abuse them.

If a client is aware of the destructive feeling of jealousy and willing to work on it, typical goals that can be set are to reduce his or her sense of insecurity in a relationship and to reduce the level of dependency. Self-talk can be helpful. For instance, a sister bothered by sibling jealousy may tell herself, "I don't need to feel jealous. Mary may be my mother's favorite, but I have a special relationship with my mother also. She is very proud of me as a person. After my mother dies, Mary and I will only have each other, and we need each other."

In couples counseling, it is important to help the individuals separate "old" feelings evoked in them from past relationships from what is happening in current relationships. As they own up to their own projections, clients will develop greater control of their feelings and their relationships. In the event that one or both members of a couple are having affairs, the affairs can be reframed as a desperate attempt to call attention to the fact that the relationship is in serious trouble; in this way, the affair can be viewed as an unconscious effort to get some help.

THE SPIRITUAL DIMENSION

In the life of an alcoholic, there is found a certain void or emptiness. Loss and grief are active components in alcoholism. The ability to come to terms with loss and grief, and thus to transcend them, is a major factor in the alcoholic's successful recovery (Goldberg, 1985).

Recovery can be regarded as a kind of journey. It is a journey from isolation to intimacy, from alienation to meaning, and from running away to reaching toward. In other words, it is an achievement of serenity and of spiritual health.

Spirituality, defined as "a capacity to relate to the infinite," is, according to Royce (1989), the number-one means of coping with stress. Citing two research studies, Royce notes that an overwhelming majority of alcoholism patients complained that their spiritual needs were not met in treatment programs. That alcoholism is a spiritual as well as a physical and emotional illness, few would deny.

Maria Carroll (1987) conceptualizes the spiritual journey in terms of breaking the bonds to earthly attachments and achieving a mastery of oneself through strengthened virtues. For the recovering alcoholic, an earthly attachment is to the substance alcohol. Only when the bond to their addiction is broken can alcoholics move to higher things and embark on "a journey home." To Carroll, the journey home entails constructing a personal reality, becoming disillusioned with this reality, letting the ego-self disintegrate, surrendering, reframing the old reality, and then allowing a new reality to develop as the transformed state. Through *surrendering* to the reality of the present, the recovering alcoholic moves through a spiritual awakening process toward wholeness and a larger humanity. Drawing on her exploratory and in-depth research on spirituality and recovering alcoholics, Carroll (1993) suggests that the Twelve Steps can offer a guide toward increasing self-knowledge, giving to others, and reaching a higher state of consciousness. Other ways of achieving spiritual well-being and belongingness include religious faith and a sense of harmony with nature and the universe.

Writers on spirituality have made a contribution to the alcoholism literature in their conceptualization of alcoholism as a spiritual illness, a condition that "results from man's striving for the divine" (Carroll, 1987: 46). As Royce (1989) suggests, alcoholics may be unconsciously seeking to fulfill their spiritual needs with alcohol. This is an important issue in need of further research.

For the alcoholic, merely being well does not provide enough protection to withstand future temptations of alcohol and/or other addiction. Mantell (1983) believes that in order to ensure sobriety, alcoholics must achieve a level that is "weller than well." Spiritual well-being is considered by Cowley (1993) to be the epitome of health. It may come from a sense of unity with the cosmos, from a personal closeness to God or to nature. The experiences of wholeness and integration are not dependent on religious belief or affiliation. Fulfillment of the spiritual dimension is important in providing a sense of meaning in life.

Wordsworth depicts such an appreciation in "Lines Composed a Few Miles above Tintern Abbey" (1798).

> I have learned to look, not as in the hour
> Of thoughtless youth; but hearing oft-times
> The still, sad music of humanity . . .
> A presence that disturbs me with the joy
> Of elevated thought, a sense subline . . .

SUMMARY

The road from loss and grief to spiritual healing is a long one. As eloquently expressed by Langston Hughes, "Life . . . ain't been no crystal stair; It's had tacks in it; and splinters, And boards torn up. . . ." (Hughes, 1958). The passage to sobriety is rough. And there are the *feelings*, the deep, dark feelings of anguish that accompany the loss of alcohol and, later, the recognition of all the other losses along the way. Grief work must be done early in treatment and more or less continuously, as the facts from early life become progressively revealed. For dealing with the future, in order to develop a resilience for weathering the storms ahead, the alcoholic in treatment can benefit from specialized feeling work. Implicit in the philosophy of feeling work is the belief that feeling and thinking are in constant interaction with each other, that it is not the *event* itself that is significant but one's view of the event that shapes its impact. Whether a person is the victim of his or her life or a survivor may be shaped more by the *definition* of the situation than by the situation itself.

Anger, guilt, depression, fear and anxiety, and jealousy are feelings which may be problematic in recovery. These feelings have a bearing on issues, past and present, that emerge during key moments in the treatment process. The feelings orientation of this chapter can be considered within the context of the ecological or ecosystems framework, which is the organizing framework of this text. The ecological framework utilizes a here-and-now focus on the immediate reality (see Germain, 1982, for a classic formulation). This focus would seem at first glance to be at variance with the precepts of this chapter. Germain, in fact, advises against an exploration of "regressive forces pulled to the past" (p. 22) and prefers an emphasis on growth and health. It is important that ecological theory arose out of a reaction to the psychosocial approach that dominated the 1960s and 1970s and to the earlier Freudian conceptualization. My recommendation is for a further expansion of the ecological, holistic approach so that it is multidimensional in terms of *time* (past, present, and future foci) as well as *space* (person-in-the-environment). Willingness to help clients reword past issues is essential for effective feelings work in social work practice. The roots of the problematic feeling need to be discovered and explored; growth work (for future issues) and healing work (for past issues) are inextricably bound.

Chapter 6 has explored the *feelings* dimension of addictions work. For the primary feelings presented, visceral and other physical responses, situational attributes, and healthy and unhealthy styles of expression were discussed. Special attention was paid to ways of reframing destructive and self-defeating thoughts. The chapter ended with a discussion of ways to achieve solace through the spiritual dimension of understanding. Spirituality is an area of alcoholism treatment that is most subject to neglect. Yet the strength that can come from a "higher consciousness of being" can help provide a sense of meaning to an otherwise meaningless life and a sense of comfort in times of despair.

REVIEW QUESTIONS

1. Describe the process and purpose of the ritual of burying old whiskey bottles.

2. Relate the loss of alcohol to pathological grief reactions.

3. What are tasks for the early period of recovery?

4. What are some of the themes of feeling work? Delineate several guidelines for helping clients think in a healthy fashion.

5. Describe the behavior of the jocose drunk, bellicose drunk, lachrymose drunk, and amorose drunk.

6. Provide some typical visceral and other physical responses to feelings of anger, guilt, and depression.

7. Discuss Tavris's criticism of myths pertaining to anger. What are some typical client goals pertaining to the emotion anger?

8. Discuss the three basic kinds of guilt feelings that may accompany grieving. What is the difference between guilt and shame?

9. Name some of the activities that can reduce feelings of depression.

10. Differentiate between fear and anxiety. What does fear feel like physically? List some common goals pertaining to lessening anxiety.

11. Discuss the dynamics of jealousy and its relationship to alcoholism.

12. How is alcoholism a spiritual disease? How does the obtaining of spiritual health help prevent relapse? What does "weller than well" mean? What are some ways that spiritual healing may be achieved?

Part Three

SOCIAL WORK PRACTICE WITH THE ALCOHOLIC CLIENT

What are some of the cultural factors in treatment? Why does Country A seem to inculcate addictive drinking almost deliberately through the mass media and then pass severe laws to punish the individual who gets into trouble thereby? Why does Country B take a decidedly more moderate approach? What are the dynamics of alcoholism in the family? And how is the "addictive organization" like one big, sick family?

These are only a few of the diverse considerations to be taken up in Part Three. The everyday reality of *doing* alcoholism therapy is the theme of this final portion of the text. Chapter 7 surveys treatment specifically designed for special populations: men, women, racial and ethnic minorities, gays and lesbians, the young, and the old. Chapters 8 (family work) and 9 (groups) provide exercises and schemes for direct therapy work.

Whether or not such diversified programming is possible is determined by forces *external* to the treatment itself. Thus, the personal (treatment availability) becomes political, and the political, personal. Such is the argument of chapter 10, which examines economic, legal, and political forces shaping alcoholism treatment in the United States today. The final chapter moves away from the treatment center into the traditional areas of social work practice affected by alcoholism and addiction: mental health, child welfare, corrections, and school social work. Assessment and prevention are discussed as strategies relevant to all areas of social work. Finally, the epilogue pulls together substantive concepts from the text as a whole. Two contemporary, opposing paradigms of alcoholism, the one overly medicalized, the other, overly moralized, are contrasted. Each offers, at best, a one-sided view of human behavior. Through acknowledging both the medical side and the moral side of alcohol addiction but not blinded by either, the social worker can reach beyond theory to the *person* whose pain may be carefully concealed beneath a mask.

7

SPECIAL GROUPS AND
SUBSTANCE ABUSE

Perspectives on alcohol problems and alcoholism tend to be based on observations or research limited to white males. "The alcoholic" in most study designs and treatment programming is the white male alcoholic. Yet, as we have seen in chapter 2, the patterns of alcohol use—the character of the substance, the frequency and meaning of drinking—are shaped by time, geography, and culture. How these drinking patterns are shaped by various social groups within this, the most heterogeneous of societies, is the subject of this chapter. For lack of a better term, I refer to these social groups as *special groups*. The word *special* is used to refer to certain characteristics—ethnic, biological or behavioral—that differentiate these populations from others.

Of all the groups studied in this chapter only the white male is not subject to stigma by virtue of his group affiliation (although the white male may be subject to other social pressures by virtue of his gender, as we will see shortly). This stigma is strong for populations who may be in an unfortunate position in the social structure already and who then abuse alcohol. For example, the young alcoholic when drinking may be in direct violation of the law; the lesbian may experience a double stigma for being both alcoholic and homosexual. Black families, in particular, suffer severely from alcohol abuse. Members of these diverse populations have special treatment concerns that are often overlooked in a treatment environment designed for the needs of the white, heterosexual, middle-class male. For this reason, a separate chapter is included to present data on alcohol consumption patterns, cultural orientations, and innovative treatment programs pertaining to each of these special groups.

Eight groups have been selected for this overview of specialized treatment needs: men; women; the racial and ethnic minorities of Native Americans, African Americans, and Hispanics; gays/lesbians; the young; and the aged. Although this list is hardly exhaustive, these particular groups were chosen in light of their frequency of encounters with alcoholism treatment agencies. There is no way one short chapter can do justice to any of these groups; yet, I hope that the brief summaries and literature reviews offered will encourage readers to seek the additional resources that are available.

THE MALE ALCOHOLIC

Of all the texts on drug use and alcoholism in circulation, to my knowledge not one includes a section on treatment of the male of the species. The male has already received sufficient attention, if not all of the attention, as some researchers suggest (e.g., Babcock and Connor, 1981; Nichols, 1985; Sandmaier, 1992; Wallen, 1992). One could complicate the point by arguing that men have received all the attention and, at the same time, none of the attention. The absence from the alcoholism literature of research and studies relating to male-gender issues is readily apparent. (My description [van Wormer, 1989b] of a group design for male-specific sex role work is still the only one to my knowledge on this important subject.) In contrast, dozens of articles on women's "special needs" highlight the literature. The unique behavior of the female is to be explained, evidently, and that of the male simply to be taken for granted. This section will focus in on the male in all his maleness and discuss his treatment in terms of the three basic dimensions of social work's biopsychosocial model.

BIOLOGICAL FACTORS

Cloninger's classification scheme contrasting Type 1 and Type 2 alcoholics (1987), described in chapter 4, though simplistic in its drawing of a dichotomy, provides a useful framework for the matching up of alcoholics with suitably individualized programs. The large majority of men (like women) in treatment are in the standard alcohol addiction classification of the first type (similar to Jellinek's *gamma* variety; see chapter 3). Such men are inclined to need work in developing confidence, feeling secure, and learning new ways of dealing with stress other than through use of alcohol. A slow-paced, feeling-based treatment orientation should bring positive results. This type of alcoholic does well both in mixed group settings and in individual therapy work.

Cloninger's Type 2 alcoholic is very masculine; his variety of alcoholism is highly hereditary (father to son). The onset of addiction occurs immediately with the first drink, often in childhood. The traits of hyperactivity, antisocial personality, and propensity for high-risk-taking behavior create major challenges for the group therapist. Involvement in buying and selling illegal drugs is common. Corrections programs—confrontive, cognitively oriented, and run by counselors who are considered "street wise"—are geared for work with this type of hard-to-reach individual. Narcotics Anonymous is the self-help group with experience and success in working with high risk takers.

The practitioner with much experience is working with alcoholics will be aware of major differences in personality types and addiction patterns among clients. The gentle approach, so effective with some, may be a dismal failure with others. Treatment matching of type of alcoholic and program are absolutely essential to achieve the results desired.

PSYCHOLOGICAL FACTORS

Trauma from early childhood (e.g., homosexual molestation, physical abuse, or loss of a sibling) is widely found in the background histories of male alcoholics. Unresolved grief and guilt issues will need to be addressed at some point when clients have become relatively secure in their sobriety.

War veterans may express or need to express deep feelings concerning horrifying wartime experiences. Post-traumatic stress disorder is defined by DSM-IV (1994) as the development of characteristic symptoms such as obsession or repression of the extremely disturbing event and increased emotional arousal such as outbursts of anger. Chapter 6 explored how the anger on the outside is often a cover for hurt and pain under the surface. The role of the counselor working with men is basic and didactic: to teach an awareness of the range of emotions and what feelings that seem obvious actually *feel* like. The assumption is that to be human is to feel all the feelings and to know *what* one is feeling *when*.

Also subjects of chapter 6, depression and suicide attempts figure in male as well as female alcoholism. While depression may precede the drinking, this condition certainly is not helped by the depressant alcohol. A cognitive approach to recovery may bring a turnaround in the sense of lessening despair and hopelessness.

Sex and sexuality are areas of major concern to the male alcoholic. Alcohol's bizarre effect on the male was identified by the porter in *Macbeth* (II, iii, 34) who said that drink provokes lechery, sleep, and urine; "it provokes the desire but it takes away the performance." A history of negative or forgotten experiences with drug-induced intimacy may leave men feeling anxious in their anticipation of sex without alcohol. Many may have used alcohol to alleviate anxiety in the first place. This matter is further complicated as sobriety brings with it a new sexual interest and awareness. In the exclusively male treatment group, an educational presentation on primary and secondary sexual dysfunction can open up a discussion on what is likely to be a major area of concern. A related area where information is needed concerns birth defects caused by damaged sperm. The group presenter can draw on animal and human studies to show evidence of environmental damage to male sperm because of drug use or chemical exposure (see *Economist*, 1991).

SOCIAL ASPECTS OF MEN'S DRINKING

The sex-role requirements for the male in our society are every bit as rigid and stultifying as the role requirements for the female. The boy is to be tough, athletic, strong, fearless, and dependable. Society deals out its harshest sanctions to those who do not abide by the culturally accepted norms ("sissy" and "cry-baby" are two of the milder appellations used).

Men carry with them into treatment the cultural baggage of the "man's man" role. They also bring into treatment pride in their ability to "hold their liquor" and "to drink others under the table." "I spilled more than he drank" is a commonly heard boast in treatment and A.A. circles.

The link between stress on the male in our society and escape into drinking can at least be inferred from the following statements made by ex-loggers and preserved in my case notes.

> I lost my job and my wife told me to "hit the bricks." That's when the drinking got really bad.

> What's wrong with today's men? I remember how those loggers could drink. Kegs of beer, real heavy stuff! And no one got staggering drunk. Those men were strong; they were tough. Today, men get drunk on nothing.

> The pressure's rough at work. I get tense; it builds up inside me. On the weekends I drink. But never to the point of affecting my job.

> Where is the hope in today's world? Where can a man of my age find a job? Who would hire me? They all say, "You're overly qualified."

> I have to drink to prove I can control my drinking. When I tried to stop, they [the baseball team] all said, "You don't even know if you can handle it or not."

Finally, social factors pertaining to prescribed sex-role behavior vary from culture to culture. According to Langton (1991), surveys of Hispanic drinking behavior show that Mexican American, Puerto Rican, and Cuban American males are heavy drinkers about eight times as often as females. Irish men, similarly, drink much more then Irish women, most often in pubs away from hearth and home. Young males are initiated into the drinking patterns of their sex and culture. Heavy drinking among Russian males is normative. The rate of violent alcohol-related crimes against persons in Russia is over ten times as high as that of the United States, according to statistical data analyzed by Segal (1986).

Drunken car rides, date rape, wife rape, incest, wreckage of furniture, and physical assault are among the reports given in "list exchanges" by family members of male alcoholics in treatment. The widespread nature of these kinds of occurrences can be confirmed in the typical police station's records of incidents reported to the police.

Before returning men to the post-treatment world, they must be prepared emotionally to face the reality of their previous drunken behavior. Instead of being sobering, the harsh reality of one's guilt can lead to a drunken binge in short order. The disease model and selection of an A.A. sponsor with a strong record of sobriety are extremely helpful for psychological support. Consultation with a minister, rabbi, or priest can also be of enormous value.

THE FEMALE ALCOHOLIC

The extent of scientific research on the female alcoholic in no way matches the volume of newspaper and journal articles purporting to provide an accurate description and yet failing to do so in the absence of solid research. Thus, we hear both that alcoholism is not hereditary for the female *and* that it is inherited mother to daughter; that the female alcoholic works outside the home *and* tends to be hidden in the closet; that there are as many female alcoholics as there are male *and* that there are fewer female than male alcoholics. Responsibility for fetal alcohol syndrome is placed solely with the mother. In short, the "facts" are conflicting. Yet, today, with a new importance attached to health studies including women and with the substantial numbers of women researchers gathering and analyzing data, the facts gradually are being made known. To debunk the myths that still dominate the literature, this section will draw on the most recent scientific information (from medicine and social sciences); the approach is biopsychosocial.

BIOLOGICAL ASPECTS

A special report from NIAAA (National Institute on Alcohol Abuse and Alcoholism) (1990) summarizes important recently collected physiological data on women's alcoholism. From this report we learn that compared to men, women tend to:

1. Have a much shorter interval between onset of drinking-related problems and entry into treatment; women in treatment tend to be older than men.
2. Experience a higher rate of physiological impairment than men earlier in their drinking careers. The consequences associated with heavy drinking may be accelerated or "telescoped" in women (problems of the liver, heart, and reproductive organs).
3. Become intoxicated after drinking smaller quantities of alcohol than men. The reasons may be: lower body water content than men of comparable size, diminished activity of the primary enzyme involved in the metabolism of alcohol in the stomach, fluctuations in gonadal hormone levels during the menstrual cycle.
4. Have a much higher mortality rate than men from alcohol abuse, with death rates 50 to 100 percent higher. Suicide rates are higher for female than for male alcoholics.

Writing in the *Journal of the American Medical Association*, Blume (1986) confirms the high rate of mortality for the alcoholic female. The decrease in life expectancy for the average woman suffering from alcoholism is fifteen years. Women who had successfully achieved abstinence, however, experienced far fewer deaths than expected.

Previous studies into the etiology of alcoholism in women are scarce and contradictory. A systematically conducted study of 1,030 female twin (both identical and fraternal) subjects by Kendler et al. (1992) examined the role of genetic and environmental factors in the etiology from the Virginia Twin Registry. A total of 185 women met the *DSM-III-R* criteria for alcohol dependence. The correlations for alcoholism were substantially higher in identical than fraternal twins. The inheritability of alcoholism was estimated at 58 percent (approximately the same as for men); that is, if one of a set of twins is alcoholic, the likelihood is 58 out of 100 that the other twin will be alcoholic also.

Additional biologically based factors with special relevance to female alcoholism are pill use, fetal alcohol syndrome (FAS), and anorexia/bulimia. Pill use, according to Nichols (1985) may be the housewives' "methadone maintenance." Doctors often prescribe sedatives to anxious and nervous women to "help them cope." Because sedative withdrawal is one of the most difficult withdrawals (symptoms beginning to occur approximately one week after abstinence), the implications for treatment of women are considerable. An excerpt from *A True Story of a Drunken Mother* depicts the typical doctor/patient scene (Hall, 1990: 120).

"Six (children)? No wonder you're nervous. Here's a prescription for some pills that should help." From then on I made regular trips to the hospital to get my prescription refilled at the pharmacy. The pills saved me when I wasn't drinking. Some of the people in the quonsets were taking pills too and I borrowed all I could from anyone I could and stashed them away like a squirrel preparing for winter. Hiding and taking pills became just as much of an obsession as alcohol. Now it was one or the other or both. (Reprinted with permission of South End Press.)

Fetal alcohol syndrome is today considered the leading cause of mental retardation. This cause, unlike others, is entirely preventable. Considerable media attention in North America and throughout Europe has been given to FAS (alcohol-induced birth defects were discussed in chapter 4). In any large alcoholism treatment group, there may be women present who drank at critical periods during embryonic development. Some may have given birth to infants of low birth weight who evidenced hyperactivity, jitteriness, and poor food intake. Disturbances in the mother-child bonding may have occurred. Alcoholic women thus may experience extreme defensiveness or guilt feelings of an overwhelming nature. Because of the barrage of attention in the media to FAS babies, the stigma of the alcoholic mother has been magnified. Writing from a feminist point of view, Ettorre (1992) provides a thoughtful cautionary note. The attacks on drinking pregnant women which have occurred in recent years, asserts Ettorre, have important social implications. In contrast, a body of literature advising that male heavy drinkers stop drinking to avoid testicular atrophy is nonexistent. Prevention of FAS will take place when constructive preventive programs including the setting up of nurturant halfway houses for addictive pregnant women are provided. As the role of damaged sperm in causing birth defects is further defined, perhaps some of the alcoholic-woman bashing that has taken place under the guise of preventing FAS will subside. Perhaps the required warnings placed on labels of alcoholic products will one day apply to both sexes.

In women, bulimia/anorexia and chemical dependency often coincide. Hudson et al. (1992) studied 386 consecutive male and female patients hospitalized for substance abuse problems. Of these, 15 percent of 143 women had a lifetime diagnosis of anorexia or bulimia compared to only 1 percent of the men. These findings give some indication of a correlation for women between eating disorders and other addictions. Studies also report high rates of prior substance abuse in patients with eating disorders (Fellios, 1989; Mitchell et al., 1990). The female propensity to weight obsession would seem to indicate a cultural dimension in the widespread existence of phobias about being fat among women in Western society (Wolf, 1991).

PSYCHOLOGICAL ASPECTS

The psychology of female substance abuse is reportedly different from the male variety. Whereas depression and low self-esteem are more widely represented in women as a forerunner of alcoholism (Sandmaier, 1992), hyperactivity is said to be the predisposing characteristic in the male. Indeed, the extremely high suicide rates among female alcoholics would seem consistent with the evidence of depression. Women who drink heavily compound their psychological problems with feelings of shame, guilt, and self-disgust. Recent research in the area of sexual victimization is providing a revised explanation of the origin of these feelings of shame, guilt, and self-disgust. More research is needed in the area of male victimization before any direct male/female comparisons can be drawn on the role of abuse in the development of drinking problems.

Prior to the early 1980s, the literature revealed no awareness of the role of childhood sexual abuse in the lives of women alcoholics. Still today, the major sources on alcoholism in women fail to mention the factor of early childhood abuse in the etiology of alcohol problems (e.g., Ettorre, 1992; Fellios, 1989; Sandmaier, 1992). The facts are revealed instead in occasional specialized journal articles.

According to these articles, the rate of incidence of early childhood sexual abuse and of serious physical abuse among alcoholic women is staggering. In fact, every study that has explored this issue has consistently reported a high rate of childhood abuse among clients or subjects. Whether the sample size is 10 or 472, and whether the account is mere journalistic reporting or a carefully executed research survey, the findings are similar. I found (van Wormer, 1989a) that about half of my twenty female clients had been sexually victimized in childhood. These mostly high socioeconomic status women had been victimized by fathers and grandfathers. Similarly, utilizing a very small sample of ten inpatient substance abusers, Rohsenow, Corbett, and Devine (1988) found that the estimated rate of disclosure of child sexual abuse increased significantly from initial reports when extensive follow-up interviews with patients were provided. A more scientific assessment of the extent of the problem is presented by Wallen (1992), who found that 32.6 percent of women in her inpatient sample of forty-eight women were sexually abused as children compared to 9.4 percent of a sample of 181 men. Approximately 27 percent of the alcoholic women were raped at some point in their lives.

A study with the added advantage of a control group is that of Miller, Downs, Gondoli, and Keil (1987). Drawing on a sample of forty-five alcoholic women in comparison with a random selection of forty nonalcoholic women, 67 percent of the alcoholic women, compared to 28 percent of women in the control group had experienced sexual abuse. Most of the perpetrators were outside the immediate family circle. Fifty percent of those who were victimized had alcoholic fathers. The authors argue that the alcoholism in the family left the children vulnerable to being taken advantage of by outside predators.

Writing in a special supplementary edition of the *Journal of Studies on Alcohol*, Miller, Downs, and Testa (1993) provide a much more extensive and empirically rigorous study of childhood victimization as a factor in the development of women's alcohol problems. This study of 472 women aged eighteen to forty-five found significantly higher rates of childhood victimization among female alcoholics than among women in the general population. The figures were 87 percent for alcoholics and 59 percent for nonalcoholics who reported having been sexually abused as children or having suffered severe violence at the hands of parents. The high rate of victimization of women in the general population is an indication of the extent of child abuse in our society. In order to separate out the variable of treatment from alcoholism itself, a further comparison was made of women who were alcoholic and in treatment with women who were nonalcoholic and in treatment (such as at a mental health center). There were higher levels of father to daughter sexual abuse among the alcoholic women than among the nonalcoholic women.

What is the meaning of all this? If childhood sexual abuse can be considered a factor in the later development of alcoholism, there must be some intervening variable resulting from the abuse and leading to the drinking later in life. My hunch is that the combination of a general sense of shame and self-disgust prevails but that specific events (and feelings associated with them) may be repressed to make survival possible. The child survives, but the adult may appear emotionally stunted; there is little resilience for ordinary life crises. There is no "talking things out" or "laughing it off." The discovery of alcohol, often in the teenage years, may seem to offer relief.

A client I once had (I'll call her Mary) seemed as cold as ice. Her mother, also in treatment as a result of a court-ordered referral, told me that Mary had once been a sweet and affectionate little girl. But at age eleven, "when her father started messing with her," she began to change. When Mary initially told about her father's activities, her mother did not believe her. For years Mary was thought to be a liar. Then one day the mother discovered the truth. By then, the daughter, overwhelmed by the original feelings, plus the anger at her mother and, perhaps, at her own helplessness, had built up her own wall of defenses. Now a mother herself, Mary was verbally abusive and suspicious. Although Mary learned to control her drinking as a practical matter (her mother did not), she never learned to trust or to love. Unable to love herself, she could not reach out to others. Her extremely low self-esteem is characteristic of both alcoholic women and incest survivors; perhaps this connection occurs because of the overlap between these two categories.

Low self-esteem because of early abuse is associated with gravitation into situations of further abuse. Domestic violence has been shown to be considerably higher for alcoholic women than for a control sample of nonalcoholic women of similar socioeconomic class (Miller, Downs, and Gondoli, 1989). Over half of the women in alcoholism treatment programs are rape victims; their drinking associations heavily enhanced their vulnerability, according to Sandmaier (1992). Martin and Hummer (1989), in an article on fraternities and campus rape, discuss the use of alcohol as a deliberate weapon against women's sexual reluctance. "Candy is dandy, but liquor is quicker," goes the popular saying.

What are the treatment implications? How can addictions specialists incorporate the burgeoning research findings and new understandings into their everyday practice?

In my interviews with practitioners in the field, I find there is a great deal of work to be done before the treatment reality will reflect the research findings. Both the kind of intensive individual counseling and separate women's groups that are needed continue to be rare offerings in treatment programs. Under the influence of the disease model of alcoholism, women (like men) have been geared toward a present-only focus; claims of past abuse having been dismissed as attempts at denial of responsibility for the drinking. Many are still prevented from doing the real therapy work so desperately required. My attempts to help women work through incest issues were met by strong initial resistance from colleagues trained in an earlier day. Today, increasingly one reads in treatment center newsletters of the importance in recovery of coming to terms with issues of the past. It is also recognized that the mixed recovery group may not be the place for sharing intimate details about one's life. At Hazelden, for instance, individual psychotherapists are available for private sessions if requested. Same-sex groups prevail.

The most significant outcome of the research verifying the role of early childhood abuse in addiction hopefully will be professional training in unconscious processes, internalization of pain, and the timelessness of early childhood trauma.

SOCIAL FACTORS

Demographics

Some social factors play a role in the development of alcoholism among women, and other social factors pertain to women once they have become an alcoholic. First, we will consider the demographics of drinking alcohol.

In the NIAAA report "Alcohol and Women" (1990), a review of the literature reveals that fewer women than men drink, about one-third as many. Drinking behavior differs with age, life role, and marital status of women. Whereas younger women drink more than older women, the incidence of alcohol dependence that develops over time is greatest among middle-aged women. Married women who drink outside the home may have lower rates of alcoholism than women with less active roles.

Compared to white women, black women are more likely to abstain. Hispanic women are infrequent drinkers, although this pattern is changing among young, North American born Hispanic women. Women of all ethnic backgrounds typically enter treatment at the urging of their parents or grown children. (Men typically enter treatment at the urging of their wives, bosses, or the criminal justice system.)

According to Sandmaier (1992), alcoholic women are inclined to be married to alcoholic men or to be divorced. Many more nondrinking women will stand by an alcoholic husband than nondrinking husbands will stand by an alcoholic wife.

The Stigma of Alcoholism
In relation to men, women alcoholics tend to experience a stigma that is at once more distressing and more destructive than that suffered by men (Ettorre, 1992). The notion that the woman who drinks is sexually promiscuous echoes the double standard for men and women in the society. The image of the alcoholic woman as a deliberately bad mother is so entrenched that it is hard for the recovering female alcoholic to live down behavior from a former life-style. This harsh treatment of women who drink has its roots in history as far back as classical Greek and Old Testament days, when there was great concern about the effects of a woman's drinking on her unborn children, yet no concern for the woman herself.

Does the woman alcoholic experience a special stigma? The literature confirms that she does. Royce (1989: 173) sums up the situation in these words, "A false sense of chivalry and the harsh stigma attached to a woman with an alcohol problem tend to perpetuate her problems by weaving a protective circle around her rather than urging her to seek treatment." Sandmaier (1992: 8) concurs: "She [the alcoholic woman] is likely to internalize her culture's harsh judgement of her and learn to view herself with hopelessness and hatred."

In order to get some straightforward opinions from the clients themselves, I surveyed my two treatment groups (one composed of males and females, the other, women only). The plan was to ask for comments on women alcoholics and to record responses directly. The comments surprised me; in the mixed group there was a consensus that women who drank were a bad lot, that to some extent they deserved to be put down by society. Comments made in the women's group, however, were more thoughtful and compassionate.

171

The mixed treatment group consisted of five men and three women the day I asked: "Is there a special stigma given to the female alcoholic?" Using the following excerpt from my case notes, I think I can provide a sense of the group's somewhat rambling but provocative exchange. The words of the group members transcend the findings of the literature. Note the remarks against women in the following dialogue.

MALE: An old gal in a meeting I was in said the only difference between a male and a female alcoholic is the plumbing. Women hide their drinking more out in the country where Aileen and I come from. Aileen used to drink in the closet to keep the booze away from me. I didn't give a damn who knew I was drinking.

FEMALE: I think there is a stigma for a woman to drink if she is head of the household.

MALE: It don't look very good—pregnant women sitting around getting gassed in a bar. That's the part I can't stomach. I never seen men hanging around a pregnant woman in a bar.

MALE: There is nothing as low as a pregnant woman who will drink. I think the women drinkers, in general, are worse than men. You should hear them sometimes.

FEMALE: When I got drunk I was a real bitch. I think a woman has a more drastic personality change when she gets real drunk. A man maybe gets in a fight. One woman I know gets real foul-mouthed. She paws over every man she sees. She would fall all over men.

MALE: I think the general public looks differently at a female drunk than a male drunk. A lady drunk is a tramp. That's what people think of it.

FEMALE: She's a pick-up, but it's changing. People look at a female alcoholic in a different light. To me a drunk's a drunk. I don't care if they wear a skirt or not.

MALE: My drinking woman [girlfriend], she pays her board and room. She's drinking every day. She didn't start until she was thirty-five. I call her a drunk slob.

FEMALE: What do you buy her booze for?

MALE: I only buy her a six-pack. I've been through that for seven years. She works her butt off cleaning up the house.

FEMALE: Do you love her?

MALE: Good food, good sex. If I loved her, I'd marry her. When she's sober, she's sweet. She's Ms. Jekyll and Ms. Hyde. I met her in Jenny's tavern. When she sleeps, she's passed out.

The comments in the women's group also pertained to the theme of the woman-alcoholic stigma.

M.: I think it's kind of a putdown when it's a woman.

S.: You see more closet drinkers with women than you do with men. You'll see a man in a bar.

T.: They turn their noses down on a lady who is drinking.

S.: Not very ladylike to be an alcoholic.

M.: When Sonny and Jenny quit, everyone talked about Sonny and no one mentioned Jenny.

The last sentence sums up beautifully a double standard in recovery where the recovering man is given credit for courage and sensitivity and the woman is blamed for her previous undisciplined life.

A related issue rarely mentioned in the literature but tackled by Burman and Allen-Meares (1991) is the discrepancy between attitudes of children of alcoholics toward the drinking parent and the other parent. Negative social stereotypes of the woman alcoholic are often held by children of an alcoholic mother. While children may view their mother's drinking as disgusting and unforgivable, they may be ready to excuse the drunken rages of their father.

Prosecution of women who drank or took drugs while pregnant is the latest in a long history of punishment of the woman alcoholic or drug abuser. Several states have enacted laws requiring health officials to report women whose newborns test positive for drugs, even if the mother is already in treatment (Sandmaier, 1992). Many women have lost custody of their children when there is evidence of drug use. In Norway, the state may seize custody of the children, a right which may never be returned even though the mother may later achieve a good recovery. In short, the stigma of the woman's past alcoholism is a real concern of the woman in treatment.

TREATMENT IMPLICATIONS

Women represent approximately 25 percent of alcoholism clients in traditional centers in the United States (NIAAA, 1990). Women face many barriers to entering treatment. Limited financial resources, the lack of adequate child care arrangements, and the stigma attached to the woman alcoholic are among the barriers faced.

Because of the low self-esteem experienced by female alcoholics and the internalized victim blaming, women can be expected to do better in a treatment center (such as Hazelden in Minnesota) that runs separate women's groups and men's groups and provides recovering women as healthy role models. Short-term women's groups or single-sex groups for individuals with histories of childhood sexual abuse might help individual clients come to terms with childhood sexual abuse issues (Wallen, 1992). Women need to know such issues are not unmentionable, but that they can be shared and worked through. *The Courage to Heal Workbook* (Davis, 1990) is an immensely useful resource to the counselor leading a women's treatment group. The exercises contained in this book aid the traumatized women to get from *then* to *now* and to move from self-hatred to self-love in a nurturant setting. My experience as leader of a women's group confirms that women tend to be very hard on other women. Some women entering the treatment program made a special request for a male counselor. This request was never granted. Gradually, through intensive work with the help of other women, most of these women grew to like themselves and to develop strong relationships with members of their own sex.

Kay, who had been severely victimized by men, summed up her progress in these words to a hostile newcomer in the women's group:

> They put me in this group because I couldn't trust women. All my life, it's the men that have hurt me, but I couldn't trust women. Now I'm learning to trust both men and women. I have a wonderful sponsor; she's always there when I need her. Even when I think I don't.

RELATED ISSUES

Practitioners need to be aware of the heated controversies pertaining to the relevance to women of the Twelve Step approach. Through knowledge of the major criticisms, counselors can make whatever modifications are necessary to meet some of the contemporary concerns without knocking the faith of others who have found that "The Program" works for them.

Kasl (1990: 30) expresses the feminist position with the insight and concern of the psychologist "who has been there":

> The steps were formulated by a white, middle-class male in the 1930s; not surprisingly, they work to break down an overinflated ego, and put reliance on an all-powerful male God. But most women suffer from a *lack* of healthy, aware ego, and need to strengthen their sense of self by affirming their own inner wisdom.

According to Wilke (1994), the Twelve Steps of A.A. use sexist language and reinforce traditional gender-role stereotypes for women. For a thoroughly unorthodox and even sarcastic approach, read Sonya Johnson's (1989) iconoclastic chapter, "Twelve Steps into the Fog." I would opt for a few fundamental changes in the wording of the Twelve Steps to bring them up to date for the multidimensional membership of the A.A. in the 1990s and beyond. Troubling concepts (which are often misunderstood) such as *admitted, powerless, humble, God as we understand Him,* and *defects of character* could be altered quite simply (refer to The Twelve Steps in chapter 3). If the Bible can be reinterpreted and often is, then surely the Twelve Steps can be modernized. Some treatment centers are quietly doing their own revisions already. The alternative is to get bogged down in politics when there are lives at stake and when treatment time is of the essence.

RACIAL AND ETHNIC MINORITIES

In this text, *minority group* is defined as "an identifiable segment of the population that is disadvantaged because of prejudice or discrimination." This section of the chapter focuses on three minority populations—Native Americans, African Americans, and Hispanic Americans. These groups have all been subjected to extreme degrees of exploitation and vilification by the dominant groups in society. Alcohol and alcoholism policies have reflected their oppression by the wider society. Oppressive history plus present-day ruthless marketing schemes (targeting the minority community) and discriminatory health care opportunities unite to perpetuate drinking problems and alcoholism among these minority groups.

NATIVE AMERICANS

Alcoholism constitutes the most critical health and social problem confronting the American Indian today. Alcohol abuse is involved to varying degrees in eight out of the ten leading causes of Indian deaths—heart disease, cancer, accidents, cirrhosis of the liver, diabetes, pneumonia, homicide, and suicide. More specifically, according to Young (1988), alcohol is involved in 90 percent of all Indian homicides and in as many as 80 percent of all Indian suicides. In summing up these grim statistics, Young draws the conclusion that 75 percent of all Native American deaths can be traced to alcohol in some way.

Alcohol and drug use, however, vary tremendously from one tribe to the next (May, 1986). Even though there are different Native American drinking styles, a common drinking pattern emphasizes dangerous binge drinking. Indian mortality from alcohol and drug-related causes is most frequent among young males and is a major concern for prevention. A second concern for both sexes is the high rate of fetal alcohol effects found in some tribes, such as the Plains Indians.

To account for the high susceptibility of Native Americans to alcoholism, studies have looked to the physiology of alcohol metabolism and/or to sociocultural explanations. The early European settlers and fur traders gave accounts of Indians who would trade anything they had for a few evenings of drunken debauchery. On "demon rum" (the major coin of commerce in seventeenth century North America) the Indian was said to "go out of his mind."

From the Indian's point of view, this white man's disease was an evil imposed from without. It arrived with the same early settlers who transmitted smallpox, tuberculosis, and syphilis to a basically healthy and stable population. May (1989) summarizes a series of systemically conducted experiments on Indians' rate of metabolizing alcohol. The re-

175

sults are contradictory. Furthermore, liver biopsy results reveal no difference between Indians and Caucasians. At present, there is no reason, concludes May, to believe that American Indians are any different from other Americans as far as the physiology of alcohol metabolism is concerned.

What *is* unique about the Indians' experience with alcohol is their history. Identity trauma is the term utilized by Gunther, Jolly, and Wedel (1985) to describe the impact of Anglo culture on Indian tribal society. In the seventeenth century there was a ready market for Indian-produced fur pelts which were sold to buyers in the Far East and in western Europe. Recently distilled Jamaican rum was used in the exchange, once a demand was created for this "sacred water" (Weibel-Orlando, 1989). Two significant factors were at work here. One was the high potency of the alcoholic beverage introduced—rum, like gin, was wreaking havoc in Europe as well. The other factor was that alcohol was imposed upon these tribal cultures; there were no rituals, ceremonies, or norms to regulate their use. As we have seen in chapter 2, the society without cultural controls of alcohol use is the society with high rates of alcoholism. An additional factor operating in Native Americans was the simultaneous sociocultural breakdown of the cultures of Indian people (Gunther, et al., 1985). The Anglo culture in various ways tried to enslave the Indians (unsuccessful), take their lands (successful), annihilate them (almost worked), and assimilate them (it might have worked without the other attempts). Finally, the new national government, through its strict legislative enactments, settled on external regulation as a means of social control. In 1790, a series of prohibition acts were passed. Until as recently as 1953, the United States and local and state bodies were still trying to enforce abstinence. Today, many reservations have elected to stay dry. Interestingly, an analysis of various reservation policies indicates that legalization of alcoholic beverages is associated with significantly fewer alcohol-related deaths and arrests than is continued prohibition (May, 1986). A long-term change in social values affecting the social control of drinking apparently accompanied the reality of legalization, according to May.

Strategies directed toward American Indians range from the medical model approach, to the indigenously evolved A.A. program, to traditional Indian healing modalities. NIAAA funding and IHS (Indian Health Service) funding have made the Indian alcoholism treatment programs possible. The trend has gone from the pure A.A. phase of the 1950s and 1960s to the more holistic and culturally sensitive programming of today.

The success of the A.A. program, if Indian-centered, is revealed in the powerful story told in the film *The Honour of All*, which tells of the Alkalai Lake Village people of British Columbia. Indian actors play themselves as residents of an alcohol-infested village—sarcastically referred to by white Canadians as Alcohol Lake because of the amount of drinking that had gone on there. Through the gradual winning over of the residents to A.A. and the proud medicine man's teaching, the village goes from 100 percent alcoholic to 95 percent sober. As a result of the wide distribution of this uplifting film, the example of a people helping themselves has spread to other North American reservations.

Anthropoligist Thomas Hill (1990) reviewed the history of the Peyote religion and the curious connection between Peyotism, which involves the ingestion of a psychoactive drug, and abstinence from alcohol. Hill's research was conducted using records of the Winnebago Indians of Nebraska from the 1860s until 1920. Although the religion contained ritualistic Indian traits, it was actually a modified Christian religion. Followers of the religion neither smoked nor drank. A great deal of social support was provided. The religion's code helped institutionalize a set of traditional values. Ceremonial use of singing, beating drums, and eating psychoactive peyote (a vision-inducing chemical derived from a certain cactus plant) created a situation of social control and security. The lesson from the study of this tradition, according to Hill, is that any group capable of achieving these effects would be a potent force in controlling and preventing heavy drinking.

Modern therapies must be offered in ways that are consistent with indigenous values and customs. For instance, Brainerd State Hospital, at its Four Winds Lodge, offers a holistic approach for treating alcoholism among Indian residents. Powwows, Indian art, cleansing at the sweat lodge, and feasts of venison and wild rice are a part of the curriculum offered by an all-Indian counseling staff. Because of programs like this, there is room for optimism.

Today the Indian Health Service oversees 340 Native American-run treatment programs. Recent alcohol-related mortality rates point to a marked decrease in the death rate from alcoholism among American Indians and Alaska natives (Rauch, 1992).

AFRICAN AMERICANS

Alcohol abuse is a primary health problem contributing to reduced longevity in the black community. From the literature on alcohol use and abuse among African Americans, the following facts emerge:

- Data from national surveys indicate that black high school youths drink less and have fewer reported problems with drinking than their white peers.

- Heavy drinking and associated social problems typically occur after age thirty for black men. There is a larger percentage of heavy drinkers among black males than among white males.
- Far fewer black women than white women drink; those who do drink, however, drink in public more heavily and at younger ages than white women.

BOX 7.1: Australian Aborigines Turn to Anti-Drinking Programs

RON SCHERER
Nowra, Australia

Twenty-six years ago, at the age of nineteen, Bobby McLeod had the dubious ability to consume a pint of beer in six seconds. Today, Mr. McLeod, an Aborigine, is a nondrinker, and is also helping other native Australians get "off the grog."

Instead of handing out jail sentences, judges are sending Aborigines to McLeod's beach-side "self-healing" center, called Doonooch. McLeod says all the Aborgines who have gone through his treatment "properly" are now nondrinkers.

McLeod is part of a refreshing wind shift within the Aboriginal community. Grass-roots movements now are springing up as Aborigines become increasingly distressed by the violence and damage excessive alcoholic consumption causes their communities. This revulsion has resulted in women patrolling the streets at night to discourage drinking, concerts designated as grog-free, Aboriginal sports days and, in some cases, the shutting down of beer canteens.

These grass-roots efforts are likely to receive some financial backing March 31, when the government is due to release its response to a Royal Commission that looked into the deaths in custody of ninety-nine Aborigines. The commission singled out alcohol abuse as an issue the government must address.

Tourists visiting Alice Springs look out at groups of Aborigines drinking on the town's fringes. In February, drunken rioters in Queensland caused $80,000 (Australian; US$61,160) worth of damage and menaced police with spears and axes.

Anti-grog groups, inspired by the success of Canadian Indians at Alkalai Lake in British Columbia, now say change is possible. Residents used to call the community "Alcohol Lake." Both Native Americans and Aborigines developed patterns of binge drinking in groups, imbibing as long as they had money. Neither culture had much experience with alcohol and did not receive the right to drink until the 1960s.

About fifteen years ago, Canadian Indians began returning to tribal

- The Protestant church is a major force for abstinence in the black community.
- Black males are more often victims in alcohol-related assaults and homicides, arrests for intoxication, and accidents than white males. Black males are admitted far more often to hospitals for medical problems associated with drinking compared to white males.

---

customs and developed twenty-eight-day Alcoholics Anonymous-type programs. A key feature of their programs is the continuous training of instructors to prevent burn-out.

The founder of a number of those programs, Eric Shirt, has been hired by at least two Aboriginal groups as a consultant, and several anti-grog activists have gone through Mr. Shirt's training programs in Canada.

The movement coincides with some changes taking place in governmental attitudes. In November 1991, Marshall Perron, chief minister of Australia's Northern Territory, announced a major crackdown on alcohol sales. Among the measures was a new tax, a tightening of liquor license laws, and an education program. The Northern Territory has the largest number of Aboriginal residents in Australia.

At the same time, the federal government in Canberra is reviewing its policies on alcohol and Aborigines. In the 1980s, Canberra funded residential treatment centers, most of which are now closed. It then shifted its focus to prevention through education.

That policy is now under review after a Royal Commission investigation into the deaths of ninety-nine Aborigines while in jail. Alcohol was involved in all the arrests, the commission found. Its report last May stated that alcohol was having "a devastating effect" on the Aboriginal people of Australia, including "sickness and death, violence and despair, exclusion from education and meaningful employment," and "families and communities in disarray."

The report suggested the government focus on solutions devised by Aboriginal people and geared to their lifestyle.

Robert Tickner, the Minister for Aboriginal Affairs, said in a Monitor interview that the money spent on alcohol programs today is "woefully inadequate." The Aboriginal and Torres Strait Commission has budgeted A$5.4 million for substances abuse programs out of a budget of A$42.6 million for this financial year.

- Rates for alcohol-related injuries and diseases soared among blacks after World War II.
- The black community is likely to regard heavy drinking as normal as opposed to being a symptom of an illness.
- Liquor stores and dealers are very often located in black residential neighborhoods.

In short, one can characterize attitudes toward alcoholic beverages and their consumption in terms of ambivalence (Herd, 1985). A strong anti-alcohol sentiment among African Americans persists in the present time. In order to understand the conflicted history of the black American experience with alcohol, one must look to historical antecedents.

Harper (1989) contrasts the use of alcohol on the western African continent and the use of alcohol under the cultural breakdown that occurred during slavery. The extensive black African beer-brewing culture was well-integrated into agrarian subsistence rites. As with much of the African culture of the times, alcohol was employed as part of religious and cultural rituals and regulated by norms of social etiquette.

Under conditions of slavery, alcohol was alternately forbidden and supplied in copious amounts for rare, wild celebrations. Excessive drinking, however, was not a problem. In fact, it was drinking by the slaves' masters and overseers that created a significant problem for their charges. The stage was set for the period following emancipation. A large proportion of newly freed blacks continued the tradition of heavy weekend and holiday drinking. By the early 1900s, blacks drank at black-owned speakeasies and taverns.

A counterstrain—the strong anti-alcohol sentiment—is summarized by Herd (1985). Following their mass involvement in the antebellum temperance movement, blacks abstained from alcohol, which was seen as a symbol of slavery and oppression. Temperance workers drew vivid parallels between enslavement in antebellum society and enslavement to a substance. Black religious women were at the forefront of the temperance and abstinence movements. And the black church was at the heart of the social and political life of the black community. Affiliation with fundamentalist Protestant religions reinforced the aversion to alcohol. The racism and political hostility of the Southern prohibition movement, however, set the stage for the modern-day ambivalent attitudes of blacks. The so-called "Negro problem" became a central issue in liquor reform. Alienation from the mainstream prohibition forces continued with the increasing urbanization of the black population. This, in turn, paved the way for some blacks to enter into the illicit manufacturing and trading of liquor. The nightclub culture of the 1930s began to make substantial inroads into many areas of black life. Statistics from this era indicate an increase in deaths from alcoholism, particularly in the migrant black population. Profound generational differences in drinking patterns are evidenced in morbidity and mortality data on cirrhosis of the liver rates.

Today, the pull of the black Protestant church is in the direction of abstinence, while, as a holdover from Prohibition, liquor plays a key role in the economy of black communities. The ambivalence of today, concludes Herd (1985), must be understood in the historical pattern of coexistence of two different and opposing worlds of black drinking patterns. Alcohol is simultaneously esteemed and despised.

A recent issue of grave concern to African Americans is the deliberate targeting of blacks by the liquor industry for special advertising and promotions. Scott, Denniston, and Magruder (1992), through an analysis of the quantity and content of the advertisements targeted to African Americans, examined the marketing practices of alcohol producers. Their findings are striking. A large percentage of ads in African American oriented magazines were for alcohol. A recent St. Ides malt liquor promotion uses themes of sex, hedonism, and violence to entice inner-city youth of both sexes. For example,

> Get your girl in the mood quicker, and get your jimmy thicker with St. Ides malt liquor.

> Tell your man to get you a six pack, and don't be afraid of what it does to you . . . cause it will get you in the mood. (1992: 460)

According to Scott et al., the above commercial was aired in June 1991 on a nationally syndicated television show of rap music. Numerous other shocking illustrations are provided by these authors. The advertising influence is rendered more insidious by the huge contributions made by leading liquor companies toward the United Negro College Fund and other educational and cultural organizations. In exposing the attempt at exploitation, the authors hope that leadership from the African American community will insist on high standards for promotions of alcoholic beverages. Such leadership is indeed emerging. My preference would be for tightened regulations banning exploitative advertising of the beverage alcohol. Black church leaders and politicians would be hard put to fight corporate America unless empowered by the force of law.

A second policy issue of concern to the African American community is the need for culture-specific prevention and treatment programs including halfway houses. Adequate funding for the institution of such programs and for the training of minorities to staff these programs is essential. Because of societal barriers and limited knowledge in the treatment field about sociocultural and race-specific treatment models, blacks utilize traditional alcoholism treatment facilities less often than whites. The major referral source for bringing blacks into treatment is the judicial system (McRoy and Shorkey, 1985).

A comparative analysis of two consecutively run treatment programs established by a midwestern metropolitan community to meet the needs of black alcoholics is provided by Maypole and Anderson (1983). Both minority alcoholism programs evolved out of a wider community concern that the available alcoholism treatment programs were not providing services to the black population. An interracial committee evaluated the needs of the community to include:

1. A minority program model that recognizes the need to establish a meaningful relationship between the minority alcoholic and his or her environment.
2. A strong outreach component.
3. A youth development program that focuses on education and prevention.

The original program was an Afrocentric, entirely indigenous program that developed a high degree of community trust but failed at the level of administrative work necessary for continued funding.

The second program attempt involved a merging of the original program with a large, financially secure provider of treatment for low-income persons. The merger allowed for the existence of the innovative culture-centered model within the sound fiscal structure of the parent organization. Because of the degree that it has been integrated into the black community's natural support system, the program has been effective and well received. For continuing success, the emphasis is on working with extended families and other neighborhood care givers, such as church and youth leaders. A strong minority representation on the board of directors of the parent organization is essential to continuing progress.

An exemplary community-focused approach has been successfully adopted by the Northeast Council on Substance Abuse (NECSA) serving northeast Iowa. The culturally specific outreach office was described by program director JoAnn Qualls-Carr in a classroom presentation as "very different from traditional treatment programs." The traditional setup emphasizes red tape and billing procedures. Clients may become suspicious, angry, and resentful. The minorities- oriented counselor, in contrast, must be prepared to be an advocate, for instance, to help a client get money to get a tooth filled, to cut through the paperwork and build up trust. Qualls-Carr presented a differentiation between culturally specific and traditional treatment (see table 7.1).

TABLE 7.1

Culturally Specific Outreach versus Traditional Treatment

Culturally Specific Outreach	Traditional Treatment
1. Goes to client	1. Client comes to treatment
2. Allows for drop-in clients	2. Appointment centered
3. Building rapport and trust come first in initial appointment rather than paperwork	3. Focus is on getting paperwork done at initial appointment

Traditional treatment centers around an agency in the community and is focused on the individual and immediate family. Cultural specific treatment centers around the community. More focus is put on collateral involvement, and the family is expanded to include extended family and very close friends.

My interview with a recovering crack user from NECSA reveals the culture-centered content of a treatment group. The group consisted of fifteen men and five women, all African American. The group leader, himself a recovering drug user from the community, drew a parallel between addiction and slavery. Under both conditions there is a total lack of control over one's body and mind. "Do we want to go back into a slave frame of mind or do we want the control our forefathers fought for?" the leader asked.

The perinatal program from People's Clinic of Waterloo refers high-risk pregnant women and mothers to NECSA's culturally specific outreach office for counseling. Such programs are vital in keeping conflict-ridden black families intact. Similarly, Meharry Medical College in Nashville, Tennessee, sponsors a community-based substance abuse treatment program (called Sister), with a team of twelve women helping women (Ryan, 1993). These women work in the local housing developments. Therapeutic day-care activities are provided in addition to full residential care. When a woman needs detoxification, arrangements for child care are made. Authorities cooperate, not by evicting mothers with drug problems but by encouraging them to get help. This multifaceted program, according to Ryan, is considered to be life saving and highly successful in keeping families intact.

Anderson and Maypole (1989), in a fairly recent assessment of minority alcoholism programs, call for community implementation of such programs to include active involvement of minority community representatives at every level. The appointment of a permanent minority advisory group to the board of directors has proven to be a valuable resource both in restructuring services to minority groups and in ensuring the survival of a culturally specific program. For the employment of sufficient full-time personnel, adequate government funding is essential.

HISPANIC AMERICANS

The diversity of groups collectively known as Hispanic Americans makes generalization difficult. The three major subgroups of American Hispanics—Mexican Americans, Puerto Ricans, and Cuban Americans—do not share a common history, ancestry, or socioeconomic status. They do share a common language—Spanish.

A common theme that transcends these differences, however, is the Latin American cultural heritage. Community surveys in most Latin American countries indicate a high level of excessive alcoholic drinking, especially among males (Smart and Mora, 1986). No Latin American country has a history of legal attempts at prohibition of alcoholic beverages, however (Canino, Burnham, and Caetano, 1992). Men enjoy drinking together after work, during sports activities, or in connection with cultural activities. There is an association of control of one's liquor, heavy drinking, and *machismo*. Excessive drinking by women is frowned upon.

An empirically based survey of drinking patterns across the three major Hispanic groups in the United States was conducted by Caetano (1986). While Mexican American males were found to include the highest percentage of both heavy drinkers and abstainers, a more moderate pattern was found among the Puerto Ricans and Cuban Americans. Women in all three groups tended to favor abstinence or drink only lightly. Cuban American women drank the most moderately, while among the Mexican American women who drank, heavy drinking was common. Among the Mexican American population, cultural attitudes toward drinking show more tolerance of female drinking as the level of acculturation into the norms of North American society increases (Canino, et al., 1992).

Mexican Americans, especially males, make extensive use of alcoholism treatment services, according to Gilbert (1985). Discriminatory law enforcement, the tendency to drink in public places, and the high percentage of driving-while-intoxicated offenses all contribute to the frequency of their referral to alcoholism treatment. Yet across the United States, treatment offerings for Spanish-speaking Americans have been notably deficient.

For treatment effectiveness, Hispanic-focused, culturally sensitive, and bilingual alcoholism services are a must. Bureaucratic requirements such as the filling out of multiple forms must be kept to a minimum. Assurance that treatment is confidential is a fact of vital importance to immigrants who may be in the country illegally. The fact that information will not be shared with the authorities without the client's permission (unless certain release-of-information forms have been signed) needs to be explained very carefully.

The element of shame attached to seeking treatment within Hispanic cultures is an important cultural trait that needs to be taken into consideration (Rebach, 1992). Because Hispanic men and women are constrained from disgracing their families in any way and because Hispanic males are expected to be able to control their alcohol intake and to provide for their families, a treatment encounter may be an event of extreme disturbance. Confrontation techniques, accordingly, should be carefully avoided. Positive strategies such as drawing on family support, religion, and folk healing help shape the intervention within the natural support systems of the Hispanic communities.

Trotter's (1985) description of the Midway House Program in the Lower Rio Grande Valley of Texas is the prototype of a culturally sensitive halfway house program for the diverse population of the region. Mexican Americans and Anglos do equally well in the program, which has achieved an externally evaluated success rate of 60 percent. Language, values, and ideals are starting points on a broad cultural spectrum. Therapy modalities are mixed, with various options available. A bilingual client may attend both English-speaking and Spanish-speaking groups. A Spanish language A.A. group meets at the facility. Because of the rapid growth of the Hispanic community and the youthfulness of this population, alcoholism services, research, and evaluation efforts into effective treatment modalities such as this one are badly needed. Future planning should include the training and hiring of Hispanic counselors to offer culturally sensitive treatment to Hispanic Americans and their families.

ALCOHOLISM AMONG GAYS AND LESBIANS

The alcoholism rate among gays and lesbians is high, staggeringly high. Most studies report an estimate of 30 to 35 percent, with comparable levels for both sexes (Kus, 1988; Saghir and Robins, 1973; Sandmaier, 1992). Faderman (1991), however, believes that for lesbians a new culture of sobriety is developing to replace the bar culture that had been so pivotal to their lives in the past. In any case, a rate of alcohol problems that is four to five times higher among homosexuals than among heterosexuals must be explained.

The prevalence of gay bars is the explanation for the high alcoholism rate given most frequently in the literature. In this relatively safe, sociable atmosphere, men meet men and women meet women; the alcohol lowers any inhibitions that might accompany the situation.

The alcoholism rate is high, I believe, for the same reason the suicide rate is so high among gays and lesbians (a 1989 government report gave a suicide figure for gay youth several times higher than that for their non-gay peers). Both heavy drinking and suicide attempts can be considered forms of escape that are used when "the going gets too rough." Because of society's hostility, young gays and lesbians may try to reject their own inclinations, and the going can get very rough. Living a secret life is not without its psychological consequences.

While lesbians and gays have achieved greater equality and visibility in recent years, a counterresistance has impeded progress. For every social revolution, there is a backlash; for every movement forward, some stumbling back. The book *Violence Against Lesbians and Gay Men* (Comstock, 1991) provides jarring quantitative information on victims and perpetrators. Violence against gays and lesbians is committed most often, it seems, by male family members. Alienation from family, church, and society combine to close avenues of much-needed social support. The resistance, anger, and hatred are surface indicators of the depth, intensity, and pervasiveness of *homophobia* (the irrational fear of homosexuality) in the society (Hartman, 1993).

Because of the homophobia present in the typical treatment group as elsewhere, few gays and lesbians will take the risk of disclosing their sexual orientation. The danger is that if they do disclose their sexual orientation, this fact comes to dominate treatment instead of the illness— alcoholism—which is the reason they are there. In a predominantly heterosexual treatment center, the client can discuss his or her sexual orientation issues in individual sessions. To encourage sharing, I have found it helpful to display literature of gay A.A. meetings in my office. The presence of such literature is a clue that this is a safe place to talk. The effective counselor is one who has both self-awareness of his or her sexual orientation and empathy for the human condition. To meet the needs of gay and lesbian clients, every large agency should make a point of having one or more openly gay or lesbian counselors on the staff.

Pride Institute, a thirty-six-bed facility in Eden Prairie, Minnesota, near Minneapolis is a gay-specialized treatment center. Ratner (1988) provides a detailed description of this unique program. A holistic Twelve-Step-based model is adapted to the special needs of chemically dependent gays and lesbians. A great deal of work is done with self-esteem. Because gay and lesbian clients may have internalized the homophobia of society, the Pride program provides help in self-acceptance and building long-term relationships. An educational family program is provided.

Among the first one hundred patients assessed at Pride, it was found that 38 percent of the men and 40 percent of the women had been sexually molested before the age of fifteen. Individual therapy sessions are geared toward helping clients see the relationship between chemical dependency and sexual abuse in childhood. Specialized groups also are provided for work on issues stemming from the past. A bereavement group is available for those dealing with grief and loss, especially as a result of the AIDS epidemic. Some of the male clients have been diagnosed as HIV-positive themselves. Assessments of patients indicate that 22 percent of the women and 18 percent of the men suffer from serious eating disorders. Accordingly, good nutrition and body image work are provided in treatment. See Box 7.2 for a rare glimpse into the life and struggles of a male gay anorexic.

A follow-up study done by external evaluators indicated outstanding results, according to *Our Voice* (1991). In short, this pioneering program at Pride Institute helps gays and lesbians recover from their own internalized homophobia as well as from the presenting problems of addiction. Where insurance policies allow for inpatient treatment, referral to such a gay/lesbian-oriented treatment center is highly desirable.

ALCOHOL AND YOUTH

Underage Americans (those under age twenty-one) drink, and they drink heavily (Clark, 1992). In the United Kingdom, where the legal drinking age is sixteen in a restaurant and eighteen to purchase alcohol beverages, underage drinking is perceived as just a normal step in growing up (Foxcraft and Lowe, 1991).

Data from the National (U.S.) Adolescent Student Health Survey administered by the American School Health Association (1989) were used to study the prevalence of drinking among American teenagers. A representative sample was taken of eighth grade students and tenth grade students. The figures for the twelfth graders had been obtained in a previous survey. The data are presented in table 7.2 (compiled by Windle, 1991).

This survey of heavy drinking revealed that approximately 36 percent of tenth and twelfth graders had consumed five or more drinks consecutively in the previous two weeks. Although gender differences were apparent, these differences were not as pronounced as formerly. The results showed that white and Hispanic adolescents were much more likely to drink heavily than were black adolescents.

Potentially preventable causes—accidents, homicide, and suicide—account for at least two-thirds of adolescent deaths. *The Prevention Report* from the U.S. Public Health Department (1993) indicated today's youth start using tobacco, alcohol, and often drugs on an average at age twelve; the initiation of risky behaviors is thus occurring at progressively younger ages, according to this report.

On university campuses, the dangers of heavy alcohol consumption are especially pronounced. Clark (1992) cites the results of a nationwide college survey implicating alcohol in 70 percent of the cases of campus violence, 90 percent of hazing deaths, and 59 percent of sexual assaults on college campuses. The bombardment of advertising aimed at college youth by the alcoholic beverage industry undoubtedly aggravates the problem. The college campus newspaper is a regular source of enticing drinking ads.

BOX 7.2: Obsessed with Shape: Men Are the Forgotten in Eating Disorder

DEBORAH CUSHMAN

In Daniel Selby's nightmares, potato chip bags have chased him down the street screaming, "Eat me! Eat me!" In others, he's been trapped in an avalanche of Ho-Ho's.

The 26-year-old Nevada resident is anorexic. At 6 feet 1 inch, he weighs 115 pounds and has trouble maintaining his weight. Once he weighed as little as 102; he couldn't walk.

Shoulder length hair frames a gaunt face and brushes a small wooden cross on a neckchain. His fingers are long and slender, more likely those of a surgeon or violinist than those of someone who used to stick them down his throat regularly. He wears an elaborately fringed denim jacket with ease. But his legs look as though no jeans will hug them. His front teeth are visibly false, the originals ruined from years of acidic vomiting.

On a warm autumn day Selby, who is unemployed as a result of his eating disorder, is wearing layers, one of which is a dark sweater. He says he wears a sweater year-round. Surrounded by books on his illness, he studies his half-finished diet cola and seems to want to shut out the cafe around him.

On the infrequent occasions he eats out, he feels like "a million eyeballs" are watching him. "I've been anorexic for at least thirteen years; I don't think I ever will be cured," he says.

The former fashion model, born Mormon, wants to help men know they can be treated for a disease inappropriately identified as afflicting "women only." The percentage of men suffering from eating disorders is about ten, and likely growing.

Too many men remain undiagnosed. Male cases should be treated differently from women's but remain subject to the same standards, say Iowa eating disorders specialists. The field has suffered atypically in the scientific world, says Psychiatrist Arnold Andersen, director of eating disorders treatment and research at the University of Iowa.

"This is one of the few disorders in which there has been a research prejudice against men," he says, unlike heart disease, recently singled out for lack of research on females. "This is one in which men have suffered from relative neglect and the male role has been trivialized."

References exist from the 1800s, says Andersen, "but from about 1900 to 1950, there was a relative neglect of men because of theories that certain problems are definitely single-sex." By the 1960s, interest was picking up again but still lagged.

Andersen and Diane Alber, an Iowa Methodist Medical Center eating disorders specialist, say research has mostly been done on women because men are a small percentage of the picture.

Physicians often overlook eating disorders symptoms in men, attributing low blood pressure and heart rate, obsession with exercise and a very lean figure as signs of fitness and attention to good health, Alber says.

Men are more reluctant to discuss depression and dissatisfaction with body image than women, and they are more embarrassed by an eating disorders diagnosis and angrily resist treatment, she says.

Selby, a San Francisco-area native, says a doctor told his mother he had anorexia in 1977, but he didn't learn it until 1983. "California and all the emphasis on slimness and body type wasn't good for me," he says.

At one time or another, he has had most of the standard eating disorder symptoms: hoarded food, thrown out groceries bought for the family, binged by downing liquids by the gallon. He has devoured whole cakes and boxes of graham crackers while hidden in the shower, only to throw them all up later and end up taking speed for energy; then he needed "downers" to counteract the speed. His behavior has led to heart and joint trouble and esophageal burns.

Selby, who says he always knew he was gay or at least confused about his sexuality, comes from a troubled background. He says he was sexually abused by his father, an alcoholic and drug abuser.

His parents were married and divorced from one another five times. When he was fifteen he says he had to wrest an eight-inch knife from his father who was trying to stab his alcoholic mother, a part-time club singer. Selby threw his father out of the house.

He has been hospitalized three times, once for several months after attempting suicide when his friend and therapy group mate, singer Karen Carpenter, died.

"It really threw me. . . . We used to meet for lunch and talk. Of course we didn't really eat much."

He has every recording Carpenter made, even those not available for sale in the U.S.

He's compulsive, he says. "I love cleaning and used to get in trouble for cleaning my room after lights-out. Everything in my closet is organized, according to color and size." His 800-some record albums are kept in alphabetical order.

Selby's case seems far more brutal than the more familiar story of anorexia—a middle-class teen-age girl who thinks she needs to be thin to be popular.

Andersen says puberty isn't the same weight trauma to men as it is to women, and neither is perception of obesity. "For example, men tend to feel fat when they are actually fat," he says, "whereas women feel fat when they're normal."

(continued on next page)

BOX 7.2 *(continued)*

Women feel obese at 10 percent above their ideal weight, he says, but men feel fat when they are actually obese, at 20 to 40 percent overweight. Researchers have found that men are preoccupied with shape, while women obsess over weight, says Andersen.

"Men would be happy to stay the same number of pounds if they could redistribute it, while many women don't want the same number of pounds no matter what they look like."

Andersen theorizes that males don't acquire eating disorders the same way women do.

"With guys, the onset of eating disorders tend to be later and at a higher weight and often in the service of a "functional" goal like sports or gender identity, like wanting to be attractive to a homosexual lover," Andersen says. "I've seen very few women with eating disorders dieting to be slim to be attractive to homosexual lovers."

Selby's Ames psychotherapist, Craig Groehn of Central Iowa Mental Health Center, says he's observed more male anorexics than female

---

In contrast to the marketing efforts of beer and liquor companies, alcohol education efforts have been immeasurably enhanced in recent years. The U.S. Department of Education's requirement that colleges and universities set up anti-alcohol programs in order to receive federal funding for education has created a climate increasingly conducive to sobriety. Some college presidents have banned alcohol advertising from the campus newspapers. At the student level, the Interfraternity Council has begun a serious monitoring of all fraternity activities to help lower the traditionally high alcohol consumption rate for this group.

For male adolescents, a correlation between drug use and the use of anabolic steroids is a finding of concern. Steroids hold a special appeal for adolescent males because of their muscle-building and endurance-enhancing effects. The results of an extensive survey are reported by DuRant et al. (1993) in the *New England Journal of Medicine*. Since many of the steroid users share needles, according to this article, HIV transmission becomes a major risk. Other serious side effects are acne and testicle shrinkage caused by the hormonal imbalance associated with this drug.

Youths who are risk-takers are in considerable danger from polydrug complications. Adolescents with antisocial personality disorder, impulsive behavior, and learning disabilities, such as Attention Deficit Hyperactivity Disorder, are at heightened risk of developing alcoholism (Pihl and Peterson, 1991). O'Connell (1991) surveys effective programs and interventions with the high-risk adolescent to prevent further problems from developing. School-based programs help youths who have behavioral and

with "ambivalence connected to gender identity and whether they are going to be sexual beings or not." U of I's Andersen concurs.

"It's not exclusively a gay men's disease, but there's 20 to 25 percent probability that an eating disorders male will have a bisexual or gay orientation. Maybe because that group is more tuned into and dedicated to slimness, body physique and weight loss."

Or, maybe it's simply that gay men are less embarrassed to talk about it, Albers says, theorizing that the disease affects equal numbers of gay and heterosexual men.

Andersen suggests men belong to "male mini cultures" in which thinness is demanded such as those of homosexuals, some athletes (wrestlers and runners, most notably jockeys) and models and media people.

Source: *The Des Moines Register*, Oct. 30, 1991. Copyright 1991 The Des Moines Register and Tribune Company. Reprinted with permission.

learning problems to keep functioning in school. The Yes Program in San Francisco is a community-based prevention effort that provides interesting recreational activities. The goals are to enhance self-mastery and self-esteem in participating youths.

Cognizant of the need for adolescent alcoholics to be treated in facilities geared for teenagers, Royce (1989) stresses that merely applying an adult program to adolescents is ineffective and unethical. A.A. groups, similarly, lack appeal because of the inability of the young to identify with the stories and folk wisdom of older alcoholics. Adolescents, according to Royce, seem to need longer treatment than adults, and they have a higher relapse rate. And because of their inability to resist their peer group, youths find it very hard to break off ties with their former friends.

Adolescent treatment is effective to the degree that the young are linked up to a new peer group with interests other than experimenting with drugs or drinking "until you drop." Adequate treatment planning further involves matching individual clients with medical, psychological, and social problems identified in diagnostic testing and family interviews with appropriate therapies. Above all, work on how to handle feelings (besides drowning them in alcohol) and work on communicating feelings and needs to others should be primary.

ALCOHOLISM IN THE AGED

In contrast to the young alcohol abuser, the elderly drink smaller amounts at one time, use drugs prescribed by doctors—licit as opposed to illicit

TABLE 7.2

National Adolescent Student Health Survey

Adolescents Who Consumed Five or More Drinks Consecutively on at Least One Occasion During the Past 2 Weeks[1]

	8th-Graders	10th-Graders	12th-Graders
Total number of students in sample[2]	1,947	1,842	70,560
Percent of students who drank	23.7	36.6	36.2
Males			
Total in sample	920	945	33,942
Percent who drank	23.5	40.0	45.0
White			
Number in sample	662	673	28,056
Percent who drank	23.4	42.2	48.1
Black			
Number in sample	107	119	3,688
Percent who drank	15.1	26.9	24.0
Hispanic			
Number in sample	78	94	2,198
Percent who drank	35.9	46.8	41.0
Mexican-American			
Number in sample	*	*	1,518
Percent who drank	*	*	45.3
Puerto Rican and Latin American			
Number in sample	*	*	680
Percent who drank	*	*	31.4
Females			
Total in sample	1,016	891	36,618
Percent who drank	23.9	33.0	28.1
White			
Number in sample	744	663	29,808
Percent who drank	24.1	33.3	31.3
Black			
Number in sample	106	118	4,499
Percent who drank	16.8	27.1	9.3
Hispanic			
Number in sample	92	64	2,311
Percent who drank	33.7	39.1	20.8
Mexican-American			
Number in sample	*	*	1,599
Percent who drank	*	*	23.6
Puerto Rican and Latin American			
Number in sample	*	*	712
Percent who drank	*	*	14.5

Source: Windle, *Alcohol Health and Research World*, 15 (1993): 5.
1. Values for 8th-grade and 10-grade students are from the National Adolescent Student Health Survey (NASHS) (American School Health Association et al. 1989). Values for 12th-grade students are from Monitoring the Future studies and include data combined from 1985 to 1989 (Bachman et al. 1991).
2. Numbers in columns may not add up to totals or to 100 percent, as not all data for all subgroups are reported.
* Hispanic subgroups were not assessed separately in the NASHS.

drugs—experience a hidden alcohol problem, and drink in connection with a number of late-life stresses, including bereavement from the loss of family and friends and loss of occupational roles through retirement. Unlike young adults who seek out drugs for recreational use, the elderly may be seeking a therapeutic effect such as relief from pain (Schonfeld, 1993).

A recent government report (U.S. Congress, 1992) provides data on the dimensions of the problem. Estimates indicate that as many as 37 percent of the over-fifty-five population have a severe problem with alcohol or medication. About 60 percent of older people are likely to be daily drinkers. Widowers over the age of seventy-five have the highest rate of alcoholism in the country. Estimates of older persons in hospitals or other health care facilities who evidence illness or other serious consequences of alcohol abuse range up to 70 percent; for all ages the figure is 25 percent. The alcoholism pattern for males is much different from that for females. Up to 88 percent of the total elderly population who receive treatment are male. Solitary drinking is the pattern for older women but not for the men.

Investigators have distinguished two types of elderly alcoholics— the early onset and the late onset. The early-onset alcoholics are those who began to have drinking problems early in life and have carried them into old age. Approximately two-thirds of the elderly alcoholics are of the early-onset variety (Lawson, 1989). In an empirically based comparative study, Schonfeld and Dupree (1991) matched twenty-three early-onset alcoholic abusers admitted for treatment with twenty-three late-onset abusers in treatment. Early-onset subjects were likely to have changed residence, to have been intoxicated more often, and to have experienced more severe levels of depression and anxiety. For both groups, depression, loneliness, and lack of social support were the most frequently reported antecedent to readmission drinking behavior. In contrast to the long-term drinkers, late-onset subjects were more likely to remain in treatment. Their drinking, according to Royce (1989), is *reactive* and springs from the losses of old age. These alcoholics have not experienced the organic damage of the long-term drinking group.

In my experience, the late-onset group has close family ties; initially, they are overcome with the stigma of the alcoholism diagnosis. After a life of sobriety, a tainted self-image in old age is an unexpected blow. An empathetic therapeutic environment is essential.

As the number of elderly persons in the population increases, the number in treatment is going up also. Many treatment programs are targeting older alcoholics through special outreach efforts and by setting up senior support groups. To date, the funding resources for programs geared toward the aged alcoholics have been quite small (U.S. Congress, 1992).

Some inroads are being made to offer counseling services in the community. Blackmon (1985) notes the convenience to the social worker of the development of housing complexes for the elderly. A collaborative network of staff in the housing site and the appropriate community workers enhance the possibility of early intervention.

The elderly enter formal substance abuse treatment when referred by concerned relatives, the family doctor, or a court referral due to a driving offense. Most often these clients join the regular treatment groups; usually they do quite well. The most appreciative and best motivated of clients are often those of advanced age.

Some commentators, such as Chernoff (1991), believe that elderly people need their own programs where they can discuss their special needs. One often-heard objection of older alcoholics is the level of profanity sometimes tolerated in the regular support group. Moreover, the drugs of choice may be alien to seniors in the group, who may disapprove of the polydrug involvement of younger participants in the group. Regardless of the specifics of treatment provided (more research is needed to define which patients do better in age-specific programs and which do better in programs that include all ages), the elderly respond well to treatment, and often thrive in an active, dynamic therapeutic group. In short, alcoholism among the elderly is highly treatable. The challenge for society is to find the resources that make treatment and prevention efforts available.

CONCLUSION

As alcoholism treatment has grown (in the United States and throughout the Western world) to become a viable health-care activity, the kinds of treatment offerings have grown commensurately. The original program, whether a Twelve Step plan as in North America, or a psychological/ religious oriented approach as in Norway, was designed to cater to the white, middle-class male alcoholic in his young to middle years.

Today, there is a realization that the one model does not fit all. There are varieties in treatment needs among males, depending on their personality characteristics and the character of their alcoholism, and there are the special needs of women of childbearing age, of older men and women, and of gays and lesbians. Culturally specific programs are necessary for treatment effectiveness with each racial and ethnic population.

Hiring culturally diverse staff helps ensure the presence of role models for the diversified populations who enter treatment. At least one employee should be fluent in Spanish; a gay client should have access to a gay therapist to work on issues such as sexuality and gay support systems. A woman who was sexually abused in childhood may want to engage in psychotherapy with a woman well trained in dealing with early childhood trauma. Alcoholics in treatment, in short, can benefit by a treatment approach that is flexible, holistic, and individualized to meet the diverse needs of today's treatment population.

REVIEW QUESTIONS

1. How can one justify including men in a chapter on special groups?
2. How would treatment needs vary for the *Type 1* male alcoholic and the *Type 2* male alcoholic?
3. How does early childhood trauma or wartime experience figure into possible alcohol abuse?
4. What are the special needs of men with regard to sex issues?
5. How do the statements by the ex-loggers tie in with men's concern with pressures from society on men?
6. What are the physiological differences between males and females in regard to alcoholism?
7. Discuss the findings of studies of female twins and alcoholism.
8. Discuss FAS and prevention efforts for both males and females.
9. Discuss the scientific research findings on early childhood sexual abuse and how this may lead to alcohol abuse.
10. Is the stigma of alcoholism different for women than for men? Explain.
11. Analyze the content of the Twelve Step Program in terms of feminist objections.
12. How is alcohol abuse a major health problem for Native Americans?
13. Recount the history of American Indians' experience with alcohol.
14. Describe Alkalai Lake Village.
15. What are the facts of African American alcohol abuse?
16. What was the slave experience with drinking? Is there a carryover today?
17. Describe the deliberate targeting of blacks by the liquor industry.
18. Discuss the culture-specific treatment program and how such a program can be successful.
19. What is the Latin American drinking pattern? Contrast Cuban American and Mexican American drinking customs.

20. What are some treatment considerations in working with Hispanic alcoholics?

21. Explain the high alcoholism rate among gays and lesbians. Define and discuss homophobia. What does Pride Institute offer?

22. Which youths are at high risk for alcoholism? What are their *treatment* needs?

23. What are the two types of elderly alcoholics? What is the prognosis for treatment of older alcoholics?

8

ALCOHOLISM AND THE FAMILY SYSTEM

Maybe we are both father. . . . Maybe happen is never once but
like ripples maybe on water after the pebble sinks, the ripples
moving on, spreading, the pool attached by a narrow umbilical
water-cord to the next pool which the first pool feeds . . . let this
second pool contain a different molecularity of having seen, felt,
remembered, reflected in a different tone the infinite unchanging
sky, it doesn't matter: that pebble's watery echo whose fall it did
not even see moves across its surface too at the original
ripple-space to the old ineradicable rhythm.
—William Faulkner, *Absalom, Absalom!*, p. 261

The family has a pattern, a rhythm that is more than the sum of
its parts. From generation to generation, the rhythm persists. So the culture
of addiction—the urges, the emotions, the escape—are echoed down the
line.

The Greek philosopher Aristotle recognized the alcoholism link between generations as did Plutarch. Yet, only in recent years has the family
role in addiction and recovery been recognized. The ecological approach
looks at the family members as an interactive whole that is greater than
the sum of the individual parts. Because of the emphasis on both human
ecology and family systems, the term *ecosystems model* is sometimes used.
This is the predominant framework of social work today.

This chapter will examine the alcoholic family (or family in which
one or more members are alcoholics) from an ecological or ecosystems

197

perspective. Just as the biopsychosocial approach can provide an understanding of the alcoholic, the dynamics of the alcoholic family system can also be understood in terms of biology, psychology, and social analysis. What addiction does to family rules, roles, and communication patterns will be considered. The starting point is a historical overview of the literature and theoretical paradigms.

Because of the stigma of alcoholism, the family therapy field has devoted little effort to developing techniques to deal with the problems of families that have problems with alcoholism (Kaufman and Pattison, 1981). While alcoholism treatment centers give little more than lip service to family treatment, inpatient centers often are located too far away from a client's home to offer intensive family therapy.

CLASSIC FAMILY SYSTEMS THERAPY

The leading proponents of family systems theory have tended to focus almost exclusively on interpersonal transactions (Johnson, 1986). From the *classic systems perspective*, a disorder such as mental illness, anorexia, or alcoholism is viewed as stemming from faulty family communication or functioning. The systems therapist in this tradition accordingly does not do individual therapy, that is, try to fix "the identified patient." Rather, the patient is viewed only within the context of the family where the symptoms or problems presumably evolved (Becvar and Becvar, 1982; Hanson, 1994). Relationships and communication are stressed. The fact that the designated sick person in the family could truly be sick and be the source of the family's stress and malfunctioning is not recognized. Thus, Minuchin (1974) and Nichols (1984) placed the source of anorexia in the tension within the family. Ellis-Ordway (1992) more recently adopted this perspective in her article "The Impact of Family Dynamics on Anorexia." Satir worked with Bateson on the role of family interaction in the "development of mental illness in a family member" (Chase-Marshall, 1976). Similarly, alcoholism was conceptualized by Bowen (1978) as a symptom of a problem in the larger family or social unit. Alcoholism was not viewed as the problem but as the *solution* to the problem. Family therapy divorced from alcoholism treatment was the answer.

Kaufman and Pattison (1981: 952) articulate the traditional family therapy premise:

> The use of alcohol is purposeful, adaptive, homeostatic, and meaningful. The problem of alcoholism is not just the consequences of drinking, per se, but more important, the system functions that drinking fills in the psychodynamics of the family system.

The drug addict, likewise, is seen as the symptom carrier of the family dysfunction. The addict, in his or her aberrant behavior, helps maintain the familial balance (Kaufman and Kaufman, 1992). For all these systems thinkers, the key to changing the drinking behavior lies in working on weak points in the relationships among family members. Then, as the addiction loses significance in maintaining equilibrium in the family, it presumably will become unnecessary.

The correctness or effectiveness of this theoretical orientation is not grounded in research. In fact, there is some evidence of harm done through this orientation. Medical needs may be overlooked; needed intervention may not be offered; and the family-blaming aspect can arouse feelings of guilt and anger in family members (Johnson, 1986). In an extensive ethnographic study of the families of the mentally ill, Jim Hanson (1994) records the utter frustration of family members whose contributions were continuously devalued by family therapists.

Fortunately, this variety of family systems theory, which views the family as the source of pathology, has not been adopted by the alcoholism treatment enterprise. In fact, with the disease model firmly entrenched and the focus on the *individual* alcoholic, the wonder is that the family is incorporated into treatment programming at all. That the family needs do get addressed is probably a reflection of the increasingly interdisciplinary nature of the chemically dependent treatment field. Practitioners schooled in family counseling techniques have brought to addictions work a modified and highly useful understanding of family pain and dynamics. Hiring large numbers of counselors from alcoholic family backgrounds further ensures a sensitivity to family needs and concerns. In short, a gradual paradigmatic shift in thought from family-as-enemy to family-as-potential-treatment-ally has occurred. Work with the whole family is now recognized, at least theoretically, as a vital component in alcoholism treatment.

According to the cliché in social work, "There is nothing so practical as good theory." By the same token, one could argue that there is nothing so impractical as bad theory. Understanding of the biological and psychological dimensions of addiction has contributed to the demise of some of the extreme family systems rhetoric from the past and the emergence of the new family treatment models. Some specific modalities for everyday treatment demands will be presented later in the chapter.

ENCOURAGING RECENT DEVELOPMENTS

Sharon Wegscheider's (1981) ground-breaking writings and films on "the family trap" marked a departure from the earlier atomistic and individualistic approaches of alcoholism specialists. In her depiction of typical roles

BOX 8.1: Creativity: Working the Medium

When my father was in his early twenties, completely untrained in voice and self-taught in music, he walked into an open audition at the New York Opera company and was accepted into the chorus. But he turned the job down. I had just been born, he was holding a strenuous fulltime day job, and getting to the evening rehearsals downtown by subway would have been just too much.

I first heard this story when I was about seven, and I was not only impressed, but surprised. He certainly enjoyed music, but he was never one to burst into song, especially songs in languages you couldn't understand. But I never doubted his creativity. As a teenager, he designed, built, and flew model airplanes. He expanded our house by several rooms, even building fireplaces and chimneys. One Christmas, he painted choir boys, candles, and Santa in his sleigh on our living room window. He bailed me out of a science fair panic by designing and helping me build a plaster model of a cross-section of Earth, complete with oil rigs.

The time I remember best was a winter day after a heavy snowfall. He and I had just rolled up a jumbo, three-ball snowman on the front lawn, and I was scouting about the backyard for sticks that could become arms. When I finally returned with branches torn off a holly bush, I found the snowman in the process of metamorphosis. With karate chops, my father lopped off the round edges. Snow from the midsection became the stuff of muscular arms and legs. Eyes and eyebrows, a nose and lips were gouged and carved into the no-longer-basketball-shaped head. When my father finally stood back to admire his work, the snowman was gone; in its place stood a sculptured, seven-foot man of snow. Throughout the day, we looked out from the livingroom window and watched the warm sun work its own transformation. By late afternoon, the shoulders drooped, and the head, resting upon a slushy neck, tilted back so that its eyes met our own.

Through his example, my father convinced me that everybody has talent and that the task is to find your medium and work with it. My father usually chose media that he could hold and move with his hands—wood, snow, paint. Early on, I realized that my medium was different; for me, words, especially written language, were my best form of self-expression. This difference created some distance between us. Despite my father's best efforts to entice me into his building projects, I quickly became bored and wandered off to my bedroom to read. While my poems were regularly printed in the school literary magazine, my father felt embarrassed by the awkward, clunky-sounding letters he occasionally wrote to his family and friends.

Although our creative media were different, it is from my father that I learned about creativity as more process than product, filled as much with mistakes and pragmatism as inspiration. Watching him, I saw that creativity is effort: doing, pushing, experimenting, trying. Only by working his chosen media did he find their limits; only by trying to express his vision—however trivial, simple, or extraordinary—did he ever fully see it.

It is from my father that I also learned the difference between giving up and letting go. Giving up does not always mean defeat: it is the process of choosing, of weighing commitment, of determining how well something fits one's vision, cutting the cord to that commitment and vision if necessary. Perhaps because he also intuitively realized that other media were better suited to him, he gave up the opera to use his time elsewhere.

Letting go is something else. Rather than moving away from commitment, letting go during the creative process allows one to hold on. Watching my father, I learned that letting go can be deeper, more risky, and more magical than the quiet, tucked-away image suggested by the notion of incubation.

When my father became stuck with a problem in the middle of a project, when all his tinkering and trying, prodding, pounding, and pushing left him only more frustrated and exhausted, he would put down his tools, go into the kitchen, and make spaghetti sauce. Like a diligent parent nursing a sick child, he would from time to time drift back into the room where the tools and project lay and stand for a few moments as if checking to see if anything had changed. Usually, it hadn't, and he would go back to stirring the sauce. He knew that during some point in the process of watchful neglect, a solution would, on its own, come into his head. My father's trust in himself taught me to trust myself; seeing the creative process work for and within him made me confident that it could be the same for me. As with most questions of faith, having the firm belief that something will happen is often enough to find that it does.

A couple comes to my office. After nine years of marriage, they are blunted by the rub of their everyday lives; the vision that they once shared has become cloudy, maybe lost. They sit on opposite ends of the couch; I sit facing them both.

The wife speaks, and words flow effortlessly, spilling over both me and her husband. Her medium is language. Her husband, a furniture maker, has large muscular hands like my father, he looks stiff and awkward in what he probably senses is his wife's space. Unable to move about, he leans on his silence.

I am there to help them work their mediums. Like the conductor of an operatic orchestra, I am down in the pit, ready to signal an

(continued on next page)

BOX 8.1 *(continued)*

entrance, ready to augment and support their own voices so that their drama can go forward; like a stage manager, I stand ready to hand them whatever props they may need. I am less concerned with their marriage and more concerned with how they can express their visions.

The wife begins again. Although she sounds more frightened than angry, it is mostly about the anger that she speaks. Arguments over nothing, arguments over everything, arguments that are not really arguments but battles between words and silence. She describes their last vacation together: What she remembers most is how depressed she felt by the seemingly endless expanse of dry prairie.

Like a painter overworking the same square of canvas, the color of her words soon becomes muddy, the outlines blurred. I look for untouched white spaces of emotions and ask her about her past so she can begin from a different perspective. Most of all, I focus on her words, and I push to have her consolidate the shower of chatter into something more solid. I feign misunderstanding, hoping to drive her into forging new images.

Impasse. Her husband's silence stretches out, filling the room, keeping her words suspended in mid-air. I ask him to speak, and it is immediately clear just how difficult this is. As his words slowly

---

that members of the chemically dependent's family play, Wegscheider (now Wegscheider-Cruse) conceptualizes alcoholism in terms of both its physical and social dimensions. Her approach is highly practical in its implications.

Popular author and public speaker Claudia Black was influenced by the writings of fellow social worker and systems theorist Virginia Satir. Black's thought-provoking book *It Will Never Happen to Me!* (1981) applies some of the fundamentals of systems theory concepts to family alcoholism treatment. Dulfano, in her less widely known *Families, Alcoholism, and Recovery* (1982), offers a brief but dynamic ecological interpretation of the alcoholism syndrome. Edited by social workers Daley and Rasken (1991), *Treating the Chemically Dependent and Their Families* is a practical guide to various aspects of addictions work. Helpful information on family intervention with an addicted family member is included. A broad-based social work perspective is offered by Metzger's *From Denial to Recovery* (1988). This book summarizes the writings of popular authors and includes a step-by-step guide to counseling children of alcoholics. Several other academic offerings are indicative of the family focus which is a part of standard social work practice. Using a stage format, Starr (1989) presents a tripartite model of recovery for families affected

cut into his silence, his hands move, carving, patting, squeezing, cupping pieces of air, sculpting the images his words cannot.

Words are not his medium. I hand him a pad of paper and black marker, and ask him to draw, rather than say, what he feels. He looks surprised, then uncomfortable, and shifts from side to side, finally retreating once again into silence.

After much hesitation and encouragement, he finally draws lines. He holds up a stark drawing of two figures looking out from different windows at the same street below, His wife begins to cry.

Exhaustion replaces anger in the room. It is not time to give up, I tell them, but it is time to let go, to give up old images of themselves and of the relationship, to make way for new visions.

Something new has been set in motion, but I'm not sure yet that their fear and impatience won't overrun this fragile connection. I must give up any visions with which I am tempted to fill the void they now sense. I, too, must let go.

Source: R. Taibbi, "Creativity: Working the Medium," *The Family Therapy Networker,* Sept./Oct. 1992, 42–43. Reprinted with permission of *The Family Therapy Networker.*

by alcoholism. Alcoholism is perceived as an integral part of the family dynamics. Flanzer and Delancy (1992) present a family case study of work with a multiple-member addicted family. Specific interventions are detailed.

AL-ANON AND ALLIED GROUPS

The influence of Al-Anon cannot be underestimated. Founded in the 1950s to serve the families of A.A. members, Al-Anon groups today meet in over seventy countries. Al-Anon meetings are found, as well, in virtually every North American community large enough to have several bars and half a dozen A.A. meetings. Throughout the years, membership has stayed unwaveringly at 88 percent female (Robertson, 1988). Through growing meetings and widely distributed pamphlets, Al-Anon has spread the message that family members are powerless over the alcoholic's addiction. Al-Anon members learn, through supportive and shared interchange, that they can achieve serenity, a serenity that is independent of whether or not the drinker recovers from alcoholism. Royce (1989) sums up Al-Anon's purpose as threefold: to offer comfort, hope, and friendship to the families of compulsive drinkers; to teach members to grow spiritually by living the Twelve Steps; and to give understanding and encouragement to the alcoholic in his or her recovery.

The Twelve Steps used by Al-Anon are modified slightly to pertain to persons who are powerless not over alcohol but over another's use of alcohol. Individual work is directed toward independence and self-awareness. Learning that attempts to shield the alcoholic from the consequences of his or her addiction are futile and counterproductive helps free the family members from the emotionally wearing attempt to control what cannot be controlled. Members are aided in achieving detachment from the active alcoholic. Al-Anon members rave about the close psychological bonds that develop from membership in this group. Recognition of one's powerlessness over another's addiction goes a long way toward reducing one's guilt feelings.

One of the most significant referrals the alcoholism counselor can make to family members of alcoholics is to a local Al-Anon group. They should be prepared for a kind of ritualistic openness and friendliness that may at first seem intrusive; they should be encouraged to visit several different meetings before making a decision on whether or not to join.

Alateen is the organization for children of alcoholic parents. Children are helped to achieve understanding of alcoholism and awareness of a severe family problem. *Nar-Anon* is the comparable group for family members of narcotics users. Adult Children of Alcoholics (ACOA) is a rapidly growing group for those who grew up in alcoholic homes and who may have many unresolved feelings and issues pertaining to their family life. Members are encouraged to give full vent to their repressed feelings. As emotions may be intense, newly sober alcoholics may be advised to achieve a lengthy sobriety first before joining such an endeavor.

THE ECOLOGICAL FRAMEWORK AND THE FAMILY WITH ALCOHOLISM

Recall the key concepts of the ecological approach introduced in chapter 1. The starting point is the idea that the whole consists of a pattern which has emerged out of the synchronized activities of the individual components. The system, which is stationary, is composed of parts in simultaneous and mutual interaction. Relating this framework to the family, we can see that the family members compose a system. Their way of doing things is the pattern. Members of the system perform *roles*; roles are *reciprocal* and depend on *feedback* from other roles to give them form and purpose. The system adapts to internal or external *stresses*, such as the loss of an individual member. Or, in failing to adapt, the system experiences *entropy* or breakdown.

The family affected by alcoholism in one or more of its members is a family in stress. As the addiction progresses, the alcoholic's need for the alcohol takes precedence over all other concerns. As the addicted person learns to adapt his or her life-style to accommodate to the tremendous demands of this illness, so the family unit adapts to the stress that has been imposed upon its functioning. As various individuals come forward to fill the essential family *roles*, the integrity of the family is preserved; equilibrium is maintained but at the expense of one or more of the individual members. If the alcoholic later recovers, the operating family system will be "thrown out of whack," a crisis will occur, and individual and group adaptation will be required.

In summary, according to ecological theory, the individual alcoholic is not viewed in isolation but as someone in dynamic interaction with the environment. Attention is paid to the complex ways in which individual persons in the roles that they perform are linked with each other.

THE FUNCTIONAL FAMILY

An estimated 28 million children are growing up today in alcoholic homes. Some will develop special strengths of survival; others will get caught up in the web of alcoholism. The strongest predictor of alcoholism, in fact, is a family history of alcoholism (Goodwin, 1979). In order to study the extreme pressures put upon a family affected by chronic illness such as alcoholism, let us first consider what is meant by the *functional* family.

The following list of characteristics are provided by family members in treatment and college students in alcoholism treatment courses. The so-called functional family is generally considered to be characterized by:

- Open communication
- Respect for individual differences
- Love for children as they are, rather than for what they can do
- Having fun and doing things together
- Stable routines and rituals

Let us imagine a family with such characteristics and inflict one of the members with alcoholic binges and/or some other addiction and examine what happens to the system.

Open Communication

Claudia Black has singled out three rules for the alcoholic family: don't talk, don't trust, don't feel. The *don't talk* rule is enforced as the children tell their friends and their grandparents. They are scolded severely and given a mixed message, such as: "We don't have a problem, and don't tell anybody either!" As children try to *express their feelings*—"I'm afraid of Daddy when he's drunk"—they are told they do not feel this way and

205

to quit sniveling. They are told there is no reason to be afraid, just stay out of Daddy's way. Gradually, over time, because children are told they don't see what they see, their *trust* is broken.

Respect for Individual Differences
When alcohol moves into the family, the system tightens as members come to play more rigidly defined roles. The alcoholic member regresses into childlike behavior, and one of the children may become a miniature parent. Coalitions occur between family members; boundary lines can become obscured. Ultimately, respect for individuality gives way to pressure for conformity and closeness.

Love for Children as They Are
This is another quality that goes out the window when the alcohol comes in the door. To compensate for the disturbance within the family unit, high achievement by offspring may be stressed to the exclusion of unconditional love.

Having Fun Times Together
This is impossible when the worry is constant that one family member will get drunk. The sober parent becomes increasingly anxious and frustrated. Family outings are destroyed with bickering and humiliations.

Stable Routines and Rituals
Plans and traditions are interrupted by the compulsion of drink. In the alcoholic household, the only thing that is consistent is inconsistency. Where there once was trust, now there is doubt. The taken-for-grantedness of the healthy family is no more.

THE DYSFUNCTIONAL FAMILY

With the introduction of hard and relentless drinking into the picture, the functional family becomes dysfunctional. As Tolstoy once wrote, "All happy families are alike, but every unhappy family is unhappy in its own way" (*Anna Karenina*, 1876). Often it is helpful to draw the structure of the relationship patterns in the alcoholic family.

The alcoholic family is isolated from the outer world by shame. Excuses are made to cover up for the ailing member. There is isolation from feelings, too, as members avoid talking about or identifying the problem.

STAGES OF PROGRESSION INTO ILLNESS

The family's stages of progression into the illness of alcoholism was first noted by Jackson (1954). Jackson delineates seven stages, from denial

FIGURE 8.1

Family Forms

A. The enmeshed family: Spouses are estranged; one child is enmeshed with the father, one with the mother.

B. The isolated family: Lack of cohesion and social support. Each member is protected by wall of defenses.

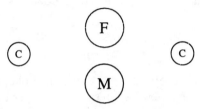

C. The healthy family: All are touching, but their boundaries not overlapping.

Key: F = father, M = mother, C = child

---

and isolation through disorganization to reorganization, with or without the alcoholic. In dealing with family groups, I have found Kübler-Ross's (1969) scheme for adjustment to the reality of terminal illness to be especially meaningful to the afflicted family members. The five stages of adjustment are denial, anger, bargaining, depression, and acceptance. Each stage represents an emotional response to pain and to the acknowledgment of pain.

DENIAL

The fact that one of the family members has developed drinking problems is a huge shock to the family unit. The implications are too threatening to face. The facts are denied; feelings are denied. Embarrassing public episodes are often followed by explanations and vows of "never again." The long sober intervals provide grounds for minimizing the problem and denying the pain: "My wife is *not* an alcoholic; she goes to work every day and is a good wife and mother."

Downs (1982) takes a crisis approach to the onset of alcoholism in the family. Early stages are marked by an inconsistency that throws family interactions out of balance. The amount of stress is heightened by the constant change of state from sober to drunk and back again. Ultimately, the sober partner's behavior comes to vary with the level of intoxication of the drinking partner; role confusion results.

Denial is a normal response to an abnormal or painful situation. When one is psychologically prepared to face the facts or when the evidence is too overwhelming to be denied, the denial stage will give way to anger.

ANGER

Now *feelings* emerge. There is anger at the alcoholic, anger at the self. "Why did I marry such a man? Didn't I say I'd never do like my mother and marry an alcoholic?" If the alcoholic is belligerent when drunk and touchy when sober, the anger of the family member is internalized. The children may experience the alcoholic's anger directly themselves or indirectly through the sober parent, who displaces anger onto them.

The family becomes socially isolated; invitations to the homes of friends become less frequent (Royce, 1989). Viewed as interfering, friends and relatives are effectively excluded from the family circle. Now the nuclear family must draw on its own resources, resources that are increasingly weakening under the strain of isolation and resentment. With one partner now "married to the booze," the other partner feels that all love is dissolved in a glass of alcohol. Reacting to the tension in the family, the children are prone to whining, crying, and acting-out behavior. Their constant disappointment at the string of broken promises is internalized as anger.

BARGAINING

A human response to a near-impossible situation is to try to negotiate a way out of it. In the Kübler-Ross configuration, this stage is when the dying person bargains with God for more time, for life itself. In the alcoholic's family, bargaining occurs as frantic attempts are made by the family to get the alcoholic to stop drinking. Visits to religious revivals and treatment centers may be made. "Choose us or choose the bottle" is the typical ultimatum.

For parents of the addicted teenager, bargaining takes on a truly pathetic character. "If you stop using drugs, we will get you that motorcycle you want." Such bargaining almost never works. The teenager gets a motorcycle and uses it to transport drugs. The son gets a car and wrecks it. The alcoholic may stop drinking for awhile. But hope is dispelled when the new sobriety is put to the test in an inevitable tempting situation. The children of alcoholics, of course, suffer also. The astute teacher will be alert to such difficulties. The author of *A True Story of a Drunken Mother* recounts what the school day was like for her children:

> The three older children were ready to go back to school. They said goodbye and I could see in their eyes they didn't expect very much from me. Every day they sat in the classroom, worrying about me and the younger children, and trying to pay attention to the teacher. Would I forget to feed the baby? Would I watch David and Susan? Or would I possibly get drunk and set the house on fire? (Hall, 1990:118–19. Reprinted with permission of South End Press)

The shifting of roles among family members to adapt to the under-functioning partner or parent increases markedly over time (Downs, 1982). Secondary stresses, including loss of income, violence, and sexual abuse, may become apparent. Hope persists, at least sporadically, that the drinking will stop. The solution is so obvious; even the youngest child can see it. Royce (1989: 145) depicts the scene of the typical alcoholic family:

> All behavior becomes oriented around the drinking, and the thought of family members becomes obsessive on this subject. As no action seems to be successful in achieving its goal, the wife persists in trial-and-error behavior with mounting frustration.

The more the sober wife nags and worries, according to Royce, the more the children turn their affection to the childlike and needy drunken father. I have heard divorced fathers in treatment both in Norway and the United States express wonderment that the children chose to live with them rather than with the mothers. I have heard the older children respond, "But *he* needed me, she didn't."

For a compellingly real expression of anger by a once-loving wife, read the poem in Box 8.2. This poem was translated from Swedish (Tikkanen, 1984).

DEPRESSION

There comes a time when hope gives way to despair. The atmosphere brought about by continuous and consistent drinking may be one of stunted emotions. Children may evidence a "lack of affect." This is an adjustment of sorts; equilibrium in the family may be restored. Other members now "pick up the slack" from the one who is "there, but not there."

BOX 8.2: The Alcoholic Family

How's Dad?
No smell of brandy
around?
Are you really sure he won't drink
tonight?

While you're crying yourself to sleep
because you feel sorry for yourself
who had a father who was
an alcoholic

I sit wondering when
my hatred
will burn you
to white ashes

while you're lying there, sobbing
without thinking for one second
that your kids, too, have
a father

At one time
I was hiding bottles
and quickly emptying
dregs
into flower pots and ashtrays
and through the window
as soon as you turned your back

Sexual problems between partners abound. Drunken sexual advances may not be remembered by the alcoholic the next day. The sober partner may be too disgusted to want to remember. The marriage is dead. Much of the family life is dead also. Hall (1990: 44) recalls the following exchange:

"No, I'm not going to buy you a martini," Joe calmly said.
"Why?"
"I've wanted to tell you something for a long time and I hope it doesn't hurt your feelings. Nancy, I love you very much and I'd like to marry you some day when the war is over, but you're in trouble with your drinking."
"Oh, Joe, do you mean that? We'll have to have a drink to celebrate!"
"I don't think you heard me, Nancy. From now on you'll have to buy your own drinks. I can't stop you."
"Everybody drinks, Joe. I don't drink more than anyone else."
"You were just sick. Do you know what was wrong?"

Nowadays I don't give a damn
The quicker you pour the stuff into yourself
the sooner you'll pass out
and the sooner I'll be able to continue with
the things I'd rather be doing
than sitting and listening to your monologues

Besides, it isn't necessary
to wait long anymore
since you get drunk
on just a few drops
and vomit right away
and pass out

Practical
One saves both time
and money

Earlier
you were nasty and sardonic
only when you drank

Nowadays you are
even nastier and more sardonic
when you are sober

Source: *Århundradets Kärlessaga (Love Story of the Century)*, by Märta Tikkanen. Reprinted by permission of Bokförlaget Trevi, Stockholm, Sweden.

"Yes. I had the flu."

"I talked to the doctor. You had alcoholic paralysis."

"That's nonsense. I don't drink that much, and besides I can stop anytime I want to."

"Okay. Then you don't have to drink tonight, do you?"

"No. No, I don't."

The rest of the evening was difficult because I had nothing to falsify my inadequate feelings. I was in a position where Joe made all the decisions. He drove to his apartment, turned on soft music, and took me in his arms again, tenderly. He asked me if I wanted to sleep with him, and I was afraid and full of old guilts. It had been years since I had had sex without any alcohol first. I wanted to, but I didn't even know how without a drink. Oh God, this was all wrong. Something was all wrong.

Reprinted with permission of South End Press.

Downs (1982) includes this stage in the category *reorganization.* The drinking partner, in this scenario, is defined out of the parental and marital roles. There will be mental or physical separation. Family members are racked with guilt and anguish over "giving up" on an apparently helpless and sick person. The stigma from the outer world echoes the shame felt by the now tainted and isolated family. Although the alcoholism may be recognized, it is not discussed.

ACCEPTANCE

During the acceptance stage of terminal illness, according to Kübler-Ross, a kind of calmness comes over the person. The ill person and the patient's family accept his or her forthcoming death. The hysteria is over. Tikkanen (1984: 47) articulates the universal reality:

> I live my life
> and the kids live theirs
> yes, you're bothering us
> the hours you're awake
> stumbling around
> nagging
> but you don't concern us
> you are no longer
> part of our lives.

In the alcoholic family, the members may decide to break up and function without the alcoholic. Or, thanks to the crisis and perhaps intervention by professionals and/or A.A., the alcoholic may have come to accept the need to quit drinking. In rare cases, the addictive drinking may be replaced by moderate drinking (Fingarette, 1988). Because I know of several cases personally, I am including the very real (if unsettling) possibility that some alcoholics may learn to drink moderately.

Family members come to recognize their powerlessness over another's illness and that life must go on. Family members can sleep and eat at this stage. As time passes, they may look back. In the following poem, the son of an alcoholic father speaks to his late father (Upshaw, 1993).

> The days are short and easy to fill.
> My life, once a dream, now is real.
> I'm glad that part of my life is over.
> It was not fun.
> My life started when yours was done.

Acceptance of the past comes as clients learn to change the things they can change (the present) and accept the things they cannot change (such as the past). Through treatment, they may come to a therapeutic understanding of the things that were and reconcile themselves to the reality of these truths—for example, "My father was from the old school. He never knew how to express his love for me. He never hugged me. He tried to mold me into the tough fighter that he never was. I realize he did love me. With my son, I can express the love that my father felt for me."

The stage of acceptance for the alcoholic family can be summed up as "peace at last." Social support from a self-help group such as Al-Anon is tremendously helpful in getting family members to realize that the problem is in the situation and not in themselves. Being able to talk about "the problem" and give it a name—"alcoholism"—helps restore sanity to the family. The acceptance by family members of the alcoholism—may parallel the acceptance by the alcoholic, following treatment, of the fact that he or she is an alcoholic.

Because the family is a system, alcoholism treatment presents a new crisis. Concomitant with the hope of recovery is the risk of pain if the promises are not fulfilled. Even in the event of recovery, the mistrust that has built up for years cannot be dissipated overnight (Royce, 1989). Family members must be warned by counselors that sobriety will not be easy. The title of a well-known book on psychotherapy with a troubled girl, *I Never Promised You a Rose Garden*, offers an apt description of the rough road ahead. According to systems theory, the equilibrium of the family is broken once again through the storm and stress of recovery.

FAMILY ROLES

According to the systems formulation, a social system is composed of roles. Roles that individual family members play are interactive and reciprocal with other roles in the family. Clearly linked to the ongoing maintenance and functioning of the family system, roles include caretaker, explorer, jester, and family historian (Hartman and Laird, 1983).

In all families, individual members play roles. In a dysfunctional family system, in conjunction with the rigidity of the structure, members tend to get stuck in these behaviors. The roles described in this section are mere generalizations, abstractions that are oversimplified for the sake of presentation. While, for purposes of illustration, the assumption is made that the roles are mutually exclusive, family members may play various combinations of roles or different roles during different stages of life.

The labels used here are taken from Wegscheider's (1981) characterizations. In her depictions of family roles, Wegscheider was influenced by Virginia Satir. The following presentation of the roles is based on one that I gave in Family Week presentation. To include all members of the family, I would start with the chemically dependent person. Three illustrations are provided; these are copies of actual drawings made by children of Norway who lived the roles depicted. Interestingly, there was no representation of "the lost child."

The Chemically Dependent Person. This member of the family is gripped by contradictions. Sensitive to the point of touchiness, the chemically dependent person is selfishly preoccupied with the sources of addiction. Often charming and talented, this family member tends to see life events and personalities in terms of black and white, all or nothing. There is a tendency to escape the scene when very high expectations (of relationships, work, studies) are not realized. When a man occupies this role, he is often treated with great fondness by his children. The woman alcoholic/addict is inclined to be either divorced or married to a fellow alcoholic/addict. She is subject to strong criticism of her neglect of motherhood responsibilities.

The Family Manager. Because Wegscheider's term "chief enabler" has acquired pejorative connotations in disregard of the survivorship nature of this role, I prefer the term *family manager.* The individual who occupies this position is often a sober partner of an alcoholic/addict. The role that the family manager assumes is to overfunction to compensate for the partner's underfunctioning. As the family sinks along with the alcoholic/addict into near ruin, this individual worries and nags and struggles to balance the checkbook. His or her denial in the early stages of the partner's addiction may be replaced by a frantic and bitter awareness later on. The person who occupies this position in the family structure suffers from a bad press that relates to the games he or she often ends up playing in conjunction with the games of the alcoholic. Counselors at treatment centers are quick to condemn the sober partner for some of the covering-up devices that make survival as a family possible. If not accorded a great deal of sensitivity, family managers are often plagued by feelings of shame and guilt.

The Hero. Often the firstborn child in the family, this high achieving and very competent individual is constantly seeking approval. The family labels this child as the star—scholar, football hero, or performer. Inclined to suffer from low self-esteem, the child in this position tends to feel loved for what he or she *does* rather than who he or she *is*. Accustomed to babysitting and caring for younger siblings, this child often grows up to work in the helping professions. Perfectionism is a key risk, as is marrying an alcoholic; such a marriage preserves the caretaking role from the family of origin.

A thirteen-year-old Norwegian girl, who drew herself fastidiously (see figure 8.2), was a child in the hero role. The caption over her head reads "I am a wonderful girl," and the one on her chest reads "everybody loves me." In the original drawing, there were six erasures (indicative of perfectionism), while the colors were very neatly within the lines. There

FIGURE 8.2

The Hero

is a strained quality about the expression on the child's face. When I discovered this self-portrait hanging on the Family Room wall, I was immediately struck by its solemnity and constraint. This drawing seemed to be a clear personification of the hero role. Later, therapists who knew the child confirmed my classification. Their role with the girl's family consisted of trying to get all the family members "to loosen up," to relax and learn to have fun. The child was encouraged not to keep trying so hard to be perfect. Everybody does not have to love her, she was told.

FIGURE 8.3

The Scapegoat

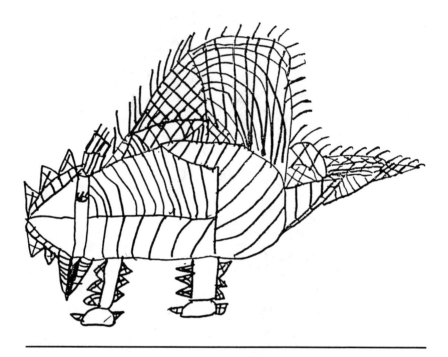

The Scapegoat. This is the child, often the second-born, whom ev-eryone loves to blame. The negative label is applied and seems to stick. The irresponsible behavior that accompanies this role often lands the perpetrator in trouble. Early pregnancy is a risk for girls and delinquency for boys. School performance is poor. Drug use and alcoholism are com-mon. A ten-year-old boy, Alf, drew the remarkable self-portrait in figure 8.3. Tough on the outside and soft on the inside, this child had constructed a heavy coat of armor around his feelings. In family therapy, his family was encouraged to tell him that *he* was not the cause of the family problems; alcoholism was. He was helped to express his feelings and to develop hobbies so as to express himself in a more positive fashion. Of all the pictures on the wall, this was my clear favorite.

The Lost Child. This child lives in a fantasy world and is said to be little or no trouble. Although he or she may be lonely, this younger child can entertain him- or herself through endless playing with dolls or television or computer games. When family members fight, the lost child has an excellent escape mechanism. In order to grow into a responsible, mature adult, the boy or girl in this role requires a tremendous amount of help with self-expression and facing problems realistically.

The Mascot. Forever clowning, the occupier of this role helps provide comic relief for the family unit. Encouraged to be cute and to kid around, the mascot can attract much positive attention while distracting members from serious matters. Often hyperactive, this child has a short attention span, which may be linked in some way to the needs of the family. The means of escape is through laughter. Figure 8.4 was drawn

FIGURE 8.4

The Mascot

by a little girl who always wore a grin. The inside faces, however, have varied expressions. In family therapy, her parents were helped to allow this child to express feelings long suppressed. When the parents continued to insist that this child smile, this fact was brought to their attention.

In all of these ideal-typical categories, there is a discrepancy between outward expression and behavior and the deep feelings within. The designated roles can be regarded as effective defense mechanisms in a sick environment. Flexibility in role playing is a helpful recovery goal: the caretaker can be cared for; the scapegoat can be praised; the lost child can demand recognition; and finally, the clown can show anger.

Families who participate in family programs respond well to the role descriptions. Members are often forthcoming about which roles they assumed in their families of origin and which ones their children assume now. Exercises pertinent to the role classifications are found at the end of this chapter.

THE CO-ALCOHOLIC PARTNER AND "CODEPENDENCY"

The partner of the alcoholic or other drug abuser receives a bad press. Usually the partner who remains in a long-suffering relationship is a woman. The wife-mother in the play *Long Day's Journey into Night* speaks for many women who have loved an alcoholic. See Box 8.3 for Mary's chilling reminiscence.

Whereas early systems models blamed wives for their husbands' alcoholism, the most recent theoretical frameworks are more cautious in their formulations. The emphasis in family therapy, according to Simon, McNeil, Franklin, and Cooperman (1991), has shifted away from blaming the family for the *etiology* of the disease to blaming the family for the *perpetuation* of the disease. *Codependent* and *enabler* are labels that were once neutral or even positive but that now have acquired derogatory meanings. These terms as used today suggest complicity. Some go so far as to claim that the nonalcoholic spouse or partner has a disease separate from his or her partner's alcoholism. An editorial from a leading treatment center's newsletter, reprinted in Box 8.4, challenges this view.

Ellis et al. (1988) define the enabler as an individual who appears to help the substance abuser sustain his or her addiction. These authors single out three types of enablers who require therapy. The "joiner" openly supports the addict's habit. The "messiah" intervenes for the addict in such a way that prevents him or her from receiving the natural consequences of his or her act. A third type is the "silent sufferer."

A barrage of criticism has been launched against these classifications. Frank and Golden (1992), in an editorial in *Social Work*, deride use of a

BOX 8.3: *Long Day's Journey into Night*

MARY: But I must confess, James, although I couldn't help loving you, I would never have married you if I'd know you drank so much. I remember the first night your barroom friends had to help you up to the door of our hotel room, and knocked and then ran away before I came to the door. We were still on our honeymoon, do you remember?

TYRONE: (With guilty vehemence.) I don't remember! It wasn't on our honeymoon! And I never in my life had to be helped to bed, or missed a performance!

MARY: (As though he hadn't spoken.) I had waited in that ugly hotel room hour after hour. I kept making excuses for you. I told myself it must be some business connected with the theater. I know so little about the theater. Then I became terrified. I imagined all sorts of horrible accidents. I got on my knees and prayed that nothing had happened to you—and then they brought you up and left you outside the door. (She gives little, sad sigh.) I didn't know how often that was to happen in the years to come, how many times I was to wait in ugly hotel rooms. I became quite used to it.

EDMUND: (Bursts out with a look of accusing hate at his father.) Christ! No wonder—! (He controls himself—gruffly.) When is dinner, Mamma? It must be time.

TYRONE: (Overwhelmed by shame which he tries to hide, fumbles with his watch.) Yes. It must be. Let's see. (He stares at his watch without seeing it. Pleadingly.) Mary! Can't you forget—?

Source: Eugene O'Neill, *Long Day's Journey into Night* (New Haven, CT: Yale University Press, 1956). Reprinted with permission of Yale University Press.

nomenclature that can compound the problem. Are we looking at a codependent woman, they ask, or are we looking at the results of traditional feminine training? My earlier contribution (van Wormer, 1989) examined use of the label as an attempt to find a diagnosable, treatable illness.

A rare find in the literature is *Women Married to Alcoholics* by Kokin (1990). That women who live with alcoholics are survivors is the basic theme of this book. These women, declares Kokin, do whatever is necessary to protect themselves and their families from potential consequences of their mates' abusive drinking. The condition of living with an alcoholic is likely to bring on feelings of shame, guilt, anger, pity, fear, worry, and depression. Much of the current family treatment that goes under the name of codependency treatment, according to Kokin, only perpetuates these feelings.

BOX 8.4: Some Thoughts on Codependency

There is no doubt that people who are involved emotionally with chemically dependent individuals are likely to suffer more emotional problems than people who are not. In fact, any chronic illness creates stress within the family system. Certain patterns of similar responses emerge.

Our predilection, as trained clinicians and as individuals, is to try to classify these patterns, define them, identify their cause, and prescribe a solution. This tendency rises out of our cultural bias toward a biochemical approach to health problems: if we find the cause of a problem, its solution is not far behind. This model also fits within the current health care system, which requires diagnosis in order to justify reimbursement for treatment.

The difference in these two approaches becomes apparent when we compare the views of the seventeenth-century philosopher, Descartes, with those of contemporary systems thinkers. Descartes saw the body as a machine which, if fully understood, could be taken apart and reassembled. In contrast, systems thinkers view health as an integrated state of mental, physical, spiritual, and emotional well-being. Both views are helpful.

We think that the controversy over the term *codependency* is one manifestation of the conflict between these two views. Support for the concept arises, in part, out of our culture's biomedical bias. We can't help people who aren't diagnosed, and the term is one way of describing the distress that chemical dependency creates for people who live with it.

At the Hazelden Family Center, we have consciously chosen not to label problems that occur within the family system with any diagnosis, including the word *codependency*. We have made this choice because:

Despite the fact that the partners of alcoholics do not have a disease—only the symptoms of struggling against someone else's disease—individual and family therapy can be extremely beneficial in the healing process for these survivors. Work in the area of self-esteem can do much to help resolve powerful feelings accompanying years of abuse and unshared pain.

AN ECOLOGICAL ASSESSMENT OF THE FAMILY WITH ALCOHOLISM

From the ecosystems perspective, the social worker views the recovering family as one seeking a new adaptation in the aftermath of a member's

- Our clients exhibit a remarkable variety of responses to the problems of chemical dependency within the family. For us, these responses are too varied to classify into a single phenomenon.
- The family exists as a system, and problems within that system have complex, multiple levels of interaction causation that resist diagnosis.
- Emphasizing a particular diagnosis and its symptoms may lead clients to focus on problems rather than solutions.
- Clinically, most of the clients we deal with are "normal," experiencing levels of distress appropriate for their situation.
- The research that we have seen tends to support the position that while people involved with chemically dependent individuals do experience more emotional problems, no clearcut syndrome has emerged.

The view we take at the Hazelden Family Center is rooted in health promotion, a systems approach to health problems. We believe that each member of the family has an innate power of self-healing, and we try to awaken that power within our clients. Our practices are based on a combination of Al-Anon principles and the family systems theories developed by Murray Bowen, Ph.D. Both de-emphasize the need for a diagnosable sickness, instead requiring a sincere desire to change.

There are many ways to help families return to health, and we respect the philosophical differences that shape various practices in our growing field. *Codependency,* both as a clinical and popular term, brings some of these differences into focus. We look forward to hearing your views.

Source: *Hazelden Professional Update,* 5(3) (1987): 2. Reprinted with permission of Hazelden.

active alcoholism. After years of living with illness, family members' relationships have become strained; communication has become stifled. The challenge for the social worker is to conduct an ecological assessment of the family in question to promote a full understanding by all parties of the persons in their reciprocating environment. The following scheme focuses on three major areas of concern—environmental links, boundary issues, and inside-the-family dynamics. This format is modeled on the suggested ecological assessment of Hartman and Laird (1983). These specific areas of investigation bring theory to the level of intervention and provide a focus for social work assessment. The underlying assumption on which this framework is built is the systems premise that each family is bound together in an intricate balancing act.

1. Environmental Links
   - What are the external sources of stress facing the family?
   - How do the events leading up to the treatment and the treatment process count as stressful events?
   - What are the economic and working-world constraints?
   - What are the sources of stress in the extended family?
   - What are the sources of support?
   - What are the organizational sources of support (e.g., A.A., religious affiliations, clubs)? Which members of the family are linked to which support systems?
   - How did the use of alcohol affect these areas of stress or support?
2. Boundary Issues
   - Are members free to link up to people and groups outside the family?
   - What are the explicit rules of dating for teenagers? The unwritten rules?
   - Does the family bond together for protection against hostile outside forces?
   - Who sits where at home? Which members are close to which other members?
   - Is the home open to visitors? What are the restrictions?
   - What impact did the use of alcohol have on these rules and relationships?
3. Inside the Family
   - What roles do individual members play? Who actually does what? Is there role flexibility? When something is amiss, who gets the blame?
   - Do all members take care of each other or is one person the designated caretaker?
   - Is there cultural conflict between parents (such as in child-rearing techniques)? What are some intergenerational issues? Is alcoholism a pattern across generations? Is teetotalism?
   - Can power be questioned? Who decides what?
   - Who listens to whom?
   - How did the presence of alcohol change any of this?

Engaging family members in the assessment process is a means of teaching the family how they operate together as a family unit. Such analysis offers a means of revealing strengths and weaknesses in the family structure. Much of family interaction over the space of years becomes background, and it is the province of therapy to throw light into the shadows for all to see. There will be many revelations for the people who compose a family. In looking at themselves as they have become under the stress of a member's alcoholism, members will come to see what the level of functioning might have been had alcoholism not occurred.

FAMILY TREATMENT TECHNIQUES

Holistic treatment is geared toward the family's biopsychosocial needs. Interventions with the family can be directed toward the biological aspects of addiction, the psychological ramifications, and the social dimensions. While these three areas are in reality intertwined, they are treated separately here for the sake of clarity.

BIOLOGICAL FACTORS

Interventions to address the physiological problems of alcoholism and other addictions are education and confrontation. At the beginning of each family session, the therapist can provide information on physical aspects of addiction and recovery, including hereditary factors and matters of relevance to the particular family. Often family members attend lectures on such topics as "Alcoholism and the Brain." Educational films commonly are shown. The ABC News close-up, *Addiction: Alcohol and Cocaine*, is a popular choice at many treatment centers.

An advantage of the disease concept of alcoholism is that it alleviates guilt feelings in alcoholics and provides a reason for their behavior. Nutritional information and facts about other drugs with cross-addictive attributes are often provided. The educational sessions can be tremendously informative to the families of alcoholics. If the content of the material is not overly complicated, participants can be expected to be attentive and even amazed at some of the information provided. The knowledge acquired empowers family members to help the alcoholic and each other in the period of recovery (which in a real sense lasts a lifetime).

Sometimes alcoholics in treatment obsess about every detail of a scientific presentation. Their very obsessiveness, typical of early sobriety, can be a hindrance to recovery. Consequently, speakers must have mastery of the subject material, which then can be presented in a straightforward way. The focus should be on the main points with a great deal of summarizing provided. Often a client's obsessiveness and worry over one small aspect of a lecture is a sign of impending relapse. For example, I once spoke at a treatment reunion. An ex-client became extremely perturbed over the issue of the possibility of detecting alcoholism susceptibility in the genes. "Wouldn't this lead to population control?" he kept asking. His disquiet was clearly apparent to everyone. This client had a "slip" or relapse at the end of the week, at which point he decided to return to the treatment center. There his tendency to "catastrophize" could be addressed.

Confrontation as used in family therapy is pointing out contradictions, such as those between goals and behavior. A family member might be confronted on why he or she filled the refrigerator with beer as the alcoholic entered the second week of sobriety. Or the alcoholic might be confronted on his or her plans to go on a starvation diet at a time when moderation in life-style is so crucial to sobriety.

An example of a therapist's (T.) confrontation with a father (F.) inclined to be overbearing is as follows:

T.: Bill, I'd like you to stop for a moment and check out what you're doing. You expressed concern that the children don't talk to you more openly. Right?

F.: Yes.

T.: Let's think about what just happened with Steve. He began to tell you how he felt about those speeding drives in the car and you cut him off with "Not now." Did you notice how he pulled back then? How did you feel, Steve, when your father cut you off in this way?

PSYCHOLOGICALLY BASED INTERVENTIONS

Interventions that are psychologically based are those geared toward thinking and feeling. Assessment of family rules is a key opportunity to explore the rules, the meaning of the rules, and the reasons for them. Faulty and healthy belief systems can be examined in this way. Some rules may be utterly unrealistic, not age appropriate, and seemingly made to be broken. Often mixed messages are sent, and family members are set up for failure.

An analysis of role expectations in the family is another area ripe for psychological investigation. Roles and feelings about roles can be explored. Finally, the relationship between feelings and drinking on the part of the alcoholic can be discovered. Ways of controlling the negative feelings and irrational actions can be shown. All the family members can be helped to develop better coping skills.

SOCIALLY BASED INTERVENTIONS

Interventions that are psychologically based and those that are socially based overlap. Focusing on the process of interaction in the system falls within the realms of social psychology. Interventions directed at the family system are educational and change oriented. Rarely are the participants themselves aware of the patterns of interaction. When the therapist, as outside observer, reveals these interactional patterns of behavior, members are catapulted in the direction of change. The stage is set for a shared groping for solutions to problems that may never have been identified without outside help. Ideally, the family therapist is a nonparticipant in the immediate, emotionally charged issues within the family (such as who takes responsibility over what and the division of labor). The focus of the therapist is not on the *content* of the interaction but on the *process* itself. Through skilled and friendly questioning the therapist imparts awareness of the form of the interaction: "Have you noticed how whenever the two of you argue your son leans over backwards in his chair until you have to stop him?" "I notice when you cry, Mary, your daughter's eyes start watering up too. Does this suggest a strong closeness of feelings between the two of you?" "Who interrupts whom in this family?"

I once attended a family session in Norway with an American colleague whose favorite advice was, "Let it all out." One time, the whole family, as if on command, became hysterical, and verbal communication was brought to a standstill for the rest of the afternoon.

Instead of excessive emotionalism in family sessions, a calm, intellectual atmosphere should be encouraged. Members are helped to listen to each other. Heavy emotion can be defused. For example, if a mother becomes distraught, other members can be asked what they can do to provide support, or how they feel about the outburst. In an intervention with the mother, the focus can be on the thoughts that accompany her feelings.

Emotions may need to be defused when couples shout at each other. A helpful intervention is to interrupt with a loud "Stop!" Each person is then requested to address the therapist individually and to take turns. To reinforce listening, the therapist can ask the nonspeaking partner to reiterate what he or she heard the speaker saying.

Conversely, couples who are not connecting emotionally with each other can be asked to look at each other and speak directly to each other, not to the therapist. To encourage engagement in a mutual undertaking or to introduce new forms of communication, homework assignments can be given to strengthen the communication process.

Through the various intervention devices described in this section, the family systems therapist guides a family with a recovering member toward its own process of recovery. As a newly sober member regains responsibility within the family, other members have to adapt accordingly. Acting as a coach or guide, the therapist can help map the course of this adaptation. The entire family must be prepared to accept as a member a sober and somewhat changed person. Every person's role in the family changes in the process.

The culmination of the Family Week program in Norway was a lecture for all departing family members: "Life after Treatment." Together, family members were given guidelines on what to expect and not to expect in early recovery. Members were told about medications the alcoholic should avoid. Alterations to expect in the newly constituted family system were described. The area of sexuality was given attention: recovering alcoholics may anticipate difficulty expressing their sexual needs without the help of alcohol. Meanwhile, the sober spouse may have lost sexual interest in the partner because of the unpleasantness associated with making love night after night to (in Father Martin's *Chalk Talk* terminology) "a drunken pig."

CASE HISTORY: KATHY AND ED

This story is reconstructed from the archives of my memory. I can still picture clearly in my mind these two intriguing clients.

A court-referred client, Ed, had been assessed as an alcoholic following an arrest for domestic abuse. Ed was a middle-aged African American from Alabama. His common-law wife, Kathy, was white and a recovering alcoholic, who led the local Women for Sobriety group. While Kathy was college educated, Ed had only an eighth grade education. The couple had two small children. Ed was my client. For months he had complained of being victimized by Kathy's manipulations. From his description, Kathy was one of the most treacherous women who ever existed. Her case history, however, told a different story: Kathy was a woman involved with a man who abused her. The couple had separated and gotten back together numerous times. Their means of financial support was a substantial sum of money from her late husband, who had died in a freak accident. Racism in the community compounded the couple's relationship problems. Counselors writing case notes on Kathy seemed impressed by her sincerity.

More out of curiosity than for therapeutic reasons, I insisted that Ed bring Kathy to meet me and that they work out some kind of living contract. Ed and Kathy had never been seen together by a counselor. Counselors at this agency, as at many others, avoided marriage counseling "like the plague."

Before I met Kathy, Ed warned me not to be taken in by her charm. He told me the story of a recent episode in which they had been screaming and yelling at each other, and Kathy had called the police. "You're in real trouble now," Kathy said. Just before they walked in the door, he watched her look in the mirror and with her fingernails claw scratches down her neck and chest. The police carted Ed off to jail. Ed suspected racism in their refusal to hear his side of the story.

This was just one example, Ed said, of Kathy's manipulations. Her jealousy of Ed's ex-wife was such that Ed felt compelled to sneak money for child support to this first wife. And only two weeks before, Kathy had pulled all Ed's clothes out of the closet and put them in the car. As she drove away, she threw them out of the car window one at a time all along the street. Ed, running behind her, had to scoop them up.

I *had* to know more about this relationship. During the joint session I found Kathy to be articulate and extremely angry at Ed. As a standard counseling assignment, I had the couple write on a sheet of paper the advantages and disadvantages of being together. Within minutes, Kathy had filled up an entire page. Ed was more subdued in his responses. When I compared the two papers, it was clear that sexual compatibility was the only area of satisfaction between the two of them.

This couple came to see me off and on for several months. This seemed to be the classic case of the lovers who could not live together but could not live apart. Most of the sessions turned into shouting matches. Later, I would hear from startled colleagues who had heard the commotion through the walls and had wondered what on earth had been going on in my office.

As with most fighting couples, the greatest source of tension was money. Virtually all their screaming at each other had to do with Ed's lack of earning power ("laziness") and the fact that he could not account to Kathy for "every cent that he spent." A secondary issue was incompatible child-rearing practices. While Ed favored a spontaneous, relaxed approach, Kathy stressed scheduling and routine.

An ecological analysis of this relationship indicated that the emotional energy in this family was being drained by the constancy and intensity of the conflict. Because of the continued fighting and earlier alcohol abuse, this nuclear family was socially isolated. Racism in the local community and the education and class differences between the partners exacerbated the stress and social isolation. The best hope for connection to the wider community was through active participation in self-help groups.

My focus was to help Ed and Kathy reach a decision concerning what was best for them and for the children. Our mutually agreed-upon goal was for the couple to alter their pattern of communication. To enhance this process, I drew up a special Fighting Fair program (presented in Box 8.5). We practiced the rules in the office; Kathy and Ed were to follow these guidelines at home and whenever they conversed. Finally, because of mutual distrust and hurtful actions, the couple volunteered for a trial separation. Ed seemed happy with his new-found freedom. But every so often, Kathy would call him, tell him that the children were crying for him, and lure him back. When Ed left for lengthy inpatient treatment at a Veterans Administration (V.A.) hospital, this period of enforced time apart was a time of much personal growth for both of them. Ed was urged to make friends of his own through the local A.A. meetings.

Because an ecological assessment of pressures on this family revealed a high source of external stressors without relief from extended family supports, greater ties with friends and relatives were encouraged. Matters of racism in their small town were shown to exacerbate this family's isolation. Cultural differences in child-rearing expectations were revealed as typical sources of dispute in joint parenting. This helped the couple recognize that what were thought to be personal differences were really cultural matters, not issues of right or wrong.

Although Kathy and Ed were still going back and forth in their living arrangements when Ed's period of court-ordered treatment grew to a close, I felt that some definite progress had been made. Ed maintained his sobriety and found an A.A. sponsor who was always available to guide him in his thoughts and actions. Kathy continued her activities in the Women of Sobriety group and began to visit Al-Anon to work on detaching herself from her near-obsession with Ed and Ed's doings. The level of communication between Kathy and Ed improved dramatically. An end to the name-calling and attending to the rule "Don't rehash the past" made for significant improvement in their relationship.

Throughout my counseling of this enmeshed couple, my attention was focused on the *process* of the interaction, not the *content*. I did not try to determine who was telling the truth (although I suspected that Ed was the more accurate of the two). A compromise was worked out over money so that Ed could make some spending choices on his own. The case was one where a wide variety of treatment approaches were called for, few of which had any direct bearing on the diagnosed problem—alcoholism.

FAMILY INTERVENTION

How do you get a drinking family member into treatment against his or her will? "The Intervention" is the method developed at the Johnson Institute in Minnesota for bringing resistant alcoholics into treatment. An intervention of this sort is a formal confrontation by family, friends, and employer under the guidance of a skilled alcoholism counselor. The earlier way was to "let the alcoholic hit bottom" (Royce, 1989). This highly dangerous practice of doing nothing until something drastic happens (such as a car crash or losing one's job) is now seen as counterproductive. The intervention itself creates a crisis through the group process, which hopefully is of sufficient strength to compel the alcoholic to enter treatment at once. Betty Ford and Elizabeth Taylor are two famous persons who were encouraged to sign up for treatment through a formal intervention process.

Local treatment centers often have a policy of intervention done free of charge, a good business practice. This therapeutic process also offers an opportunity for providing much-needed help to the family members of the alcoholic. The counselor experienced in intervention gathers a team of caring and concerned individuals who believe strongly that their loved one needs professional help. A team consisting of five members is the optimal number (Kokin, 1990). Children over the age of six are included, a doctor if there are health problems, and the employer if there are work problems that can be documented. For teenager interventions, it is essential to include other teens who are concerned about their peer. Respected adults other than the teen's parents should be included also (Treadway, 1989). Preliminary meetings are held with the counselor to prepare the stage for the confrontation. The task for the counselor is to put the family members' minds at rest, to assure them that they are doing the right thing in confronting the alcoholic.

Data are collected substantiating the claims of addiction, and a rehearsal is set up. Participants are taught to take turns reading facts from a prepared statement and to include their feelings about the incidents described. Each team member lists specific times, events, and dates. Examples are provided, such as:

> Daddy, last week was my graduation party. You promised you wouldn't drink until after the guests had left. When you arrived you smelled of beer. You flirted around with my friend Nancy, and asked to dance with her. Nancy later said, "Your father must have had a lot to drink." When you did that, I felt embarrassed.

Sometimes a reservation at an inpatient treatment center is made, and the husband or wife of the alcoholic arrives with a suitcase all packed. With a woman alcoholic, child care arrangements often must be made. Sometimes the person confronted proposes his or her own option of stopping drinking and attending an A.A. meeting regularly. If this is agreed to, a written contract is drawn up. What to do in the event that drinking continues—a second option—must be spelled out. The success rate for such formal intervention is reportedly very high. The highest successes occur when the boss is included on the intervention team (Hacker, 1990).

A treatment center with which I was affiliated in Norway had a more controversial plan. Family members reported the person in urgent need of help. A team of strong-armed counselors arrived and forced the individual into their car, which was well supplied with hard liquor. By the time the journey was over, the alcoholic was in no shape to resist. The next day the person woke up in an inpatient bed and often couldn't remember how he or she got there. One man thought he was in a resort hotel in Finland; another thought he was on a ship and rushed out to jump into the water. After a public scandal ensued—one person sued the center for "kidnapping" him—the practice was discontinued. Family

BOX 8.5: Rules for Fighting Fair

Roommates and married partners bring to living situations a lot of cultural baggage from their families of origin and from previous marriages. Kids in the family are often influenced by the norms of their peers as well as by the wider culture. Often, the differences that arise between people can be understood in terms of a clash in cultural background. These differences may not be personal at all. Some conflict in the home is inevitable in a pluralistic society such as the United States. In any case, everyday conflicts between partners can be alleviated or prevented through developing skills in communication techniques for resolving differences. Skills in conflict resolution can be learned and practiced with a teacher or social worker and applied in actual situations. These techniques have been found to be helpful in resolving conflict and restoring goodwill between opposing groups or factions as well as in subduing heated marital disputes.

Here is the step-by-step framework for resolving a problem with a partner. The theme of this approach is to bring about the most change while doing the least amount of harm.

Step 1. Formulating the Problem

Meaning of the Behavior

Before putting your concern into words, try to get at the *root* of what is really disturbing you. Do you object to your partner's behavior because he or she reminds you of someone else? Is your own insecurity or intolerance causing distress? Think about what is bugging you, and be sure you are not being unreasonable, possessive, or overly protective, or are snooping. Sound out your complaint with trusted friends to make sure it is a reasonable one. Analyze the objectionable behavior in terms of possible cultural or class patterns in upbringing of both yourself and your partner. Consider the participant's family background and family situation (birth order).

Choose an area where the partner can make a change. An area such as a serious illness or a handicap would not be negotiable. Financial planning, division of labor, child rearing, sexual behavior, family traditions, sleeping patterns, or bathroom sharing are examples of negotiable areas.

Feelings Aroused by the Behavior

Identify your overt feelings (e.g., anger) and underlying feelings (e.g., hurt, guilt). Try to identify where these feelings are coming from. *Be specific.*

Wrong	*Right*
"You're secretive with me."	"When you plan a trip without discussing it with me first, I feel left out."
	"I feel rejected when you don't tell me where you've been."
"You're messy."	"I'd like you to squeeze the toothpaste from the bottom, not the top."
"Your drinking is getting out of hand."	"Last night you threw the chair across the room; and now you don't remember."
	"Last night you drank six cans of beer."

Step 2. Choose an Appropriate Time and Place

Don't approach a partner who is tired or intoxicated (or engaged in the bathroom). Choose a private time and place and say, "I'd like to talk. If now isn't convenient, let's schedule a time later."

Step 3. Keep These Rules in Mind

- Attack the *behavior,* not the *person* or his or her background. Use a pleasant tone of voice; avoid yelling, hitting, cursing, or name-calling. Deal with one issue at a time—don't let your partner counter with, "Well, if you think I'm bad you ought to see how you come across." Or, "When you get a decent job, I'll think about it!"
- No mind reading. Don't say, "You are jealous," or "You're just angry because you . . ."
- Narrow the problem down to a manageable size rather than focusing on vague wholes.
- No accusations and put-downs, such as, "You're just like your father!"
- Don't rehash the past.

Step 4. Make the Request

Sentence 1: I'm feeling troubled about

- the amount of money we've been spending lately.
- the way the work load has been distributed around here.
- hearing all these lies.
- finding someone's been here while I'm gone.

Sentence 2: I want a change in the situation so it's more fair.

(continued on next page)

BOX 8.5 (continued)

Sentence 3: I'd like your help.

Respondent: I'll try to . . .

Sentence 4: I'd like something more definite. What I would like from you is . . .

Respondent: I'll cook on Mondays and Wednesdays . . .

Sentence 5: That would help a lot.

Step 5. Use Active Listening Skills

When you discuss the matter with your partner, listen to the response. A good technique is to rephrase what the person said by beginning with, "What you're saying is . . ." or "What I hear you saying is . . ." Ask your partner to play the request back to you to make sure he or she hears what you are asking.

Follow-up Questions

This "growth-fight" was successful if:

1. You feel better now than you did and you feel better about your partner.

---

members were then encouraged to follow the routine themselves: get the alcoholic very drunk and drive him or her to the center.

Sometimes, when the treatment center is a for-profit business, strategies to get new recruits can get out of hand. The *planned*, professional family intervention of the kind described earlier, however, is both therapeutic and within ethical bounds. Even if unsuccessful in getting an alcoholic into treatment, the intervention process is of value to family members in getting them to communicate their feelings with one another.

FORCES WORKING AGAINST FAMILY TREATMENT

Despite the well-recognized treatment effectiveness of family therapy work, agencies often resist including families in treatment. Hartman and Laird (1983) spell out some of the obstacles to family treatment created by the work environment. Offices are often too small and sufficient office furniture is scarce. The treatment center may require that additional forms be filled out for each family member. The building may be closed evenings and weekends.

The lack of training that alcoholism counselors and social workers receive in family counseling is another factor in an agency's reluctance to engage the whole family in alcoholism treatment work. A distrust of family members who may be viewed as *enablers* who will resist the treatment process

2. Your relationship has been helped.
3. The behavior in question has improved.
4. There are no hard feelings.
5. You expressed your feelings.
6. There is greater trust in the relationship.

This fair-fighting scheme can be used for a variety of relationships, such as mother/son, colleague/colleague, husband/wife. When misunderstandings are cleared up early in a relationship, the bad feelings have less time to fester. It is unfair to yourself and to your partner not to point out the things that can be changed.

> God grant me the Serenity
> To accept the things I cannot change,
> Courage to change the things I can,
> And the wisdom to know the difference.
> —Serenity Prayer

A single light dispels darkness.
—Gandhi

---

causes some counselors to avoid close contact with them. A reciprocal distrust is often voiced by family members who may feel that they will be blamed and who therefore are reluctant to participate in treatment. Working with larger groups of people can be stressful and time-consuming. Usually, there is no extra pay for this additional work. If cotherapy is involved, the request for the extra therapist may seem an unproductive use of resources.

Despite the drawbacks to bringing friends and relatives into treatment, I have found that the information collected in this manner is invaluable. My work with Ed, in the case history cited earlier, for instance, would have been extremely limited without the inclusion of the person with whom he was most directly involved. I needed to see the two of them engaged in interaction before I could help shape this interaction. Simply talking to Ed about Kathy and reinforcing his sense of victimization would have gotten us nowhere.

If the inpatient treatment center is far away from the client's home, family programs may be poorly attended because of the distance. In the United States, especially, it is difficult to take a week off from work to attend a Family Week at a treatment center. In Norway, each client could be required to have at least one family member attend for one week. Though the treatment center was miles away from the home of most clients, family members came in large numbers. Work leave was easy to obtain. One week of concentrated treatment seemed especially gratifying to these participants. Many said upon leaving, "I have learned more this week than I ever have in my whole life."

FORCES WORKING IN FAVOR OF FAMILY THERAPY

The trend toward outpatient treatment in the United States should encourage family programming. The opportunity is available for practitioners to invite significant others living nearby to attend individual sessions. Sometimes the significant other is only as far away as the waiting room. With the permission of the client, a useful strategy is to invite this person to join the session. Conversely, couples may be invited to attend a couples group to work on communications and coping skills. (Kaufman [1985] has a chapter in his book describing this dynamic approach.)

Another area with great potential for future growth is adolescent treatment with a family focus. Working with and within a family system where a child and often one of the adult members is abusing alcohol is a major challenge. To alleviate crushing guilt feelings in the parents of an alcoholic adolescent and to help them recognize their role in recovery, a strong family-oriented program is essential. An excellent resource on family treatment of adolescent substance abuse is found in Treadway's *Before It's Too Late* (1989). Referral to Al-Anon is helpful for parents, while Al-Ateen is a superb resource for children whose parents are alcoholics. Young people can also attend a youth group of A.A. or N.A. (Narcotics Anonymous), which they often prefer.

EXERCISES FOR FAMILY GROUPS

1. Family Sculpture
   Purpose: To portray roles in the family; to portray roles as frozen in time. To help reveal feelings that accompany each role.

   The worker begins by explaining the technique to the family. This is a non-verbal technique that involves physical placement of persons in a symbolic fashion. The "sculptor" moves various family members into particular positions. The exercise begins with everyone standing up. Talking is not allowed. A family member volunteers to be the sculptor. The therapist instructs the sculptor to arrange the family members to show who is close to whom and what people do together. The setting reproduced may be the family at home in the evening or on an outing such as a picnic. Following the sculpture display, participants discuss the meaning of each sculpture and how each felt about the role he or she played.

   Family sculpture can be effectively used in a Family Week program. Volunteers are asked to play the roles they play in their families or, in another variation, to play a very different role. The roles of alcoholic, family manager, hero, and so on are given to participants. With the help of the therapist as sculptor, each arranges him- or herself in a way that best represents the role. For instance, the alcoholic may be put high on the chair or seated stooped over the table. The lost child may stand in a corner or watch television. The family manager may extend his or her arm around the alcoholic. All members freeze as for a portrait. Afterward, each person is asked to recapture the feelings of being in the role. The audience and players discuss the meaning of what they saw.

2. Drawing Family Maps
   Purpose: To open discussion about family lines of communication and closeness and to help the family gain insight into where the boundaries are.
   The therapist draws a circle on a chalkboard or flip chart to represent a hypothetical family. For example, an alcoholic mother and daughter could be represented by two circles with boundaries that overlap. If the mother cries, the daughter cries, too. The sober father and the other daughter are also close, but these two, represented by two more circles, are apart from the others. Family members are asked to take turns drawing their families.

3. Family Relapse Prevention Plan
   Purpose: To help the alcoholic and the family identify the warning signs of pending relapse.
   A list of warning signs is written by each participant. Signs must be clearly spelled out. Family members discuss these warning signs, such as extreme and obsessive devotion to work. They discuss what these symptoms meant in the past and reach agreement on what to do if they recur. An action plan is drawn up.

4. Genograms, or Family Trees
   Purpose: To provide information on patterns in families; to reveal possible hereditary and cultural themes that have been passed from generation to generation; to reveal similarities and differences across families joined by marriage.
   Hartman and Laird (1983) show how diagrams can be constructed through the use of symbols. A marital pair is indicated by a line drawn from a square (male) to a circle (female). Divorce is indicated by two slash marks on the line. Words can be used for events, occupations, dates, and ethnic origins (refer to figure 8.5 for an example).

235

FIGURE 8.5

Genogram

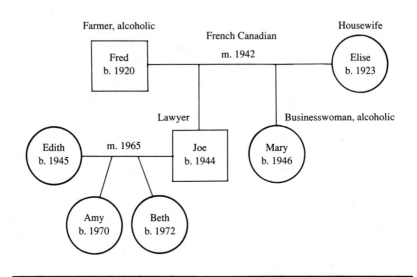

SUMMARY

Social workers and those in related counseling fields have a systems orientation to treatment that is especially relevant to working with alcoholics and their families. A background in interactionist-systems training is invaluable for recognizing how the affected individual is influenced by family dynamics and how family dynamics are influenced by the affected individual. The family systems approach offers a view of the family as a system of interdependent parts. The most commonly used metaphor is that of a mobile suspended from a ceiling. If one part moves, the other parts shift simultaneously. Social workers and other helping professionals are familiar with the boundary concept, with the reciprocity of role playing, and with the development and enforcement of rules in the family.

The family systems paradigm offers to alcoholism treatment a way of conceptualizing alcoholism as an intergenerational phenomenon. The family is perceived of and treated as a valuable resource in the treatment of alcoholism. Unfortunately, some potential for blaming the family still persists. The emphasis has shifted from family factors that *cause* alcoholism to those that *perpetuate* it. The careless use of terms such as *codependent* and *enabler* can compound the negativism associated with being in a family with an alcoholic member.

Family therapy is an exciting dimension of alcoholism treatment. Family work with alcoholics is an area especially amenable to the biopsychosocial framework. Systems therapists can utilize a didactic focus to teach biological and physiological factors of alcoholism and the link with other addictions. The psychological realms can be addressed through work on the thinking-feeling dyad. The social aspect relates to the systems component, which can offer a shared assessment of the structure and interaction patterns in the family. In all these ways, the social worker as family therapist guides the family toward welcoming back a member who, in words of the old Scottish hymn; "once was lost, but now is found." Through the use of various communications exercises or of listening skills, workers can help family members deal with their own feelings of anger, shame, and guilt that have plagued them for a long, long time.

REVIEW QUESTIONS

1. Relate family systems theory to William Faulkner's words, "the old ineradicable rhythm."

2. How would *classic* systems theory explain mental illness? Does this take into account biological explanations? Explain. Why are recent systems theorists modifying their use of the systems metaphor?

3. What are some encouraging developments (generally) in terms of recent contributions to the family-of-alcoholics literature? What was the impact of Al-Anon?

4. Discuss the family with alcoholism using systems terminology. Include the concepts of *roles, adaptation, stresses,* and *feedback.*

5. What are the characteristics of the functional family? When you "throw in the booze" what happens to this hypothetical family?

6. What is the connection between the enmeshed family and alcoholism?

7. Discuss the family with alcoholism in terms of the Kübler-Ross stages of facing terminal illness.

8. Describe the roles of members in a family with an alcoholic parent. How can these roles be considered defense mechanisms against pain?

9. Discuss the concept *codependency.* Why do some critics raise objections to this term?

10. How can an ecological assessment of the family with alcoholism be conducted? What are the key areas of focus?

11. Which treatment interventions address biological realities? Which address psychological factors? Which interventions are geared toward the social dimension?

12. How does the therapist confront an overbearing father in family therapy without losing the respect and cooperation of the father? Give an example.

13. What does the case history of Kathy and Ed show about relationships in the addicted family?

14. What are the necessary steps in conducting an intervention with an alcoholic when the goal is to get him or her into treatment?

15. How does the family sometimes show resistance to the process of family treatment?

16. Review the rules for fighting fair. How can they be used in helping family members to communicate. How do members' feelings come in? How is a request made without causing offense?

9

GROUP THERAPY WITH SUBSTANCE ABUSERS

At first, I loathed these sessions. I was uncomfortable, unwilling
to speak up. Then one day another woman said she didn't think
that her drinking was a problem. I became very emotional and got
to my feet. "I'm Betty," I said. "I'm an alcoholic and I know my
drinking has hurt my family." I heard myself, and couldn't believe
it. I was trembling; another defense had cracked.
—Betty Ford, 1979, p. 85.

A working therapy group has about it a certain glow, an aura that
is infectious. One person speaks, sometimes several speak at once; all
heads nod in unison. Eyes move, too, from speaker to speaker. And the
expression on one member's face, whether a grin or a look of pain, is
mirrored on all the faces. A oneness of feeling and mood permeates the
air. Should the group progress falter, the group leader prompts the players
and helps get the group back on track. The leader's hardest work was done
earlier, however. Now it is time to sit back and enjoy the performance.

Most of the excitement at an alcoholism treatment center takes place
in the group. The essence of healing and recovery is centered in the group
process. And the essence of effective group therapy is in the level of skill
and training of the group leader.

Accordingly, in terms of practical knowledge and applicability, this
chapter may well be the most important one. For the addictions worker,
everything comes together in the group—all his or her knowledge of disease characteristics, psychology, and, of course, social skills. The ability

to impart this knowledge in a meaningful and relevant way to group members is a requirement of an effective leader. Whether the social worker as group leader takes the initiative or is passively moved along by the whims of the group is the test of group leadership. As an aid to individual therapy and as a treatment modality in its own right, the group process is a powerful agent for change. It is through this kind of therapy session that many of a client's old ways of thinking and believing are broken down. And here, hopefully, new strides toward healthier thinking and believing take place.

To introduce the group as a treatment vehicle, this chapter provides a brief literature review and surveys the principles of group dynamics. Specific therapeutic activities are introduced at significant points. Interventions are organized according to the developmental or phase approach. But such an approach is only a structural construct for organizing reality. According to this simplified conceptualization, clients are perceived as collectively moving along, all members mastering one step before going on to the next one. In reality, of course, most treatment groups consist of individuals at different levels of sobriety, awareness, and need. Conceiving of treatment in terms of the phase approach allows for a structured presentation of carefully selected exercises for ever-increasing levels of wellness.

The group activities, views of alcoholism, and practical methods of recovery form a totality. As applied to the group process, the person-in-the-environment conceptionalization—the ecological framework—focuses attention on the wholeness of the group. In the group, a collective consciousness emerges.

Material presented in this chapter is geared toward the development of a powerful group experience for individual members who, at the moment at least, are in recovery. The material is drawn from the wealth of treatment knowledge that is passed along from counselor to counselor, across generations and across treatment centers. Much of this material comes from the folklore of the treatment world.

HISTORICAL PERSPECTIVE

Social workers have been involved in doing group work since the settlement house days. The history of specialized group work with alcoholics, however, has been more limited. After the 1920s, when the psychoanalytical approach dominated the field of social work, the emphasis shifted to long-term, individual psychotherapy. Through the 1960s and later, social workers simply referred clients with drinking problems to the local A.A. meeting. In some cases, this worked. In others, the alcoholics became lost to the system (see Googins, 1984).

The paucity of research reports of successful group therapy efforts with alcoholics or other addicts reflects the social workers' general avoidance of work with this population. In the early days of systematic alcoholism treatment, the few studies done came largely from outside of social work and mostly from a single source, the *Quarterly Journal of Studies on Alcohol*, the predecessor to today's *Journal of Studies on Alcohol*. An argument for the effectiveness of active group psychotherapy with alcoholics was provided by McCarthy (1946). Other early writers on the usefulness of alcoholic groups were Pfeffer et al. (1949), Scott (1956), and Armstrong and Gibbons (1956). *The International Journal of Group Psychotherapy* published papers on group therapy efforts with alcoholics. In the 1960s, the technique of group therapy was praised as a powerful means of breaking the power of resistance. In understanding and confronting others, alcoholics could come to know themselves.

Krimmel (1971) wrote a textbook—*Alcoholism: Challenge for Social Work Education*—for the Council on Social Work Education (CSWE). A significant section of the book was devoted to group therapy techniques. Clients at the Cleveland Center on Alcoholism were shown to thrive in the sanctuary of the small group in a safe setting where they could test their relationships with one another. Publication of this text represented a breakthrough; social work professionals for the first time were brought face to face with the problem that they had taken such pains in the past to avoid.

In the years that followed, traditional social work journals, such as *Health and Social Work* (Nov. 1979), *Social Work with Groups* (Jan. 1982), and *Social Casework* (June 1989) have all devoted special issues to alcoholism and its treatment. Among special topics addressed have been assertiveness in recovery, stress management for relapse prevention, partner therapy, and women in groups. The attention given by these journals to group counseling of alcoholics is a reflection of the fact that thousands of social workers are involved with and contributing to all aspects of the burgeoning field of alcoholism counseling.

During the time that social work and psychology professionals were doing little or nothing to treat the alcoholic, specialized treatment centers on the "Minnesota Model" plan were developing a group therapy format derived from the principles of A.A. self-help programming. Recovering alcoholics at the early treatment centers, such as Hazelden in the 1940s and 1950s, revolutionized the way therapy was performed (Anderson, 1981). Groups became informal and client centered; counselors alternately led the group in harsh confrontation of a recalcitrant client and joined in with the group to offer intimate self-disclosures from drinking days. "I have been there too" was the theme of the group leadership. Instead of *I* and *you*, there was a sense of *we*, the *we* of the treatment group.

241

In these early treatment centers, social workers, psychologists, and active A.A. members worked side by side. Group leaders were referred to as *counselors*; first names were used; strong group confrontation was encouraged. Counselors trained in various schools of group work, or not trained at all, borrowed styles and interventions from each other, and over the years constructed their own professional traditions and knowledge base.

Working with professionals from the traditional disciplines, counselors of the A.A. school benefited from exposure to basic therapy techniques such as the psychosocial focus on the person in the system and strategies of active listening, role playing, and providing empathy and nonpossessive warmth. Meanwhile, social workers have been enlightened through exposure to counselors' knowledge of the disease concept of alcoholism, work from the Twelve Steps of recovery, and demonstrated democratic models of group leadership. Such interdisciplinary collaboration has led to the possibility of integration of alcoholism treatment into the mainstream of social work practice and of social work practice into standard work with alcoholics (Cook et al., 1983).

With the growing recognition that alcoholism is treatable if not curable, therapists have employed a variety of innovative techniques for reaching the client. Family therapy, couples groups, senior citizen groups, children of alcoholics groups, women's therapy, and anger management are examples of areas of special focus.

In summary, this review of the alcoholism literature reveals both an early pattern of neglect, especially by social work literature, and much recent attention to exciting new trends in the field. Contemporary textbooks on group therapy typically include a chapter on alcoholism and other addictions (see Zastrow, 1990). Books on alcoholism, however, whether written by psychologists, physicians, or social workers, rarely include chapters on the group process.

GROUP DYNAMICS

Group therapy with chemically dependent persons has as a major goal helping people find new nonaddictive ways of coping. Helping clients trust and communicate their feelings to others is a secondary goal of therapy. The scarcity of available psychiatric personnel during World War II encouraged a rapid growth in treating mental patients together rather than separately (Lieberman, 1975). The theory and techniques of current group treatment practices derive from the pioneering work of Kurt Lewin. Lewin (1947, 1952) did much experimental work on the group process, studying the interdependence of persons in a group as well as factors in group leadership and cohesiveness.

Of special relevance to the treatment of chemical abusers is information about the impact of group standards and values on the individual. The group outlook can have a powerful molding influence. When group norms emphasize sobriety and sober thinking, the individual alcoholic may be influenced accordingly. A group high in cohesiveness or group identity is especially potent in shaping individual behavior and attitudes. When the client is exposed to the judgments of not just one person but a *host* of people, obvious defenses crumble.

Groups are used for treating alcoholic clients in nearly all types of treatment centers—inpatient units, outpatient settings, prisons, and mental health centers. The preference for the group modality is due, no doubt, to cost effectiveness as well as to the recognized power of groups to mold the behavior and thinking of chronic alcoholics.

The newly sober alcoholic typically joins a treatment group because of some external, coercive force (Cunynghame, 1983). A bout with the law, an ultimatum from his or her spouse, a plea for help: These are the kinds of events that bring the clients in. For the client and family, the precipitating crisis can be a fortuitous and healthy "turning point."

Alcoholism therapy has as its aim individual change. Ways of thinking and behaving do not change overnight. According to Yalom (1974) change occurs by means of the group process and is an outgrowth of what he terms "*the curative factors.*" Relevant to chemical dependency treatment are the following seven curative factors of the group process singled out by Yalom. The first of these is the *interpersonal learning* that takes place in a group of persons engaged in satisfying interaction. Second is *group cohesiveness*, which is defined as the degree of bonding among group members based on their identification with each other and their liking for each other; this creates the unity needed for change. Third is *catharsis*, the much needed ventilation of feelings and sharing them with others. Next is *universality*, the sense of recognition that holds group members together. Then there is *altruism*, or the joy of helping others through unselfish giving of oneself. Through observation of others' progress comes the *instillation of hope* that is essential to progress. Finally, *imitative behavior* is the opportunity to model others in the group. These interrelated properties of the functioning group keep clients coming back for additional sessions.

How are these curative factors relevant in group treatment of alcoholics? The individual alcoholic has a great deal to learn about the physical and psychological disabilities associated with alcoholism. With group support and through modeling of others, group members can reach a decision as to whether or not they will take that first drink. Anxieties about treatment are alleviated through group cohesiveness and the sense of similarity. Self-esteem and confidence are generated through positive feedback in a group that functions as a microcosm of the wider world. The instillation of hope is a vital curative factor to those who have turned to drink when under stress and now must seek new avenues of relief. Joining with others who have "turned their lives around" can be an exhilarating and uplifting experience. In sharp contrast to the mood of bereavement groups and groups for the mentally ill and terminally ill, the group of recovering alcoholics can find reason to celebrate. Through shared joys and sorrows, individual group members are facilitated in their personal growth and relationships.

GROUP THERAPY VERSUS THE A.A. MEETING

The powers of the group in molding the behavior and self-concept of the individual are well evidenced in any A.A. meeting. Here are people very different from one another (according to age, social class, and culture) linked by a common identity and experience. The ritual of shared storytelling functions as a way of reconstructing one's past and therefore one's identity. Out of horrendous biographical stories comes meaning, a kind of light in the darkness. Feelings of guilt and loss associated with the ravages of drinking are diminished in the realization that maybe these things all happened for a purpose.

A.A. programming has become a cornerstone of virtually all contemporary rehabilitation efforts (Tournier, 1979). Examples of A.A. principles used in North American professional treatment programs are the view of alcoholism as a disease, the belief in total abstinence for an alcoholic, the reliance on group support, and the take-one-day-at-a-time strategy for dealing with stress. Unfortunately, much of what passes for group therapy at chemical dependency centers is ritualistic, highly structured, and tightly controlled (Matano and Yalom, 1991). The focus is on standardized responses to standardized questions, rather than on the easy give and take of a working, client-oriented therapy group.

As Matano and Yalom (1991) indicate, most contemporary group therapy with alcoholics fails to take advantage of a powerful therapeutic element: the *interactive* group process. Such a process includes social and psychological factors. If the disease model emphasis is too overwhelming, interpersonal problems of addicts will remain untreated. And previous maladaptive behavioral patterns may go unchallenged.

A clear distinction between the Twelve Step format of the A.A. group and the therapy group should be made. Flores (1988: 126) contrasts Alcoholics Anonymous and the professionally oriented therapy group. A.A. is characterized by:

- A focus on abstinence.
- An emphasis on the "how" of recovery.

- Ritualized readings.
- Structured use of life stories, or "drunkalogs."

The professionally run group, on the other hand, is:

- Focused on many issues.
- Concerned with the "why" of drinking.
- Based on development of group cohesiveness.
- Geared toward feeling work.
- Led by a traditional group leader, often with a topics format.

A.A. meets some needs that a group therapy does not: It is always there; the sponsor, ideally, will come any hour of the day or night. Group therapy, on the other hand, meets some needs that go beyond mere sobriety and togetherness. Group therapy involves hard work in certain specified areas (other than the Twelve Steps), including patterns of coping, thought processes, and familial relationships. Group therapy should be in the hands of a paid professional trained in the skills of effective group management. (The trend toward utilizing volunteer group leaders is a practice laden with pitfalls because of the complex nature of group therapy with addictive populations.)

Professional group therapy is highly effective for many introverted, depressed individuals for whom the active A.A. meeting is an alien and painful experience. The skilled group leader can "pull out" the seemingly resistant and unresponsive member with sometimes remarkable results. At the same time, many others are made ready, through the personal growth experience, for participation in various self-help groups in the community (e.g., parenting groups, grief recovery groups, and groups for women who were sexually abused).

THE FUNCTIONING THERAPY GROUP

For me, the ideal working group is seven clients of various ages seated in a circle; one male and one female cotherapist are seated across from each other. The session lasts two hours, with a brief break at the end of the first hour.

Consider the format of a "beginners' group" for persons newly admitted to treatment. Each group member, after encouragement, is wrestling with the question: *Do I want to continue going as I am going, or do I need to make a major change in my life?*

Or perhaps some of the members are seasoned group members; they operate as a core group, modeling appropriate behaviors for newcomers to the group. In the fully functioning group, members are enabled to take risks, disclose feelings, and become fully responsive to each others' needs and concerns. The functioning group meets clients where they are, rather than forcing errant individual members to subscribe unconditionally to group beliefs, such as the disease concept of addiction (Matano and Yalom, 1991). Insisting that clients label themselves as alcoholics or addicts can lead to a "battle of wills" (Vannicelli, 1992) that accomplishes nothing. Abstinence is not the primary topic of discussion; rather, discussion centers on the needs of the group members at that particular time.

COTHERAPY

Heap (1985) notes the increasing popularity of the coleadership of groups in Scandinavia and Britain. In the United States, cotherapy is most often employed as a training device; the student or intern helps with the group as a means of learning the skills of group therapy. Many group therapists believe that coleadership requires equality of status between leaders. Vannicelli (1992), however, believes that a difference in status, such as between leader and trainee, can be handled as long as the novice therapist is encouraged to use his or her clinical skills in tandem with the chief therapist.

Cotherapy offers many advantages to the group. Two heads are generally better than one; it sometimes takes two experts to handle difficult situations in the group. If one member is out of control or leaves suddenly, one of the group leaders can attend to the troubled person, leaving the group process unabated.

Having one man and one woman conducting therapy is an optimal combination for covering different points of view. Interracial and intercultural representation are also desirable. One leader may be a recovering alcoholic steeped in the principles of A.A.; the other may take a more cognitive approach. Although the potential for conflict is high, this combination of viewpoints can enhance group work. Many interdisciplinary combinations—such as a nurse and a social worker or a psychologist and a social worker—are possible. Above all, at the personal level, coleaders must be compatible to the point that they can tolerate disagreements that arise.

The advantages of dual leadership are many. One leader may observe a participant's body language while the other focuses on the words that are spoken. Both therapists are present for support and feedback during the group meeting and afterwards for follow-up. A strange twist on cotherapy is when the lead therapist does not speak the language of the group. An interpreter may then help lead the group and translate the words of the "outsider." The power balance can shift gradually over time toward the translator, however, as it is he or she who controls the flow of the interaction. Americans who were brought into Norway to teach "Minnesota Model" techniques experienced this strange phenomenon of the "tyranny" of the "native" translator. Group cotherapy can become something else entirely under such conditions.

THE PHASE APPROACH FOR BIOPSYCHOSOCIAL WORK

In order to demonstrate the basics of group treatment, I will tamper with reality and make a basic assumption: the hypothetical treatment group con-

---

BOX 9.1: You Don't Have to Tear 'Em Down to Build 'Em Up

There was a time when the dominant mode of chemical dependency treatment was based on a "tear 'em down, build 'em up" philosophy. This technique was used at Hazelden and a number of other treatment centers. While many of us discontinued its use years ago, it still persists in other programs across the country.

Aggressive, confrontational counseling was regarded as the only way to get an alcoholic to listen. A good counselor needed a loud voice and an arsenal of four-letter words. "Encounter" groups emphasized dealing with feelings with the volume cranked up all the way. Counseling sessions sounded disrespectful and dehumanizing. And they were.

Legislation in the early 1970s forced a change in style at Hazelden and many other treatment centers. Licensing regulations in Minnesota mandated *individualized* care, as did the standards of the Joint Commission on Accreditation of Hospitals. As a result, we took a good look at how we had been practicing treatment.

What we found was that individualized care meant respectful care. Patients, we discovered, can and will deal with information presented and discussed in a reasonable environment. They don't need to be "put down" to deal with symptoms such as grandiosity. Nor do they need to be hit over the head with a two-by-four. They need to be nurtured, to have their health built up. Most importantly, they need to be treated as individuals, with the same rights and respect we expect for ourselves.

We're concerned because many treatment programs still use these confrontational techniques. Some even call themselves Hazelden or Minnesota models. It's true that we once used confrontation. But we found a better way, and we went with it.

None of us can afford the assumption that our program is as effective as can be. It's our responsibility to continually evaluate ourselves and our techniques. That's the best way to ensure the most humane, respectful treatment for patients. It's also the best way to continue our own growth.

Source: *Hazelden Professional Update*, 4(2) (Nov. 1985): 2. Reprinted by permission of Hazelden.

---

sists of a *single* group of clients who begin and end an outpatient program at the same time. The length of treatment is approximately one year. The scheme presented can apply also to inpatient treatment. In this case, treatment progress takes place in a concentrated form, all formal work being completed in a mere twenty-eight days. The phase approach assumes, second, that the clients have all experienced a similar length of sobriety and therefore that everyone is working more or less on the same issues. Most actual working groups, however, have a combination of newcomers, relapsed former clients, and experienced group members. Sometimes even the group leaders come and go. The individual therapist, therefore, will have to make allowances for the discrepancies between the reality of everyday work and the ideal conditions imposed by this descriptive scheme.

The phase approach views treatment needs in terms of three precise intervals: initiation (relates to biological issues); working stage (relates to psychological factors); and termination stage (prepares client for new social supports). The group structure, goals, and session formats vary according to the length of time in treatment. A tremendous advantage of outpatient treatment is the greater length of sobriety that occurs with this treatment design. A client with six months of physical recovery and six months' practice in acquiring new social skills is clearly in better shape to work on emotionally troubling issues than a man or woman with ten days of sobriety. Inpatient programs, in fact, move along so fast that severely poly-addicted clients, such as the pill-users, may be in a still-toxic state for the first third of treatment. Fortunately, for reasons external to treatment, the trend has shifted in the direction of the community outpatient, long-term model.

The theory behind the phase system is that alcoholics' needs vary with the length of sobriety. This system also rewards sobriety by offering progressive treatment. Cohen and Spinner (1982) recommend this model as an extremely helpful tool in *outpatient* treatment for maximizing the chances for long-term sobriety. Progression is from some kind of orienta-tion-entry groups through problem-solving groups of various sorts. Grouping may or may not be on the basis of some special characteristic such as age, sex, or marital status, or on individual needs.

At the intensive *inpatient* treatment program, within a matter of weeks, the same population of clients may go through the basic stages of group process. At various times in the day, clients may attend homogeneous groups organized, for instance, by age and sex.

A much different group treatment plan operates, typically, at the *mental health agency*; here, alcoholism treatment is more limited in scope. The group may meet once or twice a week for an extended period, and there may be a waiting period for treatment to begin. Early, middle, and late stages of treatment may all take place within one group setting with one group leader and the same, stable population of members.

WORK AT THE INITIATION STAGE

Whatever the particular arrangements may be, the general tenets of the *initial* treatment process apply during the early sessions (first through fifth) of the group. In the early stages, members are tentative; the group leader is somewhat formal and very active in his or her role; emotional bonding is weak. Emotions, however, are strong beneath the surface.

GOALS OF INITIAL TREATMENT

The focus during the first part of treatment is on the *biological* side of alcoholism and recovery. The question "How do you feel?" is apt to be answered at this time in terms of how the members slept last night, what they are eating, and what kind of mood they are in.

The basic function of initial treatment is to provide basic education on the addictive process and to impart a sense of hope—hope that the alcoholic can somehow overcome and prevail against this addiction that has created so much havoc. Group structure is tight; the group leader lectures, uses diagrams, and generally fulfills the information-giving function of early treatment. Information must be provided on particulars of the total program and of the legal requirements, if any. Finally, a wealth of information concerning the physical illness of alcoholism is given. As a supplement to lecture material, educational films are often shown. Such films teach the effects of alcohol abuse on the mind, body, and relationships. Because of the newness of the material, it is often advisable to show each film more than once.

The importance of abstinence from all chemicals is emphasized; an exception is made for clients being medically treated to prevent withdrawal symptoms. Necessary attention must be given to reducing the defensiveness and externalization that are a concomitant of early recovery. Caring confrontation is essential. Emphasis is not on placing blame or on tearing people down but, rather, on helping individuals to accept responsibility for their own behavior. This is the time, too, to impart new ways of coping with stress other than through use of the drug alcohol.

A final aim of the early group sessions is to prepare members for later, active group membership. The early period is when one learns how to share, listen, and respond warmly in the group context.

DEALING WITH DENIAL

Coerced into treatment by crisis or by family, group members draw on all their denial defenses to stave off the pain of reality. During early recovery, the "rude awakening" period, the client's mental state is apt to be one of shock if not bewilderment. This is the *feeling* aspect of the postdrinking phase. Feelings control and are controlled by the cognitive dimension. Cognitively, the dry alcoholic is wrestling with yesterday's sins and omissions. Denial, minimization, and rationalization are basic themes of an alcoholic's logic, and they are still very much apparent in the early stages of treatment. These defenses should be understood in terms of the mind's attempts to adjust to a new reality. Adjustment takes time. Until reality has set in, there will be a period of resistance to the threatening information. Patience and warm encouragement are essential.

Members' acknowledgment of alcohol problems is the central organizing theme of all early group work. Related issues characteristic of early alcoholism treatment are grief and loss, social isolation, and dependency. Grief may ensue over the loss of the alcohol itself—"my worst enemy and my best friend"—or over the toll the alcohol has wrought (e.g., job, home, reputation). (A thorough discussion of the role of grief work in recovery was provided in chapter 6.) Social isolation from loved ones is a familiar part of the addiction experience. Emotional dependency is a paramount issue during this difficult time (Brown, 1985). Spouses and partners of alcoholics often minimize the severity of any problems that exist. Parents of acting-out teenagers are often the worst minimizers. Yet the families and/or significant others often need help too, every bit as much as do the alcoholics.

Outpatient treatment is designed to include concerned others at the preliminary stages of treatment. Edwards (1982) has developed a group work strategy based upon the developmental approach, the purpose of which is to enhance the social functioning of spouses and increase the likelihood that clients will maintain their level of progress following treatment. A further goal is the inculcation of factual information to reduce fear and confusion on the part of family members.

IMPLICATIONS FOR GROUP LEADERS

The basic skills of effective alcoholism group work are the same general skills of group leadership taught in counseling and social work practice courses. These skills include: initiating group interaction and guiding its direction; elaborating upon and underscoring significant individual contributions; paraphrasing; pulling inhibited or concerned persons into the action; drawing out helpful feedback from the group members; and providing commentary on the group process.

The leader of a group of chemically dependent persons draws on these basic skills and tailors them for work with persons who may or may not want recovery help. Anxiety and suspiciousness are two elements in every new alcoholism treatment group. "What are we going to have to do here?" is the common question. Members need to feel safe and accepted in the group; they need to be encouraged to trust and respect each other and the group leader.

Experts in the field recommend a highly structured approach in the initial sessions (Vannicelli, 1982; Yalom, 1974). Group leaders have to contend with denial, defensiveness, and ingenious avoidance tactics (avoidance of emotionally painful areas). Under the circumstances, leaders have to closely monitor the discussion and continually be prepared to shift the focus back to the therapeutic goals. A helpful strategy in lengthy group sessions is to vary group size. Many individuals who are noncommunicative in large groups will work well in dyads, triads, and groups of four or five. To maintain a sense of unity in the large group, the small groups may choose a spokesperson to report on what they accomplished in their discussion.

The group norms that develop early can "make or break" the evolving alcoholism therapy group. The leader's role in developing therapeutic group norms is essential. The norms desired are those that promote sharing in the group, sobriety, and individual change efforts. Norms *not* desired are those that sanction complaining about the courts, the police, or the program, or those that reinforce externalization and fatalism. Since norms arise out of the group context and cannot be imposed from without, it is advantageous in every alcoholism treatment group to have several recovering alcoholics who are firm in endorsing abstinence from alcohol as an important goal (Panepinto et al., 1982).

As clients begin to trust the leader and the group, they will begin to self-disclose. As they increasingly take risks and get supportive feedback, they come to trust the group more. In working with male alcoholics on gender-based issues, the group leader might first model the desired behavior, then encourage sharing. This process assists members to realize that they are not alone in their anxieties and inhibitions. Dave Clark, certified alcoholism counselor in Washington state, discloses how the process works (van Wormer, 1989: 238).

> I self-disclose at how effective I was about putting on a front; I fooled everyone. We [men] have feelings. It's a heavier brick [expression of feelings in men] because men aren't allowed to burst into tears like women do. Anger—this is the one thing we can express. So even feelings of hurt and rejection and loneliness have to get channeled around and come out as anger. I tell the men in my group, "You can open up. You're not less of a man because you admit you have feelings like women and that you are human." The flood gates may not open up; the men may just sit there. But I know they *had* to hear what I said.

The group leader can help members set their own rules; then he or she can help the group enforce these rules. First the leader lists the agency rules, such as:

- No smoking or drinking pop in the group
- No admission of intoxicated members into the group

Then group members are asked to suggest rules they would like to set for their group. Invariably the following suggestions are made and approved:

- What is said in the group stays in the group
- No put-downs or attacks on individuals
- No interruptions when someone is speaking; don't all talk at once
- No name-calling; no shouting

When the leader must remind the group that rules *they* have set are being violated, group members are often relieved to have this form of external protection. They make the rules, and they can rely on the leader to help enforce them.

What is the alcoholism counselor's role in promoting appropriate group norms? The trained leader makes use of effective group interventions at key points in the group process. Early in the group's life, skillful intervention serves as a model for group members who are thereby being groomed to assume responsibility for this function at some later stage of the group process. Significant, well-timed interventions help to keep members working on their goals and to give everyone a sense of security and structure. In reality this is much more difficult than it sounds. Hostility can run high; clients will blame the leader for their failure to get out of the session what they need. One angry young woman's unsolicited commentary haunts me still: "Frankly, I find the group process here a farce," she said.

In *The Practice of Social Work with Groups*, Ken Heap (1985) describes the role of the leader in helping the group move from a collection of isolated and estranged individuals to what sociologists term "a consciousness of kind." Based on his personal leadership experience with groups in England and Norway, Heap (1985: 49) expounds upon the universals in group management:

> Members' awareness seems initially to be focused either on their private distress or on their attempt to place the worker and to relate in some individual and personal way to him. It seems to require both time and freedom for members to register and relate more to the others in the group. The worker, however, being oriented towards the group as a whole, hears many signals about commonality which the members, who initially are inwardly directed and guarded, tend to miss. He comments on these by "linking" them together, indicating commonality and aiding the exploration and discovery necessary for the development of the group bond.

WHEN INTERVENTION IS CALLED FOR

The group counselor can expect to "step in" with an appropriate question or comment when:

1. A group member monopolizes the group and other members either seem uncomfortable or too comfortable (common in groups of involuntary clients) with this role;
2. A group member focuses on external events (court, parents, spouse, loss) in ascribing blame and fails to take any personal responsibility;
3. A group member falls into the widely recognized "all-or-nothing" thinking fallacy. Typically heard "all-or-nothing" statements are these: "There are two types of people—the weak and the strong"; "If you don't get an A in a course, why bother?"; "If you can't be the best then why bother at all?";
4. The recovering member expresses an abnormally high degree of guilt or self-blame over the alcoholism and its consequences;
5. Members fail to confront someone or to indicate their concern for one who is "setting him- or herself up" for personal tragedy;
6. Group members are sidetracked and turn the session into a "gripe session";
7. A member fails to see any *positive* thread in his or her attempt to grow and needs appropriate reinforcement for the small steps taken;
8. A client arrives at a group intoxicated or expresses views conducive to drinking behavior;
9. The mood of the group is too heavy and should be lightened. Or conversely, the mood is too light and thoughts should be moved into a more serious direction;
10. Effective individual and group maneuvers are observed; these should be positively reinforced as a model to all participants.

GROUP EXERCISES

Group exercises during the beginning of treatment focus on getting acquainted, building trust among members who will be sharing parts of their lives with each other, and setting the stage for deeper, more intensive work to follow.

1. Communication
   Purpose: To get acquainted; to explore levels of communication.
   Clients divide into groups of four. They are told to communicate for the first three minutes at a superficial level: talk about the weather, food, clothes. The second three minutes they will talk of a recent event—a movie or sports. The third three minutes, they express opinions on controversial topics. The next three minutes they will fill out cards that say:
   I feel *scared* when _____.
   I feel *happy* when _____.

I feel *jealous* when _____.

I feel *rejected* when _____.

Clients take turns filling in with their responses. The fifth period of time is the peak experience. Each member describes a peak moment of time of great revelation in his or her life.

While the interaction is taking place, the leader rotates visits among the various groups. He or she announces the end of each period of time and beckons members to move on to the next level. Following the last exchange, the groups rejoin each other. The leader may engage the participants in discussion by introducing such questions as: *At which level did you feel the least, the most comfortable? Did you learn something meaningful about each other? What surprised you about this exercise? At which level do you usually communicate throughout the day?* Discussion ensues.

2. Use of Cards

Purpose: To get acquainted; to learn to feel safe; to begin to learn to express feelings in the group. Group members fill out cards on which questions or statements are written. Some sample statements and questions are:

Say something positive about yourself!

My favorite childhood memory is _____.

Something I value highly is _____.

Name a famous alcoholic and tell this person's story _____.

If I could have three wishes, I would wish _____.

My advice to a young person is _____.

My understanding of alcoholism is _____.

3. Positive Feedback

Purpose: To boost self-esteem.

Sometimes a group member who is relating well to others puts himself or herself down. Group members are asked to say positive things about the member. The person records the messages. In later sessions, the person is asked to repeat these positive comments. This exercise helps provide substance for improved "self-talk" and to replace negative thoughts with positive ones.

We have considered basic elements of the group during the early stages, not only in the group treatment process but also in the alcoholic's sobriety. In many ways the early period of therapy is the most difficult—individual resistance is at a maximum, relapse is common, and defensiveness is a characteristic. Next, we come to the "working stage" of the group therapy with alcoholics.

THE WORKING STAGE OF GROUP WORK

Whereas the unifying theme of the early stage of treatment is the biology of alcoholism, during this, the middle period, the unifying theme is the *psychology* of alcoholism. Emphasis in this phase of treatment is on the frame of mind—the cognitive components—of sobriety. This phase, according to Kaufman (1985), may last from six months to several years. The working stage of group treatment begins when members are firm in their sobriety. Having already achieved some stability in using coping devices other than alcohol, they are psychologically ready to do some *real* work, to engage in risk taking. Whereas the mood of the newcomers' group is inclined toward anger (in the mandatory programs especially), the mood of seasoned group members is more apt to be depression punctuated with some moments of joy and possibly even humor.

Though he was not concerned with the group modality, Goldberg (1983: 43) provides an apt description of middle stage alcoholism work:

> It is a period in which alcoholics move from recognizing that they can have an impact on their own lives, strengthened by their continuing sobriety, to the recognition that they can have an impact on the world around them. The patient realizes that he, himself, rather than dependency, anxiety, and depression, can be the motivating force in his life.

Goldberg's (1983) middle phase recovery work utilizes a psychosocial task-oriented framework. The abstinence focus has now taken a back seat. Learning to drink responsibly may be the selected goal. Goldberg singles out five focal areas for recovery: sobriety, separation and loss (of alcohol), self (low self-esteem), success (and failure), and sexuality (resumption of sexual interest).

The working phase of the group occurs relatively quickly in the intensive inpatient treatment center where group members are together daily in a world, *sui generis*. They are living together, eating together, sleeping together. Members of alcoholism groups at the typical outpatient center or mental health clinic can be expected to remain at the initial stages for a longer time period for two reasons—the long lapses of time between sessions and the inflow and outflow of individual members.

Writing about prison group therapy, Fenton (1957) notes the gradual change in emotional tone over time. Initial resistance and uncertainty give way to sharing of personal problems presented for group discussion. Feedback is given to the member who speaks; eye contact is with the entire group, not just the group leader. Group work, in a real sense, has begun.

The focus in this more advanced group setting continues to be on learning new ways of thinking and behaving to replace the old ways of thinking and behaving. Specific interventions are directed toward heightening the alcoholic's perception of him- or herself and increasing insight into others. The focus is on insight, self-concept, and members' feelings and emotions. As the therapy group becomes more sophisticated, the members grow more introspective. They grow more empathic of others' needs also.

Substance abusers, according to Kaufman (1985), can be expected, during this period, to show alternating cycles of improvement and retreat into former patterns of behavior. Emphasis should be more on taking responsibility for one's life and less on the illness itself.

During the middle stage of treatment, emotional crises abound. Early, too-high expectations for a smooth recovery may affect both the client and the client's family. Impatience and distress may replace the earlier euphoria.

Long ago, Shakespeare (*Hamlet*, II, ii) noted that "there is nothing either good or bad, but thinking makes it so." In order to help clients accept their lives and learn to cope with future stress without the use of alcohol, the group leader may adopt the technique called *cognitive restructuring*, which relates to the way one looks at things. By reframing clients' unhealthy thoughts into a more positive direction, the group leader can teach clients to ward off stress. Thus, the thought "I've wasted my life" can be replaced with "I'm going to take advantage of each day that's left" or "I believe this all happened for a reason, so that I can help others." The latter comment is one I have occasionally heard from clients.

Individual problems are broken down into manageable steps to reduce anxiety. Social workers call this *partializing* the problem. Assertiveness training may be provided to enhance coping skills and expression of feelings. Behavioral rehearsals may take place in the group. The group leader may instruct, "Now I will play the employer, and I want you to practice the job interview." Following a rehearsal, the real-life experience is usually easier. At the next session, the client can report on how the job interview went. Anxiety-ridden clients often can be helped by trying to answer the question "What's the worst thing that can happen?" Usually, the worst possible occurrence is an event that could be lived with. The imaging of this event aids the client to cope with any eventuality.

General themes that crop up in advanced treatment groups are the stigma of being an alcoholic, depression, holidays, dealing with criticism, loneliness, fear, love, and endings.

Women alcoholics need to explore, in all-female settings, their relationships with men (a favorite topic in women's groups), patterns of self-destruction, their relationships with other women (a topic that the therapist may have to introduce), self-esteem issues, and patterns of victimization. Individual therapy is often indicated for more intensive work with emotional trauma.

Male alcoholics need to explore similar issues. They also need to work on the issue of sexuality. Alcoholics may find that sex, like dancing, is a major undertaking without the fortifying effects of alcohol. Gays and lesbians, likewise, report sexual inhibitions in the absence of "90-proof courage."

GOALS OF THE WORKING STAGE

The primary purpose of alcoholism therapy groups at the working stage is to ensure continuing progress toward personal growth and development. Although abstinence remains a basic requirement for group participation in most North American programs, it should now more or less fall to the background of group concerns. Improving one's self-image and getting "in tune with" one's true emotions are the major goals at this stage. As stated by Forrest (1984: 142):

> The later stages of treatment involve focused and intensive affective work. Primary alcoholics experience a great deal of difficulty in the realm of managing feelings and affects. . . . Many alcoholics are unable to correctly label their various emotions. . . . Primary alcoholics are able to openly explore and express their various repressed feelings and emotions later in the psychotherapeutic relationship.

A major goal of therapy is to help modify the behavior pattern that alcoholism counselors term "stuffing" of strong emotional reactions. Participating in group treatment sensitizes members to the fact that their feelings and problems are not unique. As a means of behavior modification, the literature on alcoholism treatment recommends that specialized work be done with each individual group member on his or her own special needs and issues. Individual goals are set in the group; goals are unique to each individual and geared toward personal self-improvement. Work on anger control or assertiveness or stress management are examples of popular individual goals.

Dyer and Vriend (1975) correctly warn against the leader's getting sidetracked into having the group set collective goals. Contracts are more effectively set on a case-by-case basis. According to their scheme, each individual sets a goal (e.g., to learn to deal with stress, to get the confidence to look for work, to learn assertiveness) and pursues work toward that goal in the group. By asking each individual member to set personal goals and by helping individuals to set new goals as the group progresses, the group leader removes the obstacle of *group* goals, goals that are time-consuming and irrelevant in a counseling group.

In summary, specific tasks for the group leader at the middle phase of treatment are to:

- Reinforce the alcoholic in his or her sobriety and close affiliation with sober support systems; help the individual identify him- or herself as a part of a larger whole—the recovering alcoholic community.
- Reduce guilt reactions to past alcohol abuse; help group members internalize the role of addiction in past, uncharacteristic behavior.
- Aid group members to make the important leap from "I can't drink" to "I won't drink" (Lawson, et al., 1983: 23).
- Continue to help clients develop healthy interpersonal relationships and to gain from the weekly treatment group a sense of belonging and oneness.
- Encourage trust and bonding among members of the support group so that emotional expression may be enhanced; help group members express and correctly label feelings in hypothetical and real situations.
- Teach practical skills of cognitive restructuring and other effective coping devices.
- Help group members to cope with their disturbing moods and feelings without turning to alcohol.
- Work with family members to explain some of the realities for an alcoholic in recovery, and encourage family members to develop strong personal interests apart from the alcoholic; recommend attendance at Al-Anon meetings.

IMPLICATIONS FOR GROUP LEADERS

Having laid the proper groundwork in the initial sessions, the group leader can now enjoy a less directive, more relaxed facilitative role. Ideally, every member of the group is both client and therapist. The leader's role is to facilitate the group's work and to keep the group focused on work conducive to individual growth. Growth is directed toward the general area of feelings. Dave Clark (quoted in van Wormer, 1989) describes his leadership role as follows:

> The role I play is not didactic. My role is less obvious than that. Ideally, I will not have to say anything. I introduce the topic; I might say, "The ideal man in our culture is Superman."
>
> I moderate the discussion and rely on the core group of experienced members to follow through. After someone speaks, I might say, "What do some of the rest of you guys think?"
>
> I intervene when the discussion stalemates or when we get into a real touchy area, like being scared. . . .
>
> I also intervene when members fail to make eye contact with the group but just talk to me, one-to-one. I say, "Tell the group; don't tell me."

Yalom (1974) spells out the specific intervention techniques required in conducting alcoholic groups in the working stages. The focus is on the *here and now* of the small group experience. The stress is not on relationships external to the group. As people get to know each other in the group, they are instructed to state how they feel about certain behaviors of these people.

Yalom (1974: 90) explains his concept of the leadership function:

> The leader should strive to transfer the responsibility of the content and direction of the meetings onto the members. In other words, the therapist should aim to help the group become self-monitoring. . . . I usually ask certain people about their reactions at that specific moment (when subject too abstract): How do you feel about what's happening to the group?

Through the use of videotape equipment, Yalom provides a ten-minute playback of important segments of the previous meeting. Through centering on the group process itself at moments when "things are going slowly," Yalom causes members to be conscious of their own interaction, of the *form* the interaction is taking. This has the effect of moving the interaction along and preventing such stagnation in the future.

Yalom's conceptualization of the group is as an experimental society, though one with a unique etiquette. The role for the leader is continually to build and to monitor such an experimental but very real creation.

Alcoholism treatment modalities tend to center upon education of the disease concept and the early stages of sobriety. Much more than this is required, however, for late-stage treatment. Orosz (1982) has introduced a much-needed specialized program to, in her words, "enhance the quality of sobriety." Orosz utilizes the rational-emotive approach with alcoholics. One of the tasks for the therapist is to mobilize the entire group to the assistance of the individual member in working through thoughts and feelings. In one example presented, members helped a member construct I-statements to express her terror at her husband driving while intoxicated. The type of I-statement used begins, "I feel _____ when you _____." This standard format has wide applicability in the working-level group.

Much of the work done in traditional alcoholism groups is directed toward the ventilation of anger. As Tavris (1982) correctly suggests, anger that is ventilated tends to build on itself and to thereby grow. This snowballing effect is one good reason for the alcoholism counselor to strive to quash the gripe session as soon as it gets started.

Themes of the early portion of treatment—separation and loss— are also dominant themes in the middle phase of treatment (Goldberg, 1983). There are two kinds of loss relevant to alcoholism—the loss of a job or loved one and the loss of the crutch, alcohol, to deal with the original loss. For satisfactory resolution of grief, alcoholics are helped by social workers to develop appropriate grieving mechanisms. Similar work is done by the counselor in other areas of equal relevance to chemical dependents—for example, in the areas of self-image and sexuality. Experienced alcoholism counselors have at their disposal a battery of exercises to keep clients actively participating in shaping their lives.

EXERCISES

The focus of the following activities is on allowing deep feelings to arise spontaneously in a warm, supportive setting.

1. Art Therapy
   Purpose: To reveal feelings that may not be expressed. May bring out perfectionism as a secondary function.

   Have clients draw their world during the time *before* they came to treatment, *during* treatment, and *after* treatment. Clients are told they can draw stick-people—no need for talent. This exercise, seriously undertaken, gives an indication of future hopes and fears. Those who, because of lack of confidence or anxiety, resist this exercise can have someone else draw what they describe in words.

   Ask clients to draw pictures representing three feelings from a list: jealousy, anger, joy, grief. Note which feelings are *not* chosen as well as which ones are chosen. Women may not choose anger, for instance, an indication of possible inhibition of this emotion.

   Following the drawing activity, each client holds his or her picture and shares it with the group. Clients likely will give thoughtful feedback on the meaning of their drawings.

   While I was working in Norway, a beautiful and refined young mother drew representations of jealousy, joy, and anger (figure 9.1). Under "anger," there is a knifed television set and a coffin. This woman, who seemed so happy on the surface, stayed beyond the inpatient phase in the halfway house. Some months later, when the state refused to return her children to her, she committed suicide. The message had been in her artwork, yet tragically, we on the staff had failed to address the feelings revealed in the telltale picture.

2. Faces
   Purpose: To elicit discussion of feelings.
   Use a sheet of faces with diverse expressions on them. Simple cartoon faces, including duck faces, are effective. This exercise works with nonreaders and equally well with men and women.

   The following instructions are given: "Choose the face that shows how you feel today and also one that shows how you felt earlier in the week. Each of you will share your selection with the group."

FIGURE 9.1

Feelings Drawn by Client

Jealousy

Happiness

Anger

FIGURE 9.2

Faces

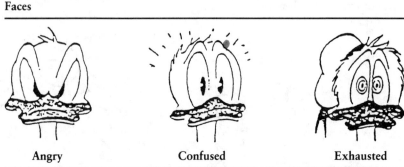

| Angry | Confused | Exhausted |

3. Grief and Loss
   Purpose: To reveal underlying feelings of grief and guilt over loss.
   On a sheet of paper have clients:
   a. Identify a significant loss. (This can be a person, a job, or some other loss.)
   b. Describe the support you have received for the loss and what you have learned from this experience.

4. Quiz Cards
   Purpose: To share in the group; to elicit a wide range of responses.
   This exercise is a continuation of the card game described in an earlier group exercise. These questions call for deeper level responses.
   Examples:
   When I think of my mother _____.
   When I remember my father _____.
   Alcohol was for me _____.
   Sobriety is _____.
   As a child, if only I had _____.
   Love is _____.
   I feel depressed when _____.

5. Movie/Television Titles
   Purpose: To help group members review their lives with perspective; work on past and present issues, and share with others; to see where clients are headed; to have an enjoyable session. (Some of my favorite sessions flowed from this exercise, which I created in a desperate search for some activity for a particularly unresponsive group.)
   Clients are given a list of movies and television programs. Each client chooses the title that best describes his or her life yesterday, to-

day, and tomorrow. Example: "I had *Great Expectations*, but today it is all *Gone with the Wind*. Tomorrow I will follow *The Journey* to sobriety." Explore meanings with the help of group members.

Examples of Titles

Search for Tomorrow	*The Brady Bunch*
Days of Wine and Roses	*The Good Mother*
The Lost Weekend	*A Farewell to Arms*
Remains of the Day	*The Children's Hour*
Gone with the Wind	*The Witness*
Loss of Innocence	*Great Expectations*
Crime and Punishment	*Superman*
The Journey	*Rebel without a Cause*
Pride and Prejudice	*Basic Instinct*
An Affair to Remember	*Presumed Innocent*
The Outsiders	*Fatal Attraction*
Add your own titles.	

6. Awareness Wheel

   Purpose: To reveal thought patterns, feelings, and irrational interpretations of life experiences and the behavior that may follow.

   A circle is divided into four wedge shaped sections; each section is labeled: interpretations, feelings, intentions, and actions. At the top of the pie is written "The Event."

   Clients list a key event such as a breakup with a girlfriend or boyfriend. They write in the pie their responses to this event, then share their responses with group members.

All of these devices are means of getting otherwise reluctant clients to reveal their feelings of anger, hurt, and anxiety and to identify them. The trained alcoholism counselor has a repertoire of strategies to use as the situation requires. In addition to introducing the strategy and setting it up, the therapist helps group members to label, recognize, and experience the basic emotions that arise in the course of a session. The therapist-leader helps the individual as well as the other group members to both laugh and cry. The use of humor is an essential component in the treatment group in which so many of the primary emotions are disguised as anger, and incorrectly identified as such. Associated with a good sense of humor is the ability to step back and observe the self objectively. Humor breeds a sense of perspective; a sense of perspective breeds humor. The following case history shows how anger can serve to cover up another emotion. The example reveals the kind of interaction that close exploration of emotions may entail.

CASE HISTORY OF LOVE DISGUISED AS ANGER

"I was sent here by my parole officer." With those words, Butch entered the alcoholism support group, and the group was never quite the same again. Butch was an ex-convict from a maximum security prison. Although Butch denied he was an alcoholic, because "I am a strong person," he said, he was unlike most other members, who were willing to take real risks in the group. An American Indian, Butch always wore a cowboy hat and boots. After I requested that he remove his sunglasses in group, he pulled the brim of the hat down over his eyes. I saw them once, and they were blue.

The striking thing about Butch was that he was so full of contradictions. He dressed tough, and all his talk was tough. Yet underneath was a loving, gentler self. The group seemed at once intrigued and outraged by Butch.

The following exchange took place approximately six weeks into treatment. The therapist's goal was to help Butch recognize his emotions for what they were.

BUTCH: When my nephews stole from others, I could accept that. But then when they stole from me, that was another thing entirely. I can't wait for them to go to jail. They'll be picked out by those homosexuals right away!

GROUP MEMBER: (Laughing) Don't reach down for your bar of soap!

BUTCH: I'll give them a bar of soap myself.

THERAPIST: So, Butch, what do you *feel* about your nephews right now?

BUTCH: I feel they deserve a licking. I'd like to take them out to the woods and tan their hides, both of them.

THERAPIST: No, how do you *feel*? Where are you emotions right now?

BUTCH: Mad! I'm as mad as hell. After all I've done for those two boys. I'd like to knock some sense into them. Of course they'll serve their time. But that's not what I want to see. I'd like to handle it in my own way.

THERAPIST: So, going back to your feelings, what you are saying is you have mixed feelings. Anger, but something else too?

BUTCH: I helped raise those boys.

THERAPIST: Did you love them?

BUTCH: I loved them like my own.

THERAPIST: That explains the anger. Love turned to hatred, or at least to anger. (To group) I wonder if some of you can find any other feelings here?

GROUP MEMBER: Hurt, maybe. Butch, do you feel hurt that they let you down?

BUTCH: Yeah. You're damn right I do!

In summary, the focus in group work on emotional expression is not to encourage ventilation of violent emotions but, rather, to show clients the way to verbalize thought and impulses that represent a wide range of feelings. The effective leader strives to get group members to appreciate the difference between thoughts and feelings. Use of group dynamics to "bring the message home" to the client is a vital part of meaningful group interaction.

Over the months, as he faced situations and his feelings more fully, Butch grew toward greater maturity and control. He moved from a position of attacks on authority and expression of personal rage to gaining understanding of his own personal concerns. And as Butch moved forward, the group moved forward with him.

ENDING-ONGOING PHASE

The ending phase of a group frequently offers the highest potential for important work (Zastrow, 1990). The concerns that have gone before—sobriety, feelings, control—are still concerns in the third, the ongoing stage of recovery. (I consider this phase *ongoing* because it continues beyond the life of the group.) Strong feelings are elicited in group members as they contemplate dealing with events and emotions without group support and clarification.

Separation and ambivalence are two themes singled out by Heap (1985) as instrumental to group interactions during the final period of treatment. "Ambivalence which is not recognized and separation anxiety which is not articulated and resolved hold people in positions of dependency and confusion." The time spent together is drawing to a close. Dealing with mixed feelings concerning ending the group is a major task of building the bridge between the microcosm of the group world and the wider world outside. Not only a sense of loss but some sense of relief may accompany the leaving process. Heap (1985) would anticipate relief when areas of privacy will no longer be invaded and interpersonal conflicts and rivalries will be no more. The end of stress caused by imposed intimacy of persons that would never have freely chosen each other as friends is another positive aspect to breaking the ties.

On the other hand, feelings of loss and a sense of emptiness may prevail. Some members can even be expected to bargain for an extension of the group as new problems are suddenly "discovered." Whatever the feelings that arise, clients should be encouraged to face them. Counselors can help members get in tune with their feelings by having the group reminisce about highlights and learning experiences in the group. The group therapist might ask, "Mary, what did you learn that surprised you from the group experience?" "John, what do you wish had happened that didn't happen in the group?" "Kirsten, what's the best thing about the end of these sessions?"

As Heap (1985: 174) eloquently describes the parting process, he sums up the essence of the whole experience:

There may have been laughter in the group, for people who have become strangers to it. There may have been tears, giving to distressed people a freedom and release which is forbidden by the controlling norms of our denial-ridden culture. The group may have been an island of meaning and challenge in lives which lack these qualities.

Termination is not an event but a process. I have heard it said that the moment of inception of the group is the time to plan for the ending of the group. The final sessions are a time to put the meaning of the shared experience into words and to help members deal with realized and unrealized emotions.

Exercises at this stage are often of the "learning to have fun while sober" variety. Public outings and potlucks may be enjoyed. The style of leadership employed at this stage (sometimes the group is renamed "The Grad Group") is more relaxed and nondirective than in previous sessions. There may be a rotation in group leadership.

Major tasks for the termination period are:

- To help clients acknowledge painful realities of the past that still have a bearing on the present; to help them explore ways to get beyond these realities.
- To enable clients to move from the "I won't drink" stage to the "I don't have to drink" stage (Lawson et al., 1983: 23).
- To help prepare the members for a level of intimacy in their relationships in the group and elsewhere.
- To help clients be aware of and analyze their rigid ways; to help them learn to be more flexible; to address the question "Why not?" as well as "Why?"
- To prepare clients and their families for healthy personal autonomy; to relax the tight structure of the group and encourage autonomy here also.
- To utilize exercises for relapse prevention; to explore key emotional responses that trigger relapse; to indicate how to rebound in case of relapse.
- To encourage affiliation with a relevant self-help group for lifelong protection and support.

SOME COMMON PITFALLS IN ALCOHOLISM COUNSELING

The literature on group therapy with chemical dependents points to major pitfalls peculiar to this variety of group work. An excellent resource for "removing the roadblocks" in this kind of specialized treatment is provided in Vannicelli (1992). Vannicelli provides suggestions concerning all the common problems in group leadership, problems that are encountered again and again in the group process. From this source and others, and from my own group leadership experience, I have assembled the following pitfalls of alcoholism counseling.

1. *Coercion, denial, and resistance.* The element of coercion and related factors of denial and resistance that are characteristics of the disease alcoholism impede easy group progress. The group norms likely to arise in a group of willing clients are likely to be nontherapeutic norms. The beauty of the group setting, however, is that what individuals cannot see in themselves they can often recognize in others. The trained therapist is able to draw on the insights of the various members.

2. *Character disorders and alcoholism.* Character disorders associated with, but not unique to, alcoholism—rigidity of personality, "all-or-nothing" reasoning, hypersensitivity—render treatment of some alcoholics in the group especially difficult (Cunynghame, 1983; Forrest, 1984; Levinson, 1979).

Alcoholics in the typical treatment group face an "unceasing staccato of crises" (Yalom, 1974: 92). Relapses are a well-known phenomenon in an alcoholic group. Levinson (1979) mentions problems for the leader in groups with members who are suffering from brain damage and serious emotional problems as well as a sense of loss without alcohol. The task for the therapist is to effectively utilize the experience of the healthier members as examples for the less healthy ones. The ongoing therapeutic work needs to be ego-supportive and reassuring.

When a verbally abusive interaction takes place, the group leader may redirect attention away from the disruptive client onto the group as a whole. Vannicelli (1992: 165) offers a response: "John has been pretty forthright with some of his feelings this evening. It seems as if others in here are having more difficulty right now sharing their feelings. Perhaps we can understand what it is about what John has shared or the way in which he shared it that makes it hard to respond."

3. *Getting every member to work.* A few members do all the talking. Sometimes one individual, week after week, is allowed to dominate the group. Such a pattern must be broken at once. The therapist can encourage group members to summarize this person's problem and comment on it. A technique I have found to be successful when all else fails is to ask another group member "Why are you allowing [Gary] to do all the work?"

4. *Separate groups for women.* A common pitfall in alcoholism counseling is the failure to provide a separate arena for *women* alcoholics, who have their special and often unidentified concerns. A woman in a group of other women has an opportunity to look to other women as role models for breaking the pattern of self-defeating and sex-role stereotype behaviors. Often, in the mixed group, these behavior patterns go unno-

ticed or are reinforced (Joyce and Hazelton, 1982). The worst treatment scenario for a woman is to be the lone woman in a group. This often occurs because males are so much in the majority in alcoholism treatment.

5. *The nonalcoholic professional.* There is a certain suspiciousness by the recovering alcoholics of the nonalcoholic professional; sometimes this creates a sense of inferiority on the part of the professional. "How can you lead a group like this when you have never been drunk?" is typical of the kind of remark that is made. The recovering alcoholic group leader does not have this "bridge to cross" between his or her world and the clients'. The nonalcoholic professional would do well to self-disclose on a wide range of situations presented. He or she can utilize empathy to identify with the alcoholic person just as he or she would in working with the physically or mentally challenged. Some of the attacks at the capabilities of the nonalcoholic counselor are simply a sign of reluctant group members' resistance to counseling of any sort.

6. *Limits of confidentiality.* The therapist must make clear that although there is confidentiality of information shared in the group, there are limits to the agreement, "What's said in the groups stays in the group." Exceptions are: reported ongoing injury to children, endangerment of oneself or others by certain planned activities, and reports of recent substance abuse. If the group leader fails to clarify the limits of the confidentiality rule, clients may feel a trust has been violated when information is reported or written up in treatment records.

7. *Dealing with scapegoats.* One member or an entire group may be scapegoated; members sometimes displace aggression and anger onto vulnerable persons. The group leader must be alert to any moves in this direction. To prevent the herd instinct from taking over, the scapegoating must be stopped at the earliest moment. Role playing in the group can be discussed by members of the group as a whole. Those who identify with the scapegoat role can be encouraged to express the feelings aroused by this treatment. As treatment progresses, the leader can inconspicuously help the group member move into a more positive role in the group by drawing him or her out in a positive way. When a whole group or culture is scapegoated, an effective approach is to ask a question that arouses empathy for members of the out-group (e.g., What is it like growing up as a gay or lesbian in our society?). In this way, members of the out-group are shown to be people too. Only when group members are secure within themselves will they no longer feel it necessary to attribute their problems to other people. The best discussion of scapegoating that I have found in the literature is from Heap (1985: 98):

> A member who is vulnerable, or new, or less identified with the group, or who has in fact done or said that which is forbidden, is chosen as a scapegoat. By clearly ostracizing him, the group as a whole both relieves the tension of

suppressed conflicts and vicariously punishes and asserts their disapprobation of that which they in fact feel but which is forbidden. . . . Thus the most liberating contribution is one which is aimed not at protection, not at mediation, not at judgment of the scapegoat, but at relief of the feelings of guilt, deviance, inadequacy, fear, or whatever qualities arouse the need for projection and expiation.

Vannicelli (1992: 125) provides a response to a member who is attacking another member: "It must be hard for you to hear Sally doing this stuff. I wonder if it might bring back memories that are quite uncomfortable to think about—things about yourself. . . ."

8. *Issues best kept private.* Some issues that arise in the group are best dealt with privately, in an individual session. If gay and lesbian members are prompted to be "open and honest," for instance, they may be labeled and even scapegoated by other members. Former prostitutes and incest survivors also may feel somewhat tainted after sharing highly personal material with the group. Whether or not sharing intimacies with the group is appropriate depends to a great extent on the degree of cohesiveness of the group and the sense of trust that develops.

Above all, the wide range of legal concerns of court-ordered candidates for treatment tends to crop up in the group discussion at the most unsuspecting moments. The frustration inherent in the Driving While Intoxicated (DWI) cluster as well as the hostility felt by persons sent by the court for domestic violence or child neglect charges are the most real and immediate issues to many of the members of an alcoholism therapy group. Far-reaching topics like sobriety and relationships are apt to be of less immediate concern in the group. Hence, the effective addictions specialist plays the directive and active role of keeping the group discussion on target. Group norms may develop that are antithetical to treatment; when this happens, changes in group composition and tighter structuring are necessary.

CONCLUSION

This chapter has examined the theoretical roots and current practice of group therapy with particular emphasis on its applicability to chemically dependent individuals. In light of practical and therapeutic considerations, use of the group modality has secured a dominant position in inpatient and outpatient alcoholism treatment centers.

Group therapy with alcoholics and other substance abusers utilizes the scientific principles of group dynamics to effect changes in individual self-concept, feelings, and behavior. We have seen how social support mechanisms in the group can be mobilized toward the particular needs of chemically dependent people. A survey of the literature reveals a variety of innovative techniques to serve the alcoholic client and to offset tactics of resistance characteristic of the "captive" client. Such approaches can be directed to the newly sober and often suspicious client group as well as to the group of conscientiously working individuals.

We have seen how group therapy complements Alcoholics Anonymous. In focusing on personal and interpersonal dynamics that at once support and go beyond sobriety, both varieties of treatment are compatible. Group therapy, furthermore, is compatible with individual psychotherapy. Ideally, each group member receives intensive personal counseling to reinforce progress made in the group and to address personal issues unique to each client. Consultations between the group leader and the primary therapist are crucial in assessing the individual's progress in achieving his or her chosen goals.

Group treatment occupies an important part of any comprehensive approach to individuals in trouble with alcoholism "whose lives have become unmanageable." Regardless of the diversity of the population afflicted with alcoholism, the treatment group can address members' common needs in getting a handle on the curse of addiction. In any treatment group, an overwhelming array of personal, social, and financial problems associated with alcoholism occupy the highest mental resources of the group. The individual member in the group can benefit from the wealth of knowledge and experience represented. For the group leader the challenge is to channel this collective energy into positive and creative directions. Activities and exercises appropriate to each stage of the treatment process are included.

The kind of personal and relationship growth that occurs in a group cannot be measured scientifically. Sometimes the growth must be experienced to be realized. The reality of the interpersonal change that takes place in a long-term therapy group was made evident in a surprising comment of one female member: "Oh, I wish my husband could come up here and be in a group like this," she said.

"I didn't know he was an alcoholic," I replied.

"Oh, he's not," she said. "I just want to see him learn what these other men have learned here in this group, so he can be caring like them."

REVIEW QUESTIONS

1. Give three reasons why group work is so widely used in alcoholism treatment today.

2. Describe what is and is not in the literature on group practice with substance abusers.

3. List several of the "curative factors" included by Yalom in his discussion of individual change through the group process.

4. Which needs does A.A. meet that group therapy does not? Which needs does group therapy meet not met by A.A.?

5. Describe the well-functioning therapy group at the early stage. Observing the group, what would you *see*? Listening, what would you *hear*?

6. Discuss factors in doing cotherapy. What is the ideal arrangement? What are the hazards?

7. What are tasks for the leader in addressing denial and other resistances?

8. How are drinking issues—"slips" or relapses and negative attitudes—handled?

9. Compare new and former confrontational styles of doing group therapy.

10. What are the major tasks for the group during the early stage of treatment?

11. What are the major issues facing the group therapist during the "working stage" of group treatment?

12. How are games and exercises used to get group members to deal with feelings? Describe some of these exercises and the purpose of each one.

13. Explain how hurt can be disguised as anger. How does the case example demonstrate this?

14. What are some common pitfalls for the social worker in alcoholism counseling?

10

ECONOMIC, SOCIOLOGICAL, AND LEGAL DYNAMICS

Drug use, licit and illicit, is big business in America.
—Langton (1991), p. 9

The notion of "the alcoholic society" was formulated by sociologist Norman Denzin (1993). In providing the arena for the production of alcoholics U.S. society, according to Denzin, promotes an atmosphere in which the mass media create demands for certain products like alcohol. Our society then creates laws that persons violate when they get into trouble with alcohol and the treatment centers that deal with the resultant alcoholism. To study alcoholism, then, is to study the relationship between individuals and the social structure, and between the treatment center and the economic and social forces that create and sustain it. In other words, marketing of the legal drug alcohol has as its parallel the marketing of treatment services. For the purposes of exploring the linkages among the political economy, the alcohol beverages industry, and the alcoholism treatment apparatus, this chapter employs a macro (structural) perspective. Among the topics addressed are the *business* aspect of alcohol consumption and the *policy* aspect of provision of treatment services. Business and policy are viewed as intertwined. The role of third-party payment schemes will be shown to be crucial in shaping the course of alcoholism treatment. Detoxification, inpatient treatment, and outpatient community-based services are modalities for the provision of much-needed services. Their survival is linked to factors in the political economy.

Moving from the economic into the more purely sociological realm, a sociological analysis of alcoholism counseling will be provided. What is a profession? And to what extent does alcoholism counseling qualify as a profession? How do codes of ethics and the certification process relate to professionalization? These and related issues consume the middle portion of this chapter. The legal constraints on professional activities relevant to alcoholism treatment will be described. Finally, a controversial exploration of the social organization of the alcoholism treatment center, often a house divided against itself, will complete the chapter. Insight into characteristics of "the addictive organization" is provided.

THEORETICAL FRAMEWORK

Alcohol problems drastically affect the U.S. economy; over $85 billion is wasted each year in alcohol-related lost productivity, crime, accidents, and health-care costs, according to the Department of Health and Human Services (1993). The economy also shapes alcohol use in myriad ways. Langton (1991) offers an addictions commentary concerning the wider, social context. In the tradition of radical sociologist C. Wright Mills, Langton's text, *Drug Use and the Alcohol Dilemma*, examines personal problems in terms of public issues. Among these public issues, economics emerges as paramount. The rhetoric that Langton uses is not the rhetoric of pathology and treatment; her focus is entirely structural. Such an approach is highly applicable to the macro concerns of this chapter.

The form, shape, and availability of alcoholism treatment are shaped less by science or custom than by sharp economic realities. Since the alcoholic clients themselves can rarely pay for the intensive treatment they need, funding must be sought from external sources. For public agencies, third-party payments may consist of federal grant money or, more frequently, money obtained from state and local sources. Private treatment centers often rely on health insurance reimbursement for clients with comprehensive policies as well as contracts from the county or city to perform specialized services. Cutbacks at any one of these levels reverberate throughout the entire system. Thus, if the federal government or the states reduce coverage, the treatment industry must appeal to the county for support. Therefore, the provision of revenues and services is a highly political and volatile phenomenon. Public opinion and interests may reach a consensus that substance abuse is a top *social problem* in this country (Akers, 1992). Conversely, the public and the media may concentrate on crime and increasing various punishments for drug- related offenses. The way in which social problems are prioritized, government budgeting, and demands of competing interests all come into play in determining treatment offerings and duration and the forms of treatment (e.g., outpatient versus inpatient modalities).

By way of contrast, the Canadian system attempts to offer universal care to individual citizens through medical insurance corporations owned by provincial governments. The insurance corporations are funded generally through the work place and subsidized from the general task pool (Todtman and Todtman, 1991). For a comparative view of another system, the Swedish welfare system, see Box 10.1. Because the Swedish public, through their elected officials, plays a role in guiding health-care costs, costs have risen less rapidly than in the United States. Private inpatient treatment for substance abuse has been rare.

THE BUSINESS SIDE OF TREATMENT IN THE UNITED STATES

In order to maintain financial solvency and to offer comprehensive services, treatment centers must engage in political lobbying—wheeling and dealing at the local community level—and marketing of services to local entities such as the Department of Corrections. Centers solicit support from key community leaders such as judges who can be encouraged to mandate assessment and treatment for substance abuse related offenses. Potential consumers may be the state, the local community, or individuals with adequate insurance coverage. Major target populations are those individuals fortunate enough to have generous insurance reimbursement payment plans. Unrestricted insurance policies, however, are becoming increasingly rare.

Administrators of alcoholism treatment centers today would do well to have a solid business background and superb public relation skills in addition to counseling education. The major part of the director's time and energy, in fact, goes into soliciting funds, writing grants, and balancing budgets. Even decision-making about hiring and retaining employees is largely financially based. The director often works closely with an accountant, who may be a full-time member of the staff. Board members with good fiscal backgrounds and connections are often highly sought after by board and agency directors.

The big business aspect of alcohol addiction, therefore, must not be overlooked. Previously, health-care entrepreneurs joined with chronically underused hospitals to turn empty wards into profitable addictions treatment clinics (Seligmann, 1984). Today, in light of growing fiscal restraints, sheer economic survival rather than accruing profits may receive the major emphasis. Babcock (1992) blames the earlier crass commercialism of the alcoholism treatment industry of the 1980s for many of the problems of today. The switch from a "pass the message" mentality to a "promote the facility" phenomenon was associated with a lack of accountability for treatment effectiveness. Counselors, according to Babcock, pay more homage to commercially popular viewpoints than to the findings of science. The extremely competitive nature of the field is taking its toll.

THE POLITICAL DIMENSION

Since the late seventies, with some help from highly publicized celebrities who courageously acknowledged their own problems with drug dependency, the demand for drug and alcohol rehabilitation services has been seemingly insatiable. In fact, checking into a drug or alcoholism clinic for treatment has become almost chic in some circles (Akers, 1992). Appearances on the lecture and talk-show circuits combined with the production of unlimited, dramatic autobiographies has helped reach a wide range of persons who were encouraged to follow suit.

The public perception of addiction as a disease coupled with admiration for persons striving to straighten out their lives has paved the way for generous third-party reimbursement schemes. But the climate of public opinion is subject to rapid and unpredictable changes. With regard to illegal drugs, federal revenues and activities have been directed toward the supply side of the drug/alcohol problem in the United States (Fields, 1992). Public opinion and media attention have begun to change. Now, as the "war on drugs" has become a war *against* drug users, the stigma of chemical dependency has returned. Treatment for chemical dependency seemingly is no longer a high priority item for the health care system. The contemporary emphasis on individual responsibility and punishment rather than rehabilitation (evidenced in unprecedented prosecution and incarceration rates), coupled with scientific criticism of the disease model (see Fingarette, 1988, Peele, 1989, and Peele and Brodsky, 1991), augurs poorly for continued expansive (no questions asked) coverage. Cost containment is the *sine qua non* of all treatment modalities.

Managed care companies hired by self-insured employers or by insurance companies increasingly monitor the costs of care. The private chemical dependency field has been almost decimated as a result: Since 1989, two-hundred private residential centers in the country have closed down (Duda, 1992). As insurers become increasingly restrictive in the kinds of alcoholism they will cover, marketing becomes more crucial than before. Today's addiction treatment advertising is aimed less at the alcoholic (who rarely wants treatment, anyway) than at "the significant other." Typical promotionals show a person proclaiming his recovery as a beaming wife looks on.

A subsidiary avenue for the treatment industry is the sale of self-help books and products such as coffee cups. The themes of "the inner child," bulimia, and incest survival are highly marketable topics. As Peele (1989) convincingly argues, the treatment corporations have worked hard to cast a wide net, to increase the number defined as ill—including codependents

---

BOX 10.1: The Worker Stumbles: A Comparison of Sweden and the United States

The difference between benefits that are work-related and those that are not is illustrated in the following realistic account of the resources provided to two workers and their respective families confronting similar situations in Sweden and the United States.

The situation is the following: A forty-five-year-old researcher with two teenage children and a spouse who is employed by a consulting company becomes permanently disabled because of alcoholism and related medical problems. The spouse, like the worker, is also employed outside the home in a full-time professional-level position. The strains on the family result in a nervous breakdown for one of the two teenage children. Both the worker and the teenager have to be hospitalized, the worker several times for serious medical complications related to alcoholism. In such a situation, what resources are available to this family?

As we shall see, the resources available in Sweden and the United States are quite different. In Sweden, government disability, pension, and health programs provide nearly comprehensive protection for workers and their families. Benefits in the United States are much less comprehensive and tied to employment, leaving workers much more vulnerable.

Sweden

In Sweden, the researcher, once diagnosed as suffering from chronic alcoholism, is declared disabled and begins receiving a monthly government disability payment. This money, along with the spouse's income, ensures the family's continued economic security. Hospital care for both the researcher and the teenage child is free, while the cost of longer-term medical and psychiatric care and prescriptions is minimal. The family's only medically related expenses are a very small set fee for each of the first ten visits to the doctor and the first ten prescriptions. Thereafter, all medical care and prescriptions are free. The researcher's spouse makes use of the five-week annual vacation to which all Swedes are entitled by law to help care for the researcher and the teenage child. In addition, the spouse is able to use paid sick leave as needed to deal with any additional family crises.

and members of dysfunctional families. A facetious cartoon, which made the rounds of treatment centers several years ago, showed a drawing of a convention room with one speaker at the podium. The sign overhead proclaimed, Association for Adult Children of Functional Families. There was only one person seated in the audience.

As a result of the benefits available to Swedish workers, the family's lifestyle is preserved while its disabled members struggle to reestablish themselves.

Should the researcher's disability become permanent, both spouses, upon reaching retirement age, will still receive their individual government pension based on their own work history. Thus the researcher's interrupted earnings will not reduce the spouse's pension.

United States

As in Sweden, the researcher is diagnosed as suffering from chronic alcoholism and determined to be eligible for disability benefits from the government. This, along with the spouse's income, protects the family's economic security to some degree. The disabled worker qualifies for health insurance through the employer's private plan. Under this plan, the family is reimbursed for 80 percent of the cost of all medical and hospital care, but receives no reimbursement for prescription costs. Fifty percent of the cost of the teenager's psychiatric care is covered by the spouse's health insurance plan provided by the spouse's employer. This plan, however, limits hospitalization coverage to thirty days and outpatient treatment to one year. The spouse's employer also provides two weeks' paid vacation and twelve days of sick leave that the spouse is able to use during the course of dealing with the family's medical crises.

As a result of its circumstances, the family amasses large medical and drug bills that force severe economies in its lifestyle. A second mortgage is used to help pay the medical bills, and the second child has postponed graduate school to work and help support the family. Throughout the crisis, the amount of time the spouse is able to spend with ill family members is limited by the amount of the available vacation time and sick leave.

Should the researcher's disability become permanent, the family's retirement income will be reduced because the working spouse's pension will be tied to the worker's now-interrupted work history.

Source: R. Federico, *Social Welfare in Today's World* (New York: McGraw-Hill, 1990). Reprinted with permission of McGraw-Hill.

The vast resources spent on marketing and expanding treatment, however, are minuscule compared with the resources invested in the beverage alcohol itself.

THE ADVERTISING OF ALCOHOL

The importance of advertising in our culture cannot be exaggerated. Market research investigates attitudes and responses in order to establish which imagery will be effective in selling products. Advertising both reflects culture and helps shape it. Alcohol promotion targeting of carefully selected vulnerable populations involves vast sums of money, over $2 billion each year since 1990 to advertise alcoholic beverages in the United States. The message is clear: alcohol advertising is influential. Well-financed public relations efforts, including the sponsoring of public service campaigns and lobbying of influential legislators, ensure alcohol availability and affordability at every level of society.

With 10 percent of the drinking-age population consuming over half of all alcoholic beverages sold, the heavy user, not the moderate drinker, is the primary target of the ads (Kilbourne, 1991). In 1990, beer companies spent about $190 million on sponsorships, about 70 percent involving sports. Just one beer company, Anheuser-Busch, helps finance all major league baseball teams and most National Football League teams (Nelson, 1991). Budweiser alone spends more on its annual advertising campaign than the U.S. government spends researching alcoholism.

Although correlation studies to examine the relationship between the amount of consumption and exposure to alcohol advertising have yielded mixed results, according to Jung (1994), the targeting of special groups such as women, African American males, and young males seems to be generating sales.

Findings from a random sample of 468 California school children give credence to the argument that awareness of advertising—in this case beer advertising—is related to favorable beliefs about drinking and intentions to drink as an adult. Grube and Wallack (1994), in probing the relationship between the effects of beer advertising and children's attitudes, support the argument that alcohol advertising is a major contribution to underage drinking. Heise (1991) provides a shocking and well-documented account of the ravages of "market-generated alcohol abuse" in Third World countries. In conjunction with the huge cigarette multinationals, alcohol producers portray their products as tickets to glamorous western life-styles. What consumers see is an image of health, wealth, sophistication, and power. What they do not see are the images of broken homes, violence, and impoverishment. Many of the developing countries look to alcohol as a generator of revenue; alcohol provides tax money, a source of income, a use for agricultural products, and an escape from personal problems. Meanwhile, the death rate from alcohol-related traffic accidents and acts of violence is soaring.

TREATMENT MODALITIES

While the high-powered marketing practices of alcohol manufacturers create an atmosphere conducive to high consumption, the prevailing tendency to regard alcohol problems as the fault of the individual (Jung, 1994) galvanizes action in after-the-fact remediation. Create a climate for addiction, in other words, then treat the individuals who succumb. For such individuals, there is a wide range of program alternatives, varying from detoxification units to hospital wards to residential and nonresidential programs (Akers, 1992). The *National Directory of Drug Abuse and Alcoholism Treatment and Prevention Programs* (1992) lists 11,632 federal, state, local, and private facilities in the United States and its territories. This brings us to a consideration of the role economics plays in determining how treatment services are organized and delivered.

The standardized twenty-eight-day inpatient treatment plan was once decreed by insurance reimbursement schemes. The hospital that offered detoxification and other medical services became the preferred provider. The intensive residential plan evolved not as a result of empirical study but as the negotiated arrangement between hospital corporations and insurance companies (Fields, 1992). Without insurance, the cost of getting "the cure" through residential treatment can be truly prohibitive. Today, the trend is toward less costly outpatient treatment in its *least restrictive* form. In the last ten years there has been a turnabout in treatment coverage, and many of the inpatient centers have been forced to close as a consequence. The extent to which third-party payment schemes shape the essence of program offerings is one of the most striking aspects of alcoholism treatment.

As McNeese and DiNitto (1994) observe, there are two completely separate systems of alcohol and other drug treatment—one for the rich and one for the poor. The rich have financial resources and/or private insurance. This tier developed primarily from private hospital units. Public-tier providers, in contrast, receive the bulk of their operating funds from governmental sources. Treatment for the public sector is given in small community outpatient clinics across the nation in addition to a number of large residential facilities.

While it is usually possible to get immediate admission into the private facilities, public programs are likely to have long waiting lists. Many public and nonprofit private facilities are crowded, underfinanced, and inundated with court-referred and criminal cases (Akers, 1992).

Homeless persons, one-third of whom have severe substance abuse problems, often fall between the cracks of service delivery by the public tier. It is common for them to get caught in the revolving door—to be "recycled" from detoxification centers to homeless shelters and back to the streets (McNeese and DiNitto, 1994).

DETOXIFICATION

Only a small minority of alcohol abusers develop the kind of physical complications associated with withdrawal from the drug alcohol. Hospitalization for all "drying out" alcoholics is thus unnecessary. Traditionally, holding facilities such as jails have kept a supply of whiskey on hand to prevent the detained alcoholic from going into delirium tremens (the DTs). The typical medical treatment involves the use of sedatives to diminish the hyperexcitability of an alcoholic's nervous system.

The standard twenty-eight-day treatment program of the past typically kept all patients in *detoxification* for the first several days of treatment. Intensive counseling and psychotherapy, however, are often completely ineffective during the first week, when the patient may be clearly toxic and/or under the influence of sedative medication.

Many of those who appear in the detoxification wing of a hospital never enter treatment. Chronic alcoholics periodically turn themselves in to "dry out" not in order to enter treatment but so that they can resume their drinking after a quick recovery. Such patients typically lack insurance coverage (they are listed as "self-pay" in the medical records). Many such patients are homeless and estranged from family members. Hospitals are often reluctant to admit such patients when they are seen in the emergency rooms. If they are admitted, hospitals either write them off as charity cases or get reimbursed from the city or county. The treatment accorded them may range from professional to extremely punitive.

Though readily covered by insurance policies because of the life-threatening nature of such a crisis, "detox" is rarely a high profit area of treatment. Thus, there is no marketing of detoxification services and certainly no effort to recruit patients as customers for such emergency treatment.

INPATIENT TREATMENT

There was a time when it was believed that the only way to "break the alcoholic's denial" and to remold his or her thinking was in a closed facility offering round-the-clock seclusion and supervision. Insurance companies were far more willing to reimburse agencies or, more often, hospitals offering this modality. The medical technology available in a hospital ward provided a credibility that won the sanction of the medical community. From the hospital standpoint, the ability to fill empty beds with high-paying but low-cost patients (no advanced medical technology required) was a godsend. Professionals who worked in hospital-based programs were relatively well paid; health benefits to the alcoholic were excellent.

The Minnesota plan was the taken-for-granted treatment plan in the United States. This consisted of a unicausal model of alcohol abuse with singular interventions based on "doing the Steps" of A.A. This plan was popular only in the United States. In countries such as England, Canada, and Australia, hospital referral was limited to patients with medical complications or those in dire need of detoxification (Goodwin, 1991). During the 1980s, academically trained counselors introduced differing types of interventions and approaches into the treatment setting (Rivers, 1994).

The twenty-eight-day residential program format survived as long as the insurance companies endorsed it. With health costs soaring, however, and cries for "accountability" going up, insurance companies began to take notice of research published in scholarly journals indicating that outpatients treated for alcoholism did as well as inpatients on six-month follow-up studies (Miller and Hester, 1986; Hayashida et al., 1989).

Nevertheless, there are clear therapeutic advantages to four weeks of intensive residential care that should not be overlooked. Residential treatment is indicated: when outpatient treatment has been tried and failed; when an individual needs time away from the family and the family from him or her; and when medical supervision is required. Alcoholics from actively drinking environments must be removed to a sober placement. People will try harder to "make it," moreover, in outpatient treatment when inpatient treatment is a viable option.

One systematically conducted study that was widely publicized in the mass media goes against the trend favoring outpatient treatment. In a 1991 study (Walsh, et al.) 227 General Electric workers were randomly assigned to three treatment protocols: hospitalization in an alcoholism treatment unit followed by participation in A.A.; participation in A.A. only; and a treatment of their choice. The number of persons who abstained completely from drinking during the two-year follow-up period was considerably higher in the hospitalized group than in the other two groups. Because of the high rates of relapsing workers who had to be re-treated, the costs of initial inpatient treatment proved to be a sound economic investment by the company. One must be careful in generalizing this study of well-paid workers with the general population of alcoholics. Nevertheless, the results indicated that the cheapest treatment is not necessarily cost effective in the long term.

BOX 10.2: Mayo Clinic Finds Benefit and No Harm in Treating Nicotine in the Setting of Other Addictions

The Sixth National Conference on Nicotine Dependence was held in Atlanta in November. A highlight of the conference was the report by Richard Hurt, M.D., of the Mayo Clinic about his study of treatment for nicotine dependence among patients hospitalized for the treatment of another chemical dependency problem.

The Mayo study team followed a control group of fifty patients who were treated for their drug or alcohol problem in the usual way with no special attention paid to their tobacco use and an intervention group of fifty-one patients who were given treatment for smoking as well as for the drug or alcohol problem which had prompted the inpatient admission. At one year follow-up, both groups had identical outcomes for the alcohol or other drug problem. None of the control group had stopped smoking, however, while six of the intervention group had. Three of the 101 subjects had died. All the deaths were from the control group, and two of the deaths were from diseases which can be caused by cigarettes. Dr. Hurt also noted that, during the study period, in which smoking was permitted in a designated area on the unit, at least four patients who had been abstinent from tobacco for years relapsed to smoking while they were in residence.

Source: *The Nicotine Challenger,* 2(2) (1994). Reprinted with permission of The Nicotine Challenger.

An intriguing experimental design offered by the Mayo Clinic treated nicotine dependence in conjunction with other chemical dependence (see Box 10.2).

OUTPATIENT TREATMENT

The most commonly conducted form of alcoholism treatment in the United States and Britain is performed at regional outpatient treatment centers. Group therapy work is often conducted in the evenings, sometimes following intensive week-long, eight-hour-day sessions. Such treatment can be up to two years in duration as in the state of Washington. Sometimes clients spend one or two weeks at a residential program, then join a weekly outpatient group. Sobriety may be monitored through Antabuse use and random urinalysis checks.

The advantage of the outpatient modality is that it offers community-based drop-in crisis counseling centers. Programs that are locally based can easily link welfare and social services with treatment activities. The outpatient program staff can act as a liaison between the center and criminal justice and human service agencies. After-care treatment can be provided at the same facility as intensive short-term programs. Women especially favor community-based treatment so that they can be near their children. Child-care arrangements for mothers with young children are more difficult for a residential than for a nonresidential stay.

A major disadvantage of the outpatient modality is the inability to provide healthful activities throughout the stay. Clients in outpatient treatment are inclined to relapse, to substitute one dependency for another, and to break their appointments. For those who do manage to adapt to a life-style of sober living, however, and who develop close friendships with other recovering alcoholics, the treatment on their home turf can compensate for the drawbacks.

PROFESSIONAL ASPECTS OF ADDICTIONS WORK

With the tremendous expansion of alcoholism services through the 1970s and 1980s, a new occupational category—*alcoholism counselor*—has arisen (Kinney and Leaton, 1991). Today, through the certification and other means of professionalization, alcoholism counseling can be considered a field in search of a professional identity. A tug of war between two competing traditions (one in science and medicine and one in self-help interventions) developed as early as the 1940s in Minnesota, when paraprofessional A.A. members were found to have a better rapport with clients than did the professionally trained psychologists (Anderson, 1981). The paraprofessionals ended up staying. Over the years they came to define and control the territory of alcoholism counseling. Today, life experience requirements assume a special importance in the world of chemical dependency treatment. This section will examine the *working milieu*, that is, the occupational culture and norms of a much maligned and widely misunderstood vocation.

IS ALCOHOLISM TREATMENT A PROFESSION?

Professions are vocational fields with special characteristics. The professional's primary commitment is to the profession itself rather than to the employer (Federico, 1990). Flexner (1915) set forth six standards for distinguishing professionals from other kinds of workers. His criteria became the standard for judging all professions and are still used to this day. According to Flexner, professional activity (1) is basically intellectual, carrying with it a certain prestige; (2) is learned and based on scientific knowledge; (3) is practical rather than academic; (4) can be taught in a higher education

BOX 10.3: Why Scholarship Should Be More Popular

MARGUERITE BABCOCK, M.ED, C.A.C.

The lack of acceptance of the validity of our addictions work, and consequent lack of adequate funding for treatment and prevention, is not just due to stigma about addictions or to problems with managed care. It is in large part due to our own commercialism.

Havens[1] writes about the booming business in addictions services from the 1960s through the late 1980s, which led to lack of accountability for treatment effectiveness and lack of motivation for change: "The economic success was so resounding that it led to many of the current problems experienced by the chemical dependency field" (p. 29). Similarly, Dwinell[2] talks about the positive element in the early tradition of using recovering people as helpers, but how that has changed "from a 'pass the message' mentality to a 'promote the facility' phenomenon" (p. 3). Dwinell expresses concern about "the potential exploitation of the addict" in this atmosphere.

Although the heavy emphasis on commercialism began with the success of private inpatient addictions facilities, the attitudes and beliefs that it fosters have infected the entire field, including public outpatient addictions agencies.

Case in Point

Recently I was talking with a bright young man who had just a few years of experience working in addictions treatment. We were discussing an area of addictions treatment in which he advocates a view that has been made quite popular in lectures and workshops, whereas I advocate of a view which, while not as popular, by contrast is substantiated by formal research and critique. The discussion was revealing because his level of knowledge and patterns of thought were virtually a portrait, for me, of the cognitive (and sometimes emotional) functioning of too many addictions workers I have encountered.

Despite his good level of intelligence, this young man genuinely had no notion that there are workers in the field other than just myself who question the validity of some popular ideas in addictions. Apparently an unwitting victim of the commercial conformity that is popular in the field, he had been in touch only with the unquestioning majority. He was also unaware of the nature of scientific research. He thought that anecdotal, clinical impressions presented by advocates of his view amounted to full research. He had no concept of experimental design as a means of rigorously exploring premises.

The young man's rigidity was another issue of concern. I offered to give him copies of scholarly articles critiquing his point of view.

He then stated that he already knew he would disagree with me even if he read the articles. This advance rejection of new ideas is ominous, but is all too common in audiences of addictions workers confronted by data that have not previously been circulated among them, perhaps due to their unprofitable complexity.

Anti-Research Bias

This anti-research and -scholarship bias shows in the material we are inundated with daily in addictions work. One piece of advertising for a monthly addictions newsletter promotes its product by categorically contrasting "clinicians" with "ivory tower types," the clear implication being that the former legitimately have no room for the latter.

As another example, extreme over-simplifications about the important issue of COAs and ACOAs are the usual workshop presentations on this subject. "Codependency" is a phenomenally popular topic, and a major example of unvalidated over-simplification.

What backs the commercialism in fueling the conformity is a pervasive censorship. Workers who challenge the common wisdom are rarely asked to speak; their work faces more hurdles in publishing; they often do not get hired.

A Professional Secret

With this background of simplistic commercialism in the addictions field, a secret that has been well kept from most workers is that extensive, substantial research has been done on a variety of related issues, and is waiting in serious journals to be looked at and used. Research on such areas as social concerns, family issues and treatment effectiveness has virtually been ignored. Gomberg[3] talks about how this happened:

> The expansion of detoxification, treatment and rehabilitation facilities for substance abusers created a demand for training in relevant skills. A surfeit of trainers, institutes, visiting "experts" and consultants developed to meet this demand. As a byproduct, a number of rather simpleminded conceptualizations developed (p. 114). . . . Unfortunately, this has *not* led to a notable increase in knowledge base training (p. 120). . . . Jellinek's idea that a knowledge base about alcohol was useful, even necessary, for the development of treatment skills, went by the board, and the chasm between researchers and scholars on the one hand, and the treatment community on the other, grew
>
> *(continued on next page)*

BOX 10.3 *(continued)*

larger (p. 123). . . . Perhaps these popularizations and the support they receive is . . . a kind of Gresham's law in which there is a need, on the one hand, and an offer of easy, simple answers. Easy, simple answers apparently tend to drive out of the market place more complex ideas which take more energy and time to master (p. 128).

The distance between treatment and the world of actual research is so wide that Ogborne[4] refers to them as two different cultures. Gordis[5] in essence makes the same point:

Most of our treatment is now based on wisdom, tradition, clinical experience, and plausibility. These are valuable ingredients; you cannot have clinical practice without them. But a treatment world based solely on intuition and plausibility is headed for trouble (p. 4).

Gierymski and Williams[6] object to the "bare assertions, intuitive statements, overgeneralization and anecdotes" (p. 7) popular in the addictions field, and to "the premature introduction of a syndrome for which there are inadequate theoretically established boundaries and meanings, and which lacks convincing empirical support" (p. 12).

Gomberg[3] throws out the challenge: "the burden of proof rests on those who posit this [simplistic] state of affairs" (p. 119). She points out that the claims of the popularizers can be stated as researchable, testable hypotheses, and so must indeed be exposed to the rigors of research exploration.

The Appeal of Being Anti-Research

The anti-research bias is especially seductive to addictions workers who come from academically unsophisticated backgrounds, in that their primary qualification for their jobs is that they are recovering from addictions themselves. It has been understandably appealing to them to believe that by grasping a few simple and popular ideas, they can attain the status of expert.

This atmosphere of rapidly attainable expertise has also been heady for the addictions workers who have joined the field with academic degrees in related areas. Even if their degree did not involve a focus on addictions, they could soon grasp enough of addictions "theory" to feel part of the crowd.

Low Status, Low Pay

It is to the advantage of the bottom line that workers subscribe to the hidden notion that knowledge of addictions is a simplified matter.

This is a fine rationalization to pay on-the-line workers relatively little, even though we are directly dealing with persons having one of the most severe disorders known to humanity.

Having been told for so long by those in power, and finally by each other, that we are indeed experts (even with little information), we workers often contribute to our staying underpaid with a defensive self-righteousness about not changing that base of information. Meanwhile, we are seen by professionals in other disciplines as being at best paraprofessional.

Time to Get Smart

It needs to become unacceptable among addictions workers to prefer unproven approaches over research-based care, or to promote ideas simply because they happen to sell well.

Some reading guideline recommendations can be made. Look at scholarly journals; do not just confine your reading to popularized books and articles. Search out articles that question the more usually held ideas in the field, such as Beidler's[7] paper challenging the distinctiveness of the ACOA syndrome. Whether or not you agree with them, such pieces make you think.

Read the more clearly explained presentations on research findings, such as those in *Alcohol Health and Research World* and NIAAA's *Alcohol Alert* series. Look for scholarly articles that are themselves reviews of research studies, such as Kaufman's[8] synopsis and critique of research on family therapy and substance abuse.

Don't assume that just because an article is several years old, it has nothing to tell you: Jackson's 1954[9] study of Al-Anon wives has yet to be matched in research on family members of addicts, and the review and critique that Bailey[10] presents in her 1961 article on alcoholism and marriage is to the point even today.

Read general science publications that give regular and understandable accounts of the latest in scientific findings, such as *Science News* or *Scientific American*. Read articles such as Moore's[11] series on statistics and research design that give accessible introductory accounts about the elements of research.

With addictions workers' busy schedules, we must also think about ways to make journal material more readily accessible on the job. Several ideas come to mind: allowing official work time for reading (and giving credentialing training credit for that): hiring staff persons specifically whose duty it is to keep all facility staff informed on scholarly material; developing a quarterly journal for addictions sub-area literature update summaries.

(continued on next page)

BOX 10.3 *(continued)*

The Price of Neglect

If the addictions field fails to address needed changes, genuinely damaging developments will occur. We will continue to spend our already inadequate treatment and prevention dollars on inefficient efforts because of the widespread use of ideas/techniques that are without solid basis. The public, continuing to be unconvinced that "treatment works," and witnessing the ongoing social problems from addictions, will be even more easily persuaded to the moralistic, law-enforcement "solution." Funders, whether government or insurance, will tighten up even more on financing what they see to be questionable service, mainly because in these arenas documentation counts. We will either deal with the shorter-term discomfort of needed change, and grow, or we will continue with short-term gratification, and fail.

But we do not have to fail. In our field we have enough resources of honesty, energy, and concern for our clients to now begin the process of change.

References

1. Havens, L. M. Understanding the trends: A guide to cooperation between treatment centers and managed care providers. *Addiction & Recovery* 1991: 11(1):28–32.
2. Dwinell, L. Don't let the clients suffer in order to boost the bottom line. *The Addiction Letter* 1989: 5(9):3.
3. Gomberg, E. S. L. On terms used and abused: The concept of "codependency." *Drugs and Society* 1989: 3(3-4):113–132.
4. Ogborne, A. C. Editorial: Bridging the gap between the two

program; (5) is autonomous and provided by an occupational group; and (6) is motivated by altruism as opposed to making money.

Professionalism is not an either/or phenomenon in reality. Instead, the attributes of a profession should be regarded, as Federico suggests, as constituting a continuum or scale. Some older professions, such as law and medicine, can thus be regarded at the top of the continuum or scale with others occupying various points down the scale. Alcoholism counseling may be considered to possess several of the ideal attributes but, clearly, not all of them. Regarding the first two criteria pertaining to prestige and reliance on scientific knowledge, the field of alcoholism counseling is extremely weak. Academic standards for certification remain significantly below the requirements for engaging in psychotherapy with any compara-

cultures of alcoholism research and treatment. *British Journal of Addiction* 1988: 83:729–733.

5. Gordis, E. A commitment to research can save the chemical dependence field. *Observer: News from the Johnson Institute* 1991: 13(1):4.
6. Gierymski, T., Williams, T. Codependency. *Journal of Psychoactive Drugs* 1986: 18(1):7–13.
7. Beidler, R. J. Adult children of alcoholics: Is it really a separate field for study? *Drugs and Society* 1989: 3(3-4):133–140.
8. Kaufman, E. Family systems and family therapy of substance abuse: An overview of two decades of research and clinical experience. *The International Journal of the Addictions* 1985: 20(6-7):897–916.
9. Jackson, J. K. The adjustment of the family to the crisis of alcoholism. *Quarterly Journal of Studies on Alcohol* 1954: 15(4): 562–586.
10. Bailey, M. B. Alcoholism and marriage: A review of research and professional literature. *Quarterly Journal of Studies on Alcohol* 1961: 22(1):81–97.
11. No information given.

Source: *Addiction and Recovery*, July/Aug. 1992, 28–30. Reprinted with permission of *Addiction and Recovery*.

Marguerite Babcock has been working in the addictions services field for over thirteen years, in both inpatient and outpatient settings. She is currently employed as Clinical Supervisor at the Center for Substance Abuse, an outpatient facility in McKeesport, PA.

ble population (e.g., the mentally ill, married couples, and the terminally ill). Babcock (1992; see Box 10.3) perceives alcoholism counselors as having been corrupted, in large part, by the earlier commercial boom in providing popularized addictions services. Additionally, much of the knowledge, the assumptions of the field represent belief systems that have not been tested empirically (e.g., "female alcoholics are harder to treat than males"; "inpatient treatment is more effective in breaking denial"). Through no fault of workers in the field, provision of services to alcoholics is not highly regarded (Duda, 1992; Googins, 1984).

On the positive side, there is a wealth of emerging knowledge of an almost esoteric nature that could form the backbone of a new profession. I am referring to the disease concept of alcoholism now supported in part

BOX 10.4: Alcohol Abuse Therapist Faces Four Sex Charges

LES SUZUKAMO

He called himself "Doc O'Connor" and he had an unusual way of helping alcoholics beat the bottle, Apple Valley police say.

He had them strip naked and he flogged them, according to police.

Alfred Joseph O'Connor, 71, faces charges that he sexually abused a 17-year-old boy by whipping him on his buttocks, hands and feet while the boy was disrobed. O'Connor told the youth the beating would help him overcome his alcoholism, police said.

O'Connor also faces charges he attempted to sexually abuse an Apple Valley police officer through similar means. The officer was posing as an alcoholic in a two-month undercover operation.

O'Connor has not been arrested, but he has been charged with two counts of criminal sexual conduct in the fourth degree and two counts of attempted criminal sexual conduct in the fourth degree in a criminal complaint filed by the Dakota County Attorney's office. He is scheduled to appear in Dakota County District Court in Hastings on June 29.

Criminal sexual conduct in the fourth degree alleges the complainant was a patient of the defendant and the sexual contact occurred during a psychotherapy session or by means of therapeutic deception. It is punishable by up to five years in prison and a $10,000 fine. Attempted criminal sexual conduct in the fourth degree is punishable by up to $2^1/_2$ years in prison and a $5,000 fine.

Police began investigating O'Connor after a man told Washington County Sheriff's investigators that O'Connor had beaten him with whips and sticks on more than 100 occasions to cure him of his alcoholism, the criminal complaint said. None of the charges are connected with those incidents.

"The discipline was 'to toughen you up.' I remember him saying that a lot," said investigator James Boyer, who visited O'Connor from Feb. 23 to March 29 posing as an alcoholic named Jerry Tarmen.

"He'd bring out the points that lives are ruined by alcohol and talk about getting on top of your problems," the investigator said.

Boyer said that O'Connor told him that he "was not a psychiatrist, he was the other," which he took to mean a psychologist. O'Connor often referred to himself as "Doc O'Connor," the officer added. Posing as a licensed psychologist is a misdemeanor.

Peter Schmitz, a Northfield attorney representing O'Connor, said his client has a doctorate in French literature with a background in psychology.

Schmitz said O'Connor "is treated as not guilty and we certainly intend to plead not guilty."

O'Connor, a Canadian citizen who was born in London, England, is single with no children, Schmitz said. He has been a lay missionary in various areas around the world but arrived in the Twin Cities about 20 years ago. He stays with a family in Apple Valley.

The complaint said O'Connor sexually abused the teen-ager in a single counseling session sometime between December 1985 and April 1986 at the Apple Valley home.

The youth ended his therapy with O'Connor after the alleged beating, the complaint said. The family that owns the house was unaware of the alleged activity, police said.

The complaint also alleged O'Connor asked Boyer at several counseling sessions to imagine he was Boyer's father and the 38-year-old officer was a young boy who had misbehaved and needed to be punished.

The imaginary punishments included floggings so severe they were supposed "to cut me to the bone," Boyer said in the complaint.

Sometimes the fantasized punishments were followed by imaginary showers and massages between the boy and his father, with O'Connor asking Boyer to imagine becoming sexually aroused.

Boyer said O'Connor told him the fantasies were therapeutic.

"It's supposed to rebuild bad memories and these are supposed to be positive memories," Boyer said.

"There is no doubt in my mind that he did this for some type of sexual gratification," Boyer said.

Boyer said a staff psychologist at the Dakota Mental Health Center in Apple Valley told him there would be no reason for a patient to disrobe for discipline except for sexual contact.

Both the psychologist and the state Board of Psychology said they were aware of no therapies for chemical dependency that required pain, Boyer said.

Police said they have been told that as many as 40 to 50 people with alcohol problems could have come to O'Connor for help.

"He would obtain people interested in further one-to-one counseling sessions," Boyer said. Only some of them would be recipients of O'Connor's alleged discipline therapy, the officer said.

O'Connor worked for the Union Gospel Mission in St. Paul in the 1970s but left in 1980, Schmitz said.

Union Gospel Mission officials could not be reached for comment, but Boyer said mission officials told him that O'Connor was a staff psychologist for a chemical dependency treatment center associated with the mission in the 1970s until it closed from lack of funds. O'Connor also helped with chemical dependency counseling sessions at the mission but was not on the staff.

Source: *St. Paul Pioneer Press*, June 9, 1987, 1,3C. Reprinted with permission of St. Paul Pioneer Press Dispatch.

by biochemical research into the physiological reactions to the ingestion of alcohol. Individual reactions are found to differ markedly. Results of recent research concerning the exact neuropsychological effects of alcohol continue to be reported in the academic and professional literature (see, for instance, regular reports in *Alcohol: Health and Research World*, published by the U.S. Department of Health and Human Services). Neurotransmitters, acetaldehyde, serotonin—these are among the technical terms that help set this occupation apart from other helping professions. From the standpoint of professional development, use of such terminology functions to define the boundaries of a new occupational group.

Alcoholism counseling is practical rather than academic; its techniques can be taught in colleges and universities (although they usually are not). The field is relatively autonomous, especially in private agencies, and the motivation of altruism is the overriding one. Yet, in spite of meeting these criteria for a profession, the low prestige of the field and the strikingly low educational requirements of entry level jobs prevent alcoholism counseling from obtaining true professional status. The lack of a unified paradigm for approaching the alcoholic in treatment is a further hindrance to professionalism.

In the recent past, abuses of the alcoholism counselor role were common. While some counselors had relapses, others engaged in bizarre and illegal behavior (see Box 10.4). Nevertheless, alcoholism counseling is making strides in the direction of professionalism. Defining educational requirements in conjunction with certification efforts at the state and national levels are significant recent developments. These trends are part of the *external validation* stage of the professionalization process that is characteristic of all new professions.

Each state has developed a code of ethics; all such codes are roughly the same and closely parallel the social work Code of Ethics. Box 10.5 contains the Practitioner/Counselor Code of Ethics for the state of Minnesota.

One obvious way of promoting professionalization is to encourage an influx of already trained practitioners from the helping professions. Saxe, et al. (1985) perceive the present reimbursement system as favoring licensed (MSW social workers, psychologists) over general counselors. As professionally trained and more highly paid personnel enter the system, the status of the field should increase proportionately.

A promising development in addictions treatment is the recruitment of those whom Bissell (1982) calls "bridge people"—individuals who are both recovering alcoholics and trained professionals, regardless of the order in which these experiences occurred. The future of this occupation will be in the hands of the "bridge people," because they combine in one person the best of two worlds.

BOX 10.5: ICDP Practitioner/Counselor Code of Ethics

To ensure the highest quality of service delivered to my clients and my professional integrity, I will:

1. Adhere to all state and federal laws and rules which govern patient care, including reporting of abuse/neglect of a vulnerable person (children/adults), misconduct by individuals or agencies, data privacy, and relationships with clients and other professionals.
2. Maintain an objective, nonpossessive relationship with clients at all times. The professional shall not exploit clients: 1) sexually, 2) financially, or 3) emotionally.
3. Adhere to nondiscriminatory behavior with clients on the basis of race, color, gender, sexual orientation, age, religion, national origin, marital status, political belief, mental or physical handicap, or any other preference or personal characteristic, condition or status.
4. Maintain a willingness and the ability to recognize when it is in the client's and/or their family's best interest to refer or release him/her to another individual or program.
5. Assist clients and/or their families to help themselves.
6. Maintain a knowledge of community resources and make appropriate referrals.
7. Respect the rights and views of other professionals and agencies.
8. Abide by the agency's policies, procedures and regulations that maintain and improve the delivery of services.
9. Assess personal competence and operate only within my skills and/or training.
10. Accurately represent my own qualifications and affiliations.
11. Continue my professional growth through ongoing education and/or training.
12. Recognize my individual responsibility for appropriate professional and respectful conduct in personal and professional areas, including the use of alcohol and other mood altering substances.
13. Maintain ongoing personal growth, recovery and/or a personal enhancement program.
14. Maintain appropriate boundaries with my clients, my colleagues, and my agency.
15. Obtain clinical supervision when providing direct client care.

Reprinted by permission of Institute for Chemical Dependency Professionals of Minnesota (ICDP).

ROLE STRAINS FOR THE SOCIAL WORKER AS ALCOHOLISM COUNSELOR

Many social workers, like other mental health professionals, enter the alcoholism counseling field because of job opportunities, not because they have special training or an interest in alcoholism (Bissell, 1982). Others come to specialize in alcoholism, often at reduced salaries, because of a recent personal experience with alcoholism in their lives. In either situation, expectations may exceed the realities. Working in alcoholism circles may be fraught with stress and difficulties.

Sociologists utilize the concept of *role strain* to denote a situation in which the behaviors associated with a position must be reconciled with daily constraints and realities. Role strain can be defined as a feeling of conflict or stress caused by inconsistent demands of a single role.

I have talked informally to numerous social workers in this field. Their satisfaction or dissatisfaction varied with the circumstances at their individual agency (i.e., client motivation, treatment facility philosophy). One social worker who had "burned out" told me: "Care Unit was more interested in money than in people. Work was too hectic, and family members were ignored." Another social worker from Care Unit stated: "I like the class of client and the level of client motivation. Previously I worked with involuntary clients in an outpatient center; that was very difficult because we had to answer to the court and police the clients."

Role strain for the social worker in the alcoholism field consists of a discrepancy between the ideal of what social workers should be doing—helping people to help themselves—and what they were actually doing. I will focus on three sources of strain: role inconsistency, training incongruity, and interprofessional status tensions. The format for this discussion is loosely borrowed from Needleman (1983) and Parsons et al. (1994).

ROLE INCONSISTENCY

Contradictory role requirements are a common occurrence in chemical dependency treatment. As a social worker, the counselor is supposed to be an advocate for the client, to protect the client's personal interests. Yet information given by the client to the social worker (for example, information concerning a recent relapse) may be used by the agency as a reason to terminate the client for noncompliance.

Another typical situation in alcoholism treatment concerns the referral by the agency of a client to a physician for Antabuse (disulfiram) treatment. Antabuse is a substance that, when ingested, makes drinking alcohol very distasteful. Taking Antabuse, as a temporary measure, can be extremely effective. In some cases, however, because of client resistance,

Antabuse may be nontherapeutic. Court or agency requirements mandating Antabuse (or urinalysis) monitoring are, from a civil liberties point of view, an intrusion into the client's right to self-determination.

Conflicts between treatment and control roles are characteristic of the addictions field and the corrections field, as well. Client attitudes reflect the coercive nature of court-mandated therapy (the court, similarly, can be said to be coercive because of client attitudes). In any case, client resistance is common.

TRAINING INCONGRUITIES

Social workers are trained to help the client who is seeking help with a personal problem or with a lack of coping skills. To the extent that alcoholic clients seek help at all, it is often to "learn how to do controlled drinking." Treatment agencies in the United States, unlike those in Europe, do not allow the counselor to consider such a goal. Many times this goal may be entirely unsuitable, in any case. The client has one agenda, such as to get his or her driver's license back; the social worker, as alcoholism counselor, has quite another goal. Some sort of confrontation is called for, a confrontation for which the typical social worker may feel poorly prepared.

Another problem that plagues social workers is lack of training for the adversarial role required for the involuntary commitment of chronic alcoholics. (This aspect will be considered later in this section.) In short, social workers tend to lack education in alcoholism and drug abuse; they lack understanding of the physical and psychological processes of addiction and, accordingly, are easily bewildered by some of the ramifications.

INTERPROFESSIONAL STATUS TENSIONS

Social workers are a minority among alcoholism treatment counselors. Often lacking certification and specialized training, they may be under the authority of someone with limited college education. Some alcoholism treatment centers are characterized by split loyalties and ideological differences, while, at other agencies, a high degree of interdisciplinary harmony exists. Depending on the administrative direction provided, social workers are variously ignored or valued, underpaid or well paid. The fact that there is no specific designation for the social worker in addictions treatment and social workers are designated by the generic term "counselors" diminishes the professional identity of the social worker at the alcoholism center.

In the alcoholism field, in short, social workers are working on the nonprofessional counselor's turf, with the highest credibility going to the *recovering alcoholic counselor*. Friction may develop between treatment personnel with social work training and those without it, as occupational and philosophical loyalties come into play.

CERTIFICATION

Alcoholism counseling is seeking to establish an elaborate system of professional development involving the institutionalization of certification requirements for individual counselors and of accreditation for the agencies involved (Royce, 1989). The importance of such external control of alcoholism counseling is needed to protect not only the client and worker but also, as Royce (1989) correctly notes, the profession itself.

The concern with credentialing alcoholism counselors began in the 1970s. There has been for many years an internal thrust within the occupation itself to establish professional standards for credentialing counselors, and a more recent external impetus to assure that all helping professionals received specialized education on alcohol problems. Within the occupation, in virtually every state, efforts are underway to establish minimum standards for counselors in alcoholism treatment (Kinney and Leaton, 1991). Meanwhile, external organizations such as the federal Alcohol and Drug Institutes and the Office of Substance Abuse Prevention have initiated programs to improve professional education among physicians, nurses, and social workers (Kinney and Leaton, 1991).

There are vast differences within the states in certification standards. Some states, such as Minnesota, are beginning to require a bachelor's degree for new entry-level positions. Other states still require only a few relevant college courses, perhaps an exam, and completion of a lengthy period of supervised apprenticeship. Most states require that alcoholism counselors be certified (certification usually is provided for work with all forms of substance abuse). At the national level, the National Association of Alcohol and Drug Abuse Counselors (NAADAC) represents the interests of 22,000 counselors who are dually certified at both state and national levels (Lubben, 1989). In some states, certification requires up to one year of supervised counseling before one can be hired. Often the result is that budding therapists volunteer their services, thus virtually working free for a considerable length of time. Social work students, in any case, do extensive field work assignments. The end result is a bonanza for agencies who can often "get by" financially by employing few staff members. Individuals who have already completed lengthy programs of professional education in their own disciplines often find the requirement for additional certification (including unpaid employment) in a related discipline to be cumbersome.

On the national level, the search for a unifying set of accreditation standards is well underway. Such standards protect "the consumer from improper care, protect the credibility of treatment providers, and are important to insurance companies and other reimbursers, who look for standards as a sign of quality care. But to date we have not found a unifying set of standards." (Hazelden Foundation, 1986:1).

A more recent article by Meacham (1991), published in the alcoholism treatment journal *Focus,* deplores the continuing inability of the field to agree on a unified credentialing process for substance abuse counselors. Meacham sees the schism between the academics and the recovering people. Any attempt to raise standards may be met with resistance by those who were alcoholism counselors from an earlier day.

LEGAL ASPECTS OF TREATMENT

Practitioners in the field of alcoholism counseling find themselves both constrained by the law and relying on the "strong arm of the law" in numerous ways. The alcoholism counselor may gain courtroom experience by offering testimony concerning the progress or lack of progress of a court-ordered client in treatment. Or the counselor or social worker may testify as an expert witness on the addictions process in criminal cases, in which alcohol abuse may be argued to have been a mitigating circumstance in the commission of a crime. Alcoholism treatment personnel may testify for the defense or prosecutor, *for* the client or *against* the client. The involuntary commitment proceeding places the treatment staff in the strange position of arguing against the client in order to help the client. All these courtroom encounters provide clear illustrations of the crucial link between alcohol abuse and the law. Yet mental health professionals involved in courtroom proceedings generally lack knowledge in legal procedure and decorum. The adversary model that is used to settle courtroom disputes in many ways runs counter to the social worker conflict-resolution model.

THE ADVERSARY SYSTEM

The adversary system is the Anglo-Saxon contribution to justice. The courtroom battle that takes place today has its origins in trial by combat and, before that, in trial by ordeal (Strick, 1978). Today the *trial* itself is the ordeal.

The adversary model attempts to resolve differences through the juxtaposition of opposing arguments; the ultimate aim of cross-examination is to arrive at the truth (Gardner, 1982). However, the process of cross-examination, because of the win-lose ethos, may be alien to members of the mental health profession.

The alcoholism counselor as expert witness may testify on the facts pertaining to the disease alcoholism or alcohol consumption. Such a witness may testify for a fee for either the defendant or the prosecution. Either role will pit the therapist against attorneys on one side or the other.

The courtroom is the lawyer's domain, not the therapist's. Mental health professionals must conform their testimony to the legal requirements of the law and of courtroom presentation. Such testimony is apt to be interrupted at any moment with heatedly contested objections.

The psychodynamic perspective of the typical mental health professional is in fundamental ways opposed to the more narrow, legalistic perspective that dominates the courtroom today. The *helping professions*, as opposed to the legal profession, have tended to emphasize informal rather than formal mechanisms of social control. And this formal legal tradition that had as its forerunner trial by combat may contain elements that are unfamiliar as well as unpalatable to the helping professions. But even though they may be unpalatable, they still must be anticipated.

What, then, should expert witnesses do to prepare themselves for effective courtroom presentation? The following guidelines may be helpful in giving the social worker a voice in courtroom deliberations:

- Watch trials at which there is expert testimony.
- Observe the "traps" that attorneys set for witnesses that diminish the impact of the testimony.
- When on the witness stand yourself, do not take the confrontation personally; the seemingly personal attack is largely staged.
- Be ready to define such terms as *alcoholism , alcohol abuse, tolerance, blackout*, and so on (see chapter 4 for definitions).

INVOLUNTARY COMMITMENT

The hearing takes place before a judge and a court reporter. In some states the client may request a jury to hear the case. A court-appointed attorney usually represents the defendant. In Iowa, a forty-eight-hour evaluation is ordered. Evidence must be presented that the individual is a chronic abuser and a danger to him- or herself or to others. The evidence must be clear and convincing. Such hearings are closed to the public; records are kept confidential.

Evidence at such hearings should be brief and specific as to dates of prior detoxes and arrests for alcohol related offenses. The witness typically presents some assurance that forced treatment is necessary, because it is the least restrictive alternative available and because uncontrolled drinking has placed the individual's life and health in severe jeopardy. Although recovery rates are quite low for those committed by the courts to treatment against their will, recovery rates are far better than for those not treated at all.

CONFIDENTIALITY AND THE LAW

Respect for client confidence is not only an important aspect of the practitioners' code of ethics but also strictly regulated under federal law pertaining specifically to "alcohol and drug abuse patient records." The law pertaining to alcohol and drug abuse treatment is unique. Rules set forth in federal regulations, entitled "Confidentiality of Alcohol and Drug Abuse Patient Records," apply to all agencies that provide alcoholism and drug abuse treatment or prevention. The rules are far more stringent than for any other category of treatment. The general rule is: No disclosure without the patient's consent. Even with consent, information may not be released that is harmful to the patient.

Involuntary commitment proceedings are fraught with ethical and legal dilemmas. The client, often hostile, is to be sent away for his or her "own good" to a jail-like facility for "treatment." In life and death situations, however, such a drastic recourse may be appropriate. Providing information to those outside the treatment program or requests for information from other sources generally requires the client's written permission (McNeese and DiNitto, 1994). Such an authorization states the name of the agency, type of information requested, how the information will be used, the agency requesting the information, the date of the request, and the date on which the release expires (usually six months later). Requests should be obtained, ordinarily, from lawyers, all family members who may be involved with the client, and relevant agencies with which the client is in communication. Legal complications occur when the client, under proper legal advice, refuses to sign the Consent-for-Release-of-Information form. It becomes impossible under these circumstances to contact family members as witnesses or for input. Should the patient be committed, based on medical evidence alone, further restrictions apply regarding communication with the state treatment facility. Treatment and hospital records may not be released to the treatment center nor may the name of the patient be revealed before his or her arrival (*Of Substance*, 1980–1984).

Exceptions to confidentiality must be explained. For instance, information obtained in group settings and from family members pertinent to substance abuse is put in the client's records and shared with relevant officials with whom reports are required to be filed. In a medical emergency, information to save a client may be released.

Until recently, there was a serious legal conflict between state laws mandating reporting of cases of known or suspected child abuse and neglect and the federal law enforcing near-absolute confidentiality concerning persons in treatment for substance abuse problems. When there is a conflict, *federal law takes precedence*. For workers in the field, however, the problem is an ethical one. Many professionals are compelled to contact children's Protective Services to report mistreatment of a child. Fortunately, this dilemma between moral and legal considerations has been clarified. In August, 1986, Congress enacted the Children's Justice and Assistance Act. Today, there are no longer federal restrictions on reporting suspected situations of child abuse/neglect where a family member is receiving treatment for substance abuse (Durby, 1987).

A treatment program may not release information in response to a subpoena even if it is signed by a judge. A court order must be issued and a hearing held before the information in question is released. Even then, treatment records may not be released, only dates and times of treatment performed. Legal counsel for the agency may be necessary to clarify difficult legal points.

Hospitals and mental health agencies, although they may offer treatment for addictions problems, do not have the same legal restrictions as specialized addictions agencies. Professionals in any of these facilities, however, may be called to testify in court at the request of and on behalf of a client. Child custody hearings, criminal proceedings, and administrative hearings may be areas where information from the addictions counselor is desired. Again, information must be offered at the request of and in the best interest of the client.

THE ADDICTIVE ORGANIZATION

Schaef and Fassel (1990) assume a systems-oriented perspective with a strong emphasis on *addiction* to analyze the work organization. Their book, *The Addictive Organization*, has come to be passed about with great interest by staff members because of the relevance of some statements and metaphors employed in this work. In analyzing the corporate structure and the individual personalities that help shape it, Schaef and Fassel introduce the notion of *process addiction* to refer to a series of activities or interactions that "hook" a person or on which a person becomes dependent. The common process addictions are work, sex, money, gambling, relationships, and certain kinds of thinking. To the individual worker who ventures there, the addictive organization is highly stress inducing and likely to cause burnout. The four major forms of addictive organizations are:

- Organizations in which a key person is an addict, for example, "the dry drunk."

- Those where individuals bring their disease with them into this structure, that is, they are workaholics and assume rigid family-like roles, as do members of a sick family.
- Those in which the organization is the addictive substance; members believe in the mission of the organization with a kind of fanaticism.
- Those in which the organization is the addict; communication is indirect and closed; consumers are manipulated.

As organization consultants to many different types of corporations, Schaef and Fassel suggest in their summary that something other than mere economic considerations must inform and motivate organizations. Yet a form of ruthless management seems to be the current creed among the business establishment today, according to Schaef and Fassel. For an organization to be healthy, recommendations are that humanistic qualities be emphasized in preserving the integrity of the organization and the morale of the staff; that utmost honesty be practiced with consumers and the community; and that leadership be diffused and situational.

SUMMARY AND CONCLUSION

This chapter has considered the alcoholism treatment center as an organization constrained by economic realities in the society. These, in turn, have been shown to be affected by political factors beyond the control of the individual clinic. Whether or not certain forms of treatment are funded by insurance companies, by governmental sources, or not at all is a constant deciding factor in the provision of treatment services. The sociology of alcoholism counseling considers such factors as professional credibility and professional loyalties and structurally-based conflicts such as that between agency norms and professional attributes. This chapter has also examined the sociological dynamics of alcoholism counseling and viewed this occupation as thriving and practitioners as professionalizing and fighting to preserve the territory. In this field, intra-agency staff struggles between lay and professional counselors may destroy the agency from within. Conversely, interdisciplinary cooperation can be achieved with excellent results.

This chapter has addressed alcohol use from a structural perspective. The focus has been on the United States with its diversified funding sources. Interactions among health-care institutions have been analyzed with a special emphasis on how these interactions have shaped and have been shaped by alcohol use. Policies that define alcoholism treatment in the 1990s are seen as laden with the basic contradictions of a society that simultaneously encourages high alcohol consumption for the masses and abstinence for the few who are defined as sick. The alcohol beverage industry, the treatment industry, and the mass media continue to focus upon individuals as "the problem" (Langton, 1991). This approach gives the marketers of alcohol "a free rein," relatively, to target vulnerable populations throughout the world. The shift in responsibility away from society's institutions onto the individual drinker is consistent with the tenets of the disease model of alcoholism.

The growth of the alcoholism treatment industry, which focuses on individuals, has been enhanced by the current ideology. As Denzin (1993) astutely notes, the discovery of the "disease" of codependency has expanded the designated treatment population considerably. Regardless of one's personal views on this issue, the close interworkings of economics and ideology cannot be overlooked.

Since the 1980s "the war on drugs"—the war against drug suppliers and users—has had two major consequences for those working with chemically dependent persons. The first consequence is mandated treatment, which is problematic not only for those given the choice between treatment and jail but also for alcoholism treatment and recovery facilities (Jung, 1994). The second consequence is the stigmatizing of drug dependents of every sort, coupled with an intolerance for increased funding at state and local levels. Insurance companies, by the same token, have been able to reduce reimbursement payments with full support of the employers they represent. Whenever reimbursement policies change, the nature of the clientele change also. For example, former hospital-based treatment centers have either closed their doors or contracted to offer services to newly designated groups such as the dually diagnosed, with mental disorders plus substance abuse problems. Private clinics often obtain contracts with the county to finance work with jail inmates.

Prospective administrators or employees of alcoholism treatment agencies would do well to pay heed to how the agency fits into the overall service delivery system in a community. Before accepting a job with a given agency, the candidate for a position is well advised to research the commitment of the community to the mission of the agency. The mission may be redefined suddenly. Sometimes a candidate gives up his or her relatively secure position only to be laid off from the new position after a short period of time because of unanticipated cutbacks. A thorough knowledge of the political, economic, and professional dynamics will help give newcomers a realistic picture of the field of substance abuse.

REVIEW QUESTIONS

1. As the public loses interest in alcohol problems and alcohol abuse, how is treatment funding affected? How do insurance enterprises reflect and define the public interest?

2. Other than health insurance, what sources of funding for alcoholism treatment are there? Explain how economic survival is often the priority of a treatment center. How do treatment centers market their product to consumers?

3. How does the commercialism of treatment in the 1980s have a negative effect today? Describe the kind of ads used in the past and the present.

4. Discuss promotion and public relations activities related to selling beer.

5. What are the two separate tiers of treatment according to McNeese and DiNitto? Describe them.

6. Discuss detoxification from the profit angle.

7. What was/is the Minnesota plan and how did economic development bring about some changes?

8. Summarize research studies on treatment effectiveness pertaining to the modality of treatment (inpatient versus outpatient). How did the insurance companies respond to the research on treatment outcomes?

9. What are advantages of the inpatient and the outpatient modalities? How should patients be matched to treatment?

10. Argue for or against alcoholism counseling as a profession. Refer to the characteristics of a profession to present your argument.

11. Utilizing the concepts role inconsistencies and conflict, compare alcoholism treatment to other fields in which social workers are engaged.

12. What kinds of high-level scientific knowledge informs alcoholism counseling?

13. Discuss codes of ethics. Show how sexual involvement with a client is a violation of this code. What are some purposes of a code of ethics?

14. How does the process of certification affect the field of alcoholism treatment? How does it reflect trends in the field?

15. What do addictions workers need to know about courtroom procedures before they testify? Under what circumstances are they likely to testify?

16. List some guidelines for testifying as an expert witness.

17. Describe involuntary commitment. Is the counselor an advocate of the client or his or her adversary?

18. Discuss the importance of confidentiality and the uniqueness of the law pertaining to substance abuse.

19. Describe how information may be shared regarding a client in treatment. List the requirements for a client consent form.

20. Summarize some of the main propositions of the book *The Addictive Organization*. What are the four major forms of organizational addictions? How are humanistic qualities crucial?

21. What do budding addictions workers need to know about external influences in addiction treatment? How can such knowledge prevent burnout?

11

GENERAL SOCIAL WORK WITH THE ALCOHOLIC CLIENT

> Alcohol as a substance is capable of permeating all the tissues of
> the human body and . . . alcohol problems permeate virtually all
> the issues of human society.
> —Robert Straus, 1974

While only about 5 percent of social workers specialize in substance abuse treatment (Gibelman and Schervish, 1993), all social workers encounter addictions and the effects of addiction in the course of everyday practice. Whether at the hospital, in a community mental health center, in a nursing home, or at the department of human services, the consequences of alcohol and other drug addictions are ubiquitous.

This survey of general social work practice starts with the most popular field of social work endeavor—mental health. The focus will be on work with the dually diagnosed—those with both mental disorders and substance abuse problems. Because assessment is often undertaken at a mental health center, guidelines for doing a proper assessment of alcohol use are offered. Next, four additional major areas of social work practice—employee assistance programs, the health-care field, child welfare, and work with criminal offenders—are examined in terms of the alcoholism component in each of these specializations. *Prevention,* the primary challenge in terms of alcoholism control, is treated separately and multidimensionally. Instead of bandaging up people who fall off a cliff, prevention attempts to keep people out of danger in the first place. There are many ways the society can go about this: giving warnings, roping off the dangerous areas, and teaching safety practices. The social work practice area with the most obvious potential for preventing future generations from developing problems with alcohol and other addictions is school social work. Possible prevention activities for social workers are spelled out.

Completing the discussion on social work with alcoholics/addicts, this chapter emphasizes the need for all social workers to receive specialized addictions training as a part of their preparatory education. Several exemplary programs are outlined. A preview of *future trends* in the field of alcoholism treatment is attempted. Clinicians working with special populations will want to be aware of areas where advancement of knowledge is anticipated as well as of political/economic developments impinging upon their work roles.

MENTAL ILLNESS AND ALCOHOLISM— THE DUALLY DIAGNOSED

Troubles tend to occur not singly but in droves. Where there is substance abuse, there is also illness and tragedy of other sorts. A widely publicized study of over 20,000 people in mental hospitals, nursing homes, and prisons found that 53 percent of those who abused chemical substances had a mental disorder such as schizophrenia, anxiety, or major depression (Holloway, 1991). Thus, practitioners who work at a mental health center would do well to assess clients for a history of chemical abuse. And for practitioners at substance abuse clinics, knowledge of the major mental disorders is imperative.

The terms *dual diagnosis* and *comorbidity* are somewhat awkward terms that denote the presence of two or more illnesses in the same person. When a hospital specializes in treatment of the dually diagnosed, this usually indicates treatment of alcoholics who suffer from a mental disorder such as major depression, schizophrenia, and bipolar personality or antisocial personality disorder. Because of the likelihood of one individual alcoholic having two or more coexisting mental disorders, Read, Penick, and Nickel (1993) suggest use of the term *multiple diagnosis* as the most accurate descriptive term.

Dual diagnosis units are springing up throughout the country, and many of the very treatment centers that earlier refused to treat these difficult cases are now developing well-publicized specializations with this population. Meanwhile, at mental health agencies, where approximately 33 percent of social workers work (Gibelman and Schervish, 1993), social workers have been working, in one way or the other, with the dually diagnosed all along.

The debate over which problem came first—the chemical abuse or the mental disorder—has gotten researchers and clinicians nowhere. Traditionally, social workers have focused on the mental disorder as the overriding problem, while alcoholism counselors have concentrated primarily on the alcohol. Indeed, one of the major explanations in recent literature hypothesizes that an underlying biological vulnerability may be responsible for a number of disabilities. An imbalance of key neurotransmitters and receptors affecting levels of serotonin in the brain has been found to be associated with poor impulse control, suicide, obsessive-compulsive disorder, obesity, and alcoholism (Wallace, 1989; Kotulak, 1993). (Chapter 4 explored this biochemical link in some depth.) Science is pointing in the direction of multiple manifestations of disturbance, all derived from a single source.

For clinicians to best help their dually diagnosed clients, they must first be able to identify and assess the conditions accurately. Use of the *DSM-IV* is helpful in providing an appropriate label, one that has received consensus by mental health professionals; the characteristics pertaining to that particular diagnosis are succinctly listed. For diagnosis and treatment of mental disorders, a close working relationship between the social worker and psychiatrist is essential. Read, et al. (1993: 150) provide an instructive case history involving collaborative work with a lesbian alcoholic suffering from feelings of depression and anxiety:

> Sylvia was referred to a psychiatrist in the clinic. It was agreed that even though she was currently drinking, her past history of depression indicated that she should be given a trial on antidepressant medication. The psychiatrist prescribed Prozac, 20 mg per day. Sylvia's initial response was not very good, in all likelihood because she continued to drink. In a series of psychoeducational therapy sessions, the interaction of alcohol with depression and anxiety was explained to her. As she became more convinced that her drinking was impeding her chances of getting better, she agreed to go to A.A. A gay and lesbian A.A. group was available. . . . After she stopped drinking (with less trouble than she had expected), she continued to have symptoms of depression. It was decided to increase the Prozac to 40 mg per day, and within a few weeks she began to feel considerably better.

In the past, alcoholics who had a dual diagnosis often "fell through the cracks" and received no help at all. In Washington state, Colorado, and North Dakota, for instance, there were separate systems for treatment of the mentally ill and the chemically addicted. Specialists at each agency sometimes refused to admit persons with additional problems. Today's willingness to deal with both disorders simultaneously is a major recent development.

Substance abuse services are most effective when provided at the location where clients are already in treatment (Henrickson, 1988). Clients referred to another agency are apt simply to get lost in the system. For this reason, substance abuse treatment should be offered, if possible, at the source of the initial contact.

In Iowa and Ohio today, as in most states, mental health agencies are anxious to have staff members trained in substance abuse assessment and treatment. Ideally, professionals work together as a team. The social worker's holistic approach is consistent with treating the individual for the many manifestations of illness rather than by focusing on one or another illness exclusively. The chief drawback to having social workers at a mental health clinic provide substance abuse treatment is their traditional lack of training for this kind of work. A major oversight of the mental health worker is in failing routinely to assess for alcohol abuse problems in clients presenting with mental disabilities.

ASSESSMENT

Before treatment can be instituted, the problem must be assessed. Assessment is also crucial in preparing agency paperwork and forms for insurance reimbursement. Many assessments are court-ordered by judges to aid in sentencing dispositions. Evaluation is required at the level of treatment to determine the nature of the problem and the appropriate individualized treatment needed, if any. Ed Fitzgerald's often amusing account of his treatment and recovery in *That Place in Minnesota* (1990: 157) gives the client view of the assessment process:

> Along with everybody else in the Rehab, I thought the unidentified hero who made up the widely circulated parody of the MMPI deserved a lot more credit than the genius who did the real thing. Some of parodist's best efforts included:
>
> I salivate at the sight of mittens.
> Spinach makes me feel alone.
> Dirty stories make me think about sex.
> I often repeat myself.
> I often repeat myself.
> Recently I have been getting shorter.
> Constantly losing my underwear doesn't bother me.
> Weeping brings tears to my eyes.
> I never seem to finish whatever I

The assessment process is only as good or as comprehensive as the underlying assumptions that shape it. Years ago, Jellinek (1960) portrayed alcoholism in many of its diversified forms, only one of which represented a disease in the medical sense. Jacobson (1989) documented the accumulated evidence pointing to several different *alcoholisms*, each with its own identifiable etiological course and recommended treatment. Similarly, Cloninger

(1987) identified two types of alcoholism characterized by distinctive personality traits—one involving too much sensitivity, one too little.

More recently, alcoholism assessment tended toward "a one size fits all" design. With alcoholism viewed as an inevitably progressive continuum, evaluation devices were geared toward determining if the alcoholic was early, middle, or late stage. *DSM-IV*, reflecting a shift in thinking, categorizes alcohol dependence in terms of degree of physical impairment and makes a distinction between substance *abuse* and substance *dependence*. The time is past, according to Jacobson (1989), for considering alcoholics a homogenous clinical group who share a single, common therapy. In fact, managed health care systems require accountability; a thorough, well-documented evaluation is now not only recommended but essential.

Two forms of evaluation are screening instruments and assessment. Several easy-to-use screening tests have been shown to be effective in identifying persons with alcohol problems. Screening is for detection purposes and is useful in health-care settings, in court services, at mental health clinics, and the like. Though only a starting point in treatment, such devices are invaluable basic tools for the human service practitioner.

CAGE

Developed by Ewing and Rouse (1974) and still widely used, CAGE consists of only four questions that can easily be remembered by the acronym:

C Have you ever tried to *cut* down on your drinking?
A Have people *annoyed* you by criticizing your drinking?
G Have you ever felt *guilty* about your drinking?
E Have you ever used alcohol in the morning as an *eye-opener*?

The first two questions cleverly encourage an alcoholic to "open up" regarding the need to cut down and the anger at family members who complain. The client who answers yes to two or more questions is considered likely to have alcoholism or what is now termed *alcohol dependence (DSM-IV)*.

MAST

The *Michigan Alcoholism Screening Test* (MAST), devised by Selzer in 1971, has become the other most widely used screening instrument (figure 11.1). The MAST is a twenty-four-item list of common signs and symptoms on a host of problems stemming from alcohol use. Although earlier researchers reported high validity for this instrument, Jacobson (1989) found an unacceptably high rate of false positives in a large client sample. I have found question number 8, Have you ever attended a meeting of Alcoholics Anonymous (A.A.)?, to be problematic. The question should be worded, "Have you ever attended a meeting of A.A. *for help with an alcohol problem?*" Iowa treatment centers have varied the wording accordingly.

FIGURE 11.1

Michigan Alcoholism Screening Test (MAST)

Points		Question	Yes	No
	0.	Do you enjoy a drink now and then?	___	___
(2)	*1.	Do you feel you are a normal drinker? (By normal we mean you drink less than or as much as most other people.)	___	___
(2)	2.	Have you ever awakened the morning after some drinking the night before and found that you could not remember a part of the evening?	___	___
(1)	3.	Does your wife, husband, a parent, or other near relative ever worry or complain about your drinking?	___	___
(2)	*4.	Can you stop drinking without a struggle after one or two drinks?	___	___
(1)	5.	Do you ever feel guilty about your drinking?	___	___
(2)	*6.	Do friends or relatives think you are a normal drinker?	___	___
(2)	*7.	Are you able to stop drinking when you want to?	___	___
(5)	8.	Have you ever attended a meeting of Alcoholics Anonymous (AA)?	___	___
(1)	9.	Have you gotten into physical fights when drinking?	___	___
(2)	10.	Has your drinking ever created problems between you and your wife, husband, a parent, or other relative?	___	___
(2)	11.	Has your wife, husband (or other family members) ever gone to anyone for help about your drinking?	___	___
(2)	12.	Have you ever lost friends because of your drinking?	___	___
(2)	13.	Have you ever gotten into trouble at work or school because of drinking?	___	___

Source: Lettieri et al. (eds.), Alcoholism Treatment Assessment Research Instruments, *NIAAA Treatment Handbook,* Series 2 (Washington, DC: U.S. Government Printing Office, 1985).

Ideally, assessment goes beyond mere screening; it is the comprehensive process designed to learn the necessary facts about individuals for the purpose of matching them to appropriate treatment. Once a referral

Points		Question	Yes	No
(2)	14.	Have you ever lost a job because of drinking?	___	___
(2)	15.	Have you ever neglected your obligations, your family, or your work for two or more days in a row because you were drinking?	___	___
(1)	16.	Do you drink before noon fairly often?	___	___
(2)	17.	Have you ever been told you have liver trouble? Cirrhosis?	___	___
(2)	**18.	After heavy drinking have you ever had Delirium Tremens (D.T.'s) or severe shaking, or heard voices or seen things that really weren't there?	___	___
(5)	19.	Have you ever gone to anyone for help about your drinking?	___	___
(5)	20.	Have you ever been in a hospital because of drinking?	___	___
(2)	21.	Have you ever been a patient in a psychiatric hospital or on a psychiatric ward of a general hospital where drinking was part of the problem that resulted in hospitalization?	___	___
(2)	22.	Have you ever been seen at a psychiatric or mental health clinic or gone to any doctor, social worker, or clergyman for help with any emotional problem, where drinking was part of the problem?	___	___
(2)	***23.	Have you ever been arrested for drunk driving, driving while intoxicated, or driving under the influence of alcoholic beverages? (IF YES, How many times? __)	___	___
(2)	***24.	Have you ever been arrested, or taken into custody, even for a few hours, because of other drunk behavior? (IF YES, How many times? __)	___	___

*Alcoholic response is negative.
**5 points for Delirium Tremens.
***2 points for *each* arrest.
SCORING SYSTEM: In general, five points or more would place the subject in an "alcoholic" category. Four points would be suggestive alcoholism, three points or less would indicate the subject was not alcoholic.

has been made, clinicians use assessment techniques to characterize the problem and to individualize treatment goals. The ecological approach offers a multidimensional framework for evaluating clients within the context of their worlds, past and present.

From the *biological* perspective, a person's health, nutrition, and medical history are explored. Which substances are being ingested into the body? What is the family history of alcohol use and addiction? A detailed *alcohol use history* should be obtained. Although the approach may be formal or informal, the information needed is: what does the client drink, how much, how often, when, where, and in conjunction with which other substances? What are the eating, sleeping, and drug-taking patterns? When did the drinking begin? Is the pattern daily or binge-drinking? How about blackouts, tolerance, DTs, and hallucinations?

From the *psychological* perspective, the evaluator would look at personality dynamics relevant to drinking. A mental health history is important here. Questions pertaining to depression, suicide, and anxiety elicit some indication of the psychological functions alcohol is serving. What does alcohol do for you? is a good basic question. Also, list the reasons for starting, continuing, stopping, and resuming drinking (Danaher and Lichenstein, 1978). MMPI test results elicit a vast amount of information about an individual; patterns that are revealed can be helpful in treatment. Persons who score high on extroversion, for instance, are likely to feel comfortable in group settings and to thrive in Twelve Step groups or their equivalent. *Socially,* the assessment surveys the person in the environment and the environment in the person. What is the role of the peer group? Who is in the family? Where are the supports in the family? Where are the stresses? What is the reality in regard to work or lack of work?

For the client, the *multidimensional* evaluation as an ongoing, interactive process can be a valuable learning experience, a powerful intervention in its own right. Rivers (1994) notes that although many clients never come back, they later say that the assessment session led to a change in the way they approached and used alcohol. For countless others, the assessment is the first step in a long road down the conventional treatment lane to sobriety.

MATCHING

Researchers are currently working to determine scientifically how to maximize treatment effectiveness through *matching*. This entails matching clients on the basis of personality (including demographic) characteristics and/or drug histories with specialized treatment efforts geared to their special needs. A study by Kadden et al. (1989) illustrates the usefulness of placing antisocial-type alcoholics into a coping skills, cognitively based treatment and the mainstream variety of alcoholics in supportive interactive group therapy. Although John Jung (1994) is cautious about expecting significant improvement with this research-based design, Miller and Hester (1986) have faith that, through systematic research, alcoholics who are likely to be successful in treatment can be identified and provided with appropriate interventions. Moreover, others could be weeded out early to prevent wasted resources. There is a consensus among alcoholism researchers that matching patients to treatments allows for individual differences and optimal therapy (Jung, 1994).

EMPLOYEE ASSISTANCE PROGRAMS (EAPs)

Within an employee assistance program, the assessment is focused on possible psychological, physical, interpersonal, and substance abuse problems in the work situation. Research evaluations indicate that the occupational environment may be one of the most efficient and economical means of providing an opportunity for early identification and treatment of alcohol abuse and alcoholism (Kinney and Leaton, 1991; Symonds, 1991). Workplace alcoholism programs have great potential for stopping people from abusing alcohol, because the risk of loss of employment is a powerful incentive to get people to change their behavior.

Reacting to the absenteeism and productivity losses due to alcohol abuse, private industry and the federal government have turned increasingly to work site employee assistance programs for identification and referral of workers with alcohol problems. Founded in the 1940s, EAPs were slow in developing until the 1960s, but expanded rapidly during the 1980s (Langton, 1991). Just under 1 percent of social workers work in this practice area (Gibelman and Schervish, 1993).

> An article in *Business Week* (Symonds, 1991: 76) presents the EAP rationale: Booze is the substance most abused in the business world. Experts estimate that it afflicts at least 10 percent of senior executives. . . . And of the $86 billion that alcoholism costs the nation every year, business pays the lion's share in extra health care, lost productivity, and absenteeism.

According to the same article, DuPont reports that about 80 percent of its alcoholic workers with long service recover with treatment. General Motors had a 65 to 70 percent success rate for 6,400 employees counseled for alcohol problems. EAPs, however, do not focus solely on alcoholism but are geared to help employees deal with any number of personal problems that could interfere with health and well-being. A broad-brush, or broad-based, approach is used today. This means that EAP counselors must have expertise in many areas, including polydrug use and mental health.

The cover story of *US News and World Report,* November 1, 1993, listed employee assistance counseling, a social work specialty, as one of the twenty best jobs for the future. It noted that more than 90 percent of Fortune 500 companies have employee assistance programs. *NASW News,* the news magazine for social workers, highlighted this article (Hiratsuka, 1994).

Across Canada and Europe, companies are introducing EAPs. Shell Canada established a full-scale program at its Calgary headquarters, assuring workers with dependency problems that they could get expert assistance without fear of discrimination (Jenish, 1993). Mandatory drug screening, uncommon in Canada, was rejected in favor of positive policies. In the United States, this issue of mandatory screening and testing for drugs as a prerequisite for being hired and continuing employment is a controversial one for employee programs. Having to submit to polygraph tests and/or urinalysis raises some serious constitutional questions about rights of privacy and self-determination (Akers, 1992). Problems with clients "beating the tests" or researchers receiving false positive results have been reported in the popular press. In the United States, the issue is being resolved in favor of allowing mandatory testing.

SOCIAL WORK IN HEALTH CARE

Medical social work, now called social work in health care, is the third largest field of practice for social workers (DiNitto and McNeese, 1990). At the present time, about 14 percent of all NASW members work in health care. The most typical settings for social work practice are hospitals, hospices, community home health-care settings, nursing homes, and health maintenance organizations. In recent years social workers have been in great demand for AIDS counseling.

Heavy and chronic drinking can harm virtually every cell in the body (see chapter 4). The standard estimate is that 25 percent of all hospitalized persons, regardless of the reasons they were admitted, have a significant alcohol problem. Yet, by all accounts, this is a conservative estimate. As Kinney and Leaton (1991) indicate, Veterans Administration (VA) estimates are that 50 percent of all VA hospital beds are filled by veterans with alcohol problems.

Health-care costs for actively drinking alcoholics and their families are high. Diseases, accidents, suicide attempts, and violence all take their toll. Accordingly, social workers in health-care settings must be able to heed the indicators of alcohol abuse and alcoholism and to make appropriate referrals in short order. Whereas patients in detoxification units are attended to appropriately, the cause of their problems being obvious, other patients are treated medically but rarely screened for alcohol problems. A great deal can be done at the time of a medical crisis to ensure that patients get help that can prevent further alcohol-induced illness and trauma. Medical screening, tests, and interviews can be used to identify and treat alcohol problems.

CHILD WELFARE

Child welfare practice has long been considered a social work domain. In their NASW-sponsored survey of the labor force, Gibelman and Schervish (1993) report that 16.3 percent of all members render services to children, while an additional 11.3 percent are employed in family services. With the United States the only industrialized nation not to have a program of children and family allowances, pressure on families for financial survival can be tremendous (DiNitto and McNeese, 1990). Children who come to the attention of agencies because of deficiencies in care of one sort or another are apt to be living near or below the poverty line. The role of social workers is to enhance family functioning and, if possible, to prevent placement outside the home. Caseworkers in the child welfare system must make important decisions about foster placement and parental rights, trying to judge which children are in danger and which are not.

In addition to poverty, another factor affecting families receiving services is alcohol abuse. Alcohol figures prominently in cases of child abuse and neglect. In 1990 the Child Welfare League of America surveyed its member agencies on the impact of alcohol and other drugs. The statistics collected give some indication of the extent of the problem. Beer, wine, liquor, and marijuana were the substances most commonly used by families served by agencies in the survey. Over 36 percent of public agencies reported children affected by substance abuse, while over 57 percent of the voluntary child welfare agencies had identified this as a problem. Curtis and McCullough (1993), in accounting for these research results, note that the voluntary agencies screen referrals for substance abuse problems more thoroughly than do state agencies. There is a lack of specialized training in substance abuse assessment and intervention throughout the field of child welfare.

Curtis and McCullough rightly conclude that the impact of chemical abuse on family functioning is profound. Many of the children in placement have developmental problems related to alcohol abuse. The results also confirm the need for immediate action to address deficits in the provision of services and training related to substance abuse. Screening procedures need to be improved and implemented.

CRIME AND ALCOHOL

Alcohol use plays a significant role in family violence and other behavior that bring families to the attention of child welfare authorities. The presence of alcohol is reflected in the national crime statistics. Alcohol is widely implicated in homicide and assault and in the crime of rape, especially date rape. According to a national survey of 13,986 state prison inmates, conducted in 1991, nearly half of the incarcerated inmates were under the influence of alcohol (32%) or of drugs exclusively (17%). The leading crime for which females were imprisoned emerged as drug offenses (reported by Hall and Watson, 1993).

Approximately half of men who batter their female partners have substance abuse problems, according to an extensive survey of domestic violence programs and substance abuse treatment centers (Bennett and Lawson, 1994). Survey participants estimated that 60 percent of the women in chemical dependency treatment were victims of domestic abuse. Yet, due to different etiological philosophies concerning the nature of the problem, cooperation between women's helpers and alcoholism treatment centers has not been forthcoming, according to Bennett and Lawson.

Canadian statistics tell the same story; drugs and alcohol play a major role in the commission of crime. Comprehensive data show that over half of the individuals given penitentiary sentences since 1990 used drugs or alcohol on the day they committed their crime. Over two-thirds had substance abuse problems, mostly involving alcohol, requiring professional treatment (Jenish, 1993). In the United Kingdom, alcohol is implicated in 50 percent of all homicides, 78 percent of assaults, and 93 percent of arrests between 10:00 P.M. and 2:00 A.M. (Sparks, et al., 1990).

Alcohol consumption tends to reduce the ordinary inhibitions that restrain people from committing acts of violence, including sexual offenses. I was shocked to read in a newspaper that one of my most dignified and courteous clients was arrested for indecent exposure, "mooning" in a bar. Later, he could recall nothing of the incident.

Drug-related violations tend to spring from illegal activities to procure money to replenish the supply of drugs. Regardless of the drug of choice, substance abuse treatment is imperative for persons in jail and prison. In order to provide coping skills and resources to insulate inmates returning to a drug-influenced environment, correctional institutions need funding for built-in treatment components. Yet, according to a national report from the U.S. Department of Justice (1993), placements for offenders needing treatment are entirely inadequate, and there is a lack of funding to hire qualified personnel to staff treatment programs. Despite the fact that over 50 percent of all state inmates reported using drugs in the month before arrest and 31 percent were under the influence of drugs at the time of arrest, only 11 percent of state and prison inmates were enrolled in drug treatment programs in institutions and community corrections facilities (U.S. Bureau of Justice Statistics, 1993).

What money is available comes from state funding. Despite the perpetual threat of budget cutbacks, exciting innovations can be found, for instance, in California, Kentucky, and Iowa. California, in 1994, allocated $100 million to build two correctional facilities to be run as therapeutic substance abuse treatment communities. The Kentucky corrections program charges inmates for the intensive Lifeline rehabilitation program. A no-nonsense drug and alcohol treatment program at Iowa's medium security prison in Clarinda reports excellent follow-up results in reducing recidivism rates for treated inmates. Despite the cost effectiveness, however, budget cuts in Iowa have reduced rather than expanded the experimental program.

In Scotland, major structural reforms in the criminal justice system beginning in the 1990s involve a link between social work departments, courts, and prisons. Noncustodial sentencing alternatives for young offenders provide for a full range of alcohol treatment services. Intensive educational program offerings to young substance abusers in prison are considered unique in Europe and have generated considerable interest in the United Kingdom (Baldwin, 1992). The strong social work influence is noteworthy.

Social workers in the United States work in juvenile and adult probation and parole, juvenile court services, correctional institutions, youth shelters, group homes, and diversionary programs. Yet there is room for expansion of social work employment in criminal justice, especially at administrative levels. Social workers who are certified as substance abuse counselors should find increasing opportunities in this rapidly expanding field.

PREVENTION

Treatment services in health care, child welfare, and corrections work are fundamentally prevention programs. However, they would be considered, in Royce's (1989) terminology, *secondary* and *tertiary prevention*. Secondary prevention is aimed at arresting the problem before the consequences are serious; early detection is paramount. In tertiary prevention, the aim is to prevent further damage to the alcoholic and to his or her family.

Primary prevention is forestalling alcoholism from developing in the community at all. The public health model seeks through education to prevent drinking problems and smoking, for instance, from getting started in the first place. Prevention of alcohol abuse is a difficult task in the United States given the mixed messages sent by advertisers and peer groups concerning the drug alcohol. Denzin (1993: xvii) provides a sociological commentary:

> A culture which respects the drug alcohol would undertake careful means to integrate that drug into its daily patterns of ritual and routine. It would not leave instructions on drug use up to novices; it would have the older, more mature members of the culture teach the novice drinkers how to drink.

Furthermore, adds Denzin, a society conducive to a healthy relationship with alcohol would encourage abstinence, but not try to force it on the young.

Societies and cultural groups tend to get the problems they anticipate, some would say deserve, with regard to alcohol. A remedy or a prevention strategy that works in one society may not work in another. For example, prohibition is highly successful in Muslim countries. And high, very high, taxation on alcohol curbs drinking in Scandinavia, although the same policy with smoking has not been effective. Successful prevention strategies would consider multiple environmental and cultural components of the system of interrelated factors, rather than choosing just one out of context (Jung, 1994). Primary prevention has traditionally focused on school and public education programs as means of providing knowledge. Such programs have been underfunded, however. Pioneering prevention programs in schools sought to educate children about alcohol and drug use and teach children to "just say no." Results were not very successful; perhaps too much focus was put on the drugs themselves (Goodstadt, 1975). More recent efforts to empower students to enhance their sense of self and to teach coping skills should help reduce the risk for developing addictions problems (Fields, 1992). The kind of stress management training provided is useful also in preventing any number of unhealthy reactions to stress and pain, including reckless driving and suicide.

Leicestershire, England, provides for the public a rare offering, an alcohol advice center. A drinker can get counseling there over the years to monitor his or her drinking. Labels such as "alcoholism" and "client" are avoided to prevent a medicalized image. Counselors see the "customers" at home and help them take responsibility for their lives and to slow down on the drinking. According to a 1993 BBC radio broadcast, the city has seen a decline in alcoholism rates. *Harm reduction* is the term for this kind of prevention strategy, popular in Europe. Instead of abstinence, reduction in the level of harm is emphasized.

In the United States, the federal government and many state governments have enacted laws to shape the sales, distribution, and consumption of alcohol. Control over advertising in the form of warning labels is one small example of the enactment of regulations for the public good. More pressure, in all likelihood, will be placed on alcoholic beverage advertising in the future.

Public health control efforts to avert alcohol-related driving injuries and death have resulted in laws imposing serious penalties for drinking and driving and laws restricting the serving of alcoholic beverages to persons under age twenty-one. Recent studies seem to indicate that such laws, perhaps because of the certainty of their enforcement, are having some success in deterring drinking-related accidents (U.S. Dept. of Health and Human Services, 1993).

The best level for a social worker role in prevention occurs at the level of school social work. Much work needs to be done as early as the primary grades level. There is a growing recognition that some children are at much greater risk of becoming substance abusers than others. Prevention programs, according to the American Medical Association (1991) should be targeted toward youths who:

- exhibit antisocial behavior;
- have unskilled and uninvolved parents;
- get failing marks or are uninterested in school;
- have friends and siblings who participate in and accept alcohol and drug use;
- are alienated from social and religious conventions; and
- are at risk of genetic predisposition to addiction.

I would add to the list those students, most likely girls, who have been victimized sexually (refer to chapter 7).

Children living in alcoholic environments can derive tremendous psychological benefits from learning about the nature of addiction and its consequences. Children tend to blame themselves for family problems and to feel weighed down by family secrets. Social workers can do much in schools to teach about life in an alcoholic home. Then individual children can later "open up" and perhaps get the counseling they need.

In summary, to prevent alcoholism is to reduce health care costs, alcohol-related traffic deaths, court costs, the school dropout rate, unwanted pregnancies, the spread of AIDS, and crime including family violence. In recognition of the important role of prevention, an Office of Substance Abuse Prevention (OSAP) was established in 1987. Today, this is a major center for prevention knowledge and other activities.

SOCIAL WORK TRAINING

Social workers in general social work practice, such as those areas discussed in this chapter, require education in the core competencies of addictions-related work. Social workers encounter alcoholism and its effects at every turn. In 1987, in recognition of the pervasiveness of substance abuse problems, the National Association of Social Workers (NASW) Delegate Assembly introduced a policy statement recommending that substance abuse knowledge, like information on cultural diversity, be incorporated into the social work core curriculum. To date, this particular proposal has not been adopted. However, in 1996, the Delegate Assembly will address this policy statement once again.

A three-year curriculum development project is currently underway to develop curriculum modules on alcohol and other drug abuse knowledge to be circulated to undergraduate programs for possible integration into the foundation courses of social work. A $500,000 contract with the National Institute on Alcohol Abuse and Alcoholism (NIAAA) is augmenting this work. If this curriculum development project is implemented nationwide, all social workers of the future will have knowledge of the basics of substance abuse problems.

At the undergraduate level, there is often little opportunity to specialize in any branch of social work, much less substance abuse counseling. A rare exception is the program at the University of Northern Iowa, which provides four specialist courses for a state approved UNI certificate in substance abuse training. That this program is rare was reflected in the extra paperwork required by Council of Social Work Education (CSWE) authorities in 1991 to justify the concentration and field placement at substance abuse centers.

Yet specialized curriculum development in this area, as Freeman (1985) persuasively argues, is sorely needed. Freeman refers to several different models of training that can be utilized by graduate schools of social work. Some programs offer specialized courses to select students; others attempt to integrate material on alcoholism into the existing core curriculum to inform all students. Finally, some programs do both. Rutgers School of Social Work, located at a university famous for its substance abuse research center, provides for a highly specialized concentration. The Human Behavior and Social Environment sequence reaches all students with an introduction to alcohol and other drugs. The specialization leads to state certification.

In New York State, where social workers have played a leadership role in providing alcoholism services and in raising professional standards for alcoholism counseling, graduate schools have shown a strong interest in providing relevant and meaningful education. At both the undergraduate and graduate levels, the University of Utah has long offered and encouraged social work students to take addictions courses. An undergraduate minor in chemical use and awareness and an addiction counselor training program are offered by the University of North Dakota.

But until CSWE requires that all social work graduates be competent for working with clients with addiction problems, clients in treatment whose lives have become unmanageable will not receive the professional help they so badly need.

THE BRITISH STANDARDIZED CURRICULUM

From an international perspective, Great Britain leads the way in ensuring social worker competence in "substance misuse" knowledge. Since 1991 a new social work qualification has been introduced throughout the national curriculum. The rationale as set forth by the Central Council for Education and Training (1991: 30) is stated as follows:

> Over the past twenty years, it has been established that every social work agency dealing with individual, family, and child care problems is likely to have contact with a great many people with alcohol and other drug problems. . . . If social workers and probation officers are unable to recognize and respond to these problems they will not be able to perform core tasks like child protection adequately.

While some university departments in the United Kingdom and Ireland integrate substance abuse course content across the curriculum, others teach specialist modules. Harrison (1992) expresses distress that, in his national survey due before the new requirements came into effect, 11 percent of the social work programs provided no formal training in responding to substance abuse problems. In comparison with American social work students, Harrison notes, those in the British Isles are much more likely to be required to attend substance misuse training. However, when American students do receive training, it is more extensive. One British program that is both required and extensive is that offered at the University of Hull.

A CHALLENGE TO THE SOCIAL WORK PROFESSION

Whether health-care funding encourages substance abuse treatment to take place at specialized treatment centers or at mental health centers or through family therapy agencies, social workers will be actively involved in the addictions treatment scene. Social workers should be at the forefront of educating mental health professionals in the creative and innovative practice methods required for effective addictions treatment. All accredited programs of social work should be required to educate students concerning the physical and psychological aspects of addiction. Practice courses should integrate skills content into the standard treatment curriculum. To provide role models for this field, university departments should actively recruit workers who have specialized in substance abuse counseling. Non-degreed alcoholism counselors should be encouraged to pursue social work training. In all these ways, social work practice should be reconceptualized to include addictions training and work as an acceptable and standard social work endeavor. With a generalist's understanding of the biological, psychological, and social components in human behavior and a specialist knowledge of clinical interventions such as family systems therapy, social workers bring a flexibility to the addictions field that is consistent with their holistic approach.

In light of the program functions that need to be performed in the substance abuse treatment field, social workers are not well represented (Magura, 1994). Across all treatment programs nationally, only 6 percent of total staff are social workers at the master's level or above (U.S. Dept. of Health and Human Services, 1993). The rationale for an expanded social work participation includes improvement in direct services to clients, evaluation and accountability of programs, research on practice issues, and development of diversified treatment models (Magura, 1994). Politically, as well as professionally, social work has done little to carve out a recognized role for itself within addictions treatment. This is in sharp contrast to nationally orchestrated efforts to be officially recognized for insurance reimbursement purposes in areas such as mental health and private practice. Social workers would find it advantageous to focus on the certification process in raising academic standards for substance abuse counselors and promoting the attainment of a bachelor's degree in a relevant professional field. Social work organizations could negotiate with the funding agencies to explore the advantages of increasing the representation of social workers in treatment programs, as Magura (1994) wisely suggests. Social work educators can benefit their students by cultivating field placement opportunities and by joining local treatment center boards of directors.

FUTURE TRENDS

POLICY

- More control of costs and services and a dramatic increase in the use of managed care. Managed care, the private regulation of health-care providers by insurers and others has evolved because of a concern over rising health care costs. Strict preadmission criteria may prevent alcoholics from getting the intensive care they need.
- Increasing emphasis on outpatient care, with special attention to problems of the dually diagnosed. Look for mental health clinics to be more active in providing assessments and treatment.
- Increased federal funding for substance abuse treatment programs within the criminal justice arena. Hopefully, the focus will shift from control of the *supply* side of drugs to a control of the *demand*.
- At the national level, congressional regulation to place stricter controls on advertising alcoholic beverages; tighter smoking regulations; and increased taxation on alcohol and tobacco.

- Recognition of prevention efforts as crucial; greatly strengthened school programs.

TREATMENT

- Development of alternative approaches to the Twelve-Step programs. Continuing legal suits will be filed on the basis of constitutional rights against the imposed religiosity of Twelve Step groups. Such challenges can be expected to have a dampening effect on coerced attendance at these meetings.
- Making treatment programs free of all addictive behavior. Addiction increasingly will be seen as a primary drive with many manifestations, including drug, nicotine, food, and gambling addiction.
- Greater requirements for evaluation of treatment interventions. This should result in an increase in the use of more cognitively based treatments.
- Continued growth of multicultural centers that are community based. The precepts of Twelve-Step recovery at these agencies will be adapted to the mores and traditions of the people in the community. Family programs will be enhanced.
- Continuing attacks on the basic premises of the disease model. Such attacks, often scientifically based, may have drastic implications for treatment. The emphasis on moral responsibility and self-control are dangerously reminiscent of the puritanical views of an earlier era.
- Managed care requirements that treatment be *individualized* to meet client needs. Attention to individual case histories will reveal widespread existence of post-traumatic stress disorder (PTSD) among individuals with addictions problems. Addictions counselors can be expected to address the needs of war veterans and survivors of early childhood sexual abuse. More psychotherapy will be provided.
- More federally and locally funded programs for pregnant alcoholic women. The impetus to prevent Fetal Alcohol Syndrome will lead to greater efforts here.

RESEARCH

- The application of new and exciting research findings concerning the workings of the brain and the role that brain chemicals play in human behavior. Serotonin uptake blockers may be administered to reduce alcohol craving. Encouragement of exercise, stress management techniques, and good nutrition will be viewed as ways to replenish the brain's chemicals naturally. More research will be forthcoming on the link between addictions and biochemistry.

- Matching of clients to appropriate treatments. Recovery rates can be enhanced through more extensive, long-term research evaluation of interventions.

- Greater acceptance of the British notion of *harm reduction* as a measure of successful treatment outcome. In measuring recovery rates, abstinence need not be the only criterion for recovery. One former client may abstain, another may drink a glass of wine a day. And a heroin addict may substitute methadone for heroin. These clients are all showing improvement; they are all reducing the harm to themselves. The treatment evaluation design can be expected to develop greater flexibility to reflect the reality of post-treatment behavior.

SUMMARY

Social workers, in their chosen line of practice, see addiction and the effects of addiction every day. Perhaps even more often, they fail to see it. Detecting addiction such as alcoholism or an eating disorder involves asking the right questions at the right time and recognizing in the answers the old, familiar pattern. The beauty about knowing the pattern is that suddenly so much of the person's history begins to make sense—the lost jobs, ill health, bizarre relationships, and other addictions. And now, at last, something can be done to alter the course.

Having examined the whole gamut of social work—the mental health office, the health care setting, EAPs, child welfare, criminal justice, school—we will now proceed to "pull it all together." Data collected from various sources, mostly from governmental agencies, show that alcohol abuse remains a major health problem, a crime problem, and a family problem. Like other addictive behaviors, alcoholism has been resistant to traditional prevention and treatment interventions, especially since the large majority of alcoholics do not want nor do they get specialized substance abuse treatment. This is where social workers can enter into the picture. Trained to approach human behavior holistically and to adopt a strengths perspective, social workers are in a unique position to help alcoholics begin to heal. As practitioners, they must utilize all their resources to assess the nature of the problem and to help clients develop good survival skills. As policy experts, social workers can work in grant writing and through state and local government to help establish the kinds of programs that are needed. A halfway house for pregnant, addicted women would be example of an assessed need. On a higher level, social workers can work to build a society that cares for its people, a society that provides for the social welfare of its members.

Social work education today is at a crossroads as far as mandating substance abuse training in all departments of social work is concerned. Courses that are introduced are invariably popular with students, many of whom are from alcoholic backgrounds and many of whom want an education that is marketable as well as meaningful.

Alcohol is involved in:

- Approximately 25 percent of all hospitalizations
- Nearly one-half of all deaths from motor vehicle crashes
- 20 to 36 percent of suicides; alcohol use is highly associated with use of firearms as a means of suicide
- 17 percent of drownings in boating accidents
- Over 50 percent of all homicides
- 38 percent of all drowning deaths
- The majority of cigarette-generated fire deaths
- Up to 50 percent of excess mortality due to cardiovascular disorders. (U.S. Dept. of Health and Human Services, 1990)

REVIEW QUESTIONS

1. What is meant by the dually diagnosed? Why is the debate over which disorder caused the other futile?

2. Discuss the role of social workers in mental health and what they can do to help alcoholics.

3. Describe the two most commonly used alcohol assessment schemes.

4. What is the biopsychosocial approach to assessment?

5. Describe the ramifications of matching for treatment.

6. What are EAPs? What is the social worker's role here? What are some research findings that relate to employee treatment outcomes? What is the *broad-brush* program?

7. How do Canadian EAPs differ from those in the United States?

8. Describe the field of social work in health care. What is the connection between alcohol and health problems?

9. Discuss the child welfare link with alcohol abuse. What are the needs of families affected by alcoholism?

10. Relate crime to substance abuse. How is the situation changing today? What do the statistics show? What is being done about the problem in prisons?

11. What type of prevention programs are there? What does Denzin say a culture should offer its youth to prevent alcohol abuse? Discuss the notion that a society tends to get the alcohol problems it deserves. What is the English approach?

12. According to the AMA, which youths should prevention programs target?

13. What are social work educators doing to address training needs of students of social work? Describe some innovative programs.

14. What is the challenge to the social work profession?

15. Discuss future trends in terms of policy, treatment, and research.

EPILOGUE

The practice of alcoholism treatment is rich in history and tradition. It would be impossible to separate the evolution of "modern day" alcoholism counseling from the development stages of group dynamics and from social psychology, disease concepts and the notion of progression, and the growth of self-help and of self-help-oriented treatment. Systems theory from the social sciences by way of social work and the cognitive approach from both psychology and Twelve-Step folklore have given rise to a treatment milieu that is exciting, innovative, and not without some ideological differences. No longer is the alcoholism counselor the drill sergeant who tears down and terrorizes in order to break denial. No longer are patients sent home under instructions to "hit bottom" and then return for more "tough-love" treatment when the time is right.

And yet, it is in these early days that some of the most remarkable and gripping tales of recovery against incredible odds occurred.

From these early days, too, comes the description of group bonding that grew out of shared suffering and endurance and raw human drama, when laughter was considered a form of escape and one had to cry to "get honest." If today, seasoned therapists are nostalgic about the past, it is because some of the pioneering spirit of the early days has been lost. Bureaucratization and professionalization have triumphed over fervor and emotionalism.

However, nostalgia for the past should not blind us to the many mistakes that were made in the name of alcoholism treatment. Removal of psychotic patients' medication, refusal to allow survivors of sexual assault to work on past issues, belief that the A.A. path was the only way to sobriety—the list is considerable.

A combination of a new multimodal treatment orientation and reduced financial resources has led to upheaval in the treatment community. Even the earlier rigid adherence to the twenty-eight-day inpatient modality of chemical dependency treatment is undergoing change. Much of the impetus for this change is political and economic. As we have seen, ideology is socially and historically constructed; the only thing predictable is change and the need to adapt. Because social agencies are political entities and because addictions work, like social work practice in general, is largely agency based, politics shapes professional life: How alcoholism is understood in the political arena, the resources allocated toward addressing perceived needs, and which approaches are promoted for intervention influence to a great extent the treatment enterprise.

Today, two paradigms shape the political thought and popular literature concerning alcohol and alcoholism. One is the *diseasing* of society—women who love too much, men who love too little, children brought up in alcoholic homes. On the opposite end of the spectrum is the *moralizing* about "drinking problems" and other "bad behavior" that can and must be corrected through the individual will. While the first approach, the medicalized (but not medical) view, is compatible with expanding the treatment industry into new areas, the second approach (which stresses moralism) parallels the national war on drugs and other punitive legislation. The overemphasis on mass labeling and treatment of the one has its counterpart in the behavioral treatment (or no treatment) by the other. The opposing dogma of the "mad" versus the "bad" reflects the maelstrom within North American society itself concerning the use of alcohol. Promoted vigorously by advertisers on the one hand, alcohol consumption is simultaneously restricted through harsh legislation on the other.

The two warring ideologies, both influential today, though with different audiences, each describe a small part of the whole. Their sole, common ground is in their narrowness. Both promote doctrine to the neglect of the *individual*, the human being described eloquently by Dennis Wrong (1976) as "that plausible creature whose tongue so often hides the despair in his heart." In this case, the forgotten individual is the alcoholic.

The pain of the alcoholic is hidden, unexpressed—hence, the reason for the alcohol. There is no other outlet. Alcoholics use alcohol, as Denzin (1993) suggests, to make peace with their fears and guilts and resentments. Alcoholics drink both to cope with feelings and to run away from feelings; they drink to dissolve guilt feelings about the past and to stave off anxiety over the future. People drink, in short, in order not to think. The decline in rational attributes associated with alcohol abuse is paralleled by a decline in moral and spiritual life.

To the extent that alcoholism involves spiritual poverty, recovery involves spiritual and social growth that often exceeds the growth of the nonalcoholic. This is not to say that alcoholics are all alike or that one person's recovery, if there is recovery, will be like another's. Just as there are many differences among alcoholics, there are many alcoholisms, far more than have been even defined at this time. These diverse alcoholisms require multiple levels of treatment. A promising new strategy involves matching patients to interventions specific to their needs. Treatment outcome research gives evidence that behavioral training, such as stress management therapy, assertiveness, and social skills training, reduces the incidence and severity of relapse.

The writing of this text was initiated as a response to recent developments in alcoholism treatment research, education, and practice. *Alcoholism Treatment: A Social Work Perspective* was written in accordance with current trends within the field of social work to identify addictions as an inevitable and worthwhile area of practice. Although attention has been paid to the reality of external constraints, the joy of alcoholism treatment work is seen in the friendliness of the treatment community and in the wealth of feelings that are expressed and shared by those (staff and clients alike) "who have been there" and who are fighting from the depths of the soul to be there no more.

In keeping with the changing currents in addictions work, this text has drawn on the social work ecological model as a framework and on the literature of social work and related disciplines, including science and medicine, for research findings. The intent has been to present a foundation of knowledge from which the student or practitioner, whether in social work or a related field, can prepare to address the needs of clients. Accordingly, the three basic components of behavior in social work theory—the physical, the cognitive, and the social—have served as an organizing framework for the presentation of alcoholism material. The physical consequences of alcohol abuse and alcoholism, the subject of chapter 4, are highly relevant to treatment and recovery. The currently evolving scientific knowledge, much of it focused on brain chemistry and pharmaceutical discoveries, has vast implications for future treatment strategies.

The psychology of addiction is another theme of this text. The chapters on alcoholism as a way of thinking, loss and grief and spiritual healing, and group therapy (chapters 5, 6, and 9, respectively) are centered on the cognitive approach derived from psychology as an approach encompassing commonly used but rarely articulated modes of therapy.

Included under the rubric of the social side of human behavior are such diversified elements as the history of alcohol use, the subject of chapter 2; the economic, sociological, and legal dynamics (chapter 10);

special groups research (chapter 7); and family systems therapy (chapter 8). An international perspective was adopted as a way to understand how alcohol use is culturally defined and determined, how the society basically gets the alcoholism it expects or, as Denzin and others would say, deserves. Throughout these sections and in the chapter on group therapy, I have included first-hand treatment knowledge, the "folk wisdom" from the field, so that practitioners of the future will have what I did not have all in one place: group exercises, feelings work descriptions, rules for "fighting fair," and suggestions for family group presentations.

Both the science and art of social work practice with alcoholics are reflected in the several major divisions of the text. Part One focuses on the theoretical context of social work addictions practice and the history and contemporary paradigm of social work. Part Two encompasses various aspects of addiction, including the somatic and psychological components in drinking. Recent scientific findings in the literature were employed to present a thorough knowledge base. The artistic and spiritual aspects of grief and recovery are covered in chapter 6, the chapter that also summarizes feelings work for all alcoholics in treatment. Part Three, social work practice with the alcoholic client, can be rightly regarded as focusing on the artistic side of alcoholism treatment work. Yet even here, emphasis is placed on social scientific research evaluation in determining which approach or approaches are correlated with treatment successes. Again, from social sciences, the framework for viewing the alcoholism treatment agency as a formal organization was borrowed from classical sociology and applied to the alcoholism treatment work environment.

The interplay between internal and external forces is most pronounced at the level of the agency where leadership style, work conditions, professional ideologies, and the selection of treatment clientèle—the internal aspects—are both situationally and politically determined. This coalescence of opposites between internal and external, like art and science, theory and practice, the disease model and "responsibility" theory, is the essence of social work's ecosystems perspective. The whole is greater than the sum of its parts; the parts are not disparate, but in constant interaction.

In scientifically informed therapy, art and science can be seen as intertwined and inseparable. The same is true of theory and practice: the situation ideally is never either/or but always both/and. Just as good theory is highly practical, good practice must be grounded in solid theory. Although proponents of the disease model of alcoholism and those who hold to the "responsibility centered" approach tend to dichotomize their views, the actual treatment scene offers an intricate combination of aspects of both designs for recovery. Good alcoholism therapy, in short, encompasses art and science, unites theory and practice, and blends the strengths of the Twelve-Step approach with its cognitively based counterpart.

REFERENCES

CHAPTER 1: THE ECOLOGICAL APPROACH TO ALCOHOLISM TREATMENT

Bell, W. (1979). The Attribution of Cause in the Assessment Process. Ph.D. diss., Tulane University, New Orleans, LA.

Dulfano, C. (1982). *Families, Alcoholism and Recovery: Ten Stories.* Center City, MN: Hazelden.

Germain, C. (1984). *Social Work Practice in Health Care: An Ecological Perspective.* New York: Free Press.

Germain, C. (1991). *Human Behavior in the Social Environment: An Ecological View.* New York: Columbia.

Germain, C., and Gitterman, A. (1980). *The Life Model of Social Work Ecological View.* New York: Columbia University Press.

Goodwin, D. W. (1976). *Is Alcoholism Hereditary?* New York: Oxford University Press.

Hartman, A., and Laird, J. (1983). *Family-Centered Social Work Practice.* New York: Free Press.

Holden, C. (1985). Genes, Personality and Alcoholism. *Psychology Today,* Jan., 38–44.

Howe, G. (1981). The Ecological Approach to Permanency Planning: An Interactionist Perspective. *Child Welfare,* 42 (July–Aug.): 291–301.

Jacobson, G. (1989). A Comprehensive Approach to Pretreatment Evaluation. In R. Hester and W. R. Miller (eds.), *Handbook of Alcoholism Treatment Approaches.* New York: Pergamon Press.

Kaufman, E., and Pattison, M. (1981). Differential Methods of Family Therapy in the Treatment of Alcoholism. *Journal of Studies on Alcohol,* 42: 951–967.

Krystal, H. (1985). Some Problems Encountered in Attempting Psychoanalytical Psychotherapy with Substance Dependent Individuals. *Drug Abuse and Alcoholism Newsletter,* 14 (Feb.): 1–3.

Kurzman, P. (1983). Ethical Issues in Industrial Social Work Practice. In R. K. Hester and W. R. Miller (eds), *Handbook of Alcoholism Treatment Approach.* New York: Pergamon Press. P. 9.

Lawson, G., Ellis, D., and Rivers, P. C. (1984). *Essentials of Chemical Dependency Counseling.* Rockville, MD: Aspen.

Lewis, D. (1977). Role of Social Worker. In *Encyclopedia of Social Work,* vol. 1, pp. 13–22. Washington, DC: National Association of Social Workers.

Miller, W. R. (1990). Alcohol Treatment Alternatives: What Works? In H. B. Milkman and L. Sederer (eds.), *Treatment Choices for Alcoholism and Substance Abuse.* Lexington, MA: Lexington.

National Institute on Drug Abuse (1990). *National Drug and Alcoholism Treatment Unit Survey.* Rockville, MD: U.S. Dept. of Health and Human Services.

Steinglass, P. (1979). Family Therapy with Alcoholics: A Review. In F. Kaufman and P. Kaufman (eds.), *Family Therapy of Drug and Alcohol Abuse.*

van Wormer, K. (1987). Training Social Work Students for Practice with Substance Abusers: An Ecological Approach. *Journal of Social Work Education, 23*(2)(Spring-Summer): 47–56.

Wallace, J. (1989). A Biopsychosocial Model of Alcoholism. *Social Casework, 70*(6): 325–332.

Wessells, N., and Hopson, J. (1988). *Biology.* New York: Random House.

Zastrow, C., and Kirst-Ashman, K. (1990). *Understanding Human Behavior and the Social Environment,* 2d ed. Chicago: Nelson-Hall.

CHAPTER 2: HISTORICAL CONTEXT

Alasuutari, P. (1992). *Desire and Craving: A Cultural Theory of Alcoholism.* Albany: State University of New York Press.

Ayto, J. (1990). *Dictionary of Word Origins.* New York: Arcade.

Brun-Gulbransen, S. (1988). Drinking Habits in Norway. In D. J. Skog and R. Waahlberg (eds.), *Alcohol and Drugs: The Norwegian Experience.* Oslo, Norway: National Directorate for the Prevention of Alcohol and Drug Problems.

Christiansen, B., and Teahan, J. (1987). Cross-Cultural Comparisons of Irish and American Adolescent Drinking Practices and Beliefs. *Journal of Studies on Alcohol, 48:* 558–562.

Davidson, R. (1991). Alcohol and Alcohol Problems. Research 16, Northern Ireland. *British Journal of Addiction, 86:* 829–835.

Douglass, F. (1845/1968). *Narrative of the Life of Frederick Douglass.* New York: Signet.

Encyclopaedia Britannica. (1993). Alcohol and Drug Consumption. Chicago: Encyclopaedia Britannica, Inc.

Giancana, S., and Giancana, C. (1992). *Double Cross.* New York: Warner.

Helzer, J., and Canino, G. (1992). *Alcohol in North America, Europe and Asia.* New York: Oxford University Press.

Hughes, H. (1979). *The Man from Ida Grove.* Waco, TX: Word Books.

JAMA (1892). Inebriety among Women in This Country. *Journal of the American Medical Association, 19:* 530–531. Reprinted in *JAMA, 268*(14): 1928.

Jellinek, E. M. (1960). *The Disease Concept of Alcoholism.* New Haven, CT: Yale Center for Alcohol Studies.

Kerry, T. K. (1973). *A History of Modern Norway, 1814–1972.* Oxford: Clarendon Press.

Kinney, J., and Leaton, G. (1991). *Loosening the Grip.* St. Louis, MO: Mosby.

Langton, P. A. (1991). *Drug Use and the Alcohol Dilemma.* Boston, MA: Allyn and Bacon.

Lender, M., and Martin, J. (1982). *Drinking in America: A History.* New York: Free Press.

Levin, J. D. (1990). *Alcoholism: A Bio-Psycho-Social Approach.* New York: Hemisphere.

Miller, W. (1986). Haunted by the *Zeitgeist:* Reflections on Contrasting Treatment Goals and Concepts of Alcoholics in Europe and the United States. In T. Barbor (ed.),

Alcohol and Culture: Comparative Perspectives from Europe and America. New York: New York Academy of Sciences.

Miller, W., and Hester, R. (1989). Treating Alcohol Problems: Toward an Informed Eclecticism. In R. Hester and W. Miller (eds.), *Handbook of Alcoholism Treatment Approaches.* New York: Pergamon.

Metzger, L. (1988). *From Denial to Recovery.* San Francisco, CA: Jossey-Bass.

Moynihan, D. P. (1993). Iatrogenic Government: Social Policy and Drug Research. *American Scholar,* Summer, 351–363.

Orford, J. (1985). *Excessive Appetites: A Psychological View of Addictions.* Chichester, England: Wiley.

Plant, M., Ritson, B., and Robertson, R. (1992). *Alcohol and Drugs: The Scottish Experience.* Edinburgh, Scotland: Edinburgh University Press.

Robertson, N. (1988). *Getting Better: Inside Alcoholics Anonymous.* New York: Fawcett Crest.

Rorabaugh, W. J. (1979). *The Alcoholic Republic: An American Tradition.* New York: Oxford University Press.

Royce, J. (1989). *Alcohol Problems and Alcoholism.* New York: Free Press.

Rush, B. (1790). *An Inquiry into the Effects of Spiritous Liquors on the Human Body.* Boston, MA.

Rusk, J. (1902). *The Authentic Life of T. DeWitt Talmage.* New York: L. G. Stahl.

Sandmaier, M. (1992). *The Invisible Alcoholics: Women and Alcohol,* 2nd ed. Blue Ridge Summit, PA: TAB Books.

Smart, R., and Mora, M. E. (1986). Alcohol Control Policies in Latin America and Other Countries. In T. Barbor, (ed.), *Alcohol and Culture: Comparative Perspectives from Europe and America,* pp. 211–218. New York: New York Academy of Sciences.

Thorton, M. (1992). Prohibition's Failure: Lessons for Today. *USA Today* magazine, March, 70–73.

Vaillant, G. (1986). Cultural Factors in the Etiology of Alcoholism: A Prospective Study. In T. Barbor (ed.), *Alcohol and Culture: Comparative Perspectives from Europe and America,* pp. 142–148. New York: New York Academy of Sciences.

Wilson, B. (1939). *Alcoholics Anonymous.* New York: A. A. World Services.

CHAPTER 3: THE CONTEMPORARY CONTEXT IN TREATMENT OF ALCOHOLISM

Akers, R. (1992). *Drugs, Alcohol, and Society.* Belmont, CA: Wadsworth.

American Medical Association. (1967). *Manual on Alcoholism.* Chicago, IL: American Medical Association.

American Psychiatric Association. (1985). *Diagnostic and Statistical Manual of Mental Disorders,* 4th ed. Washington DC: American Psychiatric Association.

Anderson, D. (1981). *Perspectives on Treatment: The Minnesota Experience.* Center City, MN: Hazelden Educational Service.

Barker, R. (1987). *The Social Work Dictionary.* Silver Spring, MD: National Association of Social Workers.

Blume, S. (1990). Alcohol and Drug Problems in Women. In H. Milkman and L. Sederer (eds.), *Treatment Choices for Alcoholism and Substance Abuse,* pp. 183–98. Lexington, MA: Lexington Books.

Bromet, E., Moos, R., Wuthmann, C., and Bliss, F. (1977). Treatment Experiences of Alcoholic Patients. *International Journal of Addictions, 12:* 953–958.

Brown, S. (1985). *Treating the Alcoholic: A Developmental Model Of Recovery.* New York: Wiley.

Brun-Gulbrandsen, S. (1990). Drinking Habits in Norway. In O. J. Skog and R. Waahlberg (eds.), *National Directorate for the Prevention of Alcohol and Drug Problems* pp. 13–27. Oslo: Universitets Forlaget.

Chernus, L. (1985). Clinical Issues in Alcoholism Treatment. *Social Casework, 66:* 67–75.

Cloninger, C. R., Sigvardsson, S., Gilligan, S., van Knorring, A. L., Reich, T., and Bohman, M. (1989). Genetic Heterogeneity and the Classification of Alcoholism. *Advances in Alcohol and Substance Abuse, 7:* 3–16.

Conrad, P., and Kern, R. (eds.). (1981). *The Sociology of Health and Illness.* New York: St. Martin.

Crowley, T. J., Chesluk, D., Dilts, S., and Hart, R., (1974). Drug and Alcohol Abuse among Psychiatric Admissions. *Archives of General Psychiatry, 30:* 183–198.

Cunynghame, A. (1983). Some Issues in Successful Alcoholism Treatment. In D. Cook, C. Fewell, and J. Riolo (eds.), *Social Treatment of Alcohol Problems,* pp. 49–60. Brunswick, NJ: Journal of Studies on Alcohol, Inc.

Duckert, F. (1985). Behandling av Alkoholproblemer. In O. Arner, R. Havge, and O. J. Skog (eds.), *Alkohol: Norge,* pp. 233–250. Oslo: Universitets Forlaget.

Duckert, F., and Aastand, O. (1988). Alcohol Related Problems. In O. J. Skog and R. Waahlberg (eds.). *Alcohol and Drugs: The New Experience;* pp. 114–225. Oslo: Enger Boktrydden, A/S.

Ellis, A., McInerney, J., DiGiuseppe, R., and Yeager, R. (1988). *Rational-Emotive Therapy with Alcoholics and Substance Abusers.* New York: Pergamon.

Fingarette, H. (1988). *Heavy Drinking: The Myth of Alcoholism as a Disease.* Berkeley: University of California Press.

Forrest, G. (1984). *Intensive Psychotherapy of Alcoholism.* Springfield, IL: Charles C. Thomas.

Forrest, G. (1985). Psychodynamically Oriented Treatment of Alcoholism and Substance Abuse. In T. Bratter and G. Forrest (eds.), *Alcoholism and Substance Abuse.* New York: Free Press.

Freeman, E. (ed.). (1992). Glossary. *The Addiction Process: Effective Social Work Approaches.* New York: Longman.

Gibelman, M., and Schervish, P. (1993). *Who We Are: The Social Work Labor Force.* Washington, DC: NASW.

Googins, B. (1984). Avoidance of the Alcoholic Client. *Social Work, 29:* 161–166.

Gordis, E. (1988). Milestones. *Alcohol World: Health and Research, 12:* 236–239.

Gorenstein, E. E. (1987). Cognitive-Perceptual Deficit in an Alcoholism Spectrum Disorder. *Journal of Studies on Alcohol, 48:* 310–318.

Hartman, A., and Laird, J. (1983). *Family-Centered Social Work Practice.* New York: Free Press.

Hazelden. (1985). You Don't Have to Tear 'Em Down to Build 'Em Up. *Hazelden Professional Update,* 4(2):2.

Hester, R., and Miller, M. (1989). Self Control Training. In R. Hester and W. Miller (eds.), *Handbook of Alcoholism Treatment Approaches,* pp. 141–152. New York: Pergamon.

Hoffman, N., and Harrison, P. (1986). CATOR 1986 Report: Findings Two Years after Treatment. St. Paul, MN: Ramsey Clinic.

Holloway, M. (1991). Treatment for Addiction. *Scientific American,* March, pp. 95–103.

Howe, G. (1981). The Ecological Approach to Permanency Planning: An Interactionist Perspective. *Child Welfare, 42:* 291–301.

Jellinek, E. M. (1952). Phases of Alcohol Addiction. *Quarterly Journal of Studies on Alcohol, 13:* 673–684.

Jellinek, E. M. (1960). *The Disease Concept of Alcoholism.* New Haven, CT: Yale Center for Alcohol Studies.

Kalish, C. B. (1983). Prisoners and Alcohol. *Bureau of Justice Statistics Bulletin,* Jan.

Kasl, C. D. (1990). The Twelve Step Controversy. *MS,* Nov./Dec., 30–31.

Klingemann, H., Takala, J. P., and Hunt, G. (1993). The Development of Alcohol Treatment Systems. *Alcohol Health and Research World,* 17: 221–227.

Krogh, P. (1988). Alcoholics Anonymous in Norway, Proceedings of the 35th International Congress on Alcoholism and Drug Dependency, July 31, Oslo, Norway.

Laberg, J. C. (1988). Concepts of Alcoholism. Proceedings of the 35th International Congress on Alcoholism and Drug Dependency, July 31, Oslo, Norway.

Lee, J. (1985). One Less for the Road? *Time,* Jan. 25, 76–78.

Lord, L. (1987). Coming to Grips with Alcoholism. *U.S. News and World Report,* Oct. 3, 56–62.

Makela, K. (1993). International Comparisons of Alcoholics Anonymous. *Alcohol Health and Research World,* 17: 228–234.

Marlatt, G. A., and Gordon, J. R. (1985). In J. R. Gordon (ed.), *Relapse Prevention: Maintenance Strategies in the Treatment of Addictive Behaviors.* New York: Guilford.

Miller, W. R. (1990). Alcoholism Alternatives: What Works? In H. Milkman and L. Sederer (eds.), *Treatment Choices for Alcoholism and Substance Abuse,* pp. 253–264. Lexington, MA.: Lexington Books.

Miller, W. R., and Hester, R. K. (1989). Treating Alcohol Problems: Toward an Informed Eclecticism. In R. Hester and W. Miller (eds.), *Handbook of Alcoholism Treatment Approaches,* pp. 3–13. New York: Pergamon.

Moncher, M., Schinke, S., and Holden, G. (1992). Tobacco Addiction: Correlates, Prevention and Treatment. In E. Freeman (ed.), *The Addiction Process.* New York: Longman.

Mother Jones. (1991). Sobering Up. *Mother Jones,* 16 (6):52–54.

National Association of Social Workers. (1987). *NASW News,* 6 (Jan.): 7.

National Institute of Alcohol Abuse and Alcoholism (NIAAA). (1988). *Sixth Special Report to the U.S. Congress on Alcohol and Health.* Rockville, MD: NIAAA.

Nordstrom, G., and Berglund, M. (1987). A Prospective Study of Successful Long-term Adjustment in Alcohol Dependence. *Journal of Studies on Alcohol,* 48: 95–103.

Oei, T. P., Lim, B., and Young, R. (1991). Cognitive processes and Cognitive Behavior Therapy in the Treatment of Problem Drinking. *Journal of Addictive Diseases,* 10(3): 63–80.

Oxford Universal Dictionary. (1955). London: Oxford University Press.

Parihar, B. (1982). Issues and Answers in Treating Alcoholism. *Social Casework,* 63: 333–339.

Pattison, E. M. (1985). The Selection of Treatment Modalities. In J. Mendelson and N. Mello (Eds.), *The Diagnosis and Treatment of Alcoholism,* pp. 189–294. New York: McGraw-Hill.

Peele, S. (1988). A Moral Vision of Addiction. In S. Peele (ed.), *Visions of Addiction,* pp. 201–233. Lexington, MA: Lexington Books.

Peele, S. (1989). *Diseasing of America: Addiction Treatment Out of Control.* Lexington, Md: Lexington Books.

Peele, S., and Brodsky, A. (1991). *The Truth about Addiction and Recovery.* New York: Simon and Schuster.

Peyton, S., Chaddick, J., and Gorsvek, R. (1980). Willingness to Treat Alcoholics: A Study of Graduate Social Work Students. *Journal of Studies on Alcohol,* 41(9): 935–938.

Plaut, T. (1977). Addictions: Alcohol. *Encyclopedia of Social Work,* vol. 1, 22–24. Washington, DC: NASW.

Powell, D., and Fuller, R. (1991). EAPs in the Soviet Union. *EAP Digest,* March/April, 27–29.

Random House Dictionary. (1980). New York: Random House.

Royce, J. (1989). *Alcohol, Problems and Alcoholism,* 2d ed. New York: Free Press.

Scherman, P. (1990). Minnesota Rules. *Star Tribune,* Dec. 9, 10E.

Selbyg, A. (1987). *Norway.* Oslo: Norwegian University Press.

Shaffer, H., and Gambino, B. (1984). Epilogue. In H. Milkman and L. Sederer (eds.), *Treatment Choices for Alcoholism and Substance Abuse.* Lexington, MA: Lexington.

Sherrid, P. (1982). Selling Sobriety. *Forbes,* Nov. 12, 59–66.

Siddons, R. (1985). Treatment Profiles of Concerned Others: Enhancing Family Therapeutic Effectiveness. *Focus on Family, 8:* 10.

Stenius, K. (1991). The Most Successful Treatment Model in the World: Introduction of the Minnesota Model in Nordic Countries. *Contemporary Drug Problems, 18* (Spring): 151–179.

Vaillant, G. E. (1983). *The Natural History of Alcoholism: Causes, Patterns and Paths to Recovery.* Cambridge, MA: Harvard University Press.

van Wormer, K. (1987). Training Social Work Students for Practice with Substance Abusers: An Ecological Approach. *Journal of Social Work Education, 23*(2): 47–56.

CHAPTER 4: THE BIOLOGY OF ALCOHOLISM AND ALCOHOL ABUSE

American Psychiatric Association. (1994). *Diagnostic and Statistical Manual of Mental Disorders,* 4th ed. Washington, DC: American Psychiatric Association.

Begleiter, M., and Porjesz, B. (1988). Potential Biological Markers in Individuals at High Risk for Developing Alcoholism. *Alcoholism, 12:* 488–493.

Biglan, A., Metzler, C. W., Wirt., A., Ary, D., Noell, J., Ochs, L., French, C., and Hood, D. (1990). Social and Behavioral Factors Associated with High-Risk Sexual Behavior among Adolescents. *Journal of Behavioral Medicine, 13* (3): 245–261.

Bower, B. (1994). Alcoholism Exposes Its "Insensitive" Side. *Science News, 145:* 118.

Cloninger, C. R., Sigvardsson, S., Gilligan, S., van Knorring, A. L., Reich, T., and Bohman, M. (1989). Genetic Heterogeneity and the Classification of Alcoholism. *Advances in Alcohol and Substance Abuse, 7:* 3–16.

Desmond, E. (1987). Out in the Open: Changing Attitudes and New Research Give Fresh Hope to Alcoholics. *Time,* Nov. 30, 42–49.

Economist. (1991). Science and Technology: Sins of the Fathers. *Economist,* Feb. 23, 87.

Encyclopaedia Britannica. (1993). Alcohol and Drug Consumption. Chicago: Encyclopaedia Britannica, Inc.

Fitzgerald, E. (1990). *The Place in Minnesota: Changing Lives, Saving Lives.* New York: Viking.

Gallant, D. M. (1987). *Alcoholism: A Guide to Diagnosis, Intervention and Treatment.* New York: Norton.

Goodwin, D. (1976). *Is Alcoholism Hereditary?* New York: Oxford University Press.

Grossman, C., and Wilson, E. (1992). The Immune System. *Alcohol Health and Research World, 16*(1): 5–14.

Harvard Medical School. (1993). Update on Cocaine. Part II. *Harvard Mental Health Letter, 10*(3): 1–8.

Jacobson, J. (1992). Alcoholism and Tuberculosis. *Alcohol Health and Research World, 16*(1): 39–47.

Kinney, J., and Leaton, G. (1991). *Loosening the Grip: A Handbook of Alcohol Information.* St. Louis, MO: Mosby.

Kotulak, R. (1993). New Drugs Break Spell of Violence. *Chicago Tribune,* Dec. 15.

Kramer, P. (1993). The Transformation of Personality. *Psychology Today,* 26(4): 42–47, 70–76.

Kruger. T., and Jerrells, T. (1992). Potential Role of Alcohol in Human Immunodeficiency Virus Infection. *Alcohol Health and Research World* 16(1): 57–63.

Levin, J. D. (1990). *Alcoholism: A Bio-Psycho-Social Approach.* New York: Hemisphere.

Martin, Fr.J. (1972). *Chalk Talk on Alcohol,* Revised. Video. Aberdeen, MD: Kelly Productions.

Mendenhall, C. (1992). Immunity, Malnutrition and Alcohol. *Alcohol Health and Research World,* 16(1): 23–28.

National Institute on Alcohol Abuse and Alcoholism. (1993). *Alcohol Alert,* 20 (April): 1–3.

Rensberger, B. (1992). Primates, Politics, and the Sudden Debate over Origins of Human Violence. *Washington Post,* March 1, B1.

Royce, J. (1989). *Alcohol Problems and Alcoholism.* New York: Free Press.

Sachs, O. (1985). *The Man Who Mistook His Wife For a Hat and Other Clinical Tales.* New York: Harper and Row.

Schlaadt, R. (1992). *Alcohol Use and Abuse.* Guilford, CT: Dushkin.

Science News. (1991). Cocaine May Piggyback on Sperm into Egg. *Science News, 140:* 246.

Sexias, F. (1975). Alcohol and Its Drug Interactions. *Annals of Internal Medicine, 83:* 86–92.

Steinmetz, G. (1992). Fetal Alcohol Syndrome. *National Geographic, 181*(2): 36–39.

Substance Abuse Report. (1987). Alcoholism a Product of Genetics, the Environment, and Drinking. *Substance Abuse Report, 18*(22): 1–4.

Substance Abuse Report. (1988). Researchers Close In on the Biological Causes of Alcoholism. *Substance Abuse Report, 19*(1): 1–4.

Sweeney, D. (1990). Alcoholic Blackouts: Legal Implications. *Journal of Substance Abuse Treatment, 7:* 155–159.

Twain, M. (1876). *Adventures of Tom Sawyer.* New York: Harper.

U.S. Dept. of Health and Human Services. (1993). *Eighth Special Report to the U.S. Congress on Alcohol and Health.* Washington, D.C.: U.S. Government Printing Office.

Varner, S. (1992). Preventing Relapse from Going Up in Smoke. *Professional Counselor;* Oct., 31–32.

CHAPTER 5: ALCOHOLISM AS A WAY OF THINKING

American Psychiatric Association. (1991). *Diagnostic and Statistical Manual of Mental Disorders,* 4th ed. Washington, DC: American Psychiatric Association.

Babor, T. (1992). Cross-Cultural Research on Alcohol: A Quoi Bon? In J. Helzer and G. Canino (eds), *Alcoholism in North America, Europe and Asia,* pp. 33–52. New York: Oxford University Press.

Beck. A. T., Rush, J. A., Shaw, B. F., and Emory, G. (1979). *Cognitive Theory of Depression.* New York: Guilford Press.

Begleiter, H., Porjesj, B., and Kissin, B. (1984). Event-Related Brain Potentials in Boys at Risk for Alcoholism. *Science, 225:* 1493–1496.

Bergreen, L. (1984). *James Agee: A Life.* New York: Viking/Penguin.

Brown, S. (1985). *Treating the Alcoholic: A Developmental Model of Recovery.* New York: Wiley.

Burns, D. D. (1980). The Perfectionist's Script for Self-Defeat. *Psychology Today,* Nov., 34–52.

Chabon, B., and Robins, C. (1986). Cognitive Distortions among Depressed and Suicidal Drug Abusers. *International Journal of the Addictions, 2:* 1313–1329.

Chaney, E. (1989). Social Skills Training. In R. Hester and W. Miller (eds.), *Handbook of Alcoholism Treatment Approaches*, pp. 206–220. New York: Pergamon.

Chiauzzi, E. (1989). Breaking the Patterns That Lead to Relapse. *Psychology Today, 23:* 18–19.

Deykin, E. Y., Levy, J. C., and Wells, V. (1987). Adolescent Depression, Alcohol and Drug Abuse. *American Journal of Public Health, 77(2):* 178–182.

Drimmer, F. (1973). *Very Special People.* New York: Amjon.

Economist. (1993). High and Hooked. *Economist,* May 15, 105–107.

Ellis, A., McInerney, J., DiGiuseppe, R., and Yeager, R. (1989). *Rational-Emotive Therapy with Alcoholics and Substance Abusers.* New York: Pergamon Press.

Fromm, E. (1956). *The Art of Loving.* New York: Harper and Row.

Glantz, M. (1987). Day Hospital Treatment of Alcoholics. In A. Freeman and V. Greenwood (eds.), *Cognitive Therapy: Applications in Psychiatric and Medical Settings;* pp. 51–68. New York: Human Services Press.

Goodwin, D. W. (1988). *Alcohol and the Writer.* New York: Penguin.

Goodwin, D. (1976). *Is Alcoholism Hereditary?* New York: Oxford University Press.

Gordis, E. (1988). Milestones. *Alcohol World: Health and Research, 12:* 236–239.

Gordis, E. (1989). Relapse and Craving. *Alcohol Alert, 6:* 1–4.

Gorenstein, E. E. (1987). Cognitive-Perceptual Deficit in an Alcoholism Spectrum Disorder. *Journal of Studies on Alcohol, 48(4):* 310–318.

Hartman, A., and Laird, J. (1983). *Family Centered Social Work Practice.* New York: Free Press.

Hatsukami, D., and Pickens, R. (1980). *Depression and Alcoholism.* Center City, MN: Hazelden Foundation.

Helzer, J., and Canino, G. (1992). Comparative Analysis of Alcoholism in Ten Cultural Regions. In J. Helzer and G. Canino (eds.), *Alcoholism in North America, Europe and Asia,* pp. 289–296. New York: Oxford University Press.

Hoffman, H., Rodney, G. L., and Kammeier, M. L. (1974). *Quarterly Journal of Studies on Alcohol, 35:* 490–498.

Institute of Medicine. (1990). *A Broadening of the Base of Treatment for Alcohol Problems.* Washington, DC: National Academic Press.

Jackson, J. (1954). The Adjustment of the Family to the Crisis of Alcoholism. *Quarterly Journal of Substance Abuse, 15:* 562–586.

Jellinek, E. M. (1960). *The Disease Concept of Alcoholism.* New Haven, CT: Yale Center for Alcohol Studies.

Kinney, J. (1983). Relapsed Alcoholics Who Are Alcoholism Counselors. *Journal of Studies on Alcohol, 44(4):* 744–748.

Kinney, J., and Leaton, G. (1991). *Loosening the Grip.* St. Louis, MO: Times Mirror/ Mosby.

Kramer, P. (1993). The Transformation of Personality. *Psychology Today, 26:* 42–47, 70–76.

Leonard, L. (1990). *Witness to the Fire: Creativity and the Veil of Addiction.* Boston, MA: Shambhala.

Ludwig, A. (1988). *Understanding the Alcoholic's Mind.* Oxford: Oxford University Press.

Lyon, J. (1992). Alcoholic Beverages and Alcoholism. In D. Ludlow (ed.), *Encyclopedia of Mormonism,* pp. 30–31. New York: Macmillan.

Mannuzza, S., Klein, R., Bessler, A., Malloy, P., and La Padula, M. (1993). Adult Outcome of Hyperactive Boys. *Archives of General Psychiatry, 50:* 565–576.

McCourt, W., and Glantz, M. (1980). Cognitive Behavior Therapy in Groups for Alcoholics. *Journal of Studies on Alcohol, 48(6):* 523–527.

Metzger, L. (1988). *From Denial to Recovery: Counseling Problem Drinkers, Alcoholics, and their Families.* San Francisco, CA: Jossey-Bass.

Milam, J. (1974). *The Emergent Comprehensive Concept of Alcoholism.* Kirkland, WA: Alcenas.

Miller, W. R. (1990). Alcoholism Alternatives: What Works? In H. Milkman and L. Sederer (eds.), *Treatment Choices for Alcoholism and Substance Abuse,* pp. 253–264. Lexington, MA: Lexington Books.

Murphy, G. (1992). *Suicide in Alcoholism.* New York: Oxford University Press.

Napier, R., and Gershenfield, M. (1981). *Groups: Theory and Experiences.* Boston, MA: Houghton Mifflin.

O'Connor, S., Hesselbrock, V., and Bauer, L. (1990). The Nervous System and the Predisposition to Alcoholism. *Alcohol Health and Research World, 12*(2): 90–97.

Orford, J. (1985). *Excessive Appetites: A Psychological View of Addictions.* Chichester, England: Wiley.

Park, J. Y., Huang, Y. H., Nagoshi, C. T., Yen, S., Johnson, R., Ching, C. A., and Bowman, K. (1984). The Flushing Response to Alcohol Use among Koreans and Taiwanese. *Journal of Studies on Alcohol, 45:* 381–485.

Peele, S. (1975). *Love and Addiction.* New York: Signet.

Peele, S. (1989). *Diseasing of America: Addiction Treatment Out of Control.* Lexington, MA: D. C. Heath.

Peele, S. and Brodsky, A. (1991). *The Truth about Addiction and Recovery.* New York: Simon and Schuster.

Psychology Today. (1992). Serotonin: Neurotransmitter of the '90s. *Psychology Today, 25:* 16.

Royce, J. E. (1989). *Alcohol Problems and Alcoholism,* 2nd ed. New York: Free Press.

Snyder, V. (1975). Cognitive Approaches in Treatment of Alcoholism. *Social Casework 56*(10): 380–485.

Sparks, R., et al. (1900). *Broadening the Base of Treatment: Alcohol Problems.* Washington, DC: National Academy Press.

Stevenson, R. L. (1886/1964). *The Strange Case of Dr. Jekyll and Mr. Hyde.* New York: Airmont.

Stockwell, T., and Town, C. (1989). Anxiety and Stress Management. In R. Hester and W. Miller (eds.), *Handbook of Alcoholism Treatment Approaches,* pp. 222–230. New York: Pergamon.

Straus, R., and Bacon, S. (1962). *The Problems of Drinking Patterns.* New York: Wiley.

Substance Abuse Report. (1987). Alcoholism: A Product of Genetics, the Environment, and Drinking. *Substance Abuse Report, 18*(22): 1–2.

Valle, S. (1979). *Alcoholism Counseling.* Springfield, IL: Charles C. Thomas.

van Wormer, K. (1988). All-Or-Nothing Thinking and Alcoholism: A Cognitive Approach. *Federal Probation, 52*(2): 28–33.

von Knorring, L., von Knorring, A. L., Smigan, L. M., Lindberg, V., and Edholm, M. (1987). Personality Traits in Subtypes of Alcoholics. *Journal of Studies on Alcohol, 41*(3): 338–346.

Zastrow, C. and Kirst-Ashman, K. (1993). *Understanding Human Behavior and the Social Environment* 3rd ed. Chicago: Nelson-Hall.

CHAPTER 6: LOSS, GRIEF, AND SPIRITUAL HEALING

Allport, G. (1954). *The Nature of Prejudice.* Reading, MA: Addison-Wesley.

Carroll, M. (1987). Alcoholism as an Attachment and a Gift on a Spiritual Journey. *Journal of Consciousness and Change, 10* (2): 45–48.

Carroll, M. (1993). Spiritual Growth of Recovering Alcoholic Adult Children of Alcoholics. Ph.D. diss., University of Maryland, Baltimore.

Cloninger, C., Sigvardsson, S., and Bohman, M. (1988). Childhood Personality Predicts Abuse in Young Adults. *Alcoholism: Clinical and Experimental Research, 12:* 494–505.

Cowley, A. D. (1993). Transpersonal Social Work: A Theory for the 1990s. *Social Work, 38:* 527–534.

Davis, L. (1990). *The Courage to Heal Workbook.* New York: Harper and Row.

Freud, S. (1922/1955). Certain Neurotic Mechanisms in Jealousy, Paranoia and Homosexuality. In J. Strachey (ed.), *The Complete Psychological Works of Sigmund Freud,* standard ed., vol. 18. London: Hogarth.

Germain, C. (1982). Teaching Primary Prevention in Social Work: An Ecological Perspective. *Journal of Education for Social Work,18*(1):20-28.

Goldberg, M. (1985). Loss and Grief: Major Dynamics in the Treatment of Alcoholism. *Alcoholism Treatment Quarterly, 2*(1): 37–45.

Gorski, T., and Miller, M. (1983). Relapse: The Family's Involvement. *Focus on Family, 6*(5): 17–18.

Hughes, L. (1985). *The Langston Hughes Reader.* New York: Braziller.

Jellinek, E. M. (1960). *The Disease Concept of Alcoholism.* New Haven, CT: United Printed Services.

Kübler-Ross, E. (1969). *On Death and Dying.* New York: Macmillan.

Lifton, R. (1967). *Death in Life: Survivors of Hiroshima.* New York: Simon and Schuster.

Lindemann, E. (1944). Symptomatology and Management of Acute Grief. *American Journal of Psychiatry, 101:* 141–148.

Mantell, M. (1983). Student and Employee Assistance Programs: A Model for Secondary Prevention. *Labor-Management Alcoholism Journal, 12:* 113–124.

Marano, E. (1993). Inside the Heart of Marital Violence. *Psychology Today, 26*(6); 48–53ff.

Miles, M., and Demi, A. (1984). Toward the Development of a Theory of Bereavement Guilt: Sources of Guilt in Bereaved Parents. *Omega, 14*(4): 299–314.

Palmer, J., Vacc, N., and Epstein, J. (1988). Adult Inpatient Alcoholics: Physical Exercise as a Treatment Intervention. *Journal of Studies on Alcohol, 49:* 418–421.

Royce, I. (1989). *Alcohol Problems and Alcoholism.* New York: Free Press.

Sheafor, B., Horejsi, C., and Horejsi, G. (1991). *Techniques and Guidelines for Social Work Practice,* 2d ed. Boston, MA: Allyn and Bacon.

Tavris, C. (1982). Anger Defused. *Psychology Today,* Nov., 25-35.

van Wormer, K. (1985). Guilt Feelings in the Spouse of the Terminally Ill. *Home Healthcare Nurse, 3*(5): 21–25.

CHAPTER 7: SPECIAL GROUPS AND SUBSTANCE ABUSE

American Psychiatric Association. (1994). *Diagnostic and Statistical Manual of Mental Disorders,* 4th ed. Washington, DC: American Psychiatric Association.

American School Health Association, Association for the Advancement of Health Education, and Society for Public Health Education. (1989). *The National Adolescent Student Health Survey: A Report on the Health of America's Youth.* Oakland, CA: Third Party Pub. Co.

Anderson, R., and Maypole, D. (1989). Policy Making and Administration in Minority Alcoholism Programs. In T. Watts and R. Wright, Jr. (eds.), *Alcoholism in Minority Populations.* Springfield, IL: Charles C. Thomas.

Babcock, M., and Connor, B. (1981) Sexism and Treatment of the Female Alcoholic. *Social Work, 26:* 233–238.

Blackmon, B. (1985). Networking Community Services for Elderly Clients. In E. Freeman (ed.), *Social Work Practice with Clients Who Have Alcohol Problems,* pp. 189–201. Springfield, IL: Charles C. Thomas.

References

Blume, S. (1986). Women and Alcohol. *JAMA, 256:* 1467–1469.

Burman, S., and Allen-Meares, P. (1991). Criteria for Selecting Practice Theories: Working with Alcoholic Women. *Families in Society, 72:* 387–393.

Caetano, R. (1986). Patterns and Problems of Drinking among U.S. Hispanics. In *Report of the Secretary's Task Force on Black and Minority Health.* Vol. 7: *Chemical Dependency and Diabetes.* Washington, DC: U.S. Dept. of Health and Human Services.

Canino, G., Burnam, A., and Caetano, R. (1992). The Prevalence of Alcohol Abuse and/or Dependence in Two Hispanic Communities. In J. Helzer and G. Canino (eds.), *Alcoholism in North America, Europe and Asia,* pp. 131–153. New York: Oxford University Press.

Chernoff, G. (1991). Treatment Programs Target Elderly Alcoholics. *U.S. Journal, 15(5):* 15.

Clark, C. (1992). Underage Drinking. *Congressional Quarterly Researcher, 2:* 219–230.

Cloninger, C. R. (1987). Neurogenetic Adaptive Mechanisms in Alcoholism. *Science, 236:* 410–416.

Comstock, G. D. (1991). *Violence against Lesbians and Gay Men.* New York: Columbia University Press.

Davis, L. (1990). *The Courage to Heal Workbook.* New York: Harper and Row.

DuRant, R. H., Rickert V., Ashworth, C. S., et al. (1993). Use of Multiple Drugs among Adolescents Who Use Anabolic Steroids. *New England Journal of Medicine, 328:* 922–926.

Economist. (1991). Sins of the Fathers. *Economist,* Feb. 23, 87.

Ettorre, E. (1992). *Women and Substance Use.* New Brunswick, NJ: Rutgers University Press.

Faderman, L. (1991). *Odd Girls and Twilight Lovers.* New York: Columbia University Press.

Fellios, P. (1989). Alcoholism in Women: Causes, Treatment and Prevention: In G. Lawson and A. Lawson, (eds.), *Alcoholism and Substance Abuse in Special Populations,* pp. 11–34. Rockville, MD: Aspen.

Foxcraft, D., and Lowe, G. (1991). Adolescent Drinking Behavior and Family Socialization Facts. *Journal of Adolescence, 14:* 255–273.

Gilbert, M. J. (1985). Mexican Americans in California. In L. Bennett and G. Ames (eds.), *The American Experience with Alcohol: Contrasting Cultural Perspectives,* pp. 255–277. New York: Plenum.

Gunther, J., Jolly, E., and Wedel, K. (1985). Alcoholism and the Indian People: Problem and Promise. In E. Freeman (ed.), *Social Work Practice with Clients Who Have Alcohol Problems.* Springfield, IL: Charles C. Thomas.

Hall, N. L. (1990). *A True Story of a Drunken Mother.* Boston, MA: South End Press.

Harper, F. D. (1989). Alcoholism and Blacks: An Overview. In T. Watts and R. Wright, Jr. (eds.), *Alcoholism in Minority Populations.* Springfield, IL: Charles C. Thomas.

Hartman, A. (1993). Out of the Closet: Revolution and Backlash. *Social Work, 38:* 245–246, 360.

Herd, D. (1985). Ambiguity in Black Drinking Norms. In L. Bennett and G. Ames (eds.). *The American Experience with Alcohol: Contrasting Cultural Perspectives,* pp. 149–167. New York: Plenum.

Hill, T. (1990). Peyotism and the Control of Heavy Drinking: The Nebraska Winnebago in the Early 1900s. *Human Organization, 49:* 255–265.

Hudson, J., Weiss, R., Pope, H., McElroy, S., and Mirin, S. (1992). Eating Disorders in Hospitalized Substance Abusers. *American Journal of Drug Alcohol Abuse, 18:* 75–85.

Johnson, S. (1989). *Wildfire: Igniting the She-Volution.* Albuquerque, NM: Wildfire Books.

Kasl, C. D. (1990). The Twelve-Step Controversey. *MS,* Nov./Dec., 30–31.

Kendler, K., Heath, A., Neale, M., Kessler, R., and Eaves, J. (1992). A Population-Based Twin Study of Alcoholism in Women. *JAMA, 268:* 1877–1881.

Kus, R. (1988). Alcoholism and Non-Acceptance of Gay Self. The Critical Link. *Journal of Homosexuality, 15:* 25–41.

Langton, P. (1991). *Drug Use and the Alcohol Dilemma.* Boston, MA: Allyn & Bacon.

Lawson, A. (1989). Substance Abuse Problems of the Elderly: Consideration for Treatment and Prevention. In G. Lawson and A. Lawson (eds.), *Alcoholism and Substance Abuse in Special Populations,* pp. 11–34. Rockville, MD: Aspen.

Martin, P., and Hummer, R. (1989). Fraternities and Rape on Campus. *Gender and Society, 3:* 457–473.

May, P. (1989). Alcohol Abuse and Alcoholism among American Indians: An Overview. In T. Watts and R. Wright, Jr. (eds.), *Alcoholism in Minority Populations,* pp. 95–119. Springfield, IL: Charles C. Thomas.

May, P. (1986). Alcohol and Drug Misuse Prevention Programs for American Indians: Needs and Opportunities. *Journal of Studies on Alcohol, 47:* 187–195.

Maypole, D., and Anderson, R. (1983). Minority Alcoholism Programs: Issues in Service Delivery Models. *International Journal of the Addictions, 18:* 987–1001.

McRoy, R., and Shorkey, C. (1985). Alcohol Use and Abuse among Blacks. In E. Freeman (ed.), *Social Work Practice with Clients Who Have Alcohol Problems.* Springfield, IL: Charles C. Thomas.

Miller, B., Downs, W., and Gondoli, D. (1989). Spousal Violence among Alcoholic Women as Compared to a Random Household Sample of Women. *Journal of Studies on Alcohol, 50:* 533–540.

Miller, B., Downs, W., Gondoli, D., and Keil, A. (1987). The Role of Childhood Sexual Abuse in the Development of Alcoholism in Women. *Violence and Victims, 2:* 157–172.

Miller, B., Downs, W., and Testa, M. (1993). Interrelationships between Victimization Experience and Women's Alcohol Use. *Journal of Studies on Alcohol,* Supplement no. 11, 115–123.

Mitchell, J., Pyle, R., Eckart, E., and Hartsukami, D. (1990). The Influences of Prior Alcohol and Drug Abuse Problems in Bulimia Nervosa Treatment Outcome. *Addictive Behaviors, 15:* 169–173.

NIAAA, (1990). Alcohol and Women. *Alcohol Alert, 10* (Oct.): 1–4.

Nichols, M. (1985). Theoretical Concerns in the Clinical Treatment of Substance-Abusing Women: A Feminist Analysis. *Alcoholism Treatment Quarterly, 2*(1): 79–90.

O'Connell, D. (1991). Treating the High Risk Adolescent: A Survey of Effective Programs and Interventions. *Journal of Adolescent Chemical Dependency, 1:* 55–75.

Our Voice. (1991). Patient Outcome Data Report. *Our Voice.* (June), 1, 5–6. (Pride Institute Newsletter)

Pihl, R., and Peterson, J. (1991). Attention-Deficit Hyperactivity Disorder, Childhood Conduct Disorder, and Alcoholism. *Alcohol World: Health and Research, 15:* 25–31.

Prevention Report. (1993). U.S. Public Health Service, Feb./March.

Rather, E. (1988). A Model for the Treatment of Lesbian and Gay Alcohol Abusers. *Alcoholism Treatment Quarterly, 5:* 25–46.

Rauch, K. (1992). How Indian Youths Defeat Addictions. *Washington Post,* March 10, Health Section, 10–11.

Rebach, J. (1992). Alcohol and Drug Use among American Minorities. *Drugs and Society, 6:* 23–58.

Rohsenow, D., Corbett, R., and Devine, D. (1988). Molested as Children: A Hidden Contribution to Substance Abuse. *Journal of Substance Abuse Treatments, 5:* 13–18.

Royce, J. (1989). *Alcohol Problems and Alcoholism.* New York: Free Press.

Ryan, M. (1993). Then You Need a Good Sister. *Parade Magazine.* Feb. 21, 20.

Saghir, M. T., and Robins, E. (1973). *Male and Female Homosexuality.* Baltimore, MD: Williams and Wilkins.

Sandmaier, M. (1992). *The Invisible Alcoholics: Women and Alcohol.* Blue Ridge Summit, PA: TAB Books.

Schonfeld, L. (1993). Research Findings on a Hidden Population. *The Counselor,* Jan., 20–26.

Schonfeld, L., and Dupree, L. (1991). Antecedents of Drinking for Early- and Late-Onset Elderly Alcohol Abusers. *Journal of Studies on Alcohol, 52:* 587–592.

Scott, B., Denniston, R., and Magruder, K. (1992). Alcohol Advertising in the African-American Community. *Journal of Drug Issues, 22:* 455–469.

Segal, B. (1986). The Soviet Heavy-Drinking Culture and the American Heavy-Drinking Subculture. In T. Babor (ed.), *Alcohol and the Culture: Comparative Perspective from Europe and America,* pp. 149–160. New York: New York Academy of Science.

Smart, R., and Mora, M. E. (1986). Alcohol-Control Policies in Latin America and Other Countries. In T. Babor, (ed.) *Alcohol and Culture: Comparative Perspective from Europe and America,* pp. 211–218. New York: New York Academy of Sciences.

Trotter, R. (1985). Mexican-American Experience with Alcohol in South Texas. In L. Bennett and G. Ames, *The American Experience with Alcohol: Contrasting Cultural Perspectives,* pp. 279–296. New York: Plenum.

U.S. Congress. House of Representatives, Select Committee on Aging. (1992). *Alcohol Use and Misuse among the Elderly.* Committee Publication no. 102–852. Washington, DC: U.S. Government Printing Office.

Van Wormer, K. (1989a). Incest av Kvinnelige Alkoholikere. *Socionomen, 16:* 14–15.

Van Wormer, K. (1989b). The Male-Specific Group in Alcoholism Treatment. *Small Group Behavior, 20:* 228–242.

Wallen, J. (1992). A Comparison of Male and Female Clients in Substance Abuse Treatment. *Journal of Substance Abuse Treatment, 9:* 243–248.

Weibel-Orlando, J. (1989). Treatment and Prevention of Native American Alcoholism. In T. Watts and R. Wright, Jr. (eds.), *Alcoholism in Minority Populations,* pp. 121–139. Springfield, IL: Charles C. Thomas.

Wilke, D. (1994). Women and Alcoholism: How a Male-as-Norm Bias Affects Research, Assessment and Treatment. *Health and Social Work, 19* (1): 29–34.

Windle, M. (1991). Alcohol Use and Abuse. *Alcohol World: Health and Research, 15:* 5–10.

Wolf, N. (1991). *The Beauty Myth.* New York: Wm. Morrow.

Young, T. J. (1988). Substance Abuse among Native Americans. *Clinical Psychology Review, 8:* 125–138.

CHAPTER 8: ALCOHOLISM AND THE FAMILY SYSTEM

Becvar, R., and Becvar, D. (1982). *Systems Theory and Family Therapy.* Lanham, MA: University Press of America.

Black, C. (1981). *It Will Never Happen to Me!* New York: Ballantine.

Bowen, M. (1978). *Family Therapy in Clinical Practice.* New York: Aronson.

Chase-Marshall, J. (1976). Virginia Satir: Everybody's Family Therapist. *Human Behavior,* Sept., 25–31.

Daley, D., and Raskin, M. (eds.). (1991). *Treating the Chemically Dependent and Their Families.* Newbury Park, CA: Sage.

Downs, W. (1982). Alcoholism as a Developing Family Crisis. *Family Relations, 31:* 5–12.

Dulfano, C. (1982). *Families, Alcoholism and Recovery.* Center City, MN: Hazelden.

Alcoholism Treatment

Ellis, A., McInerney, J., DiGiuseppe, R., and Yeager, R. (1988). *Rational-Emotional Therapy with Alcoholics and Substance Abusers*. New York: Pergamon.

Ellis-Ordway, N. (1992). The Impact of Family Dynamics on Anorexia: A Transactional View of Treatment. In E. Freeman (ed.), *The Addiction Process: Effective Social Work Approaches*, pp. 180–191. New York: Longman.

Fingarette, H. (1988). *Heavy Drinking: The Myth of Alcoholism as a Disease*. Berkeley: University of California Press.

Flanzer, J., and Delaney, P. (1992). Multiple Member Substance Abuse. In E. Freeman (ed.), *The Addiction Process*, pp. 54–65. New York: Longman.

Frank, P., and Golden, G. (1992). Blaming by Naming: Battered Women and the Epidemic of Codependence. *Social Work, 37:* 5–6.

Goodwin, D. (1979). The Cause of Alcoholism and Why It Runs in Families. *British Journal of Addiction, 74:* 161–164.

Hacker, C. (1990). Employee Assistance Programs as an Early Intervention for Substance Abuse. In H. Milkman and L. Sederer (eds.), *Treatment Choices for Alcoholism and Substance Abuse*, pp. 143–158. Lexington, MA: Lexington Books.

Hall, N. L. (1990). *A True Story of a Drunken Mother*. Boston, MA: South End Press.

Hanson, J. (1994). Families' Perspectives on the Early Years of Mental Illness. Unpublished manuscript, University of Northern Iowa.

Hartman, A., and Laird, J. (1983). *Family-Centered Social Work Practice*. New York: Free Press.

Jackson, J. (1954). The Adjustment of the Family to the Crisis of Alcoholism. *Quarterly Journal of Substance Abuse, 15:* 562–586.

Johnson, H. (1986). Emerging Concerns in Family Therapy. *Social Work, 31:* 299–305.

Kaufman, E. (1985). *Substance Abuse and Family Therapy*. Orlando, FL: Grune and Stratton.

Kaufman, E., and Kaufman, P. (1992). From Psychodynamic to Structural to Integrated Family Treatment of Chemical Dependency. In E. Kaufman and P. Kaufman (eds.), *Family Therapy of Drug and Alcohol Abuse*. Boston: Allyn and Bacon.

Kaufman, E. and Pattison, E. M. (1981). Differential Methods of Family Therapy in the Treatment of Alcoholism. *Journal of Studies on Alcohol, 42:* 951–971.

Kokin, M. (1990). *Women Married to Alcoholics*. New York: Signet.

Kübler-Ross, E. (1969). *On Death and Dying*. New York: Macmillan.

Metzger, L. (1988). *From Denial to Recovery: Counseling Problem Drinkers, Alcoholics, and Their Families*. San Francisco, CA: Jossey-Bass.

Minuchin, S. (1974). *Families and Family Therapy*. Cambridge, MA: Harvard University Press.

Nichols, M. (1984). *Family Therapy*. New York: Gardner Press.

Robertson, N. (1988). *Getting Better: Inside Alcoholics Anonymous*. New York: Fawcett Crest.

Royce, J. (1989). *Alcohol Problems and Alcoholism*. New York: Free Press.

Simon, C., McNeil, J., Franklin, C., and Cooperman, A. (1991). The Family and Schizophrenia: Toward a Psychoeducational Approach. *Families in Society, 72:* 323–334.

Starr, A. M. (1989). Recovery for the Alcoholic Family: A Family Systems Treatment Model. *Social Casework, 70:* 348–354.

Tikkanen, M. (1984). *Love Story of the Century*. Santa Barbara, CA: Capra Press.

Treadway, D. (1989). *Before It's Too Late: Working with Substance Abuse in the Family*. New York: Norton.

Upshaw, J. (1993). To My Grown Up Father. Unpublished poem shared with author.

van Wormer, K. (1989). Co-dependency: Implications for Women and Therapy. *Women and Therapy, 8:* 51–63.

Wegscheider, S. (1981). *Another Chance: Hope and Health for the Alcoholic Family*. Palo Alto, CA: Science and Behavior Books.

CHAPTER 9: GROUP THERAPY WITH
SUBSTANCE ABUSERS

Anderson, D. J. (1981). *Perspectives on Treatment: The Minnesota Experience*. Center City, MN: Hazelden.

Armstrong, J. D., and Gibbons, R. J. (1956). Psychotherapeutic Technique with Large Groups in the Treatment of Alcoholism. *Quarterly Journal of Studies on Alcohol, 17:* 461–478.

Brown, S. (1985). *Treating the Alcoholic: A Developmental Model of Recovery*. New York: Wiley.

Cohen, M., and Spinner, A. (1982). A Group Curriculum for Outpatient Alcoholism Treatment. *Social Work with Groups, 5*(1): 5–13.

Cook, D., Fewell, C., and Riolo, J. (eds.). (1983). *Social Work Treatment of Alcohol Problems*. New Brunswick, NJ: Center of Alcohol Studies.

Cunynghame, A. (1983). Some Issues in Successful Alcoholism Treatment. In Cook, et al. (eds.), *Social Work Treatment of Alcohol Problems*. New Brunswick, NJ: Center of Alcohol Studies.

Dyer, W., and Vriend, J. (1975). *Counseling Techniques That Work*. Alexandria, VA: American Association for Counseling and Development.

Edwards, D. (1982). Spouse Participation in the Treatment of Alcoholism. *Social Work Groups, 5:* 41–48.

Fenton, N. (1957). *An Introduction to Group Counseling in Correctional Service*. College Park, MD: American Correctional Association.

Flores, P. J. (1988). *Group Psychotherapy with Addicted Populations*. New York: Haworth.

Ford, B. (1979). "I Intend to Make It." *Reader's Digest*, Feb., 81–86.

Forrest, G. (1984) *Intensive Psychotherapy of Alcoholism*. Springfield, IL: Charles C. Thomas.

Goldberg, M. (1983). The "Work of Recovery" in the Middle Phase of Alcohol Treatment: A Psychosocial Task-Oriented Framework. In D. Cook, et al. (eds.), *Social Work Treatment of Alcohol Problems*. New Brunswick, NJ: Center for Alcohol Studies.

Googins, B. (1984). Avoidance of the Alcoholic Client. *Social Work, 29:* 161–166.

Hazelden. (1985). *Hazelden Professional Update*, 4(2): 2.

Heap, K. (1985). *The Practice of Social Work with Groups: A Systematic Approach*. London: Allen and Unwin.

Joyce, C., and Hazelton, P. (1982). Women in Groups: A Pre-Group Experience for Women in Recovery from Alcoholism and Other Addictions. *Social Work with Groups, 5*(1): 57–63.

Kaufman, E. (1985). *Substance Abuse and Family Therapy*. Orlando, FL: Grune and Stratton.

Krimmel, H. (1971). *Alcoholism: Challenge for Social Work Education*. New York: Council for Social Work Education.

Lawson, G., Peterson, J., and Lawson, A. (1983). *Alcoholism and the Family: A Guide to Treatment Prevention*. Rockville, MD: Aspen.

Levinson, V. (1979). The Decision Group: Beginning Treatment in an Alcoholism Clinic. *Health and Social Work, 4*(4): 200–221.

Lewin, K. (1951). Formalization and Progress in Psychology. In D. Cartwright (ed.), *Field Theory in Social Science*. New York: Harper.

Lewin, K. (1952). Group Decision and Social Change. In G. Swanson, T. Newcomb, and E. Hartley (eds.), *Readings in Social Psychology*. New York: Holt.

Lieberman, M. (1975). Group Methods. In F. Kanfer and A. Goldstein (eds.), *Helping People Change: A Textbook of Methods*. New York: Pergamon Press.

Matano, R., and Yalom, I. (1991). Approaches to Chemical Dependency: Chemical Dependency and Interactive Group Therapy: A Synthesis. *International Journal of Group Psychotherapy, 41* (3): 269–293.

McCarthy, R. G. (1946). Group Therapy in an Outpatient Clinic for the Treatment of Alcoholism. *Quarterly Journal of Studies on Alcohol, 7:* 98–109.

Orosz, S. (1982). Assertiveness in Recovery. *Social Work with Groups,* 5(1): 25–31.

Panepinto, W., Garrett, J., Williford, W., and Priebe, J. (1982). A Short-Term Group Treatment Model for Problem-Solving Drinking Drivers. *Social Work with Groups,* 5(1): 25–31.

Pfeffer, A., Friedland, P., and Wortis, S. (1949). Group Psychotherapy with Alcoholics. *Quarterly Journal of Studies on Alcohol, 10:* 198–216.

Scott, E. (1956). A Special Type of Group Therapy and Its Application to Alcoholics. *Quarterly Journal of Studies on Alcohol, 17:* 288–290.

Tavris, C. (1982). Anger Defused. *Psychology Today,* Nov., pp. 25–35.

Tournier, R. (1979). Alcoholics Anonymous as Treatment and as Ideology. *Journal of Studies on Alcohol 40:* 230–239.

Vannicelli, M. (1982). Group Psychotherapy with Alcoholics: Special Techniques. *Journal of Studies on Alcohol,* 43(3): 17–37.

Vannicelli, M. (1982). *Removing the Roadblocks: Group Psychotherapy with Substance Abusers and Family Members.* New York: Guilford Press.

Van Wormer, K. (1989). The Male-Specific Group in Alcoholism Treatment. *Small Group Behavior,* 20(2): 228–242.

Yalom, I. (1974). Group Therapy and Alcoholism. In F. Seixas, Remi Cadoret, S. Eggleston (eds.), *The Person with Alcoholism,* pp. 85–103. New York: New York Academy of Sciences.

Zastrow, C. (1975). *The Theory and Practice of Group Psychotherapy.* New York: Basic Books.

Zastrow, C. (1990). *Social Work with Groups.* Chicago, IL: Nelson-Hall.

CHAPTER 10: ECONOMIC, SOCIOLOGICAL, AND LEGAL DYNAMICS

Akers, R. (1992). *Drugs, Alcohol and Society.* Belmont, CA: Wadsworth.

Anderson, D. (1981). *Perspectives on Treatment: The Minnesota Experience.* Center City, MN: Hazelden.

Babcock, M. (1992). Why Scholarship Should Be More Popular. *Addiction and Recovery,* July/Aug., 28–30.

Bissell, L. (1982). Recovered Alcoholic Counselors. In E. M. Pattison and E. Kaufman (eds.), *Encyclopedic Handbook of Alcoholism;* pp. 810–817. New York: Gardner Press.

Braus, P. (1992). Selling Self-Help. *American Demographics,* March, 48–52.

Denzin, N. (1993). *The Alcoholic Society.* New Brunswick, NJ: Transaction.

Duda, M. (1992). Managed Care Treatment Field Seeks New Ground. *Hazelden News,* Jan., 1–3ff.

Durby, D. (1987). On Conflicting Reporting. Letters to the Editor. *Social Work, 32*(2): 271.

Federico, R. (1990). *Social Welfare in Today's World.* New York: McGraw-Hill.

Fields, R. (1992). *Drugs and Alcohol in Perspective.* Dubuque, IA: Brown.

Fingarette, H. (1988). *Heavy Drinking: The Myth of Alcoholism as a Disease.* Berkeley: University of California Press.

Flexner, A. (1915). Is Social Work a Profession? In *Proceedings of the National Conference of Charities and Correction.* Chicago, IL: Hildmann Printing Co.

Gardner, R. (1982). *Family Evaluation in Child Custody Litigation.* Cresskill, NJ: Creative Therapeutics.

References

Goodwin, D. W. (1991). Inpatient Treatment of Alcoholism—New Life for the Minneapolis Plan. *New England Journal of Medicine, 325* (11): 804–806.

Googins, B. (1984). The Avoidance of the Alcoholic Client. *Social Work, 29:* 163.

Grube, J., and Wallack, L. (1994). Television Beer Advertising and Drinking Knowledge, Beliefs and Intentions among School Children. *American Journal of Public Health, 84:* 254–259.

Hayashida, M., Alterman, A., McLellan, A., et al. (1989). Comparative Effectiveness and Costs of Inpatient and Outpatient Detoxification of Patients with Mild-to-Moderate Alcohol Withdrawal Syndrome. *New England Journal of Medicine, 320:* 358–365.

Hazelden Foundation. (1986). The Accreditation Story: CD Field Has Yet to Find National Standards. *Hazelden Update, 4,* 1,4.

Heise, L. (1991). The World in a Stupor: Alcohol Promotion and Quick Profits. *Washington Post,* July 14, C1, 4.

Jung, J. (1994). *Under the Influence: Alcohol and Human Behavior.* Pacific Grove, CA: Brooks/Cole.

Kilbourne, J. (1991). Deadly Persuasion: 7 Myths of Alcohol Advertisers Want You to Believe. *Quarterly Resource for Media Literacy,* Spring/Summer, 10–12.

Kinney, J., and Leaton, G. (1991). *Loosening the Grip: A Handbook of Alcohol Information.* St. Louis, MO: Mosby.

Langton, P. (1991). *Drug Use and the Alcohol Dilemma.* Boston, MA: Allyn and Bacon.

Lubben, P. (1989). Testimony: Causes and Consequences of Alcohol Abuse. Part 2: Hearings before the Committee on Governmental Affairs, U.S. Senate. Washington, DC: U.S. Government Printing Office.

McNeese, C., and DiNitto, D. (1994). *Chemical Dependency: A Systems Approach.* Englewood Cliffs, NJ: Prentice Hall.

Meacham, A. (1991). Positively Certifiable. *Focus.* Oct-Nov., 24–25ff.

Miller, W. R., and Hester, R. K. (1986). Inpatient and Alcoholism Treatment: Who Benefits? *American Psychologist, 41:* 749–805.

National Directory of Drug Abuse and Alcoholism Treatment and Prevention Programs. (1992). Rockville, MD: U.S. Dept. of Health and Human Services.

Needleman, C. (1983). Social Work and Probation in Juvenile Court. In A. Roberts (ed.), *Social Work in Juvenile and Criminal Justice Settings,* pp. 155–181. Springfield, IL: Charles C. Thomas.

Nelson, J. (1991). Alcohol Ads Dominate Sports on Television. *Courier Journal,* May 16, C1.

Of Substance. (1980–1984). New York: Legal Action Center.

Parsons, R., Jorgensen, J., and Hernandez, S. (1994). *The Integration of Social Work Practice.* Pacific Grove, CA: Brooks/Cole.

Peele, S. (1989). *Diseasing of America: Addiction Treatment Out of Control.* Lexington, MA: Lexington Books.

Peele, S., and Brodsky, A. (1991). *The Truth about Addiction and Recovery.* New York: Simon and Schuster.

Rivers, D. C. (1984). How to Survive in a Chemical Dependency Agency. In G. Lawson, D. Ellis, and P. Rivers (eds.), *Essentials of Chemical Dependency Counseling,* pp. 147–190. Rockville, MD: Aspen.

Rivers, P. C. (1994). *Alcohol and Human Behavior: Theory, Research and Practice.* Englewood Cliffs, NJ: Prentice Hall.

Royce, J. (1989). *Alcohol Problems and Alcoholism.* New York: Free Press.

Saxe, L., Dougherty, D., and Esty, K.. (1985). The Effectiveness and Cost of Alcoholism Treatment: A Public Policy Perspective. In J. Mendelson and N. Mello (eds.), *The Diagnosis and Treatment of Alcoholism.* New York: McGraw-Hill.

Schaef, A. W., and Fassel, D. (1990). *The Addictive Organization: Why We Overwork, Cover Up, Pick Up the Pieces, Please the Boss, and Perpetuate Sick Organizations.* San Francisco, CA: Harper and Row.

Seligmann, J. (1984). Getting Straight. *Newsweek,* June 4, 62–69.

Strick, A. (1978). *Injustice for All: How Our Adversary System of Law Victimizes Us and Subverts True Justice.* London: Penguin.

Todtman, D., and Todtman, K. (1991). S.H.A.R.E.: A Local Canadian Hospital Program for Reducing Health Care Costs and Improving Treatment for Substance Abuse Patients. *Alcoholism Treatment Quarterly, 8*(2): 93–100.

U.S. Dept. of Health and Human Services. (1991). *National Directory of Drug Abuse and Alcoholism Treatment and Prevention Programs.* Rockville, MD: National Institute on Drug Abuse.

U.S. Dept. of Health and Human Services. (1993). *Eighth Special Report to the U.S. Congress on Alcohol and Health.* Alexandria, VA: National Institute of Health.

Walsh, D. C., Hingson, R. W., Merrigan, D. M., et al. (1991). A Randomized Trial of Treatment Options for Alcohol-Abusing Workers. *New England Journal of Medicine, 325:* 775–782.

CHAPTER 11: GENERAL SOCIAL WORK WITH THE ALCOHOLIC CLIENT

Akers, R. (1992). *Drugs, Alcohol, and Society.* Belmont, CA: Wadsworth.

American Medical Association. (1991). Drug Abuse in the United States: Strategies for Prevention. Board of Trustees Report. *Journal of the American Medical Association, 265*(16): 2102–2107.

Babcock, M. (1992). Why Scholarship Should Be More Popular. *Addiction and Recovery,* July/Aug., 28–30.

Baldwin, S. (1992). Alcohol and Young Offenders: Off the Mystery Train? In M. Plant, B. Ritson, and R. Robertson (eds.), *Alcohol and Drugs: The Scottish Experience* pp. 104–110. Edinburgh, Scotland: Edinburgh University Press.

Bennett, L., and Lawson, M. (1994). Barriers to Cooperation between Domestic-Violence and Substance Abuse Programs. *Families in Society, 5:* 277–286.

Central Council for Education and Training of Social Workers. (1991). *Rules and Requirements for the Diploma in Social Work.* Paper 30. Hull, England: University of Hull.

Cloninger, C. R. (1987). Neurogenetic Adaptive Mechanisms in Alcoholism. *Science, 236:* 410–416.

Curtis, P., and McCullough, C. (1993). The Impact of Alcohol and Other Drugs on the Child Welfare System. *Child Welfare, 62:* 533–542.

Danaher, B., and Lichenstein, E. (1978). *Becoming an Ex-Smoker.* Englewood Cliffs, NJ: Prentice Hall.

Denzin, N. (1993) *The Alcoholic Society: Addiction and Recovery of the Self.* New Brunswick, NJ: Transaction.

DiNitto, D., and McNeese, C. (1990). *Social Work.* Englewood Cliffs, NJ: Prentice Hall.

Ewing, J., and Rouse B. (1974). Alcohol Sensitivity and Ethnic Background. *American Journal of Psychiatry, 131:* 206–210.

Fields, R. (1992). *Drugs and Alcohol in Perspective.* Dubuque, IA: Wm. C. Brown.

Fitzgerald, E. (1990). *That Place in Minnesota: Changing Lives, Saving Lives.* New York: Viking.

Freeman, E. (ed.). (1985). *Social Work Practice with Clients Who Have Alcohol Problems.* Springfield, IL: Charles C. Thomas.

References

Gibelman, M., and Schervish, P. (1993). *Who We Are: The Social Work Labor Force.* Washington, DC: National Association of Social Workers.

Goodstadt, M. (1975). Evaluating Drug Prevention Programs. E. Schaps, and L. Slimmon (eds.), *Balancing Head and Heart.* Lafayette, CA: Prevention Materials Institute Press.

Hall, M., and Watson, T. (1993). Typical Inmate: Abused, Abuser, Repeater. *USA Today,* May 20, 8A.

Harrison, L. (1992). Substance Misuse and Social Work Qualifying Training in the British Isles: A survey of CQSW Course. *British Journal of Addiction, 87:* 635–642.

Henrickson, E. (1988). Treating the Dually Diagnosed. *Tie Lines, 5*(4): 1.

Hiratsuka, J. (1994). U.S. News: Social Work Jobs Hot. *NASW News, 39,* 1.

Holloway, M. (1991). Treatment for Addiction. *Scientific American.* March, 95–103.

Jacobson, G. (1989). A Comprehensive Approach to Pretreatment Evaluation. In R. Hester and W. Miller (eds.), *Handbook of Alcoholism Treatment Approaches,* pp. 3–13, 17–37. New York: Pergammon.

Jellinek, E. M. (1960). *The Disease Conception of Alcoholism.* New Brunswick, NJ: Hillhouse Press.

Jenish, D. (1993). The Battlefield of Addiction. *MacLean's,* July 19, 35–39.

Jung, J. (1994). *Under the Influence: Alcohol and Human Behavior.* Pacific Grove, CA: Brooks/Cole.

Kadden, et al. (1989). Matching Alcoholics to Coping Skills or Interactional Therapies: Posttreatment Results. *Journal of Consulting and Clinical Psychology, 57:* 689–704.

Kinney, J., and Leaton, G. (1991). *Loosening the Grip.* St. Louis, MO: Mosby.

Kotulak, R. (1993). New Drugs Break Spell of Violence. *Chicago Tribune.* Dec. 15.

Langton, P. (1991). *Drug Use and the Alcohol Dilemma.* Boston, MA: Allyn and Bacon.

Magura, S. (1994). Social Workers Should Be More Involved in Substance Abuse Treatment. *Health and Social Work, 19*(1): 3–5.

Miller, W. R., and Hester, R. K. (1986). Matching Problem Drinkers with Optimal Treatments. In W. R. Miller and N. Heather (eds.), *The Addictive Behaviors: Process of Change.* New York: Plenum.

National Association of Social Workers. (1987). Proposed NASW Goals, Policies: Alcoholism. *NASW News, 6:* 7.

Read, M., Penick, E., and Nickel, E. (1993). Treatment for Dually Diagnosed Clients. In E. Freeman (ed.), *Substance Abuse Treatment: A Family Systems Perspective,* pp. 123–155. Newbury, CA: Sage.

Rivers, P. C. (1994). *Alcohol and Human Behavior.* Englewood Cliffs, NJ: Prentice Hall.

Royce, J. (1989). *Alcohol Problems and Alcoholism.* 2nd ed. New York: Free Press.

Sparks, et al. (1990). *Broadening the Base of Treatment for Alcohol Problems.* Washington, DC: National Academy Press.

Symonds, W. (1991). Is Business Bungling Its Battle with Booze? *Business Week,* March 25, 76–78.

U.S. Dept. of Health and Human Services. (1990). *Seventh Special Report to the U.S. Congress on Alcohol and Health.* Washington, D.C.: U.S. Government Printing Office.

U.S. Dept. of Health and Human Services. (1993a). *8th Special Report to the US Congress on Alcohol and Health.* Washington DC: U.S. Government Printing Office.

U.S. Dept. of Health and Human Services. (1993b). *National Drug and Alcoholism Treatment Unit Survey.* Washington, DC: U.S. Government Printing Office.

U.S. Dept. of Justice, Bureau of Justice Statistics. (1993). *Drugs, Crime and the Justice System: A National Report.* Washington, DC: U.S. Government Printing Office.

U.S. News & World Report. (1993). The Changing Professions. *U.S. News and World Report,* Nov., 78–112.

Wallace, J. (1989). A Biopsychosocial Model of Alcoholism. *Social Casework*, 70: 325–323.

EPILOGUE

Denzin, N. (1993). *The Alcoholic Society: Addiction and Recovery of the Self*. New Brunswick, NJ: Transaction.

Wrong, D. (1976). The Oversocialized Conception of Man in Modern Sociology. In L. Coser and B. Rosenberg (eds.), *Sociological Theory*. New York: Macmillan.

INDEX